An Object-Oriented Introduction to Data Structures Using Eiffel

BERTRAND MEYER, Series Editor

C. BAUDOIN AND G. HOLLOWELL
Realizing the Object-Oriented Life Cycle

D. COLEMAN, P. ARNOLD, S. BODOFF, C. DOLLIN,
H. GILCHRIST, F. HAYES AND P. JEREMAES
*Object-Oriented Development:
  The Fusion Method*

S. COOK AND J. DANIELS
Designing Object Systems

P. DUBOIS
Object Technology for Scientific Computing

B. HENDERSON-SELLERS
A Book of Object-Oriented Knowledge, 2/E
Book Two of Object-Oriented Knowledge
Object-Oriented Metrics: Measures of Complexity

T. HOPKINS
*Smalltalk: An Introduction to Application
  Development Using Visual Basic*

H. KILOV AND J. ROSS
Information Modelling

P. KRIEF
Prototyping with Objects

K. LANO AND H. HAUGHTON
Object-Oriented Specification Case Studies

J. LINDSKOV KNUDSEN, M. LÖFGREN,
O. LEHRMANN MADSEN AND B. MAGNUSSON
*Object-Oriented Environments:
  The Mjølner Approach*

M. LORENZ
*Object-Oriented Software Development:
  A Practical Guide*
Object-Oriented Software Metrics

D. MANDRIOLI AND B. MEYER (eds)
Advances in Object-Oriented Software Engineering

B. MEYER
Eiffel: The Language
Reusable Software
An Object-Oriented Environment
Object Success
Object-Oriented Software Construction

B. MEYER AND J. M. NERSON
Object-Oriented Applications

O. NIERSTRASZ
Object-Oriented Software Composition

POMBERGER AND BALSCHEK
*An Object-Oriented Approach in
  Software Engineering*

R. RIST AND R. TERWILLIGER
Object-Oriented Programming in Eiffel

P. J. ROBINSON
Hierarchical Object-Oriented Design

R. SWITZER
Eiffel: An Introduction

K. WALDEN AND J. M. NERSON
Seamless Object-Oriented Software Architecture

R. WIENER
Software Development Using Eiffel
*An Object-Oriented Introduction to Computer
  Science Using Eiffel*
*An Object-Oriented Introduction to Data Structures
  Using Eiffel*

An Object-Oriented Introduction to Data Structures Using Eiffel

Richard S. Wiener

*To join a Prentice Hall PTR Internet mailing list,
point to http://www.prenhall.com/register*

**Prentice Hall PTR
Upper Saddle River, New Jersey 07458**
http://www.prenhall.com

Library of Congress Cataloging-in-Publication Data

Wiener, Richard, 1941–
    An object-oriented introduction to data structures using Eiffel / by Richard S. Wiener.
      p. cm. -- (Prentice Hall object-oriented series)
    Includes index.
    ISBN 0-13-185588-3
    1. Object-oriented programming (Computer science) 2. Eiffel (Computer program language 3. Computer science.. I. Title. II. Series.
QA76.64.W44   1996
005.13'3--dc20   96-2186
                                                            CIP

Editorial/production supervision and composition: *Joe Czerwinski*
Interior design: *Joanne Anzalone*
Manufacturing manager: *Alexis R. Heydt*
Acquisitions editor: *Paul Becker*
Editorial assistant: *Maureen Diana*
Cover design: *Design Source*
Cover design director: *Jerry Votta*

© 1997 by Prentice Hall PTR
Prentice-Hall, Inc.
A Simon & Schuster Company
Upper Saddle River, New Jersey 07458

The publisher offers discounts on this book when ordered in bulk quantities.
For more information, contact:
Corporate Sales Department
Prentice Hall PTR
1 Lake Street
Upper Saddle River, NJ 07458

Phone: 800-382-3419, Fax: 201-236-7141
E-mail: corpsales@prenhall.com

All product names mentioned herein are the trademarks of their respective owners.

All rights reserved. No part of this book may be
reproduced, in any form or by any means,
without permission in writing from the publisher.

Printed in the United States of America
10 9 8 7 6 5 4 3 2 1

ISBN 0-13-185588-3

Prentice-Hall International (UK) Limited, *London*
Prentice-Hall of Australia Pty. Limited, *Sydney*
Prentice-Hall Canada Inc., *Toronto*
Prentice-Hall Hispanoamericana, S.A., *Mexico*
Prentice-Hall of India Private Limited, *New Delhi*
Prentice-Hall of Japan, Inc., *Tokyo*
Simon & Schuster Asia Pte. Ltd., *Singapore*
Editora Prentice-Hall do Brasil, Ltda., *Rio de Janeiro*

This book is dedicated to the love of my life, Hanne.

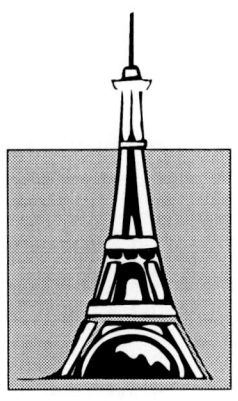

Contents

Preface . . . . *xv*

Chapter 1 . . . . ***1***
An Object-Oriented Approach To Problem Solving 1
   1.1   Abstract data types and classes 2
   1.2   Encapsulation—attributes and routines 6
   1.3   External and internal views of class 11
   1.4   Inheritance 12
           1.4.1 A more technical example of inheritance—a preview of data
                structures and the Eiffel programming language 13
   1.5   Generic classes 20
   1.6   Polymorphism and late-binding 22
           1.6.1 Application that features late binding 24
                  1.6.1.1 Specification 24
                  1.6.1.2 Analysis 25
                  1.6.1.3 Design 25
                  1.6.1.4 Eiffel implementation 26
                  1.6.1.5 A final look at polymorphism in this application 33
   1.7   Summary 33
   1.8   Exercises 34
   1.9   References 35

CONTENTS

Chapter 2 37
An Overview of Eiffel 37
- 2.1 Programming in Eiffel 37
  - 2.1.1 Creating and destroying objects 38
  - 2.1.2 Basic types 40
  - 2.1.3 Reference semantics versus value semantics 40
  - 2.1.4 Assigning objects 40
  - 2.1.5 Copying objects 41
  - 2.1.6 Cloning 41
  - 2.1.7 Basic operators 41
  - 2.1.8 Branching 42
  - 2.1.9 Iteration (loop) 44
  - 2.1.10 Routines 45
- 2.2 Basic input and output 46
- 2.3 Arrays 48
- 2.4 An overview of the components of an Eiffel class 50
- 2.5 Creation 51
  - 2.5.1 Subclass creation 53
  - 2.5.2 More advanced subclass creation 54
- 2.6 Inheritance 56
  - 2.6.1 Extension 56
  - 2.6.2 Specialization - The redefine subclause 57
  - 2.6.3 Selective export—the export subclause 58
  - 2.6.4 Renaming inherited routines—the rename subclause 58
  - 2.6.5 The select subclause 60
- 2.7 Abstract classes using Eiffel's deferred class facility 63
- 2.8 Storage versus computation: attributes versus routines 68
- 2.9 Protecting and documenting routines—assertions and programming by contract 69
  - 2.9.1 Account classes revisited with assertions 73
  - 2.9.2 Propagation of assertions through inheritance 76
- 2.10 Summary 79
- 2.11 Exercises 84

Chapter 3 87
Arrays, Sorting and Strings 87
- 3.1 ARRAY class 88

3.2 Sorting...........92
    3.2.1 Sorting problems versus their instances 92
    3.2.2 Selection-sort algorithm 93
    3.2.3 More on the efficiency of sorting algorithms 97
    3.2.4 Bubble sort 98
    3.2.5 Comb-sort—a magic number and a fast variant of bubble-sort...101
    3.2.6 Insertion-sort 105
    3.2.7 Quick-sort 108
        3.2.7.1 Partition algorithm......109
3.3 Strings......116
3.4 String searching—simple algorithm......126
3.5 Summary......128
3.6 Exercises......129

Chapter 4 131
Stacks and Queues 131

4.1 Container classes......131
4.2 Stack......133
    4.2.1 Static implementation of STACK 134
    4.2.2 Dynamic implementation 139
4.3 Queue......142
4.4 Summary......146
4.5 Exercises......146

Chapter 5 149
Lists 149

5.1 Types of lists......149
5.2 Dynamic unordered list without duplicates......150
    5.2.1 The UNORDERED_LIST data abstraction 150
    5.2.2 Interface to UNORDERED_LIST 151
    5.2.3 Implementation of class UNORDERED_LIST 156
        5.2.3.1 Discussion of class LIST_TYPE 162
    5.2.4 Details of UNORDERED_LIST 163
        5.2.4.1 Discussion of UNORDERED_LIST 167
5.3 Unordered list with duplicates 168
    5.3.1 Discussion of class UNORDERED_LIST_D 174
5.4 Ordered list 174

5.5	Doubly-linked list 176
5.6	Stack revisited 179
5.7	The queue revisited.................................181
5.8	The Deque...182
5.9	Priority queue 184
5.10	Summary 186
5.11	Exercises 187

Chapter 6 189
Recursion...189

- 6.1 The mechanics of recursion 189
  - 6.1.1 First example of recursion 189
  - 6.1.2 Second example of recursion 192
    - 6.1.2.1 Mechanics of recursion 194
  - 6.1.3 Third example of recursion 194
  - 6.1.4 Final example of recursion—permutation group 196
- 6.2 Recursion used in design 200
  - 6.2.1 Binary Search of Sorted Arrays 200
- 6.3 Summary 204
- 6.4 Exercises 204

Chapter 7 207
Applications of Stacks..207

- 7.1 Permutation iterator 207
- 7.2 Infix to postfix conversion and function evaluation 221
  - 7.2.1 Evaluation of postfix expressions 222
  - 7.2.2 Conversion from infix to postfix 223
  - 7.2.3 Implementation of system that evaluates algebraic expressions ..226
- 7.3 Las Vegas Solitaire 234
  - 7.3.1 Specifications 234
  - 7.3.2 Analysis and Implementation 235
- 7.4 Summary 255
- 7.5 Exercises 255

Chapter 8 257
Application of Queues...257

- 8.1 Queuing theory 257

8.2	Random number generator	258
8.3	Simple queuing application	263
8.4	Summary	278
8.5	Exercises	278

Chapter 9 281
Applications of Lists 281

9.1 Long integers 281
    9.1.1 The internal representation of LONG_INTEGER 282
    9.1.2 Addition of long integers 283
    9.1.3 Construction of class LONG_INTEGER 284
        9.1.3.1 Implementation of creation routine make 288
        9.1.3.2 Implementation of the addition operation 289
        9.1.3.3 Implementation of as_string command 289

9.2 Polynomials 289
    9.2.1 Class POLYNOMIAL 290
    9.2.2 Creation routine for POLYNOMIAL 294
    9.2.3 The "+" query 295
    9.2.4 The differentiate query 295
    9.2.5 The integrate query 296

9.3 Conclusions 296

9.4 Exercises 296

Chapter 10 299
Binary Trees 299

10.1 What is a binary tree? 299

10.2 Tree traversal 302

10.3 Path length 304

10.4 Implementation of binary tree 307
    10.4.1 The constrained generic parameter in BINARY_T 310
    10.4.2 Implementation of commands preorder, inorder, and postorder 311
    10.4.3 Implementation of average_internal_path_length 311

10.5 Search trees 312
    10.5.1 Insertion 316
    10.5.2 Deletion 320
    10.5.3 Search tree implementation 326

10.6 The need for tree balancing 331

Contents

    10.7 Summary 341
    10.8 Exercises 343

Chapter 11 345
Balanced Search Trees 345
    11.1 Rotations 346
    11.2 AVL trees 351
        11.2.1 AVL insertion 356
            11.2.1.1 Pattern 1 356
            11.2.1.2 Pattern 2 358
        11.2.2 Insertion algorithm 361
            11.2.2.1 Explanation of insertion algorithm 366
        11.2.3 Deletion algorithm 368
    11.3 Weight-balanced trees 372
        11.3.1 Conceptual framework 373
        11.3.2 Implementation of insertion 376
    11.4 Summary 385
    11.5 Exercises 386
    11.6 Reference 387

Chapter 12 389
Unordered Collections 389
    12.1 The BIT data type 389
        12.1.1 Summary of BIT_REF features 391
    12.2 The Set abstraction 394
    12.3 Set of integers using BIT type 394
        12.3.1 Discussion of Listing 12.3 398
    12.4 Hash functions and tables 401
        12.4.1 Design of a good hash function 403
        12.4.2 Implementation of hash function 404
        12.4.3 Collision-resolution algorithms 415
        12.4.4 Simulation that compares linear with coalesced chaining 418
    12.5 Summary 432
    12.6 Exercises 433

Chapter 13 437
Applications of Binary Trees 437

13.1 Heap sorting..437
       13.1.1 The heap data structure 444
       13.1.2 Overview of heapsort algorithm 445
       13.1.3 The procedure formheap 446
       13.1.4 The procedure rebuildheap 449
       13.1.5 Speed of heapsort versus quicksort 451
       13.1.6 Concluding remarks about heapsort 458
13.2 A "learning" tree..459
13.3 Summary 471
13.4 Exercises 472

Appendix A *473*
Interface to String Class *473*

Index..*481*

Preface

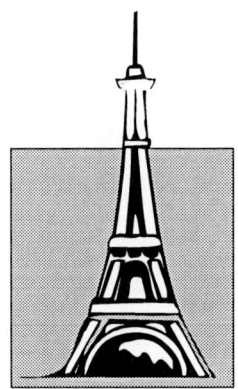

There is a strong need for a CS 2 book that from the very beginning presents the basic principles of data structures from an object-oriented perspective and is supported by a friendly, consistent, and relatively easy-to-learn object-oriented programming language. This book is directed at meeting this need. It is aimed at computer science students enrolled in a rigorous computer science curriculum taking CS 2. It is also aimed at practicing software development professionals new to the subject of data structures, Eiffel, and object-oriented problem solving.

Some computer science departments have been moving towards C++ to support CS 2. This author believes that this is a serious error. Although C++ is commercially important and widely used outside of the university, which probably accounts for its adoption as a CS 2 language, it is a poor choice to support CS 2. The C++ language is quite complex, is hard to read, and provides relatively little safety to the beginning programmer. C++ requires beginning students to master a myriad of low-level details while at the same time developing a high-level vision and sensitivity concerning the safe construction of data structures. The Eiffel language is much better suited for this task. In addition to being a viable and important language, it provides a wonderful platform for teaching the basic concepts of data structures and safe programming. Its high degree of readability, its support for generic class parameters, its assertion handling and emphasis on program correctness, and its powerful but understandable inheritance mechanisms provide a notation and foundation upon which to introduce the important data abstractions that comprise CS 2.

Chapter 1 presents a summary of an object-oriented approach to problem solving. The notions of abstract data types, encapsulation, class, external versus internal views of a class, inheritance, and polymorphism are introduced. This chapter is especially important for those readers with little or no object-oriented programming background.

Chapter 2 presents an overview of the Eiffel programming language. The major features of the language are presented and illustrated with short examples. This chapter is aimed at readers with no prior programming experience with Eiffel.

Chapter 3 presents the ARRAY and STRING classes and discusses some classical sorting algorithms. Included are selection-sort, bubble-sort, comb-sort, and quick sort.

Chapter 4 introduces the stack and queue abstractions and several of their implementations. Both static and dynamic implementations are included.

Chapter 5 presents several basic list implementations: unordered list without duplicates, unordered list with duplicates, ordered list without duplicates, and ordered list. The stack, queue, priority queue and deque are implemented in terms of a list. Portions of a doubly-linked list are shown.

Chapter 6, introduces the basic concepts of recursion. The mechanics of recursion are illustrated with several examples including the generation of permutations of an arbitrary group of objects.

Chapter 7 presents three applications of the stack. The first application demonstrates how a recursive algorithm can be implemented iteratively using a stack. The second application presents the classic infix to postfix conversion and algebraic function evaluation using stacks as the central computation engine. The third application uses a stack as a major component of a Las Vegas Solitaire simulation.

Chapter 8 presents a discrete-event queuing application. A random number class is constructed to support the queuing application.

Chapter 9 presents two applications of lists. The first application involves the partial construction of a class that manipulates extended precision integers. The second application involves the construction of a class to encapsulate the polynomial abstraction.

Chapter 10 introduces the binary tree with a focus on search trees. The need for tree balancing is explored.

Chapter 11 presents two important algorithms for balancing search trees: the AVL and weight-balanced algorithms.

Chapter 12 introduces unordered collections. The BIT data type is explored and used to implement the set abstraction. The concepts associated with hash tables are introduced. A common and important hash function is implemented using the BIT data type. Collision resolution is explored with a focus on linear and coalesced chaining. A simulation is presented that compares the efficiency of these two collision resolution algorithms.

Chapter 13 presents two applications of binary trees: heap sorting and a "learning tree" game.

Acknowledgments

I wish to acknowledge the monumental contributions of Bertrand Meyer to the intellectual foundations of object-oriented software development. Many of the seminal ideas associated with object-oriented software construction are embodied in the elegant and powerful Eiffel language and its libraries that Bertrand is the creator of. I strongly recommend that readers of this book obtain the soon to be published Second Edition of *Object-Oriented Software Construction*. This book, like the original edition published by Prentice-Hall in 1988, is destined to become an important classic.

Most importantly I wish to thank Bertrand personally for his friendship and support. This has meant a great deal to me, particularly with this project. I also thank Annie Meyer for her tremendous support.

My thanks also go to Madison Cloutier and Rock Howard of Tower Technology. This company, along with ISE, has made significant contributions to making outstanding quality Eiffel systems widely available at an affordable price. The examples developed in this book were tested with one or both of these Eiffel systems.

I would like to thank Jim McKim of the Hartford Graduate Center, my good friend and occasional Eiffel mentor, for his inspiration and help in all of my Eiffel projects.

Finally I wish to thank my wife Hanne for her tremendous help in all of my work and for her love.

An Object-Oriented Introduction to Data Structures Using Eiffel

Chapter 1

An Object-Oriented Approach To Problem Solving

Welcome to *An Object-Oriented Introduction to Data Structures Using Eiffel*. This is a book principally about data structures. It is not a book about the Eiffel language or a book about object-oriented programming. The Eiffel language is used both as an elegant notation as well as efficient implementation language to represent data structure models, concepts, and ideas. Object-orientation provides the background, the context, in which to explore and present classic data structures, their associated algorithms and their applications.

The Eiffel language was chosen to support this effort because of its clean, simple, and, in this author's opinion, elegant syntax. Eiffel, perhaps more than most modern programming languages, provides facilities that support safe programming and easy to maintain code. Its assertion handling features allow a programmer to more accurately specify the intended behavior of each module while also providing a clean and extremely useful mechanism for error detection and recovery. The reader is encouraged to look at the following references for information about the Eiffel language.[1-4] Chapter 2 presents a concise summary of the Eiffel language. Later chapters discuss interesting aspects of the Eiffel language in passing, in the context of designing data structures or applying them to practical problem solving.

An object-oriented approach to problem solving represents an evolution of a way of thinking, modeling, and problem solving that has proven to be most effective during the past 15 years. This approach to problem solving and the modeling of data abstractions in particular is embodied in the notion of **abstract data types**.

The formal linkage of a data model with its associated operations is a relatively old idea in computer science. This idea forms the basis for an abstract data type. In the 1960s, 1970s and the early part of the 1980s high-level programming languages such as Fortran, C, and Pascal provided relatively weak support for the construction of abstract data types. Strong programmer discipline was required both to construct as well as to properly use abstract data types. In the early 1980s two important languages, both derived from Pascal—Ada and Modula-2—were released. Both of these languages provided strong support for the construction of abstract data types. In both languages it is possible to separate a data abstraction into its external and internal parts. The external view or interface to the abstraction specifies the operations that may be performed on the underlying (and usually inaccessible) data model. The internal view specifies the data structure and the algorithm details (operations) that are used to manipulate the data structure.

High-level object-oriented languages, such as Smalltalk, Objective-C, and Eiffel, provide simple but powerful constructs for linking a data structure (the internal view) to the operations that support the model (the external view). In these languages, the **class** is the logical unit of abstraction that glues a data structure to its associated operations. The class becomes an embodiment of an abstract data type. In Eiffel, the class is also the basic physical unit, the module. As we will see in this chapter, the class in an object-oriented context serves as the basis for reusability. From the data model and operations defined in a class, many other more specialized classes may be spawned using the object-oriented mechanism of inheritance.

Before we get deeply involved in the main focus of this book, the construction of useful data structures and their applications, this chapter and the next one explore the rudiments of object-oriented problem and present a concise summary of the major features of the Eiffel language. Let us get on with the preliminaries!

1.1 Abstract data types and classes

The word data means "individual facts, statistics, or items of information," according to the Random House Unabridged Dictionary, Second Edition. Computer scientists are concerned with the representation of information or data; how data is stored, accessed, updated and displayed.

In many applications, complex arrangements of data must be stored and processed. The manner in which data is organized in a computer greatly affects the speed with which it can be accessed. An orderly arrangement or scheme by which to represent data is called a **data structure**. A data structure is a static entity. The actual values that are assigned to an instance of a data structure may be changed but the structure itself is invariant.

A simple example of a data structure is an integer variable declaration in a typical programming language. Suppose that in a Pascal program one declares the variable *number* to be of type INTEGER. Such a declaration might be the following

var
  number : INTEGER

The data type for the instance *number* is an INTEGER. This structure is static. But at any time this instance (the variable *number*) can have a value equal to any one of the whole numbers in a given range from some smallest negative integer to some largest positive integer (e.g., from -32,767 to 32,768). The value may of course be changed to another value through an assignment statement (e.g., *number* := 2 * *number*; here *number* is set, or assigned, to have a new value that is equal to twice its old value).

The data type INTEGER is characterized by a set of well defined operations. These include addition, substraction, multiplication, and division. These operations in fact give meaning to the data type INTEGER. The combination of the operations that form the external view of the data abstraction (a fusion of data and associated operations) with the internal representation of an integer (something that happily only the system programmer may need to be concerned about) define the abstract data type INTEGER.

In general, a data structure is defined in terms of one or more abstract data types (ADT). Each ADT has two basic components. The **data model** specifies the manner in which information is represented. Each instance of the ADT may have unique values for each component of its data model. We shall refer to these components as **fields**. The **behavior model** specifies the set of operations that can be performed to change the values of the fields of some instance. We shall call an instance of an ADT an **object**.

Let us illustrate these concepts with a simple example. Consider the geometric abstraction RECTANGLE. The data model for this ADT contains the 2 fields *length* and *width*. There are two basic types of operations that we might wish to perform on this ADT. The first type of operation is a **query**. The second type is a **command**.

A query operation accesses information and returns a value related to the current state of an object. The internal state (value of the fields) of the object are not changed by a query. A command operation updates one or more states of the object.

For the RECTANGLE ADT, the two query operations are *perimeter* and *area*. The command operations are *set_length* and *set_width*.

An informal representation of this ADT is the following:

```
ADT RECTANGLE:
  data model:
    length   : REAL
    width    : REAL
  behavior model:
    queries:
      perimeter        : REAL
      area             : REAL
    commands
      set_length (value_of_length : REAL)
      set_width (value_of_width : REAL)
```

It must be emphasized that *the only* operations that are defined for the RECTANGLE ADT are the four operations shown. This implies that it is illegal to, for example, add two instances of RECTANGLE. If such an operation were needed, it would have to be added to the command portion of the ADT. It would also be illegal to access the value of *length* or the value of *width* since there are no query operations for this in the ADT. If such access were desired, additional query operations would have to be specified.

It is useful to examine how an ADT such as RECTANGLE might be implemented in a language like Pascal. The following portion of a Pascal program shows the implementation of the ADT RECTANGLE.

```
type
  RECTANGLE = RECORD
          length    : REAL;  (* It is desired that this be private *)
          width     : REAL;  (* It is desired that this be private*)
          perimeter : REAL;  (* This is public *)
          area:     : REAL;  (* This is public *)
        END;
procedure update_perimeter_and_area (var a_rectangle : RECTANGLE);
begin
  a_rectangle.perimeter := (a_rectangle.length + a_rectangle.width) * 2.0;
```

```
    a_rectangle.area := (a_rectangle.length * a_rectangle.width);
end;

procedure set_length (var a_rectangle : RECTANGLE; a_length : REAL);
begin
    a_rectangle.length := a_length;
    update_perimeter_and_area (a_rectangle);
end;

procedure set_width (var a_rectangle : RECTANGLE; a_width : REAL);
begin
    a_rectangle.width := a_width;
    update_perimeter_and_area (a_rectangle);
end;
```

In the main portion of the Pascal program that defines the ADT RECTANGLE, consider the following code:

```
var
    my_rectangle : RECTANGLE;
begin
    set_length (my_rectangle, 20.0);
    set_width j(my_rectangle, 10.0);
    writeln ('The area of my_rectangle = ', my_rectangle.area);
end
```

The code given above, because of programmer discipline, properly uses the data abstraction of RECTANGLE. After each command (*set_length* and *set_width*), the fields of the data model *perimeter* and *area* are internally updated without the user having to manage this task.

But now consider the next segment of code, which misuses the abstract data type:

```
var
    my_rectangle : RECTANGLE;
begin
    my_rectangle.length := 20.0;
    my_rectangle.width := 10.0;
    writeln ('The area of my_rectangle = ', my_rectangle.area);
end.
```

The result that is produced is indeterminate. The *area* and *perimeter* fields of *my_rectangle* are never computed. Of course if the programmer were to explicitly invoke the procedure *update_perimeter_and_area* sending in *my_rectangle* as a parameter, the problem would be fixed. By having broken the data abstraction by directly accessing the *length* and *width* fields (in this case directly assigning to the *length* and *width* fields) the integrity of the data abstraction has been broken. The Pascal language has provided the programmer no protection against this misuse.

Another problem with this Pascal implementation relates to initialization of *my_rectangle*. The fields (*length* and *width*) of *my_rectangle* are initially undefined. Therefore it is unsafe to access the *area* and *perimeter* before invoking both of procedures *set_length* and *set_width*. If only one of these procedures is invoked, the area and perimeter would still be undefined. The Pascal programmer has many responsibilities to ensure the safe and correct use of this ADT.

Before leaving this Pascal implementation of the RECTANGLE ADT, let us summarize the main problems that we have identified:

- Inability to initialize a rectangle instance (object) at the time of its creation. This requires the user to invoke both the *set_length* and *set_width* procedures before the *area* and *perimeter* queries can be safely made.

- Inability to prevent a user from directly assigning to the internal fields of the data model, namely *length* and *width*. This causes the potential for erroneous values to be returned by the *area* and *perimeter* queries. Only when the *set_length* and *set_width* commands are used will the *area* and *perimeter* values be internally updated.

In the next section we show how both of these difficulties are easily overcome using the powerful data abstraction mechanism in Eiffel, the class.

1.2 Encapsulation—attributes and routines

The informal description of the RECTANGLE ADT is repeated below.

```
ADT RECTANGLE:
   data model:
      length   : REAL
      width    : REAL
   behavior model:
      queries:
         perimeter       : REAL
         area            : REAL
      commands
```

set_length (value_of_length : REAL)
set_width (value_of_width : REAL)

We examined a Pascal implementation of this ADT in Section 1.1. Although all of the elements of the ADT were included, the implementation offered no protection against the illegal access of data fields *length* and *width* and no assurance that the internal update of *area* and *perimeter* would occur each time a new length or width were assigned.

In the Pascal implementation, *area* and *perimeter* were defined as fields of the data model. Their values were obtained through storage rather than through computation. An alternative implementation technique would provide functions for *area* and *perimeter*. This would allow these values to be returned through computation rather than through storage. If storage is used, as in Section 1.1, *area* and *perimeter* are called **attributes**. These attributes must have read-only semantics. That is, their values should be directly accessible but not directly modifiable.

Consider the Eiffel class RECTANGLE, given in Listing 1.1.

Listing 1.1   Class RECTANGLE

```
class RECTANGLE

creation
  make

feature -- Public section
-- read-only semantics

  area: INTEGER

  perimeter: INTEGER

  make (initial_length: INTEGER; initial_width: INTEGER) is
    do
      length := initial_length
      width := initial_width
      update_area_perimeter
    end

  set_length (new_length: INTEGER) is
    do
      length := new_length
      update_area_perimeter
    end
```

```
  set_width (new_width: INTEGER) is
    do
      width := new_width
      update_area_perimeter
    end

feature {NONE} -- Protected section

  length: INTEGER

  width: INTEGER

  update_area_perimeter is
    do
      area := length * width
      perimeter := 2 * (length + width)
    end

end -- class RECTANGLE
```

The RECTANGLE class of Listing 1.1 has 2 feature sections. The first section has universal export scope. The second section is for internal use only because its scope is indicated as NONE (see Chapter 2 for details regarding the construction of Eiffel classes).

The attributes *area* and *perimeter* are declared in the public feature section. In Eiffel, *all attributes have read-only semantics*. If *my_rectangle* were declared in some client module as being of type RECTANGLE (i.e., *rectangle : RECTANGLE*), then the *area* and *perimeter* of *my_rectangle* would be accessed as follows: *my_rectangle.area* or *my_rectangle.perimeter*.

Since the attributes length and width are declared in the protected section of the class (previously called internal use only), they can be accessed only within the boundaries of class RECTANGLE. It would be illegal in classes that are a client of RECTANGLE (i.e., that use RECTANGLE but are not a descendant of RECTANGLE) to attempt *my_rectangle.length* or *my_rectangle.width*.

The routine *update_area_perimeter* is defined in the protected section of the class. Therefore it cannot be invoked outside of this class. It is for internal use only. This routine is invoked within the procedures *make*, *set_length*, and *set_width*.

As an alternative, the query *perimeter* could have been defined as a function as follows:

```
perimeter : INTEGER is
  do
```

```
    Result := 2 * ( length + width)
end
```

In this case the protected routine *update_area_perimeter* and all its references could be omitted.

The notational convention of using boldface font for Eiffel keywords and upper-case names for classes will be used throughout this book. Eiffel is case insensitive.

Readers unfamiliar with Eiffel might be asking themselves, how can this class be used in some application? How, for example, would an instance of RECTANGLE be created? Listing 1.2 shows a complete but simple application that uses class RECTANGLE.

Listing 1.2   Application that uses class RECTANGLE

```
class APPLICATION

creation
   start

feature

   start is
      local
         my_rectangle: RECTANGLE
      do
         !! my_rectangle.make (4, 5)
         output_area_perimeter (my_rectangle)
         my_rectangle.set_length (5)
         output_area_perimeter (my_rectangle)
         my_rectangle.set_width (6)
         output_area_perimeter (my_rectangle)
      end

   output_area_perimeter (a_rectangle: RECTANGLE) is
      do
         io.putstring ("area = ")
         io.putint (a_rectangle.area)
         io.new_line
         io.putstring ("perimeter = ")
         io.putint (a_rectangle.perimeter)
         io.new_line
      end
```

***end** -- class APPLICATION*

APPLICATION is an ordinary class with its own creation routine, *start*. A configuration file called Ace resides in the subdirectory that contains the source code for class RECTANGLE and class APPLICATION (files *rectangle.e* and *application.e*). The user must specify in this Ace file the name of the class that contains a creation routine that is responsible for triggering the application. The name of this creation routine must also be specified in the Ace file. The format of Ace files might vary slightly from one Eiffel vendor to another but the basic components are fairly standard. Listing 1.3 shows the ISE Ace file that allows the code in Listings 1.1 and 1.2 to compile and link successfully.

Listing 1.3 Interactive Software Engineering Ace file for RECTANGLE Application

system application -- The particular details of an ACE file are system dependent

root application (MY_CLUSTER): "start"

default

  assertion (all);
  precompiled ("$EIFFEL3/precompiled/spec/$PLATFORM/base")

cluster

  MY_CLUSTER: "/disk2/EIFFELWORK3/WORK";

end

The programmer is responsible for supplying 3 names: *applicat*, *application*, and *start*. The name *applicat* is the filename of the executable that will be produced.

In the APPLICATION class of Listing 1.2, a rectangle object, *my_rectangle*, is safely created and initialized using the creation operator, "!!". The correct initial values for *area* and *perimeter* are internally computed during this initialization.

After each change to either the *length* or *width* of the rectangle, the *area* and *perimeter* are output using the routine *output_area_perimeter* that is defined in class APPLICATION.

Readers familiar with Pascal have probably noted that Eiffel requires very few semicolons to separate or terminate lines of code. Such semicolons are allowed and would be essential if one wanted to write more than one line of code on a given line (a practice that this author recommends against). The only semicolons that have been used are to separate the parameters of a routine.

After reading Listing 1.2 you might be wondering, how does the Eiffel compiler know the meaning of the declaration, *my_rectangle : RECTANGLE*? In other words, how does the code of Listing 1.1 (that defines class RECTANGLE) get linked to the main application code of Listing 1.2? You will be pleased to learn that the Eiffel system performs automatic configuration management. Upon encountering the identifier RECTANGLE, the compiler verifies that a RECTANGLE class exists in either the working subdirectory or other subdirectories specified by the programmer in the Ace file. The compiler is also able to verify that objects of type RECTANGLE are used properly. Any attempt to violate the access rules or invoke a routine with incorrect parameter types will result in a compilation error.

The Eiffel class RECTANGLE (Listing 1.1) represents an **encapsulation** of the abstract data type for a rectangle object. The internal data model given by the protected fields *length* and *width* is glued to the operations given by *make*, *set_length* and *set_width*. The combination of data model and behavior model given in Listing 1.2 defines the complete ADT for RECTANGLE.

1.3 External and internal views of class

It should be evident from class RECTANGLE (Listing 1.1) that the interface and implementation details are mixed together in one file—the module RECTANGLE. Client code of this abstraction is generally interested only in the interface details of the class. These interface details are the external view of the class. The producer of the class and the producer of any subclasses (this idea is introduced later in this chapter) would be interested in the internal view of the class.

A useful tool has become a standard part of the Eiffel programming environment, the *short* tool. This tool allows a client to inspect only the external features of a given class—the features that can be accessed outside of the class. Listing 1.4 shows the file produced by *short* on Listing 1.1. This would be the client or external view of class RECTANGLE.

Listing 1.4   External view of class RECTANGLE produced by *short*

class interface RECTANGLE

creation
   make

feature
   area: INTEGER

   make (initial_length: INTEGER; initial_width: INTEGER)

   perimeter: INTEGER

   set_length (new_length: INTEGER)

   set_width (new_width: INTEGER)

end -- class RECTANGLE

The attributes *length* and *width* are not shown in Listing 1.4. The routine *update_area_perimeter* is also not shown. These features are in fact not part of the external view of the class.

From the interface description of the queries given in Listing 1.4, *perimeter : INTEGER* and *area : INTEGER*, it is not clear whether these quantities are obtained through computation or through storage. The Eiffel principle of **uniform access** applies here. This principle, put forth by the founder of the language, Dr. Bertrand Meyer, states that the external view of the class should not distinguish whether a query is satisfied through computation or through storage since from a client's perspective it simply does not matter. If a client needs to know this information then the internal view of the class must be examined.

1.4 Inheritance

Inheritance and the associated concepts of child and parent classes, and more generally ancestor and descendant classes, define an important logical relationship between classes. If class C is a child of class P then C should generally be "a kind of" P. For example, if CAR is a child of VEHICLE, then the logical relationship, "CAR is a kind of VEHICLE" should hold. Generally a child class (subclass) is a more specialized type of entity than its parent. A SQUARE is a kind of RECTANGLE but not the opposite. Therefore it would be logical for a SQUARE to be subclass of RECTANGLE but not for a RECTANGLE to be a subclass of SQUARE.

A subclass can redefine one or more of the routines or attributes specified in one of its ancestor classes according to a set of rules that will be specified in Chapter 2. It is rare for a subclass to redefine an attribute but fairly common for it to redefine one or more routines. Let us consider a simple example.

Suppose we define a class (ADT) FLOWER as follows:

ADT FLOWER
  queries:
    color   : STRING
    fragrance   : STRING
    petals   : INTEGER
  commands:
    make (a_color : STRING; a_fragrance : STRING; number_petals : INTEGER)
    set_color (a_color : STRING)
    set_fragrance (a_fragrance : STRING)
    display

Now we define class ROSE as a subclass of FLOWER as follows:

ADT ROSE, subclass of FLOWER
  queries:
    number_thorns : INTEGER
  command:
    redefine display
    redefine make (a_color : STRING; a_fragrance : STRING;
                   number_petals : INTEGER; number_thorns : INTEGER)

In addition to the query, *number_thorns*, defined in class ROSE, the queries *color*, *fragrance*, and *petals* and the commands *set_color* and *set_fragrance* are inherited from class FLOWER. The commands *display* and *make* are redefined in class ROSE. This implies that a ROSE object will respond differently to *display* (i.e. *my_rose.display*) than a FLOWER object (it has more features to output).

It should be clear from the simple example above that inheritance implies code reuse. If class ROSE were defined from scratch (not a subclass of FLOWER), the queries *color*, *fragrance*, and *petals* and the commands *set_color* and *set_fragrance* would have to be duplicated.

1.4.1 A more technical example of inheritance— a preview of data structures and the Eiffel programming language

Let us consider a more technical example that will provide a preview of the world of data structures and the Eiffel programming language. Some readers may wish to skip this example and return to it after complet-

INHERITANCE

ing Chapter 2. No great pains will be taken in this section to explain some of the technicalities of inheritance in Eiffel. This is done in Chapter 2.

So let the more courageous of you read on. You may find the example in this subsection interesting and useful in getting an early appreciation of inheritance.

A simple INTEGER_QUEUE abstraction is constructed. Chapter 4 deals with the subject of queues in much greater depth. The goal here is to illustrate the role of inheritance in constructing object models.

A **queue** is a container class that holds elements of some type. Elements must be accessed strictly in the order in which they were inserted. The next element that may be accessed (removed or inspected) is the oldest element in the queue (the one that was inserted before any of the remaining elements).

The commands that we wish to perform on a queue object are:

- **make**—a creation routine that requires the user to specify the capacity of the queue

- **insert**—add an element to the queue

- **remove**—remove an element from the queue and sets value of *element_removed*

The queries that we wish to make on a queue object are:

- **num_elements**—the number of elements currently in a queue

- **capacity**—the largest number of elements that can be stored in queue

- **element_removed**—set by command *remove*

To keep things simple (at least relatively simple), an array is used as an internal data structure to hold the elements of the queue. The user must specify the size of the array in the creation routine, *make*, when constructing a queue object. Also to keep things simple, we will assume that type of element to be stored in the queue is INTEGER. In Section 1.5 we show how this restriction can be removed.

Before we examine the Eiffel code for class QUEUE, let us examine the algorithms for inserting and removing elements from a queue object.

Suppose that the index *first* in the array is used to point to the array position of the oldest element. The index *last* is used to point to the array position of the most recent element inserted into the array.

A typical array, *data*, is shown below.

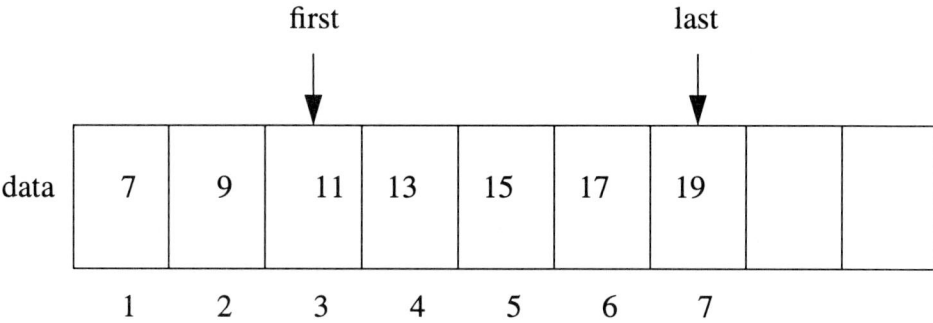

The sequence of elements inserted into the array was: 7, 9, 11, 13, 15, 17, 19. Elements 7 and 9 were removed, so the index *first* equals 3. The index *last* equals 7. The number of elements currently in the queue equals *last—first* + 1 (this assumes that *last* > *first*).

Now suppose we wish to insert element 21. The algorithm for doing this would be:

last := last + 1
if last > capacity then
   last := 1
end
data [last] := 21

The capacity for the array shown before is 9. Before allowing the insertion it is necessary to ensure that the new number of elements is equal or less than the capacity. If *last* is less than *first*, the number of elements in the queue is given by *capacity - first + last* + 1.

Suppose we wish to remove element 11. The algorithm for doing this would be:

element_removed := data [first]
first := first + 1
if first > capacity then
   first := 1
end

Before allowing a remove operation it is necessary to ensure that there is at least one element in the queue.

From the above discussion we can identify the internal data model of the queue class. It consists of an array called *data* and the integer index values *first* and *last*.

INHERITANCE

The public attribute *number_elements* is defined to allow access to the current number of elements in the queue. The public attribute *capacity* defines the size of the queue and is set in the creation routine, *make*.

The public attribute, *element_removed*, stores the most recent integer that has been removed from the queue object. The public routines *make*, *insert*, *remove*, and *first_element* take care of the remaining commands and queries.

The Eiffel class that implements class QUEUE is given in Listing 1.5.

Listing 1.5   Class INTEGER_QUEUE

```
class INTEGER_QUEUE
creation
  make
feature {NONE} -- Protected section
-- Internal data model
  first: INTEGER
  last: INTEGER
  data: ARRAY [INTEGER]
feature -- Public section
  number_elements: INTEGER
  element_removed: INTEGER
  capacity: INTEGER
  make (size: INTEGER) is
    require
      size_positive: size > 0
    do
      capacity := size
      !! data.make (1, size)
      last := capacity
      first := 1
    end
  insert (an_element: INTEGER) is
    require
      no_overload: number_elements + 1 <= capacity
```

```
    do
      last := last + 1
      if last > capacity then
        last := 1
      end
      data.put (an_element, last)
      number_elements := number_elements + 1
    ensure
      number_elements = old number_elements + 1
    end

  remove is
    require
      non_empty: number_elements > 0
    do
      element_removed := data.item (first)
      first := first + 1
      if first > capacity then
        first := 1
      end
      number_elements := number_elements - 1
    ensure
      number_elements = old number_elements - 1
    end

end -- class INTEGER_QUEUE
```

As indicated earlier, the protected section that defines the internal data model of the class is given first in the section, *feature { NONE }*. The base type INTEGER of the internal array is specified as shown (*data : ARRAY [INTEGER]*). The ARRAY class given in the Eiffel library is a generic class and requires that its base type be specified. This is explained in the next section.

The public section contains the read-only attributes *number_elements*, *element_removed*, and *capacity*.

The *require* section of each routine specifies the condition(s) that must be met by the caller of the routine. For example, in routine *make* the calling code must send in a positive integer for *size*. These are called preconditions and are discussed in more detail in Chapter 2.

The presence of preconditions simplifies the code within each routine since it can be assumed that the precondition(s) have been met. If a precondition has not been met, an exception is generated in the caller (the code that calls the routine whose precondition has not been met). If an exception handler is not present in the caller routine, the program execution stops. The tag name of the precondition that has failed is reported. This makes it quite simple to detect the nature of the fault that has caused the system to fail.

The *ensure* section, if present, specifies the condition(s) that are guaranteed to be met by the routine upon exit from the routine, assuming that the precondition(s) have been met. These are called postconditions and are also discussed in more detail in Chapter 2.

Access to the array data is achieved using either the *put* command or *item* query. The command *put* takes the element being inserted into the array as its first parameter and the index at which the insertion occurs as its second parameter. The query *item* takes the index where an item is being returned as its only parameter.

Suppose we encounter an application in which it is necessary to know the second element in the queue, if one is present. We could of course remove the first and second elements thus exposing the second element. In doing this we would upset the ordering of the queue and have to save the removed elements.

A better solution would be to define a more specialized type of queue class—one that has a query for accessing the second element, if one is present. Suppose we call this more specialized class SECOND_INTEGER_QUEUE. One option is to start from scratch and reinvent all of the protocol that has already been established for the INTEGER_QUEUE. Using inheritance this is not necessary, as will be seen below. Class SECOND_INTEGER_QUEUE is defined as a subclass of INTEGER_QUEUE. The additional query *second_element : INTEGER* is defined in this subclass. The details are given in Listing 1.6.

Listing 1.6   Class SECOND_INTEGER_QUEUE

class SECOND_INTEGER_QUEUE

inherit
  INTEGER_QUEUE

creation
  make

feature

  second_element: INTEGER **is**
    require

```
    at_least_two_elements: number_elements >= 2
do
    Result := data.item (first \\ capacity + 1)
end
```

end -- *class SECOND_INTEGER_QUEUE*

The *inherit* clause establishes class SECOND_INTEGER_QUEUE as a child of INTEGER_QUEUE. Unless redefined, all of the attributes and behavior (routines) of the parent class are acquired by the subclass and available for use on instances of the child class.

The make routine, inherited from class INTEGER_QUEUE is specified as serving as a creation routine for SECOND_INTEGER_QUEUE.

The function *second_element* (a function is a routine that returns a specified type—it is a query routine) requires that there be at least 2 elements in the queue. It is the caller's responsibility to ensure that this condition is met.

A simple application test program that exercises some of the protocol of class SECOND_INTEGER_QUEUE is given in Listing 1.7.

Listing 1.7   Test program for SECOND_INTEGER_QUEUE

```
class APPLICATION

creation
    start

feature

    start is
    local
        my_queue : SECOND_INTEGER_QUEUE
    do
        !!my_queue.make (5)
        my_queue.insert (5)
        my_queue.insert (10)
        my_queue.insert (15)
        io.putstring ("my_queue.number_elements = ")
        io.putint (my_queue.number_elements)
        io.new_line
        my_queue.remove
        my_queue.remove
        io.putstring ("my_queue.element_removed = ")
```

```
            io.putint (my_queue.element_removed)
            io.new_line
            my_queue.insert (6)
            my_queue.insert (7)
            my_queue.insert (8)
            io.putstring ("my_queue.number_elements = ")
            io.putint (my_queue.number_elements)
            io.new_line
            io.putstring ("my_queue.second_element = ")
            io.putint (my_queue.second_element)
            io.new_line
        end -- start

    end -- APPLICATION
```

The output of the program is:

```
my_queue.number_elements = 3
my_queue.element_removed = 10
my_queue.number_elements = 4
my_queue.second_element = 6
```

1.5 Generic classes

Container classes, such as the INTEGER_QUEUE class presented in the previous section, hold objects of some base type. Typically, the behavior of the class (commands and queries) can be specified without knowledge of the base type. Eiffel is the first major object-oriented language to support the construction of generic classes. This is achieved by allowing the class to specify one or more generic parameters. When an instance of the class is declared, the generic parameter must be replaced with a concrete type.

We illustrate this important concept by revisiting the INTEGER_ QUEUE class of Section 1.4 and showing how we can remove the requirement that the base type is INTEGER. We shall call the new class FIXED_SIZED_QUEUE since it is necessary for a user to specify the size of the queue at the time of its creation. The base type that is given is now arbitrary. The code for this revised class is given in Listing 1.8.

Listing 1.8 Class FIXED_SIZED_QUEUE—a generic class

class FIXED_SIZED_QUEUE [T]

creation
　　make

feature { NONE } -- Protected section

　　first : INTEGER
　　last   : INTEGER
　　data   : ARRAY [T]

feature -- Public section
　　number_elements : INTEGER
　　element_removed : T
　　capacity   : INTEGER

　　make (size : INTEGER) **is**
　　-- Details the same as in Listing 1.5
　　end -- make

　　insert (an_element : T) **is**
　　　-- Details the same as in Listing 1.5
　　end -- insert

　　remove **is**
　　-- Details the same as in Listing 1.5
　　end -- remove

end -- FIXED_SIZED_QUEUE

From Listing 1.8, it should be clear that the syntax for creating a generic class is quite simple. The protected attribute *data* is declared as *data : ARRAY [T]*. The public attribute *element_removed* is declared as *element_removed : T*. The parameter *an_element* of *insert* is of type T.

Instances of the generic class FIXED_SIZED_QUEUE can be created as follows:

name_queue   : FIXED_SIZE_QUEUE [STRING]

integer_queue   : FIXED_SIZED_QUEUE [INTEGER]

real_queue   : FIXED_SIZED_QUEUE [REAL]

Many of the data structure components that are presented in later chapters are implemented as generic classes. This provides for a much higher level of reusability.

1.6 Polymorphism and late-binding

The dominant strongly typed programming languages that have been used for the past 25 years have featured static, or early, binding. These languages include Algol, Pascal, Ada, and Modula-2. In such languages a function call is bound at compile/link time to a memory address that represents the starting location of a block of data that represents the instructions for executing the function.

In an object-oriented context, commands are invoked through objects using the structure: *some_object.some_command*. Static binding implies a compile/link time call to the body of code in the class with instance *some_object* and the routine *some_command*. This probably sounds quite innocent if not just plain natural. How else should it be?

Before answering this question, let us consider a simple application. Our software is to simulate a dog obedience exercise in which four different dogs, each of a different breed, are told to fetch a ball. The first dog, Fred, is a Collie. The second dog, Mike, is a Golden Retriever. The third dog, Mollie, is a Basset Hound. The fourth dog, Charlie, is a Husky. All four dogs have received roughly the same level of training before this exercise is performed.

When Fred receives the command *fetch*, his sheep herding instincts take over and he bounds out after the ball and proceeds to arc around the ball in shorter and shorter circles but never actually makes contact with the ball once satisfied that the ball (acting as a surrogate for a sheep) has been successfully cornered.

When Mike receives the command, he dashes out, grabs the ball and dutifully brings it back to the handler. It must be remembered that his instincts are to retrieve any object.

When Mollie receives the command she enthusiastically moves away from the handler, but in the opposite direction of the ball. She has caught the scent of a nearby rabbit and follows her scent and instincts to pursue the rabbit.

When Charlie is told to *fetch* the ball he just runs away and is never seen again. Some primeval urge causes him to just break loose.

The varying responses of these canines is attributed mainly to their differences in breeding and the behavioral characteristics that have been genetically defined. Dog fanciers have classified breeds according to both physical as well as behavioral discriminants.

In terms of a simple software model we have a hierarchy of classes given as follows:

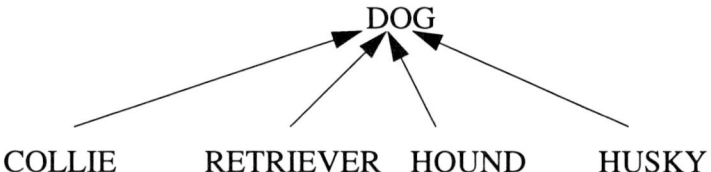

Suppose we declare an array, *dogs*, as follows:

dogs : ARRAY [DOG]

Suppose further, that we assign each dog (after it has been dutifully created) to an index of the array as follows:

dogs.put (fred, 1)
dogs.put (mike, 2)
dogs.put (mollie, 3)
dogs.put (charlie, 4)

It is legal in Eiffel and in other object-oriented languages to substitute a descendant type in place of the formal type that is expected in an expression. The array *dogs* above expects each of its elements to be of type DOG. We have substituted this type with types COLLIE, RETRIEVER, HOUND, and HUSKY.

The code that we would like to write, in order to simulate the succession of *fetch* commands is:

from index := 0
until index = 4
loop
   index := index + 1
   dogs.item (index).fetch
end

In other words, we would like to send the command *fetch* to each dog and let each dog "do its own thing." This desire flies right in the face of static-binding. How is the compiler to know which version of *fetch* to use (each class has its own unique implementation of *fetch*)? In point of fact, the compiler cannot and should not attempt to perform early binding. Here it is most unnatural.

Enter late, or dynamic, binding. With this type of binding, the particular routine *fetch* that is attached to the command *dogs.item (index).fetch* is determined at run-time and is based *on the actual type of dog* that receives the command. Late binding encourages a flexible approach to software design. Neither the programmer nor the compiler need know what type of dog is to fetch the ball at the time when the code is written. The user may in fact assign different dogs to various index locations and therefore take control completely out of the hands of both the programmer and compiler.

The binding mode in Eiffel is strictly late binding for all commands and queries. The body of the loop shown above is exactly how the four dogs would be told to fetch the ball. There is a small performance penalty associated with late binding. Because of this, an Eiffel compiler, during its "finalization" phase, will attempt to do early binding whenever there is no ambiguity regarding which version of a routine to use. The programmer may continue to think in terms of late binding regardless of what actual type of binding the compiler ultimately employs.

The fancy term **polymorphism** is used to characterize the command fetch in the above example. The word literally means "many forms." In the context of the above example, "many forms" refers to the manner in which each dog responds to a common command.

In order to more adequately convey the flavor of polymorphism and late binding in an actual software application, the next subsection presents a short but complete example.

1.6.1 Application that features late binding

1.6.1.1 Specification

Suppose we wish to simulate a simple game. In order to play the game we must first fabricate (at least in our minds) 4 different kinds of die (six-sided cubes that we assume are perfectly balanced so that each face of the cube has an equal probability of occurring when the die is thrown). These special die have the unusual property that duplicate numbers can occur in the set of 6 numbers that define the die. The four die are constructed with values on their six sides as follows:

Die 1:   4, 4, 4, 4, 0, 0

Die 2:   3, 3, 3, 3, 3, 3

Die 3:   6, 6, 2, 2, 2, 2

Die 4:   5, 5, 5, 1, 1, 1

The four die are placed into an array with *die1* inserted into the first item location, *die2* inserted into the second item location, *die3* inserted into the third item location and *die4* inserted into the fourth item location.

Player 1 always chooses the die in the first item position. Player 2 always chooses the die in the second item position.

During the first iteration of the game, player 1 "throws" her die (the program must of course simulate the throw of this die) and acquires a score equal to the value of her die (the face showing upwards). Player 2 "throws" his die and obtains a score equal to the value of his die.

Now the dice are rotated around in the array so that *die2* moves down to item 1, *die3* moves down to item 2, *die4* moves down to item 3, and *die1* moves to item 4. This operation will be called a left-rotate operation.

During iteration 2, player 1 picks the die again in index 1 (*die2*). Player 2 picks the die in item 2 (*die3*). Each player throws his/her die and adds the value to his/her current score. Iterations continue until one of the players achieves a score of 1000 points.

After each iteration, the program must output the iteration number and the current score for each player. When the first player reaches a score of 1000 or greater, the game ends and the program must announce the winner.

1.6.1.2 Analysis

There are 4 concrete classes of die (DIE1, DIE2, DIE3, and DIE4), each a subclass of an abstract class DIE. The query *value* is defined differently in each of the concrete classes (polymorphism). In addition there is a class PLAYER with attributes *score* and *a_die*, and commands *set_die (the_die : DIE)* and *throw_die_and_update_score*. Finally there is the main application class GAME that controls the flow of activities. The GAME class owns the array of die and performs the rotation after each iteration. This class is responsible for displaying the score after each iteration and announcing the winner of the game.

1.6.1.3 Design

The GAME class creates a single instance of DIE1, DIE2, DIE3, and DIE4 (*die_1, die_2, die_3,* and *die_4*). It initializes the array *dice* and inserts the 4 die into the array. It creates 2 players (*player_1, player_2*). During each iteration, it fetches the die in index 1 and places it with player_1 (using the *set_die* command). It then fetches the die in index 2 and places it with player_2. The main control loop then does the following:

```
from iteration := 1
until player_1.score >= 1000 or player_2.score >= 1000
loop
    player_1.set_die (dice.item (1)) -- fetch die in item 1 and place with player_1
    player_2.set_die (dice.item (2)) -- fetch die in item 2 and place with player_2
    player_1.throw_die_and_update_score -- player_1 throws die, updates score
    player_2.throw_die_and_update_score -- player_2 throws die, updates score
    rotate_dice -- the dice are rotated within the array
    -- Update output display
    io.putstring ("Iteration: ")
    io.putint (iteration)
    io.putstring (" Player 1 score: ")
    io.putint (player_1.score)
    io.putstring (" Player 2 score: ")
    io.puint (player_2.score)
    io.new_line
    iteration := iteration + 1
end
-- Announce winner of game
if player_1.score = player_2.score then
    io.putstring ("%NTie game%N")
elseif player_1.score > player_2.score then
    io.putstring ("%NPlayer 1 is the winner!%N")
else
    io.putstring ("%NPlayer 2 is the winner!%N")
```

Polymorphism plays a central role in the design of this simple game. Although it is not explicitly evident in the code given above, the message *throw_die_and_update_score*, which is sent to *player_1* and *player_2* sequentially, allows each player object to send the message *value* to its internal die (the die that is assigned with the *set_die* command). In the Eiffel implementation presented in the next subsection, take careful note of how this is done in routine *throw_die_and_update_score* (class PLAYER).

1.6.1.4 Eiffel implementation

Using a top-down approach (a problem-solving strategy in which the most general tasks are identified first and later smaller sub-tasks are identified), the first class that is presented is the main application class, GAME. The details of this class are presented in Listing 1.9. Readers who wish to establish a firmer grounding in Eiffel programming may want to revisit this code after completing Chapter 2. The details of routine *start* are similar to the code given above.

Listing 1.9   Class GAME

```
class GAME
creation
  play
feature
  player_1: PLAYER
  player_2: PLAYER
  dice: ARRAY [DIE]
  die_1: DIE
  die_2: DIE
  die_3: DIE
  die_4: DIE
  play is
    local
      iteration: INTEGER
    do
      initialize_objects
      from
        iteration := 1
      until
        player_1.score >= 1000 or player_2.score >= 1000
      loop
        player_1.set_die (dice.item (1))
        player_2.set_die (dice.item (2))
        player_1.throw_die_and_update_score
        player_2.throw_die_and_update_score
        rotate_dice
        io.putstring ("Iteration: ")
        io.putint (iteration)
        io.putstring (" Player 1 score: ")
        io.putint (player_1.score)
        io.putstring (" Player 2 score: ")
```

Polymorphism and late-binding

```
            io.putint (player_2.score)
            io.new_line
            iteration := iteration + 1
         end
         if player_1.score = player_2.score then
            io.putstring ("%NTie game%N")
         elseif player_1.score > player_2.score then
            io.putstring ("%NPlayer 1 wins!%N")
         else
            io.putstring ("%NPlayer 2 wins!%N")
         end
      end

   rotate_dice is
      local
         item_1: DIE
      do
         item_1 := dice.item (1)
         dice.put (dice.item (2), 1)
         dice.put (dice.item (3), 2)
         dice.put (dice.item (4), 3)
         dice.put (item_1, 4)
      end

   initialize_objects is
      do
         !! player_1
         !! player_2
         !DIE1! die_1.make
         !DIE2! die_2.make
         !DIE3! die_3.make
         !DIE4! die_4.make
         !! dice.make (1, 4)
         dice.put (die_1, 1)
         dice.put (die_2, 2)
         dice.put (die_3, 3)
         dice.put (die_4, 4)
      end

end -- class GAME
```

In Listing 1.9, routine *intialize_object*, the syntax used to create each of the 4 specialized types of die is: *!DIEn!die_n.make*, where n is either 1, 2, 3, or 4. Recall that each of the four die are defined to be of type DIE.

Let us consider the creation of *die_1*. If this die had been declared to be of type DIE1, then its creation expression would be the normal *!!die_1.make*. The notation, *!DIE1!die_1.make* is equivalent to the following:

die_1 : DIE
temp : DIE1

!!temp.make   -- an instance of DIE1
die_1 := temp -- this is legal because *temp* belongs to a subclass of *die_1*

The details of class PLAYER are shown in Listing 1.10.

Listing 1.10   Class PLAYER

class PLAYER

feature

  score: INTEGER

  a_die: DIE

  set_die (the_die: DIE) **is**
    do
      a_die := the_die
    end

  throw_die_and_update_score **is**
    do
      a_die.next
      score := score + a_die.value
    end

end -- class PLAYER

The command *a_die.next*, followed by the query *a_die.value*, allows each die type to respond in a suitable and unique manner. The player object is not concerned about which particular die object receives these messages. The responsibility lies with each die object to correctly produce an appropriate *value* according to the probabilistic rules that have been established for the given die.

If in later maintenance new die types were added, the meaning of these lines of code would remain the same.

Listing 1.11 contains the code for class DIE. This class is an abstract class. No actual instances of this class are allowed. The purpose of this class is to establish the existence of the polymorphic command *next*. The implementation details of this command are deferred (defined in concrete subclasses). In Eiffel an abstract class must be labelled a **deferred** class and, in fact, must be labelled as such if one or more of its routines are deferred.

Listing 1.11   Abstract class DIE

```
deferred class DIE
feature {NONE}
   r: RANDOM_NUMBER
feature
   value: INTEGER
   make is
      do
         !! r.initialize
      end

   next is
         -- set the attribute value
      deferred
      ensure
         value >= 0 and value <= 6
      end

end -- class DIE
```

Since class DIE in Listing 1.11 is deferred, it cannot have a creation routine. The *make* routine that is defined is inherited by the concrete subclasses DIE1, DIE2, DIE3, and DIE4. These classes declare *make* to be their creation routine.

Routine *make* creates an instance of RANDOM_NUMBER using *initialize*. The details of class RANDOM_NUMBER are presented in Appendix 1. On some platforms, some modifications may have to be made to some of the low-level details. Only the creation routine *initialize*, the command *next* and the query *value_between (low : INTEGER; high : INTEGER)* from class RANDOM_NUMBER are used here. This query returns an integer that is uniformly distributed between the values *low* and *high*.

AN OBJECT-ORIENTED APPROACH TO PROBLEM SOLVING

The postconditon, *value >= 0 and value <= 6* given in the deferred routine *next* establishes a constraint on the lower and upper bounds of the numbers on the four die. Specifically, the smallest number for a given die is 0 and the largest number is 6.

The concrete subclasses of DIE, namely DIE1, DIE2, DIE3, and DIE4 are presented in Listing 1.12.

Listing 1.12   Classes DIE1, DIE2, DIE3, and DIE4

```
class DIE1
inherit
  DIE
creation
  make
feature
  next is
    do
      r.next
      if r.value_between (1, 6) <= 4 then
        value := 4
      else
        value := 0
      end
    ensure then
      value = 4 or value = 0
    end
end -- class DIE1

class DIE2
inherit
  DIE
creation
  make
feature
  next is
    do
      value := 3
```

Polymorphism and late-binding

```
      ensure then
        value = 3
      end

end -- class DIE2

class DIE3

inherit
  DIE

creation
  make

feature

  next is
    do
      r.next
      if r.value_between (1, 6) <= 4 then
        value := 2
      else
        value := 6
      end
    ensure then
      value = 2 or value = 6
    end

end -- class DIE3

class DIE4

inherit
  DIE

creation
  make

feature

  next is
    do
      r.next
      if r.value_between (1, 6) <= 3 then
        value := 5
      else
        value := 1
```

```
        end
    ensure then
        value = 5 or value = 1
    end

end -- class DIE4
```

Each of the specialized die types in Listing 1.12 uses an inherit clause to establish a parent-child relationship. Each of these die classes declares *make* to be its creation routine. The details of *make* are inherited from deferred (abstract) class DIE.

1.6.1.5 A final look at polymorphism in this application

Before leaving this example, let us take one final look at the role of polymorphism in its design and implementation.

In class PLAYER, the simple statement *a_die.next* liberates each player from having to know anything about the type of dice it contains. Each dice instance will respond to this command in a manner appropriate to its particular subclass. In Eiffel or any object-oriented language, the responsibility for doing the dispatching to the appropriate next routine rests with the run-time system through its late-binding mechanism. All the compiler does is ensure that there exists a concrete method *next* that can respond to the expression *a_die.next*.

1.7 Summary

- The Eiffel language is used both as an elegant notation as well as efficient implementation language to represent data structure models, concepts, and ideas.

- Object-orientation provides the background—the context—in which to explore and present classic data structures, their associated algorithms, and their applications.

- Eiffel, perhaps more than most modern programming languages, provides facilities that support safe programming and easy to maintain code.

- Eiffel's assertion-handling features allow a programmer to more accurately specify the intended behavior of each module, while also providing a clean and extremely useful mechanism for error detection and recovery.

EXERCISES

- An object-oriented approach to problem solving represents an evolution of a way of thinking, modeling, and problem solving that has proven to be most effective during the past 15 years.
- This approach to problem solving and the modeling of data abstractions in particular is embodied in the notion of abstract data types.
- The external view or interface to the abstraction specifies the operations that may be performed on the underlying (and usually inaccessible) data model.
- The internal view specifies the data structure and the algorithm details (operations) that are used to manipulate the data structure.
- There are two basic types of operations that we might wish to perform on an abstract data type. The first type of operation is a **query**. The second type is a **command**.
- In these languages, the class is the logical unit of abstraction that glues a data structure to its associated operations.
- The class becomes an embodiment of an abstract data type.
- An orderly arrangement or scheme by which to represent data is called a **data structure**.
- Inheritance defines an important logical relationship between classes. If class C is a child of class P then C should generally be "a kind of" P.
- Generally a child class (subclass) is a more specialized type of entity than its parent.
- Eiffel is the first major object-oriented language to support the construction of generic classes. This is achieved by allowing the class to specify one or more generic parameters. When an instance of the class is declared, the generic parameter must be replaced with a concrete type.

1.8 Exercises

1. Identify three abstract data types and describe each one using the notation given in Section 1.1 (see the description of the ADT RECTANGLE given in this section).

2. Identify three separate examples that require inheritance and describe each one carefully.

3. List the commands and queries typically associated with the abstract data type INTEGER.

4. Consider the abstract data type for a RATIONAL_NUMBER. Describe this ADT in a manner similar to the ADT RECTANGLE given in Section 1.1. Include the data model, commands and queries for the ADT RATIONAL_NUMBER.

5. From the description of the four specialized dice types defined in Section 1.6, which player do you expect would consistently be the winner of the game? Explain your answer.

1.9 References

1. Meyer, Bertrand. *Eiffel: The Language.* Englewood Cliffs, Prentice-Hall, 1992.
2. Wiener, Richard. *An Object-Oriented Introduction To Computer Science Using Eiffel.* Upper Saddle River, Prentice-Hall, 1996.
3. Wiener, Richard. *Software Development Using Eiffel: There Can Be Life Other Than C++.* Upper Saddle River, Prentice-Hall, 1995.
4. Switzer, Robert. *Eiffel: An Introduction.* Englewood Cliffs, Prentice-Hall, 1993.

Chapter 2

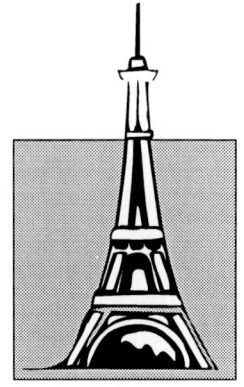

An Overview of Eiffel

This chapter presents an overview of the Eiffel language. The reader might wish to consult one or more of the references given at the end of Chapter 1. No attempt will be made to present either a rigorous or complete definition of the Eiffel language here.

Some readers may wish to skip this chapter and refer back to it as a reference whenever needed.

2.1 Programming in Eiffel

The Eiffel language was created by Bertrand Meyer in the late 1980s. His company, Interactive Software Engineering (ISE), produced the earliest commerical versions of the language. ISE continues to be a major supplier of Eiffel systems.

Eiffel is a pure object-oriented language. This implies that functions can be invoked only through objects and not as stand-alone logical entities. This is in sharp contrast to the popular but complex object-oriented language C++, which allows a mixture of object-oriented and procedural programming in the same application. C++ is called a hybrid language.

As a pure object-oriented language, the class in Eiffel is the basic logical unit of encapsulation as well as the basic physical unit, a module. Eiffel software is organized as a set of interrelated and cooperating classes.

2.1.1 Creating and destroying objects

Programs consist of classes, which create objects. These objects are created during program execution, perform their tasks and then are typically destroyed. When an object is created, storage space is allocated to hold the object. When an object is destroyed, its storage space is deallocated and may be reused by other objects that will be created later.

An object in Eiffel and in other object-oriented languages is an instance of a class. Its attributes are given by the data model of its class. The messages that it can respond to (i.e., the routines that one can invoke through the object) are specified by the behavioral model of the class (the set of routines given in the class description).

Before an object can be created in Eiffel it must be declared to be a variable of a given type. Its type is the name of the class that the object will be an instance of (after it is created). When an Eiffel type declaration such as *my_car : CAR* is given, the compiler verifies that a class called CAR has been defined. Usually the file that defines this class must reside in the same working subdirectory as the class in which the declaration exists.

The declaration, *my_car : CAR*, does not create an instance of class CAR. No memory storage for an object, *my_car*, is allocated by virtue of this declaration. In fact, the object *my_car*, like any object that has only been declared, assumes a default "value" of Void. In such a state an object cannot receive any messages or perform any useful tasks.

In order for *my_car* to become an instance of class CAR and have storage properly allocated, a creation routine or creation operator must be used.

Consider the case where class CAR does not have any creation routines specified. One could bring the object *my_car* to life (i.e., allocate storage for it) by using a creation operator as follows: *!!my_car*. The result of this expression is to allocate storage for *my_car* but provide no initialization for any of the attributes that may be defined in class CAR.

Consider the other case where class CAR provides three creation routines: *make, build,* and *construct*. A portion of class CAR is the following:

class CAR
  creation
    make, build, construct

  feature
    make (color : STRING; price : REAL; weight : INTEGER) **is**
      -- Details not shown
    end -- make

```
build (color : STRING; price : REAL; weight : INTEGER;
        horsepower : INTEGER) is
  -- Details not shown
  end  -- build

construct (color : STRING) is
  -- Details not shown
  end -- construct
```

Several expressions that would bring the object *my_car* to life include:

```
!!my_car.make ("White", 25600, 3100)
!!my_car.build ("Red", 12000, 3500, 125)
!!my_car.construct ("Blue")
```

In all three of the expressions above, the object *my_car* is created and initialized with the values given as parameters in the various creation routines. In the first case given above (i.e., *!!my_car*), *my_car* is created but its attribute values remain uninitialized.

It should be clear from this discussion that objects must be explicitly created either using the creation operator (!!) in front of the object you wish to create or using a specified creation routine in conjunction with the creation operator, as shown in the three examples above.

How are Eiffel objects destroyed? Eiffel systems provide for "automatic garbage collection." As an Eiffel application runs, a garbage collection process is running in the background and detecting when storage is no longer connected to a variable name. At an opportune moment the garbage collection process recycles (effectively, destroys) the unneeded storage. The following code segment shows an example of storage that is no longer needed.

```
my_car : CAR
!!my_car.construct( "Blue" )
!!my_car.construct( "Red" )
```

The statement, *!!my_car.construct("Blue")*, causes memory storage to be allocated and the object name *my_car* attached to this storage. The third statement *!!my_car.construct("Red")* causes new memory storage to be allocated and the object name *my_car* to be attached to this new storage leaving the old storage detached from any object name.

The detached storage containing "Blue" should be reclaimed by the automatic garbage collector while the program is running. It is not the Eiffel programmer's responsibility to do this.

2.1.2 Basic types

There are several basic object types that do not require explicit creation in order to be used. The important ones are: INTEGER, CHARACTER, REAL, and BOOLEAN. Consider the following declarations:

```
an_integer    : INTEGER
a_character   : CHARACTER
a_real        : REAL
a_boolean     : BOOLEAN
```

Objects of type INTEGER have a default value of *0*. Objects of type CHARACTER have a default value of the NULL character (ASCII value 0). Objects of type REAL have a default value of *0.0*. Finally, objects of type BOOLEAN have a default value of *false*.

2.1.3 Reference semantics versus value semantics

The basic types introduced in the previous section have "value" semantics. This implies that the declaration of objects causes memory storage to be automatically allocated and default values assigned to the objects.

Ordinary objects (non-basic type objects) have "reference" semantics. This implies that the programmer is responsible for explicitly allocating storage using a creation operator possibly in conjunction with a creation routine. The initial value of an ordinary object is Void. After the programmer creates storage for such an object the object name is attached to the storage.

2.1.4 Assigning objects

The assignment operator in Eiffel is ":=". What does it mean to assign one object to another? Here we are discussing ordinary objects with reference semantics, not simple objects such as INTEGER.

Consider the following segment of code:

```
my_car      : CAR
your_car    : CAR
!!my_car.make ("Green", 10000, 2000)
your_car := my_car
```

After the assignment of *your_car* to *my_car* both object names are attached to the same storage. This implies that if one of the attributes of *my_car* were modified by sending a message such as *my_car.set_weight*

(2500), the weight attribute of *your_car* would also be modified to 2500. There are not two independent objects but only two different names for the same object storage (only one object exists in computer memory).

2.1.5 Copying objects

Suppose that we desire the object *your_car* from the previous section to have the same values for its attributes as *my_car* but be an autonomous object that is not attached to the same storage as *my_car*. This can be accomplished as follows: (1) Create the object *your_car*, (2) Use the *copy* routine that is available to all Eiffel objects.

your_car.copy(my_car)   -- Assume that *your_car* has been created

It is essential that the object *your_car* already have storage associated with it in order for the *copy* routine to work. A run-time exception will be raised and an error reported if you invoke the *copy* routine on a *Void* object.

2.1.6 Cloning

Suppose that you wish to create storage for *your_car* at that same moment that you wish to copy the attribute values from *my_car* to *your_car*. This can be accomplished using the *clone* routine available to all Eiffel objects, as follows:

your_car := clone(my_car)

2.1.7 Basic operators

Equality operator (=): Two objects are equal if they are attached (bound) to the same storage. If one wishes to test whether the objects x and y are equal, an expression of the form *if x = y* would be used. This does not hold for simple objects such as INTEGER.

Inequality operator (/=): To test whether the objects x and y are not equal, an expression of the form *if x /= y* would be used.

INTEGER operators:
+	(Binary operator for addition)
-	(Binary operator for subtraction)
*	(Binary operator for multiplication)
^	(Binary operator for raised to power)
//	(Binary operator for integer division)
\\	(Binary operator for remainder)

<	(Binary operator for less than)
<=	(Binary operator for less than or equal)
>	(Binary operator for greater than)
>=	(Binary operator for greater than or equal)

REAL operators:

+	(Binary operator for addition)
-	(Binary operator for subtraction)
*	(Binary operator for multiplication)
/	(Binary operator for division)
^	(Binary operator for raised to power)
<	(Binary operator for less than)
<=	(Binary operator for less than or equal)
>	(Binary operator for greater than)
>=	(Binary operator for greater than or equal)

BOOLEAN operators:

not	(unary operator for logical negation)
or	(binary operator for logical "or")
and	(binary operator for logical "and")
implies	(used in assertions)
or else	(binary operator for "short-circuited" logical "or")
and then	(binary operator for "short-circuited" logical "and")

The less obvious operators presented above will be explained in context when they are first used.

2.1.8 Branching

The simplest type of branch is the *if* clause. This control structure is used when the execution of one or more lines of code, a code block, is based on the outcome of a logical test that is performed before entering the block of code. The logical test requires the evaluation of a boolean expression. Such an expression evaluates to either TRUE or FALSE. The form of this structure is:

if a_boolean_expression **then**
   statement(s)
end

Another simple control structure is the *if-then-else* structure. It is used when a choice must be made between two blocks of code. The choice is based on the evaluation of a boolean expression. This control structure is built as follows:

An Overview of Eiffel

```
if boolean_expression then
   block_1
else
   block_2
end
```

Here, *block_1* and *block2* represent one or more lines of code.

The *if-then-else* construct can be nested. Consider the segment of code below.

```
if expr1 then
   statement1
else
   if expr2 then
      statement2
   else
      statement3
   end
end
```

If *expr1* evaluates to *true* then *statement1* will be executed. Otherwise if *expr2* evaluates to *true* then *statement2* will be executed otherwise *statement3* will be executed.

Suppose that one of several alternative branches is to be executed based on the evaluation of some control expression which evaluates to *true* or *false*. The *if-elseif-else* construct might be appropriate.

This construct is formed as follows:

```
if expr1 then
   statement1
elseif expr2 then
   statement2
elseif expr3 then
   statement3
else
   statement4
end
```

The *else* clause in the above construct is optional. There is no limit on the number of *elseif* clauses.

If the number of *elseif* clauses becomes too large, the resulting expression is awkward to look at and may be inefficient to evaluate. The *inspect* construct might be more appropriate. A control expression that returns either an INTEGER or CHARACTER value is used to determine which block of code is executed.

The syntax for the *inspect* construct is given below.

inspect control_expression
when range **then**
  block_1
when range **then**
  block_2
  ...
else
  block_n
end

An actual example of the *inspect* construct is given in the code segment below.

inspect input_value
when 1 ..9 **then**
  io.putstring ("Value is a one digit number")
when 10 .. 99 **then**
  io.putstring ("Value is a two digit number")
when 100 .. 999 **then**
  io.putstring ("Value is a three digit number")
else
  io.putstring ("Value has more than three digits")
end

2.1.9 Iteration (loop)

It is often necessary to carry out a sequence of statements repeatedly until some condition is met. The construct *from-until-loop* may be used in this situation.

The general form of this iteration construct is:

from
  initialization_instructions
until
  loop_exit_conditions
loop
  body_of_loop
end

The following examples illustrate the use of iteration.

In the first example, suppose we wish to compute the sum of the finite series:

1 + 2 + 3 + 4 + 5 + 6 + ... + 1,000,000. An Eiffel code segment for computing this sum is given in Listing 2.1.

Listing 2.1   Code segment for computing sum of integers from 1 to 1 million

```
index, sum : INTEGER

from
    sum := 0
    index := 0
until index = 1000000
loop
    index := index + 1
    sum := sum + index
end
io.putstring ("sum = ")
io.putint (sum)
io.new_line
```

The initialization statements, *sum := 0* and *index := 0* are correct but unnecessary. Both objects assume default values of 0 by virtue of their declaration. Incidently, for those who are interested, the output of this segment is: *sum = 1784293664*.

2.1.10 Routines

An Eiffel routine specifies interface information as well as implementation details. The user of a class (consumer) needs access to only the interface portion of a routine. The producer of the class needs access to the implementation details when performing maintenance on the routine.

An Eiffel routine is part of the behavioral description of a class. As indicated before, a routine must be invoked through an instance of a class (an object).

Routines come in two flavors: procedure and function routines. Procedure routines do not return a value, whereas function routines do. Procedure routines are used to change the internal state of an object (the values of its attributes). Function routines are used to access state information from the object (the value of one or more of its attributes) or perform some computation that may involve the current state of the object. The result of the computation is returned. Procedure routines are used to implement commands and function routines used to implement queries.

The name of a routine should be carefully chosen. It should describe the purpose of the routine. For a procedure routine, a verb or verb phrase should be used. For a function routine a noun or noun phrase that is descriptive of what is returned should be used. For example, a procedure routine for setting the weight of a car might have the name *set_weight*. If another function routine computes the volume of the car, its name might be *volume*.

The parameter list, if present, contains the input information that is used by the routine.

The return type, if present, indicates the type of information that the function (query) computes and returns to the caller (the routine that invokes the function).

The statements contained between the delimiters *do* and *end* represent the body or implementation details of a routine.

Consider a routine that meets the following specifications for computing income tax from taxable income. The tax that is due is $0 if the taxable income is less than $6000, is 15 percent of the taxable income if the income is between $6000 and $22,000 and is $3300 plus 28 percent of the taxable income in excess of $22,000 if the income is greater than $22,000.

Routine compute_tax is shown in Listing 2.2.

Listing 2.2   Routine for computing income tax

```
income_tax (taxable_income : REAL) : REAL is
  do
    if taxable_income < 6000 then
      Result := 0.0
    elseif taxable_income < 22000 then
      Result := 0.15 * taxable_income
    else
      Result := 3300 + 0.28 * ( taxable_income - 22000 )
    end
  end  -- income_tax
```

2.2   Basic input and output

The routines that support the keyboard input and terminal output come from a class called STD_FILES. A portion of the interface to this class is given in Listing 2.3. The object *io* is automatically created when every Eiffel application is created.

Listing 2.3   Interface to class STD_FILES

class *interface STD_FILES*

  feature *-- Element change*

   new_line
     -- Write line feed at end of default output.

   putchar (c: CHARACTER)
     -- Write 'c' at end of default output.

   putdouble (d: DOUBLE)
     -- Write 'd' at end of default output.

   putint (i: INTEGER)
     -- Write 'i' at end of default output.

   putreal (r: REAL)
     -- Write 'r' at end of default output.

   putstring (s: STRING)
     -- Write 's' at end of default output.

  feature *-- Input*

   next_line
     -- Move to next input line on standard input.

   readchar
     -- Read a new character from standard input.
     -- Make result available in 'lastchar'.

   readdouble
     -- Read a new double from standard input.
     -- Make result available in 'lastdouble'.

   readint
     -- Read a new integer from standard input.
     -- Make result available in 'lastint'.

   readline
     -- Read a line from standard input.
     -- Make result available in 'laststring'.

ARRAYS

> *readreal*
> -- *Read a new real from standard input.*
> -- *Make result available in 'lastreal'.*
>
> *readstream (nb_char: INTEGER)*
> -- *Read a string of at most 'nb_char' bound characters*
> -- *from standard input.*
> -- *Make result available in 'laststring'.*
>
> *readword*
> -- *Read a new word from standard input.*
> -- *Make result available in 'laststring'.*

feature -- *Status report*

> *lastchar: CHARACTER*
> -- *Last character read by readchar*
>
> *lastdouble: DOUBLE*
>
> *lastint: INTEGER*
> -- *Last integer read by readint*
>
> *lastreal: REAL*
> -- *Last real read by readreal*
>
> *laststring: STRING*
> -- *Last string read by readline,*
> -- *readstream, or readword*

end -- *class STD_FILES*

2.3 Arrays

The basic types, INTEGER, CHARACTER, BOOLEAN, REAL, and DOUBLE, have been introduced earlier. It is often desirable to construct a collection of basic or programmer defined types in such a manner that individual elements can be directly accessed by using an integer called an *index*. For example, suppose one wishes to store the ages (rounded to the nearest integer) of the four members of a tennis doubles group. Suppose the ages of the four players are 27, 32, 35, and 29. We label the four players 1, 2, 3, and 4 and store the ages in an array.

The basic operations that one can perform on an array are insertion and access; that is, to be able to choose an index location and insert or access an element at that location. In addition, one needs to be able to cre-

An Overview of Eiffel

ate an array using an appropriate creation routine. Other operations that one might desire would include copying one array to another, resizing an existing array, and determining the current capacity of an array.

Class ARRAY supports all of these basic operations. A small portion of its interface is given in Listing 2.4.

Listing 2.4   Portion of interface to class ARRAY

    class *interface ARRAY [G]*

        creation
          make

        feature *-- Access*

          item (i: INTEGER): G
            -- Entry at index 'i', if in index interval.

          infix "@" (i: INTEGER): G
            -- Entry at index 'i', if in index interval.

        feature *-- Comparison*

          is_equal (other: like Current): BOOLEAN
            -- Is array made of the same items as 'other'?

        feature *-- Duplication*

          copy (other: like Current)
            -- Reinitialize by copying all the items of 'other'.
            -- (This is also used by 'clone'.)
            ensure
              equal_areas: area.is_equal (other.area)

        feature *-- Element change*

          put (v: G; i: INTEGER)
            -- Replace 'i'-th entry, if in index interval, by 'v'.

        feature *-- Initialization*

          make (minindex, maxindex: INTEGER)
            -- Allocate array; set index interval to
            -- 'minindex' .. 'maxindex'
            -- (empty if 'minindex' > 'maxindex').
            ensure
              no_capacity: (minindex > maxindex) implies (capacity = 0)

```
      capacity_constraint: (minindex <= maxindex) implies
         (capacity = maxindex - minindex + 1)
      lower = minindex
      upper = maxindex

  feature -- Measurement

    capacity: INTEGER
       -- Available indices

    count: INTEGER
       -- Available indices

    lower: INTEGER
       -- Minimum index

    upper: INTEGER
       -- Maximum index

  end -- class ARRAY
```

2.4 An overview of the components of an Eiffel class

The major components of an Eiffel class are displayed below in Figure 2.1. Not all of the components of an Eiffel class will be presented because their application lies outside of the scope of this book. In later chapters, if other class components are needed, they will be defined in the appropriate context.

```
  class SOME_DESCRIPTIVE_NAME
  -- Some comments that describe the semantics of the class
     inherit
        rename -- optional subclause
           -- List of inherited routines and their new names
        export -- optional subclause
           -- Used to control the scope of one or more inherited routines
        undefine -- optional subclause
           -- Will not be discussed in this book
        redefine -- optional subclause
           -- List of inherited routines to be redefined
        select -- optional subclause
```

           -- Used with multiple inheritance in conjunction with rename
    end

    creation { export scope }
        -- List of routines that can create and initialize objects of this class

    feature { export scope }
        an_attribute : SOME_TYPE
        -- Other attributes in feature section

        a_routine (a_possible_parameter_list) [: a_possible_return_type] **is**
        require
            -- preconditions
        local
            -- temporary objects
        do
            -- Algorithmic details of routine
        ensure
            -- postconditions
        end

        -- Other routines in feature section

    invariant
        -- class invariants

end

Figure 2.1 Some major components of an Eiffel class.

2.5 Creation

Creation routines provide a mechanism to dynamically allocate storage for new objects and initialize the attributes of the new objects at the time they are created. It must be recalled that an Eiffel object is not created by virtue of its declaration (a default value of VOID is assigned to an object before it is created). An Eiffel object must be created before it can be used for any practical purpose.

Creation routines may be used as ordinary routines typically to update the values of attributes for an existing object. Only if the creation operator, "!!", is used in front of a creation routine will a new object be brought to life.

If a class does not include any creation routines, instances can be created merely by using the creation operator in front of the name of an object. In such a case the attributes contained within the object assume their default values.

Creation clauses may contain an export section bounded by curly braces, "{" and "}". Objects of the given class may be created only in the classes and their descendants specified in the export section, if present. If no export section is present a default export section of ANY is implied. Since all Eiffel classes are descendants of ANY, the absence of an explicit export section implies that objects of the given class may be created from within any other class (i.e., universal export).

Listing 2.5 demonstrates the use of a creation routine that can be used for object creation but not as an ordinary routine. It would not be desirable to allow this creation routine to be used as an ordinary "mutator" (a routine that can change the internal state of an object once it exists) because this would violate the protocol that an account balance can be modified only through deposit or withdrawal. We do not want to allow a client to set the balance on an existing account once it is created.

By making the export scope of the creation routine universal (by the absence of an export scope) and then placing the creation routine in a protected section (a feature section with export scope {NONE}), objects may be created anywhere, but not modified using the creation routine.

Listing 2.5 Creation routine that cannot be used as an ordinary routine

```
class ACCOUNT
   creation -- universal export scope by default
      open

   feature
      balance : REAL

      deposit (amount : REAL) is
         do
            balance := balance + amount
         end  -- deposit

      withdraw (amount : REAL) is
         do
            balance := balance - amount
         end  -- withdraw

   feature { NONE }
   -- For internal use only
```

```
    open (initial_deposit : REAL) is
    -- Can be used only to create an account
      do
        balance := initial_deposit
      end  -- open

end -- ACCOUNT
```

2.5.1 Subclass creation

A subclass often contains more attributes than its parent. The creation routine of the parent class can often be invoked to assist in the implementation of the creation routine of the subclass. This is illustrated in the next example.

A class JET is defined as a subclass of AIRPLANE. It inherits the attributes *wingspan, weight,* and *cost* from AIRPLANE and in addition has the attribute *thrust*. As evident in Listing 2.6 , the creation routine *build* in JET uses the *make* routine of AIRPLANE. It is important to emphasize that *make* is invoked as an ordinary routine inside of *build*. An AIRPLANE object is not being created by *build*; a JET object is.

Listing 2.6   Classes AIRPLANE and JET

```
class AIRPLANE

  creation
    make

  feature
    wingspan  : REAL
    weight    : REAL
    cost      : REAL

    make (wing_size : REAL; the_weight : REAL;
      the_cost : REAL) is
      do
        wingspan := wing_size
        weight := the_weight
        cost := the_cost
      end -- make

    -- Other features not shown

end -- AIRPLANE
```

```
class JET
  inherit
    AIRPLANE
  creation
    build

  feature
    thrust : REAL

    build ( wing_size : REAL; the_weight : REAL;
      the_cost : REAL; the_thrust : REAL) is
    do
      make (wing_size, the_weight, the_cost)
      thrust := the_thrust
    end -- build

    -- Other features not shown

end -- JET
```

2.5.2 More advanced subclass creation

A descendant of a given class can be created by enclosing the name of the descendant class between each "!" operator. This is illustrated in Listing 2.7. Here a subclass CHECKING of ACCOUNT is introduced. Its creation routine, *open*, is inherited from its parent class ACCOUNT. An object *my_checking_account* is produced by using the expression, !CHECKING!my_checking_account.open (500.0).

It is essential to declare *open* in the *creation* clause of class CHECKING. Its status as a *creation* routine in class ACCOUNT does not automatically make it a creation routine in the descendant class CHECKING. This must be accomplished explicitly.

Listing 2.7   Creating subclass objects

```
class CHECKING

  inherit
    ACCOUNT -- See Listing 2.5
  creation
    open -- This routine is inherited from class ACCOUNT

  feature
    monthly_fee : REAL
```

```
    set_monthly_fee (amount : REAL) is
      do
        monthly_fee := amount
      end  -- set_monthly_fee

    apply_fee is
      do
        balance := balance - monthly_fee
      end  -- apply_fee
end -- CHECKING

class APPLICATION
  creation
    start

  feature

    start is
      local
        my_checking_account    : ACCOUNT
        my_account             : ACCOUNT
      do
        !CHECKING!my_checking_account.open (500.0)
        my_checking_account.deposit (300.0)
        my_checking_account.withdraw (100.0)
        io.putstring ("Balance in checking = ")
        io.putreal (my_checking_account.balance)
        io.new_line

        !!my_account.open (200.0)
        my_account.deposit (50.0)
        my_account.withdraw (10.0)
        -- Illegal: my_account.open (1000.0)
        -- Cannot use open as a mutator routine
        io.putstring ("Balance in account = ")
        io.putreal (my_account.balance)
        io.new_line

    end  -- start

end -- APPLICATION
```

In class APPLICATION in Listing 2.7, one would normally not declare *my_checking_account* to be of type ACCOUNT when its intended use is that of type CHECKING. This was done purely for tutorial reasons. It is noted that the effect produced is identical to the following statements:

```
check            : CHECKING
my_checking : ACCOUNT

!!check.open (500.0)
my_checking := check
```

If a class has one or more creation routines it is illegal to create a new object using just the creation operator, "!!", followed by the object name. One of the creation routines must be used. So, for example, it would be illegal to write *!!my_account*, if *my_account* were declared to be of type ACCOUNT.

2.6 Inheritance

Inheritance is an architectural property of object-oriented systems used for establishing a decomposition of a software system into classes and subclasses. Inheritance also provides the basis for software reuse. The accepted practice is for classes at the top of a hierarchy to encapsulate general properties of some domain and for classes lower in the hierarchy to extend and to encapsulate more specialized properties of the domain. As one moves down a class hierarchy, the "is-a" or "is a kind of" relationship should hold between child class and parent class. Attributes and methods defined in a parent class should make sense in all descendant classes.

In going from a parent class to its child, **specialization** involves redefining one or more of the parent's routines or attributes, **extension** involves adding routines or attributes not present in the parent, and **restriction** involves blocking one or more routines of the parent. All three may be used simultaneously, but it is most common to use only specialization and extension in going down a class hierarchy.

2.6.1 Extension

An example of extension may be found in classes ACCOUNT and CHECKING presented earlier. Class CHECKING is an extension of class ACCOUNT. The behavior of CHECKING objects includes the behavior of ACCOUNT objects as a proper subset. For example, the operations that can be performed on CHECKING objects include the following subset inherited from class ACCOUNT: *open* (for class creation only), *balance* (a read-only attribute), *deposit* (for adding funds to an account), *withdraw* (for

An Overview of Eiffel

subtracting funds from an account). The following additional behavior is associated with CHECKING objects only: *monthly_fee* (a read-only attribute), and the mutator routines *set_monthly_fee* (set the value of the attribute monthly_fee) and *apply_fee* (change the current balance by subtracting the value of *monthly_fee*).

Once the behavior of parent class instances (such as objects of type ACCOUNT) are understood, it is quite easy to understand the behavior of subtype instances (such as objects of type CHECKING). In a subtype hierarchy behaviors are additive. That is, the behavior of a descendant subtype is the strict addition of the behaviors of all its ancestor types and the immediate additions in the descendant type.

2.6.2 Specialization - The redefine subclause

In many practical class hierarchies, subclasses typically redefine as well as add to the protocol of their ancestors. When either an attribute or method of an ancestor class is redefined this must be indicated explicitly using a *redefine* subclause. Although the name of the inherited attribute or method is unchanged, the behavior associated with the inherited feature is changed.

We consider a simple example of redefinition here. Suppose class CORPORATE_CHECKING is created as a specialized type of CHECKING_ACCOUNT. This subclass of CHECKING is presented in Listing 2.8.

Listing 2.8   Class CORPORATE_CHECKING

```
class CORPORATE_CHECKING
  inherit
    CHECKING
      redefine
        apply_fee
      end

  creation
    open

  feature
    apply_fee is
    -- Monthly fee structure is changed
      do
```

balance := 0.99 *balance - 2 * monthly_fee
   end -- *apply_fee*

end -- CORPORATE_CHECKING

2.6.3 Selective export—the export subclause

The *export* subclause may be used to block or redefine the scope in which one or more routines inherited from an ancestor are visible to instances and descendants of the child class.

To continue the account classes example a bit further, suppose we wish to create another specialized class, a NO_FEE_CHECKING account, inherited from CHECKING. One way of accomplishing this is to simply use the existing CHECKING class and set the *monthly_fee* to 0. Another way would be to create the subclass NO_FEE_CHECKING and block access to the *set_monthly_fee* and *apply_fee* commands in all clients of NO_FEE_CHECKING.

Listing 2.9 shows how this can be accomplished.

Listing 2.9   Class NO_FEE_CHECKING

class NO_FEE_CHECKING

  inherit
    CHECKING
      export { NONE } set_monthly_fee, apply_fee
    end

  creation
    open

end -- NO_FEE_CHECKING

The routines *set_monthly_fee* and *apply_fee* are not available to any clients of class NO_FEE_CHECKING. If an attempt is made to invoke these commands through any objects type NO_FEE_CHECKING, the compiler will emit an error message indicating that these commands are not exported to the client class.

2.6.4 Renaming inherited routines—the rename subclause

It is often the case that the designer of a subclass wishes to utilize the behavior of a routine inherited from an ancestor class but the name given to the routine by the designer of the ancestor class may not be appropriate, suitable, or liked by the subclass designer. The *rename* subclause allows the subclass designer the freedom to reuse the behavior of the inherited routine while giving it a new name. This new name, unless changed again by the designer of a descendant class, remains in force for all descendant classes.

As an example, suppose a class designer creates a FLOWER class partially given as follows:

class *FLOWER*

  feature
    smell : *STRING*

  -- Other features not shown
end -- *FLOWER*

Suppose a subclass designer is building a ROSE subclass that inherits from FLOWER (certainly a rose "is a kind of" flower). The designer of the ROSE class does not like the choice of name given to the attribute that characterizes how the flower smells. So she renames this attribute *fragrance* as follows:

class *ROSE*
  inherit
    FLOWER
      rename
        smell as fragrance -- all clients of ROSE and its descendants must use
                -- the name fragrance
    end

  -- Other features not shown

end -- *ROSE*

Another example of renaming is shown in another revision to class CORPORATE_CHECKING given in Listing 2.10.

Listing 2.10 Another revision of class CORPORATE_CHECKING

  class *CORPORATE_CHECKING*

    inherit
      CHECKING
        rename

Inheritance

```
        apply_fee as pay_monthly_fee
      redefine
        pay_monthly_fee
      end

  creation
    open

  feature

    pay_monthly_fee is
      do
        balance := 0.99 *balance - 2 * monthly_fee
      end -- pay_monthly_fee

  end -- CORPORATE_CHECKING
```

The combination of rename and redefine subclauses demonstrates how the name of the inherited *apply_fee* command has been changed while at the same time redefining its meaning (compared to the parent class). In all instances of subclasses and clients of CORPORATE_CHECKING, the command *pay_monthly_fee* must be used. Only for instance of class CHECKING would the name *apply_fee* be used.

2.6.5 The select subclause

It might appear that renaming is strictly a cosmetic issue. Even if that were true the *rename* subclause would still be a most useful artifact. Renaming has a deeper purpose, primarily when multiple inheritance is employed in a design.

In this section, a relatively simple but important use of renaming is discussed. Suppose a method is defined in a parent class. In a subclass the method is redefined. In redefining the subclass method, the designer wishes to reuse the behavior of the parent class method but add to this behavior. That is, the subclass routine needs to be able to invoke the parent class routine. But they both have the same name. The use of the *rename* and *select* subclauses provides a way to do this. An example, given in Listing 2.11, illustrates the technique.

Listing 2.11   Use of the select subclause

```
class PARENT
  creation
    make
```

```
  feature
    attribute1 : INTEGER
    attribute2 : REAL

    make (value1 : INTEGER; value2 : REAL) is
      do
        attribute1 := value1
        attribute2 := value2
      end  -- make

    display is
      do
        io.putstring ("Attribute1 = ")
        io.putint (attribute1)
        io.new_line
        io.putstring ("Attribute2 = ")
        io.putreal (attribute2)
        io.new_line
      end  -- display
    -- Other features not shown

end -- PARENT

class CHILD
  inherit
    PARENT
      rename
        display as parent_display
      end

    PARENT
      redefine
        display
      select
        display
      end

  creation
    make_child

  feature
    attribute3 : DOUBLE

    make_child (value1 : INTEGER; value2 : REAL;
        value3 : DOUBLE) is
```

```
      do
        make (value1, value2)
        attribute3 := value3
      end  -- make_child

    display is
      do
        parent_display
        io.putstring ("Attribute3 = ")
        io.putdouble (attribute3)
        io.new_line
      end  -- display

    -- Other features not shown

end -- CHILD

class APPLICATION
  creation
    start

  feature

    start is
      local
        p : PARENT
        c : CHILD
      do
        !!p.make (10, 20.0)
        !!c.make_child (50, 60.0, 70.0)
        p.display
        c.display
      end  -- start

end -- APPLICATION
```

Class PARENT defines two attributes. The *display* routine outputs these attributes. Class CHILD introduces a third attribute. Its *display* routine calls the parent class version and then adds output for the third attribute. Although this example does nothing useful, it illustrates a common situation that occurs in many real applications.

Class CHILD inherits from class PARENT twice, using the multiple inheritance capability of Eiffel in a unique way. In the first inheritance, the parent routine *display* has its name changed to *parent_display*. In the second inheritance, the parent routine *display* is redefined. In the implementation of this redefinition, the parent version of *display* can be called directly using its new and unique name, *parent_display*. The purpose of the *select* subclause is to inform the runtime system that an object of type CHILD should use the redefined version of *display* rather than the original PARENT version of *display* when the formal type of the object is PARENT and the actual type is CHILD. It is noted that features that are the same through repeated inheritance are merged.

2.7 Abstract classes using Eiffel's deferred class facility

To motivate the need for abstract classes (to be defined shortly), the small hierarchy of two ACCOUNT classes is continued a little further. This will provide a most natural setting in which to introduce the concept of abstract classes, implemented in Eiffel as **deferred** classes.

Suppose we wish to add several additional saving account classes. Specifically we wish to add: (1) A non-interest bearing savings account, (2) A savings account in which monthly interest is based on the end of month or final balance, (3) A savings account in which monthly interest is based on the maximum balance that was achieved anytime during the month, and (4) A savings account whose interest is computed on a daily basis.

Each of the specialized types of savings accounts given above share some protocol. They all have a monthly interest rate given by the attribute *monthly_interest_rate* and behavior given by *apply_interest*. This latter routine is implemented differently in each of the savings account classes.

The common features of all the savings accounts can be factored into an abstract class, SAVINGS. The class is called abstract because no actual instances (objects) of this type will ever be created. In fact it would be illegal to attempt the creation of such an instance. Only the common properties associated with the data model and methods of the more specialized types of savings accounts are specified in the abstract class, SAVINGS.

In Eiffel a class is abstract, and can produce no actual instances, if the implementation details of one or more of its methods is *deferred*. Then the entire class is *deferred*.

The code for abstract class SAVINGS is given in Listing 2.12.

Listing 2.12 Abstract class SAVINGS

```
deferred class SAVINGS
-- An abstract class for all types of savings accounts
-- No instances of this class can be created
```

Abstract classes using Eiffel's deferred class facility

```
inherit
  ACCOUNT

feature
  monthly_interest : REAL

  set_interest_rate (value : REAL) is
    do
      monthly_interest := value
    end  -- set_interest_rate

  apply_interest is
    deferred
    end  -- apply_interest

end -- SAVINGS
```

The routine, *apply_interest*, given as *deferred* must be made effective in all non-abstract descendant classes (concrete classes). Any subclass that does not define this method is considered a *deferred* class and must be tagged as such.

Listing 2.13 shows the details of class NON_INTEREST, the first of our four specialized types of savings account classes.

Listing 2.13   Class NON_INTEREST

```
class NON_INTEREST

inherit
  SAVINGS

creation
  open

feature

  apply_interest is
    -- Null routine needed to make class effective
    do
    end  -- apply_interest

end -- NON_INTEREST
```

Listing 2.14 presents the details of class FINAL_BALANCE, the second of the four specialized savings account classes.

Listing 2.14 Class FINAL_BALANCE

```
class FINAL_BALANCE
-- A savings account with monthly interest based on final balance

  inherit
    SAVINGS

  creation
    open

  feature

    apply_interest is
        -- Compute monthly interest from final balance
      do
        balance := ( 1 + monthly_interest ) * balance
      end -- apply_interest

end -- FINAL_BALANCE
```

Class MAXIMUM_BALANCE is presented in Listing 2.15.

Listing 2.15 Class MAXIMUM_BALANCE

```
class MAXIMUM_BALANCE
-- A savings account with monthly interest based on maximum balance

  inherit
    SAVINGS
      redefine
        deposit, open
      end

  creation
    open

  feature
    -- largest monthly balance
    maximum_balance : REAL

    reset_maximum_balance (value : REAL) is
        -- Used at the beginning of every month
      do
        maximum_balance := value
      end -- reset_maximum_balance
```

```
apply_interest is
    -- Compute monthly interest from maximum balance
    do
        balance := ( 1 + monthly_interest ) * maximum_balance
    end  -- apply_interest

deposit (amount : REAL) is
    do
        balance := balance + amount
        if balance > maximum_balance then
            maximum_balance := balance
        end
    end  -- deposit

open (initial_deposit : REAL) is
    do
        balance := initial_deposit
        maximum_balance := balance
    end  -- open

end -- MAXIMUM_BALANCE
```

The additional attribute, *maximum_balance*, is introduced in class MAXIMUM_BALANCE. The *deposit* routine, inherited from class ACCOUNT (through class SAVINGS), updates *maximum_balance* whenever appropriate.

Finally, class DAILY_BALANCE, the most complex of the four specialized savings account classes, is shown in Listing 2.16.

Listing 2.16   Class DAILY_BALANCE

```
class DAILY_BALANCE
-- A savings account with interest computed daily

    inherit
        SAVINGS
            export
                { NONE } deposit, withdraw
            end

    creation { ANY }
        open_daily
```

feature
  -- day of month of last deposit
  last_deposit   : INTEGER
  cumulative_interest   : REAL

  deposit_daily (amount: REAL; day_of_month : INTEGER) **is**
    local
      daily_interest : REAL
    do
      daily_interest := monthly_interest / 30.0
      cumulative_interest := cumulative_interest +
        balance * (day_of_month - last_deposit) *
        daily_interest
      balance := balance + amount
      last_deposit := day_of_month
    end -- deposit_daily

  withdraw_daily (amount : REAL; day_of_month : INTEGER) **is**
    local
      daily_interest : REAL
    do
      daily_interest := monthly_interest / 30.0
      cumulative_interest := cumulative_interest +
        balance * (day_of_month - last_deposit) *
        daily_interest
      balance := balance - amount
      last_deposit := day_of_month
    end -- withdraw_daily

  apply_interest **is**
    do
      balance := balance + cumulative_interest
    end -- apply_interest

feature { NONE }

  open_daily (initial_deposit : REAL; day_of_month : INTEGER) **is**
    do
      balance := initial_deposit
      last_deposit := day_of_month
      cumulative_interest := 0.0
    end -- open

end -- DAILY_BALANCE

Class DAILY_BALANCE adds two attributes, *last_deposit* and *cumulative_interest*, to the data model inherited from SAVINGS.

The *deposit* and *withdraw* methods, inherited from ACCOUNT (through SAVINGS) are blocked. They are no longer applicable for adding or subtracting funds from a DAILY_BALANCE account. These methods are replaced with the routines *deposit_daily* and *withdraw_daily*. In each of these new methods, the *cumulative_interest* is incremented based on the current balance and the number of days it has been in force (of course multiplied by the daily interest rate).

The creation routine, *open_daily*, like its counterpart *open* in class ACCOUNT, is placed in a protected section in order to prevent the routine from being used as a mutator. Method *open*, inherited from ACCOUNT (through SAVINGS), is inaccessible to instances of class DAILY_BALANCE because it is not declared as a creation routine and appears in a protected section in class ACCOUNT. The only way to create an instance of class DAILY_BALANCE is through the creation routine *open_daily*.

You may be wondering why none of the descendants of class SAVINGS (i.e., the four specialized savings account classes) needed to specify the routine *apply_interest* in a *redefine* subclause. The answer is that the four definitions of this method are not redefinitions but original definitions since the abstract class SAVINGS provides no effective definition. A *redefine* subclause is required only when an effective version of a routine is changed in a descendant class.

In general, abstract (*deferred*) classes are key components of highly evolved class hierarchies such as the core Eiffel libraries. The information contained within an abstract class represents a generalization of the behavior of many more specialized classes. It is fairly typical in mature libraries to find many layers of abstract classes sitting above the concrete or effective classes that represent the actual objects of the system. Since one of the major purposes of a class hierarchy is to provide an "intellectual" decomposition of the features that represent a particular problem domain in order to manage the complexity of the domain, it should be evident that abstract classes are an important ingredient in the management of complexity.

2.8 Storage versus computation: attributes versus routines

A client of a class such as ACCOUNT (see Listing 2.5) does not need to know whether *balance* is an attribute (obtained through storage) or a routine (obtained through computation). From the client's viewpoint this information is irrelevant. Only when one or more parameters are required in a routine does the syntax make it obvious that information is being obtained through computation (the invocation of a routine).

2.9 Protecting and documenting routines—assertions and programming by contract

The routines of a class specify the behavior of the class (i.e., the behavior of the objects spawned by the class). For each routine this behavior is affected by the values of input parameters, if present, the current values of the object's attributes, and the algorithm specified in the routine.

An important issue concerns whose responsibility it is to ensure that legal values are passed to a routine? An associated question is, whose responsibility is it to handle the error that results if one or more illegal values are passed to a routine? Is it the user's or class designer's responsibility to handle errors? That is, should the producer (routine itself) or consumer (client module using the routine) be responsible for handling the errors?

Clearly, it is the client code's responsibility to ensure that legal values are provided to the routine. The designer of the routine has no control over the use of the routine. Some readers may be inclined to think that the designer of the routine has the responsibility to deal with errors committed by the user. After all it is he or she who intimately knows the requirements of the routine and indeed "owns" and controls the routine.

The designer of the routine does not typically know the best way to handle an error produced by the client. An error message emitted from the failed routine may destroy the client's carefully designed screen display. Halting program execution may bring a real-time system such as an avionic system on a Boeing 757 to a dangerous state. In fact there is no appropriate general error handling that the class designer (the author of the routine) can devise that would be satisfactory to all users. Indeed, all the routine can and should do on behalf of the user is to raise an exception (a signal that triggers an exception handling section in the client's code) so that the client code may respond appropriately to the error condition. If the client code chooses to ignore the error, program execution must be halted since it would be imprudent to continue program execution when the system is in an unsafe state.

PROTECTING AND DOCUMENTING ROUTINES—ASSERTIONS AND PROGRAMMING BY CONTRACT

The assertion handling mechanism for Eiffel routines provides the basis for this division of responsibility between the producer and consumer, that is, the class designer and user.

The preconditions section of a routine, specified by a *require* clause, precisely specifies the conditions that must be satisfied in order for the routine to successfully perform its function. The client of a routine can inspect the preconditions. They are available in both the long (full source code) or short (only attributes, routine signatures and assertions) forms that can be inspected by the user. It is the client's responsibility to ensure that every precondition required of the routine is satisfied upon entry into the routine.

In exchange, the routine may provide one or more postconditions, given by an *ensure* clause. Such an *ensure* clause specifies the state the system is guaranteed to be in as a result of executing the routine. In other words, if the client code complies with all the preconditions, the routine (class designer) guarantees the postconditions. This compact between the producer and consumer is called "programming by contract" by its originator, Bertrand Meyer. It has emerged over the years as a highly respected design tool.

Preconditions and postconditions provide a powerful, precise, and extremely useful type of self-documentation for a routine. The semantics of the routine, that is its purpose, may often be clarified by the preconditions and postconditions. To an inexperienced client, the preconditions provide the basis for accelerating the learning process associated with using features from a class. Whenever a precondition is violated, in the absence of a client-defined exception handler (to be introduced later in this section), program execution is halted with an exception trace output to the user. This exception trace indicates the exception that was violated and the errant routine that engaged in the violation. This allows the client to re-examine his or her code and make appropriate modifications so that the routine that was violated may be used legally and properly.

Listing 2.17 demonstrates the use of preconditions and exception handling in a class called MATH and a short test program in class APPLICATION.

Listing 2.17 Demonstration of preconditions and exception handling

class MATH

feature

```
silly (value : INTEGER) : INTEGER is
  require
    value_not_five: value /= 5
  do
    Result := 5 - value
  end  -- silly

load_value is
  local
    r              : INTEGER
    num_errors     : INTEGER
  do
    io.putstring ("%NEnter value: ")
    io.readint
    r := silly (io.lastint)
    io.putstring ("r = ")
    io.putint (r)
    io.new_line
  rescue
    num_errors := num_errors + 1
    io.putstring ("Error: Cannot enter the value 5%N")
    if num_errors = 3 then
      io.putstring (
         "Three strikes and you are out!%N")
    else
      retry
    end
  end  -- load_value

  -- Other features not shown

end -- MATH

class APPLICATION
  creation
    start

  feature

    start is
      local
        m : MATH
      do
        !!m
```

```
        m.load_value
    end -- start

end -- APPLICATION
```

Portions of the program output when 5 is entered three times are shown below.

```
Enter value: 5
Error: Cannot enter the value 5

Enter value: 5
Error: Cannot enter the value 5

Enter value: 5
Error: Cannot enter the value 5
Three strikes and you are out!

test: system execution failed.
```

Following is the set of recorded exceptions (implementation dependent):

```
----------------------------------------------------------------
Class / Object Routine Nature of exception Effect
----------------------------------------------------------------
MATH silly value_not_five:
<001D1BB0> Precondition violated. Fail
----------------------------------------------------------------
MATH load_value
<001D1BB0> Resumption attempt failed. Rescue
----------------------------------------------------------------
APPLICATION start
<001D1BA8> Routine failure. Fail
----------------------------------------------------------------
APPLICATION root's creation
<001D1BA8> Routine failure. Exit
```

The routine *silly* contains a precondition with the tag, *value_not_five*. If a client passes the value 5 to this routine an exception will be raised.

The routine *load_value* contains an exception handler that begins with the keyword *rescue*. If an exception is raised while in this routine, the code in the *rescue* section is activated.

In routine *load_value*, the user is prompted to enter an integer value. This value is input to the *silly* routine. If the *value* parameter does not equal 5, the *silly* function returns 5 minus the *value*.

If the user enters 5, this triggers an exception in routine *load_value* (the exception is raised in routine *silly*). Business as usual ceases. Instead of outputting the value of *r*, as would normally be done, the code in the *rescue* clause is activated. An error count, *num_errors*, is incremented by 1. The output message, *"Error: Cannot enter the value of 5"* is sent to the user's screen. If the error count equals 3 the error message, *"Three strikes and you are out"* is put on the user's screen and the program terminates. Otherwise the *retry* function causes routine *load_value* to be called again while preserving the current state of the variables *r* and *num_errors*.

2.9.1 Account classes revisited with assertions

In order to illustrate the use of preconditions and postconditions in a more meaningful context, we revisit all of the ACCOUNT classes presented earlier in this chapter and add assertions to key routines.

The short form for the revised class ACCOUNT is shown in Listing 2.18.

Listing 2.18 Short form for revised class ACCOUNT with assertions

```
class interface ACCOUNT
creation {any}
  open
feature
  balance: REAL

  deposit (amount: REAL)
    require
      non_negative_amount: amount >= 0.0
    ensure
      balance = old balance + amount

  withdraw (amount: REAL)
    require
      funds_available: amount <= balance
    ensure
      balance = old balance - amount

end -- class ACCOUNT
```

The precondition for the *deposit* routine specifies that the parameter *amount* must be non-negative. The tag *non_negative_amount* is used to indicate this condition. The postcondition in this routine specifies that the balance upon exit from the routine equals the balance upon entry (*old balance*) plus the *amount* deposited. Although the postcondition provides information that would be obviously available by directly inspecting the code of the routine, this code is not printed in an Eiffel short form. It is therefore highly desirable to include this obvious postcondition in a postcondition.

The pre- and postconditions of the *withdraw* routine are similar.

Listing 2.19 presents the short forms of the remaining classes.

Listing 2.19   Short forms for remaining ACCOUNT classes with assertions

```
class interface CHECKING
creation
  open

feature
  apply_fee
    ensure
      balance <= old balance

  monthly_fee: REAL

  set_monthly_fee (amount: REAL)
    require
      non_negative: amount >= 0.0
end -- class CHECKING

deferred class interface SAVINGS

feature

  apply_interest
    ensure
      balance >= old balance

  monthly_interest: REAL

  set_interest_rate (value: REAL)
    require
      positive_rate: value > 0.0

end -- class SAVINGS

class interface NON_INTEREST
```

creation
  open

feature

  apply_interest
      -- Null routine needed to make class effective
    ensure
      balance = old balance

end -- class NON_INTEREST

class interface MAXIMUM_BALANCE

creation
  open

feature -- largest monthly balance

  apply_interest
      -- Compute monthly interest from maximum balance

  deposit (amount: REAL)

  maximum_balance: REAL

  open (initial_deposit: REAL)

  reset_maximum_balance (value: REAL)
      -- Used at the beginning of every month

end -- class MAXIMUM_BALANCE

class interface FINAL_BALANCE

creation
  open

feature

  apply_interest
      -- Compute monthly interest from final balance

end -- class FINAL_BALANCE

class interface DAILY_BALANCE

creation {any}
  open_daily

feature -- day of month of last deposit

apply_interest
    -- Compute monthly interest from maximum balance

cumulative_interest: REAL

deposit_daily (amount: REAL; day_of_month: INTEGER)
  require
    positive_deposit: amount > 0.0
    legal_day: day_of_month >= 0 and day_of_month <= 31

last_deposit: INTEGER

withdraw_daily (amount: REAL; day_of_month: INTEGER)
  require
    positive_withdrawal: amount > 0.0
    legal_day: day_of_month >= 0 and day_of_month <= 31

end -- class DAILY_BALANCE

In class CHECKING, routine *apply_fee* contains only a postcondition that specifies that the value of the *balance* attribute upon leaving the routine is equal or less than the value of the *balance* attribute upon exiting the routine. This information summarizes essential information about the semantics of the routine. In routine *set_monthly_fee*, the precondition specifies that the parameter *amount* must be non-negative.

In deferred class SAVINGS, there are two assertions. In the routine *apply_interest*, the postcondition specifies that the *balance* attribute upon leaving the routine must be equal or greater than the *balance* attribute upon entering the routine. The precondition of routine *set_interest_rate* specifies that the parameter *value* must be positive.

2.9.2 Propagation of assertions through inheritance

A fundamental question that has not been discussed so far concerns the propagation of assertions through inheritance. Specifically, how do the assertions (both pre- and postconditions) in class ACCOUNT affect descendant classes? The same question may be asked of the assertions just discussed in the deferred class SAVINGS.

If a descendant routine redefines an effective routine in a parent class or makes effective a deferred routine in an abstract class, its preconditions are logically connected to those of all ancestor routines of the same name by the logical "or" operation. This implies that the precondition of a redefined or effective descendant routine may be weaker than that of its ancestor (i.e., the "or" condition can create a weaker condition than those inherited). This is a subtle issue. In fact, it is sensible that if a redefined descendant routine can accomplish the same task by requiring less on the part of the input parameters (a weaker condition imposed in the redefined routine's *require* clause), this implies the descendant routine is stronger than its ancestor. It should, of course, be legal to strengthen a routine through redefinition in a class hierarchy. The *require* clause in a redefined descendant routine must now be called a *require else* clause. This notifies a person performing maintenance on the redefined routine to examine the preconditions in all ancestor routines with the same name.

On the other hand, if a descendant routine redefines an effective routine in a parent class or makes effective a deferred routine in an abstract class, its postconditions are logically connected to those of all ancestor routines with the same name by the logical "and" operation. This implies that the postcondition of such a routine is stronger than that of its ancestor. This is because more conditions must be satisfied upon exit from the routine (i.e., all of the conditions given in the ancestor postconditions "and" those given in the redefined class). The *ensure* clause in a redefined descendant routine must be called a *ensure then* clause.

Class NON_INTEREST makes effective the routine *apply_interest* since this routine was *deferred* in the parent class SAVINGS. In class SAVINGS, the postcondition specifies that the *balance* upon exit is equal or greater than the *balance* upon entry to the routine. In class NON_INTEREST, the postcondition (which in the actual code is given by an *ensure then* clause) specifies that the *balance* upon exit equals the *balance* upon entry to the routine. This condition, when combined with its parent condition through the logical "and" operation, yields the same condition (i.e., *balance* >= old balance AND balance = old balance -> balance = old balance*). Had the postcondition in the parent class SAVINGS been *balance > old balance*, the postcondition in the child class NON_INTEREST could never be satisfied.

In class DAILY_BALANCE, routine *deposit_daily* specifies two preconditions. The first, with tag *positive_deposit_amount*, requires the parameter *amount* to be positive. The second, with tag *legal_day*, requires the *day_of_month* parameter to be equal or greater than 0 and less than or equal to 31. The *withdraw_daily* routine specifies similar preconditions.

Pre- and postconditions, when used in abstract (deferred) classes, provide a useful tool for imposing logical constraints on the postconditions of all descendant classes. So in addition to providing documentation about the semantics of a routine, postconditions establish constraints on the semantics of all redefined versions of the routine that may be produced in the future.

Consider again the class AIRPLANE in Listing 2.20, this time defined as an abstract class (deferred class). There is no creation routine because deferred classes cannot have instances. The *make* routine would probably be declared to be a creation routine in one of the subclasses. Its preconditions require 6000 pounds of initial fuel. This guarantees sufficient fuel to become airborne, fly for a prescribed period, and make a safe landing.

The takeoff routine, which is deferred (actually defined in subclasses), imposes the precondition that the fuel be greater than 6000 pounds (for the same reason as above). The postconditions require that upon completing takeoff the fuel remaining is greater than 5000 pounds (to provide a margin of safety for flying and landing), the altitude greater than 1000 feet (to provide sufficient glide for an emergency landing), and the speed greater than 220 knots (to prevent stall).

A subclass of AIRPLANE may weaken the preconditions (e.g., require less than 6000 pounds of fuel on takeoff if at least 5000 pounds remain after takeoff and the other postconditions are either met or exceeded—a more efficient plane might be able to achieve the same postconditions with weaker preconditions).

So the pre- and postconditions in the abstract class AIRPLANE have profoundly affected the semantics of all subclasses.

Listing 2.20 Abstract class with pre- and postconditions

```
deferred class AIRPLANE
    feature
        fuel     : REAL -- pounds of fuel
        weight   : REAL
        position : COMPASS_SETTING
        speed    : REAL
        altitude : REAL
        -- other attributes not shown

    feature { NONE }

        make (initial_fuel : REAL; initial_weight : REAL) is
            require
                sufficient_fuel: initial_fuel > 6000.0
                positive_weight: initial_weight > 0.0
            do
                fuel := initial_fuel
```

```
    weight := initial_weight
  end -- make

 takeoff is
   require
     sufficient_fuel: fuel > 6000.0
   deferred
   ensure
     fuel > 5000
     altitude > 1000
     speed > 220
   end -- takeoff
  -- Other commands not shown
end -- AIRPLANE
```

2.10 Summary

This chapter introduced the basic elements of Eiffel programming. Some of the important ideas presented include:

- The Eiffel language was "born" in the late 1980s. It is a pure object-oriented language. This implies that functions can be invoked only through objects and not as stand-alone logical entities.

- As a pure object-oriented language, the class in Eiffel is the basic logical unit of encapsulation as well the basic physical unit, a module. Eiffel software is organized as a set of interrelated and cooperating classes.

- Programs consist of objects. These objects are created during program execution, perform their tasks and then are typically destroyed.

- An object in Eiffel and in other object-oriented languages is an instance of a class. Its attributes are given by the data model of its class. The messages that it can respond to (i.e., the routines that one can invoke through the object) are specified by the behavioral model of the class (the set of routines given in the class description).

- Before an object can be created in Eiffel it must be declared to be of a given type. Its type is the name of the class that the object will be an instance of (after it is created).

Summary

- Objects must be explicitly created either using the creation operator (!!) in front of the variable or using a specified creation routine in conjunction with the creation operator.

- Eiffel systems provide for "automatic garbage collection." As an Eiffel application runs, a garbage collection process is running in the background and detecting when storage is no longer connected to a variable name. At an opportune moment the garbage collection process recycles (effectively destroys) the unneeded storage.

- There are several basic object types that do not require explicit creation in order to be used. These include INTEGER, CHARACTER, REAL, and BOOLEAN.

- Objects of type INTEGER have a default value of 0. Objects of type CHARACTER have a default value of the NULL character (ASCII value 0). Objects of type REAL have a default value of 0.0. Finally, objects of type BOOLEAN have a default value of *false*.

- Ordinary objects (non-basic type objects) have "reference" semantics. This implies that the programmer is responsible for explicitly allocating storage using a creation operator possibly in conjunction with a creation routine. The initial value of an ordinary object is Void. After the programmer creates storage for such an object the object name is attached to the storage.

- In order for the *copy* routine to work it is essential that the target object (object being copied to) be already created.

- Two objects are equal if they are attached (bound) to the same storage. If one wishes to test whether the objects x and y are equal, an expression of the form *if x = y* would be used.

- Within the body of a routine there are times when a choice must be made among several alternative blocks of code to be executed. This choice is usually based on the value of some expression that may assume a value *true* or a value *false*.

- It is often necessary to carry out a sequence of statements repeatedly until some condition is met. The construct *from-until-loop* may be used in this situation.

- An Eiffel routine specifies both interface information as well as implementation details. The user of a class (consumer) needs access to only the interface portion of a routine. The producer of the class needs access to the implementation details when performing maintenance on the routine.

- Routines come in two flavors: queries and commands. Commands do not return a value whereas queries do. Commands are used to change the internal state of an object (the values of its attributes). Queries are used to access state information from the object (the value of one or more of its attributes) or perform some computation that may involve the current state of the object. The result of the computation is returned.

- For a command, a verb name should be used. For a query a noun that is descriptive of what is returned should be used.

- The Eiffel language, like many other modern programming languages, relegates important tasks such as keyboard input and terminal output, mathematical functions, arrays, strings, and secondary storage input and output to routines available in libraries. These external routines become a typical and basic element of Eiffel programs.

- It is usually foolish and often unproductive to reinvent the wheel by creating your own basic software components especially when the language you are using already provides a fully tested and highly rationalized set of classes through several class libraries. It is important that you learn to browse and then utilize these available resources. You must become an intelligent consumer before you can become a competent producer.

- The routines that support the keyboard input and terminal output come from a class called STD_FILES.

- The class is the basic logical and physical unit of software construction in Eiffel.

- As a logical unit a class represents an abstract data type—a unification of an underlying data model with a set of operations (routines) that manipulate this data model.

- As a physical unit a class is a module

- Creation routines may also be used as ordinary routines typically to update the values of attributes for an existing object.

- Creation clauses may contain an export section bounded by curly braces, "{" and "}". Objects of the given class may be created only in the classes and their descendants specified in the export section, if present.

Summary

- If no export section is present, a default export section of ANY is implied. Since all Eiffel classes are descendants of ANY, the absence of an explicit export section implies that objects of the given class may be created from within any other class (i.e., universal export).

- Inheritance is an architectural property of object-oriented systems used for establishing a decomposition of a software system into classes and subclasses. Inheritance also provides the basis for software reuse.

- As one moves down a class hierarchy, the "is a" or "is a kind of" relationship should hold between child class and parent class. Attributes and methods defined in a parent class should make sense in all descendant classes in which they are not redefined.

- In going from a parent class to its child, **specialization** involves redefining one or more of the parent's routines or attributes.

- **Extension** involves adding routines or attributes not present in the parent.

- **Restriction** involves blocking one or more routines of the parent. All three (specialization, extension, restriction) may be used simultaneously but it is most common to use only specialization and extension in going down a class hierarchy.

- When either an attribute or method of an ancestor class is redefined, this must be indicated explicitly using a *redefine* subclause. Although the name of the inherited attribute or method is unchanged, the behavior associated with the inherited feature is changed.

- The rules of conformance require that if an attribute is redefined in a descendant class its new type be a descendant of the original type.

- The *export* subclause may be used to block or redefine the scope in which one or more routines inherited from an ancestor are visible to instances and descendants of the child class.

- The rename subclause allows the subclass designer the freedom to reuse the behavior of the inherited routine while giving it a new name. This new name, unless changed again by the designer of a descendant class, remains in force for all descendant classes.

- In Eiffel a class is abstract, and can produce no actual instances, if the implementation details of one or more of its methods is *deferred*. Then the entire class is *deferred*.

An Overview of Eiffel

- A *redefine* subclause is required only when an effective version of a routine is changed in a descendant class.

- In general, abstract (*deferred*) classes are key components of highly evolved class hierarchies such as the core Eiffel libraries.

- The information contained within an abstract class represents a generalization of the behavior of many more specialized classes.

- It is fairly typical in mature libraries to find many layers of abstract classes sitting above the concrete or effective classes that represent the actual objects of the system.

- Since one of the major purposes of a class hierarchy is to provide an "intellectual" decomposition of the features that represent a particular problem domain in order to manage the complexity of the domain, it should be evident that abstract classes are an important ingredient in the management of complexity.

- Only when one or more parameters are required in a routine does the syntax make it obvious that information is being obtained through computation (the invocation of a routine).

- The preconditions section of a routine, specified by a *require* clause, precisely specifies the conditions that must be satisfied in order for the routine to successfully perform its function.

- It is the user's responsibility to ensure that legal values are provided to a routine. The designer of the routine has no control over the use of the routine.

- All a routine can and should do on behalf of a user in the event that a precondition is violated is to raise an exception (a signal that triggers an exception handling section in the user's code) so that the user may respond appropriately to the error condition.

- If the user chooses to ignore the error, program execution must be halted since it would be imprudent to continue program execution when the system is in an unsafe state.

- The assertion handling mechanism for Eiffel routines provides the basis for this division of responsibility between the producer and consumer, that is, the class designer and user.

- It is the user's responsibility to ensure that every precondition required of the routine is satisfied upon entry into the routine.

EXERCISES

- In exchange, the routine may provide one or more postconditions, given by an *ensure* clause. Such an *ensure* clause specifies the state the system is guaranteed to be in as a result of executing the routine.

- If the user complies with all the preconditions, the routine (class designer) guarantees the postconditions. This compact between the producer and consumer is called "programming by contract".

- Preconditions and postconditions provide a powerful, precise, and extremely useful type of self-documentation for a routine. The semantics of the routine, that is, its purpose, may often be clarified by the preconditions and postconditions.

- If a descendant routine redefines an effective routine in a parent class or makes effective a deferred routine in an abstract class, its preconditions are logically connected to those of all ancestor routines of the same name by the logical "or" operation.

- The precondition of a redefined or effective descendant routine may be weaker than that of its ancestor (i.e., the "or" condition can create a weaker condition than those inherited).

- The *require* clause in a redefined descendant routine must be called a *require else* clause.

- If a descendant routine redefines an effective routine in a parent class or makes effective a deferred routine in an abstract class, its postconditions are logically connected to those of all ancestor routines with the same name by the logical "and" operation.

- The postcondition of such a routine is stronger than that of its ancestor. This is because more conditions must be satisfied upon exit from the routine (i.e., all of the conditions given in the ancestor postconditions "and" those given in the redefined class).

- The *ensure* clause in a redefined descendant routine must be called a *ensure then* clause.

2.11 Exercises

1. Add an additional subclass to the ACCOUNT hierarchy. Specify pre- and postconditions for each of its routines, if appropriate.

2. Design a small application in which it is appropriate to use one or two deferred classes (abstract classes). Explain why these abstract classes are used. Show all the implementation details in your application, some sample input, and the output.

3. Write a small example that illustrates the use of exception handling. Design the input in such a way that you demonstrate how the error handling is performed.

Chapter 3

Arrays, Sorting and Strings

The focus on data structures begins in this chapter. The emphasis shifts from the Eiffel programming language to data structures. Eiffel will be used as a precise notation to represent and implement the data structures that are presented.

The next four chapters focus on classic data abstractions whose implementation are *linear*. The word linear in this context implies a well defined beginning location, a well defined ending location and a series of elements that can be traversed in a sequence from beginning to end location (like in a straight line—thus, linear).

An array is a container—that is, it holds elements (objects) that are instances of other classes. More specifically, an array is an "indexable" collection. This implies that elements may be inserted or retrieved by specifying a particular index location. Like other container classes, an array may be static or dynamic. The dimension or capacity of a static array must be specified when the array is created. The maximum number of elements that may be held in the array is therefore fixed at the time of creation. An attempt to insert more than this number of elements causes an exception to be raised. A dynamic array may also require that a size or dimension be specified when the array is created. But if an attempt is made to insert more elements than the size of the array, the array automatically adjusts itself by increasing its size on demand. Since this occurs while a program is running the array is called "dynamic." Static arrays usually provide faster access time than dynamic arrays, but are less flexible.

3.1 ARRAY class

Most non-object-oriented programming languages such as Pascal, C, and Ada provide built-in language constructs for the array type. In contrast, most object-oriented programming languages, including Eiffel, provide standard library support for an ARRAY class.

The Eiffel ARRAY class is generic and dynamic. Elements of arbitrary type may be stored. This type must be specified when an instance of the array class is created.

In this section, we review the important features of the standard Eiffel ARRAY class. The basic command that one can perform on an array is insertion of an element at a particular index location, *put*. The basic query that one can perform on an array is to fetch the element at a particular index location, *item*. In addition, we need to be able to create an array using an appropriate creation routine. Other commands that we might desire would include copying one array to another or resizing an existing array. Another important query would be determining the current capacity of an array.

Class ARRAY supports all of these basic operations. A small portion of its interface (obtained through *short* on file *array.e* and then edited) is given in Listing 3.1.

Listing 3.1   Portion of interface to class ARRAY

    class *interface ARRAY [G]*

      creation
        make

      feature *-- Access queries*

        item (i: INTEGER): G
          -- Entry at index 'i', if in index interval.

        infix "@" (i: INTEGER): G
          -- Entry at index 'i', if in index interval.

      feature *-- Comparison query*

        is_equal (other: like Current): BOOLEAN
          -- Is array made of the same items as 'other'?

      feature *-- Duplication*

       copy (other: like Current)
          -- Reinitialize by copying all the items of 'other'.
          -- (This is also used by 'clone'.)
          ensure
             equal_areas: area.is_equal (other.area)
   feature -- Element change
       put (v: G; i: INTEGER)
          -- Replace 'i'-th entry, if in index interval, by 'v'.
   feature -- Initialization
       make (minindex, maxindex: INTEGER)
          -- Allocate array; set index interval to
          -- 'minindex' .. 'maxindex'
          -- (empty if 'minindex' > 'maxindex').
       ensure
          no_capacity: (minindex > maxindex) implies (capacity = 0)
          capacity_constraint: (minindex <= maxindex) implies
             (capacity = maxindex - minindex + 1)
   feature -- Measurement queries
       capacity: INTEGER
          -- Available indices
       count: INTEGER
          -- Available indices
       lower: INTEGER
          -- Minimum index
       upper: INTEGER
          -- Maximum index
   end -- class ARRAY

Listing 3.2 exercises only the most important routines, *put* and *item*, in class ARRAY.

Listing 3.2   Exercising the most basic operations on arrays

   class APPLICATION

   creation
       start

ARRAY CLASS

feature

    start **is**
      local
        data   : ARRAY [INTEGER]
        names : ARRAY [STRING]
        index, sum: INTEGER
      do
        !! data.make (1, 1000)
        from
          index := 0
        until
          index = 1000
        loop
          index := index + 1
          data.put (index * index, index)
        end
        !! names.make (1, 3)
        names.put ("Henrik", 1)
        names.put ("Richard", 2)
        names.put ("Hanne", 3)
        from
          index := 0
        until
          index = 1000
        loop
          index := index + 1
          sum := sum + data.item (index)
        end
        io.putstring ("The sum of values in data = ")
        io.putint (sum)
        io.new_line
        io.putstring ("The names array contains: %N")
        from
          index := 0
        until
          index = 3
        loop
          index := index + 1
          io.putstring (names.item (index))
          io.new_line

> **end**
> **end**
>
> **end** -- *class APPLICATION*

The output of Listing 3.2 is:

The sum of values in data = 333833500
The names array contains:
Henrik
Richard
Hanne

In Listing 3.2, two arrays are declared. The declaration, *data : ARRAY [INTEGER]*, specifies that *data* will hold integers (i.e., each element of the array *data* will be of type INTEGER). The declaration, *names : ARRAY [STRING]*, specifies that the array *names* will hold elements of type STRING.

The first line of code in the *start* routine invokes the creation method *make*. This method takes two parameters. The first parameter specifies the lower index limit and the second the upper index limit. For the *data* array the index range is defined as going from 1 to 1000.

The *from-until-loop* causes the *data* array to be filled with values given by the square of the natural numbers from 1 to 1000. The *put* routine is used to insert elements into the array. The first parameter of *put* specifies the value. The second parameter of *put* specifies the index. The elements inserted in the array must correspond to the base type specified in the array declaration, *data : ARRAY[INTEGER]*.

Next, the *names* array is initialized with an index range from 1 to 3. Three string values are inserted into the array: "Henrik", "Richard", and "Hanne" (Danish spelling for "Hannah"). Once again the *put* method is invoked through the array object, *names*.

The integer type, *sum*, is automatically initialized to its default value of 0. In the second *from-until-loop*, the value of *sum* is incremented by the value stored at each index location of the array. The routine, *item*, is used to access each array element. The index location containing the information that is desired is used as a parameter in *item*. The sum of all the values is then output.

The third *from-until-loop* outputs the string values stored at each consecutive index location in the *names* array.

3.2 Sorting

Sorting is a basic and well understood problem. Because of the practical importance of the sorting problem (the need to order a collection of information is quite fundamental), many sorting algorithms have been designed. Each orders an arbitrary set of elements from smallest to largest or from largest to smallest. How do these sorting algorithms differ? They differ in their efficiency, the speed and memory resources required to perform their task.

This section examines several classic sorting algorithms and their relative efficiency.

3.2.1 Sorting problems versus their instances

Consider the specific requirement of writing a function that can rearrange the five numbers, 5, 3, 4, 1, and 7 so that they become ordered from smallest to largest. Of course for such a small data set you may well wonder why one needs a computer program to perform this computation. The numbers can be rearranged by inspection! Small instances of problems can usually be solved by inspection.

The requirement of sorting the five numbers 5, 3, 4, 1, and 7 is an instance of a much more general problem called the sorting problem. The general sorting problem can be stated as follows:

Given an array of n elements (the particular type of elements is not important as long as any two elements can be compared). Write a function that outputs an array that contains the original elements in ascending order (smallest to largest) or descending order (largest to smallest).

Since an array can be of any size, n, and contain an arbitrary collection of elements, there are an infinite number of instances of the sorting problem. The particular sequence of five numbers 5, 3, 4, 1, and 7 is merely one instance from among the infinite collection of sorting problems.

The "solution" to a sorting problem is an algorithm—a finite sequence of operations—that guarantees that an array of arbitrary elements will be ordered with finite computational effort. This effort generally increases as the size of the array being sorted increases.

The functional relationship between the computational effort and the size of the array is called the computational complexity of the sorting algorithm. We examine the computational complexity of several important sorting algorithms in this chapter.

In the sections that follow, arrays of base type REAL will be used in creating instances of sorting problems without any loss of generality.

3.2.2 Selection-sort algorithm

The first sorting algorithm that is discussed, **selection sort**, is a relatively simple sorting algorithm. Informally it works as follows: *The smallest value is computed from among the n values (assume problem is of size n) in the array. The index location of this smallest value is also computed. The value in index 1 is interchanged with the value in the smallest index location. The process of computing the smallest value is repeated among the elements from index 2 to n. This second smallest value is interchanged with the value in index 2. This process is continued until eventually all of the ordered elements of the array are sorted.*

The selection sort algorithm is stated more formally as:

Selection-Sort Algorithm for Sorting Numbers in an Array

1. In a loop that iterates the index *k* from 1 to *n*.

2. Compute the smallest element and its index among the elements from *k* to *n*.

3. Interchange this smallest element with the element in index *k*.

4. When the loop is completed the elements are sorted.

The selection-sort algorithm is illustrated with the following diagrams. The total number of comparison operations that must be performed is shown after each iteration.

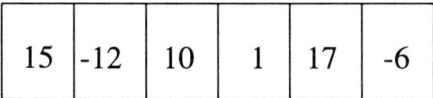

Figure 3.1 Original array.

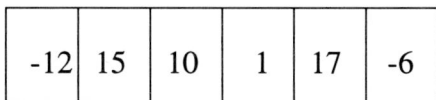

Figure 3.2 After iteration 1.

Total number of comparison operations: 6 (minimum value -12 swapped with index 1)

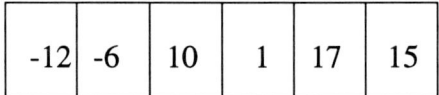

Figure 3.3 After iteration 2.

Total number of comparison operations: 11 (minimum value -6 swapped with index 2)

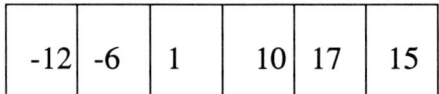

Figure 3.4 After iteration 3.

Total number of comparison operations: 15 (minimum value 1 swapped with index 3)

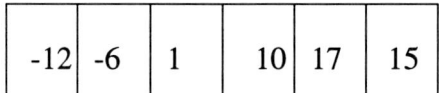

Figure 3.5 After iteration 4.

Total number of comparison operations: 18 (minimum value 10 swapped with index 4)

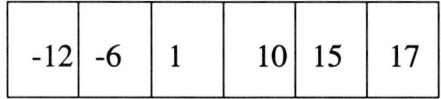

Figure 3.6 After iteration 5.

Total number of comparison operations: 20 (minimum value 15 swapped with index 5)

In general, for an array of size n, the number of comparison operations required is:

$n + (n-1) + (n-2) + ... + 2$.

For large n, the number of comparison operations is approximately $n * (n - 1) / 2$. The computational complexity of this algorithm is said to be $O(n^2)$. This implies that for large n, if the size of an array is doubled, the computational effort increases by a factor of four. The "big O" notation indicates the asymptotic complexity function. Constants of proportionality are not shown with this notation.

A support class, INFO, is presented in Listing 3.3. This class encapsulates the queries *value* and *location*. This enables the function (query) *smallest*, shown in Listing 3.4, to capture the smallest value and its index location and return both in a single object of type INFO.

Listing 3.4 shows the query *smallest* and the command *insertion_sort*.

Listing 3.3   Class INFO

```
class INFO
-- Used by function smallest to return smallest value and index location

feature

  value: REAL
  location: INTEGER

  set_value (a_value: REAL) is
    do
      value := a_value
    end

  set_location (a_location: INTEGER) is
    do
      location := a_location
    end

end -- class INFO
```

Listing 3.4   Selection-sort

```
    smallest (data: ARRAY [REAL]; lower: INTEGER; upper: INTEGER): INFO is
      local
        tentative         : REAL
        tentative_index   : INTEGER
        index             : INTEGER
      do
        tentative := data.item (lower)
        tentative_index := lower
        from
          index := lower
        until
```

```
      index = upper
    loop
      index := index + 1
      if data.item (index) < tentative then
        tentative := data.item (index)
        tentative_index := index
      end
    end
    !! Result
    Result.set_value (tentative)
    Result.set_location (tentative_index)
  end  -- smallest

  selection_sort (data: ARRAY [REAL]; size: INTEGER) is
    local
      index           : INTEGER
      smallest_value: REAL
      s_index         : INTEGER
      smallest_info  : INFO
      temp            : REAL
    do
      from
        index := 0
      until
        index = size
      loop
        index := index + 1
        smallest_info := smallest (data, index, size)
        smallest_value := smallest_info.value
        s_index := smallest_info.location
        -- Exchange the values in indices index and s_index
        temp := data.item (index)
        data.put (smallest_value, index)
        data.put (temp, s_index)
      end
    end  -- selection_sort
```

In Listing 3.4, the INFO object that is returned is constructed using the three lines of code:

!!Result
Result.set_value (tentative)
Result.set_location (tentative_index)

These lines of code create an INFO object and then set its attributes to the two desired values. If we failed to first create the INFO object using *!!Result*, the program would produce a run-time exception complaining that we were attempting to invoke the "set" routines on an uninitialized object.

3.2.3 More on the efficiency of sorting algorithms

The efficiency of a sorting algorithm is related to the speed with which it performs its work and the memory that is required to do this work. Often there are a set of distinct algorithms independently constructed to solve a given sorting problem. The computer scientist is usually concerned with determining and then using the most efficient sorting algorithm for solving a problem since computation time is valuable. It is often the case that a "brute-force" approach to solving a sorting problem (i.e., one that is relatively easy to construct and prove correct) is significantly less efficient than a more clever approach.

Various measures have been devised to indicate the computational efficiency of an algorithm. These include: worst-case asymptotic complexity and average-case asymptotic complexity. By asymptotic complexity is meant the growth in computation time as a function of the growth in problem size as the problem size approaches infinity. The worst-case complexity measure deals with a guaranteed upper bound in performance. That is, the algorithm is guaranteed to perform equal or better than this result. Such a complexity measure is quite useful. The average-case complexity measure deals with an "average" configuration of data. That is, things may sometimes be better or worse but the average-case complexity provides an indication of typical performance.

The "big O" notation is often used to express the asymptotic complexity of an algorithm. Suppose, for example, an algorithm has a worst-case asymptotic complexity given by $O(n^2)$. This implies that if it takes t units of time to perform a computation of size n, where this size is quite large (approaching infinity), then it would take $4 * t$ units of time to perform a computation of size $2 * n$. If the algorithm were of complexity $O(n)$ then doubling the size of the problem would double the computational effort required to solve the problem. If the complexity were $O(n^3)$ then doubling the size of the problem would cause the computational effort to increase by a factor of 8. It is assumed throughout that the original size of the problem is large.

It was indicated in Section 3.2 that if one doubles the size of the array using selection-sort (where the size is large), the sorting time will increase by approximately a factor of 4. This quadratic complexity is not very good and makes this algorithm relatively inefficient for sorting large data sets.

3.2.4 Bubble sort

Bubble-sort is another well known and relatively simple sorting algorithm. During each iteration, the first element is compared to the second element and if in order (the first smaller than the second) they are left alone, if out of order they are interchanged. Then the second element is compared to the third element. Again, if they are in order they are left alone whereas if they are out of order they are interchanged. Then the third element is compared to the fourth using the same logic, then the fourth element is compared to the fifth. This pattern is continued until the n-1 element is compared to the nth element. When this first major iteration is completed, the largest element in the array will have been shifted to the nth index position in the array. What about the other elements? They are not necessarily sorted, but clearly some movement in the direction of sorting will have occurred.

During the second major iteration of bubble-sort, the elements are again compared, two at a time, starting with the first and second elements. But this time the comparisons stop when the n-2 element has been compared with the n-1 element. The nth element is not touched since it is already known to be the largest element in the array. When the second major iteration is completed the second to the largest element in the array is guaranteed to be in the n-1 index location. Major iterations continue, each time involving one less element, until only the first two elements are compared. Then the algorithm ends and the numbers in the array will have been sorted.

To illustrate the workings of this algorithm, consider the following small data set of 10 integers:

Original data set: 4, 1, 5, 7, 10, 8, 2, 6, 3, 9.

During the first major iteration, the first element, 4, is compared to the second element 1. Since they are out of order they are interchanged. This produces:

1, 4, 5, 7, 10, 8, 2, 6, 3, 9.

The second and third elements are in order so nothing is done. The third and fourth elements are in order so nothing is done. The fifth and sixth elements are out of order so they are interchanged. This produces:
    1, 4, 5, 7, 8, 10, 2, 6, 3, 9.
Next the sixth and seventh elements are compared and interchanged. This produces:
    1, 4, 5, 7, 8, 2, 10, 6, 3, 9.
Next the seventh and eighth elements are compared and interchanged. This produces:
    1, 4, 5, 7, 8, 2, 6, 10, 3, 9.
This process continues until the first major iteration concludes with the new array:
    1, 4, 5, 7, 8, 2, 6, 3, 9, 10.
As stated earlier, the largest element in the array, the value 10, has been shifted to the right-most position in the array. Like a bubble, it has risen to the surface (if one rotates the array by 90 degrees so the largest element in the array is geometrically at the top of the array rather than on the right).

After the second major iteration (the same process repeated among the first 9 elements), the new array is:
    1, 4, 5, 7, 2, 6, 3, 8, 9, 10.
After the third major iteration, the array looks like:
    1, 4, 5, 2, 6, 3, 7, 8, 9, 10.
After the fourth major iteration, the array looks like:
    1, 4, 2, 5, 3, 6, 7, 8, 9, 10.
After the fifth major iteration, the array looks like:
    1, 2, 4, 3, 5, 6, 7, 8, 9, 10.
After the sixth major iteration, the array looks like:
    1, 2, 3, 4, 5, 6, 7, 8, 9, 10.
The array is completely sorted. In the general case of sorting an array of size 10, three more major iterations may have been required. Of course the algorithm should detect when no further iterations are required and not perform any additional iterations once this is determined.

In Listing 3.5, the bubble-sort algorithm is presented.

Listing 3.5   Bubble-sort algorithm

```
bubble_sort (values: ARRAY [REAL]; size: INTEGER) is
   require
      size > 2
   local
```

SORTING

```
    interchanged              : BOOLEAN
    i, j, major_iteration, top : INTEGER
    temp                      : REAL
do
  interchanged := true
  from
    major_iteration := 1
  until
    not interchanged or major_iteration = size - 1
  loop
    interchanged := false
    top := size - major_iteration
    from
      i := 0
    until
      i = top
    loop
      i := i + 1
      j := i + 1
      if values.item (i) > values.item (j) then
        temp := values.item (i)
        values.put (values.item (j), i)
        values.put (temp, j)
        interchanged := true
      end
    end
    major_iteration := major_iteration + 1
  end
end -- bubble-sort
```

Can the reader explain why it is essential to assign interchanged to TRUE above the first *from-until-loop* in Listing 3.5? What would happen if this statement were omitted?

The results of some timing runs for instances of various sizes are presented in Table 3.1. For each timing run an array of reverse ordered data was used as input. This is the worst case data set for the bubble-sort algorithm.

Table 3.1 Computation time versus array size for Listing 3.5

Array Size	Computation Time (seconds)
25	0.099
50	0.333

Table 3.1 Computation time versus array size for Listing 3.5 (continued)

100	1.383
200	5.460
400	22.08
800	Estimated time of 1.25 minutes
1600	Estimated time of 6 minutes
3200	Estimated time of 24 minutes
6400	Estimated time of 1.6 hours

The computation time appears to increase according to an $O(n^2)$ law. This is indeed the algorithmic complexity of bubble-sort as evident from the doubly nested *from-until* loops.

The estimated time of 1.6 hours of computation to sort a data set of size 6400 is quite discouraging.

Instead of looking for a more powerful computer to solve this problem we instead look for a more efficient algorithm. The "comb-sort" algorithm discussed in the next sub-section is built on the idea of bubble-sort and is, in fact, only a minor variation of bubble-sort. What is remarkable is how fast this minor variant performs. As you will soon see, what is even more remarkable is that no one, to date, fully understands why!

3.2.5 Comb-sort—a magic number and a fast variant of bubble-sort

Let us study the behavior of a small sorting problem using bubble-sort. This will set the stage for a discussion of an algorithm recently discovered that significantly improves the performance of bubble-sort.

Suppose the array we wish to sort contains the sequence: 5, 4, 3, 2, 1.

After the first major iteration, the sequence become: 4, 3, 2, 1, 5. After the second major iteration, the array contains the sequence: 3, 2, 1, 4, 5. After the third major iteration, the array contains: 2, 1, 3, 4, 5. After the fourth and final iteration the array contains the sequence: 1, 2, 3, 4, 5.

No surprise. We already know how bubble-sort works. But observe the motion of the smallest element, the number 1. It migrates quite slowly, one unit to the left during each major iteration. Until this smallest number reaches the left most index of the array, the sorting process is not completed.

Suppose a way could be devised to speed up the motion of this and other slow moving elements as they migrate from the right of the array to its left. The comb-sort algorithm does exactly this. In rough terms, here is how it works.

A gap equal to the total size of the array divided by a constant in the neighborhood of 1.3, the *shrink_factor*, is defined. This gap is rounded down to an integer (the ratio is a decimal quantity). The first element is compared to the element in index 1 + gap, the second element is compared to the element in index 2 + gap, ..., until the size-gap element is compared to the element in the right most position (index equal to size) of the array. As with bubble-sort, the numbers are interchanged if they are out of order and left alone if they are in order.

During the next major iteration, the gap is divided by the *shrink_factor* and the process continued. Eventually, the gap will become a fraction less than one. Instead of rounding down to 0 (which would make no sense), the gap is set equal to 1. When the gap reaches a value of 1, the algorithm becomes identical to ordinary bubble-sort.

In order to appreciate the effect the gap has on the sorting process, we consider another sorting problem containing 10 numbers that is similar to the one given above. The original sequence of numbers to be sorted is: 10, 9, 8, 7, 6, 5, 4, 3, 2, 1. The size of the array is 10, so the initial value for the gap is 7 (i.e., 10.0 / 1.3 rounded down to the nearest integer).

The number in the first index is compared to the number in index 8, the number in index 2 is compared with the number in index 9, and the number in index 3 compared with the number in index 10. This causes the following changes to occur in the array after the first major iteration: 3, 2, 1, 7, 6, 5, 4, 10, 9, 8. The smallest value of 1 has already been shifted to index 3 after just one iteration.

The gap is reduced to 7.0 / 1.3 rounded down to the nearest integer or 5. During the second major iteration, the number in index 1 is compared to the number in index 6, and this pattern continues until the number in index 5 is compared to that in index 10. The result of these comparisons and required interchanges after the second major iteration is: 3, 2, 1, 9, 6, 5, 4, 10, 7, 8.

The gap is reduced to 5.0 / 1.3 rounded down to the nearest integer or 3. The next iteration proceeds by comparing the number in index 1 with the number in index 4, ..., the number in index 7 with the number in index 10. This third major iteration produces the result: 3, 2, 1, 4, 6, 5, 9, 10, 7, 8.

The gap is reduced to 3.0 / 1.3 rounded down to the nearest integer, or 2. The fourth major iteration using the gap of 2 produces the result: 1, 2, 3, 4, 6, 5, 7, 8, 9, 10.

The gap is reduced to 2.0 / 1.3 rounded down to 1. The fifth major iteration produces the sorted sequence: 1, 2, 3, 4, 5, 6, 7, 8, 9, 10.

Arrays, Sorting and Strings

Not only did comb-sort require only half the number of major iterations as bubble-sort, but the number of computations required in most of the iterations were considerably less than in bubble-sort.

Listing 3.6 presents the algorithm for comb-sort.

Listing 3.6 Algorithm comb-sort

```
comb_sort (values: ARRAY [REAL]; size: INTEGER) is
  require
    size > 2
  local
    interchanged              : BOOLEAN
    i, j, top, gap            : INTEGER
    temp, shrink_factor, rgap : REAL
  do
    shrink_factor := 1.3
    interchanged := true
    gap := size
    from
    until interchanged = false and then gap = 1
    loop
      interchanged := false
      rgap := gap
      gap := real_to_integer (rgap / shrink_factor)
      if gap = 0 then
        gap := 1
      end
      top := size - gap
      from i := 0
      until i = top
      loop
        i := i + 1
        j := i + gap
        if values.item (i) > values.item (j) then
          temp := values.item (i)
          values.put (values.item (j), i)
          values.put (temp, j)
          interchanged := true
        end
      end
```

```
        end
    end -- comb-sort
```

The results of some timing runs for instances of various sizes are presented in Table 3.2. For each timing run an array of reverse ordered data was used as input.

Table 3.2 Computation Time Versus Array Size for Listing 3.6.

Array Size	Computation Time (seconds)
25	0.0166
50	0.050
100	0.117
200	0.300
400	0.717
800	1.56
1600	3.65
3200	8.97
6400	19.09

If you compare the computation time in Table 3.2 using comb-sort with the computation time given in Table 3.1 using bubble-sort you have to agree that the results are dramatic. For a problem of size 6400 we are comparing approximately 1.6 hours with 19 seconds. The computation time appears to be growing at a rate given by $O(n \log n)$. Of course to verify this more rigorously, the points need to plotted on semi-log paper. The reader is encouraged to do this as an exercise.

The title of this subsection is, "Comb- sort—a magic number and a fast variant of bubble-sort." What is the magic number? The answer is 1.3. This is the *shrink_factor* used in the comb-sort algorithm. You may properly be asking yourself, "Is there anything magical or special about the number 1.3?"

In the context of comb-sort, the answer is yes. If the *shrink_factor* is changed even slightly (e.g., by more than 0.5 in either direction) from 1.3, the performance of comb-sort degrades substantially. Only when the *shrink_factor* is a decimal value close to 1.3 does the algorithm provide a significant performance boost compared to bubble-sort. Why is the performance of comb-sort so critically dependent on the *shrink_factor*?

ARRAYS, SORTING AND STRINGS

Unfortunately, there is currently no clear explanation. It is relatively easy to understand why the structure of comb-sort works. A careful review of the sorting example presented above involving 10 numbers reveals the structural reasons for comb-sort's success. But again why is this success dependent on a *shrink_factor* that must be so carefully tuned? The magic of numbers and the mystery of the comb-sort algorithm!

3.2.6 Insertion-sort

Insertion-sort is a widely used algorithm that is considerably more complicated than either selection-sort or bubble sort.

To get a "feel" for the algorithm we walk through a small example, explaining each step.

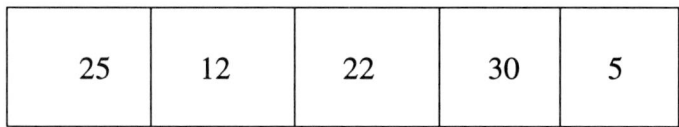

Figure 3.7 Original array for insertion-sort.

We consider two groups: the ordered group and unordered group. Initially, only the first element forms the ordered group. All the remaining elements form the unordered group. These groups are shown in Figure 3.8.

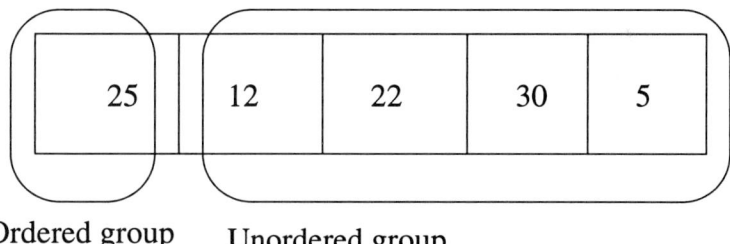

Ordered group   Unordered group

Figure 3.8 Ordered and unordered groups.

The left-most element in the unordered group (join element) is sequentially compared with all the elements of the ordered group going from right to left until the left-most element is found in the ordered group that is larger than the join element. After each comparison, if the number in the ordered group is larger than the join element, it is moved one index to the right. Finally, the join element is moved to the cell vacated by the final element in the ordered group that is larger than the join element. If the right-most element of the ordered group is smaller than the join element, the ordered group grows in size by one including the join element.

For the numbers given in Figure 3.8, the values 12 and 25 are swapped. The result is shown in Figure 3.9.

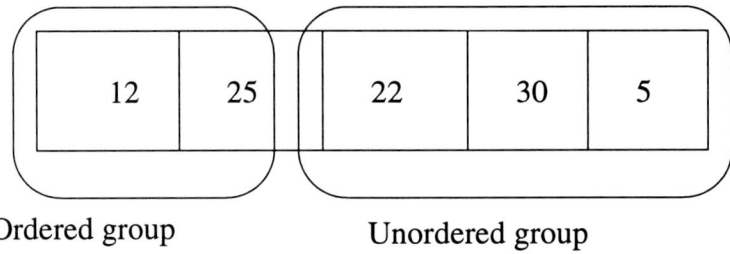

Figure 3.9 Frame 1 of insertion-sort.

Now the join element of the unordered group (number 22) is compared with the elements in the ordered group (from right to left). The value 25 is moved to the right and the value 22 is inserted in the cell vacated by 25. The results are shown in Figure 3.10.

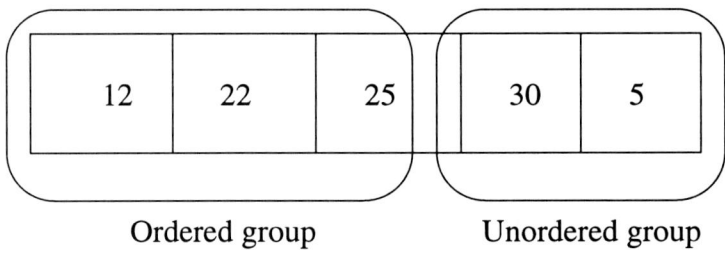

Figure 3.10 Frame 2 of insertion-sort.

Again, the join element of the unordered group (number 30) is compared with the elements in the ordered group (from right to left). Since none of the numbers in the ordered group are larger than 30, the ordered group grows in size by 1 and the unordered group shrinks in size by 1. The results are shown in Figure 3.11.

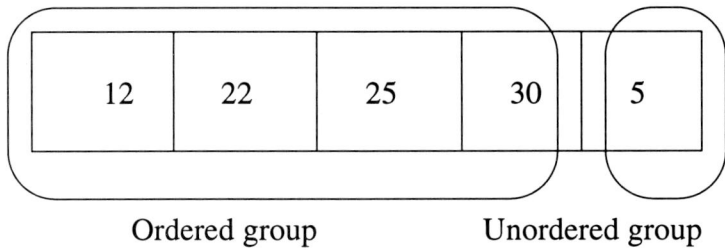

Figure 3.11 Frame 3 of insertion-sort.

ARRAYS, SORTING AND STRINGS

Finally, the last element in the unordered group is compared (from right to left) with the elements in the ordered group. The values 30, 25, 22, and 12 are each moved to the right (i.e., 30 moves from index 4 to index 5, 25 then moves from index 3 to index 4, ..., 12 finally moves from index 1 to index 2). The results are shown in Figure 3.12.

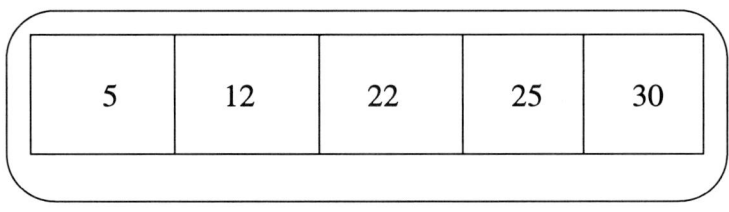

Ordered group

Figure 3.12 Final frame of insertion-sort.

Insertion-sort is completed and the numbers are sorted. The algorithm for insertion-sort is presented in Listing 3.7.

Listing 3.7   Insertion sort

```
insertion_sort (values: ARRAY [REAL]) is
  local
    index1, index2 : INTEGER
    x              : REAL
  do
    from
      index1 := values.lower
    until
      index1 = values.upper
    loop
      index1 := index1 + 1
      x := values.item (index1)
      index2 := index1 - 1
      from
      until  index2 < 1 or else x >= values.item (index2)
      loop
        values.put (values.item (index2), index2 + 1)
        index2 := index2 - 1
      end
      values.put (x, index2 + 1)
```

```
        end
    end -- insertion-sort
```

The results of some timing runs using insertion-sort are presented in Table 3.3. Once again, for each timing run an array of reverse ordered data was used as input.

Table 3.3 Computation time versus array size for Listing 4.9

Array Size	Computation Time (seconds)
25	0.00
50	0.166
100	0.645
200	2.633
400	10.73

The data appears to follow an $O(n^2)$ law for its growth.

Let us walk through the algorithm for the case when the ordered group contains all the elements except the one element, 5, in the unordered group. For this situation, the value of *index1* is equal to 5. The value of *index2* starts at 4. The value of *x* is 5. The loop is entered because the conditions *index2* < 1 and *x* >= *values.item* (*index2*) both fail. The first action in the loop is to move 30 from index 4 to index 5. The second action is to decrement *index2*. This continues until *index2* equals 0. Upon the termination of the loop the final action is to assign x (value 5) to index 1.

3.2.7 Quick-sort

One of the fastest sorting algorithms in existence was designed by Tony Hoare. Quick-sort is a classical "divide and conquer" algorithm. A large sorting problem is systematically subdivided into a series of smaller and smaller sorting problems until a large number of manageable small problems are solved. Their solutions are then merged together to form the solution to the original sorting problem.

ARRAYS, SORTING AND STRINGS

The central idea of quick-sort relates to the concept of partitioning an array around a pivot element. The concept is illustrated in Figure 3.13.

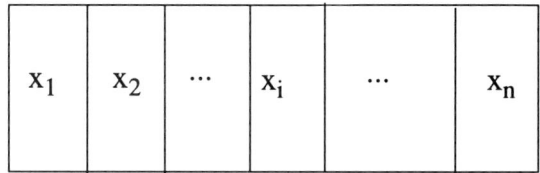

Figure 3.13 Explanation of partition.

Suppose the original elements are exchanged in such a way that all of the numbers to the left of index i (index locations less than i) contain values that are equal or less than x_i and all the numbers to the right of index i (index locations greater than i) contain values that are greater than that of x_i. We will define a command, *partition*, and demonstrate how this may be achieved.

Once the array has been partitioned with respect to the pivot element x_i, the left portion is sorted separately from the right portion. Each of these portions of the array are partitioned in the same manner so that four disjoint subarrays are sorted. Each of these is partitioned so that 8 subarrays are sorted. This doubling of subarrays continues until the size of each subarray falls below a predetermined threshold. Then each of the subarrays are sorted using insertion-sort, the algorithm discussed in Section 3.2.6. Once each subarray is sorted, the entire array is sorted because all the numbers in subarray 1 are equal or smaller than all the numbers in subarray 2, ..., which in turn are smaller than all the numbers in subarray k.

The central idea behind quick-sort is clever and relatively simple. The key is to find a simple and efficient way to partition a subarray into two subarrays separated by a pivot element.

The partition algorithm is presented in the next section.

3.2.7.1 Partition algorithm

The Hoare algorithm for partition is presented in Listing 3.8.

Listing 3.8 Partition algorithm

```
-- Queries
pivot_index: INTEGER

data: ARRAY [REAL]
```

```
-- Command
partition (low: INTEGER; high: INTEGER) is
  require
    low < high
  local
    first, second    : INTEGER
    pivot_element : REAL
    temp             : REAL
  do
    pivot_element := data.item (low)
    first := low
    second := high
    from
    until
       data.item (first) > pivot_element or first >= high
    loop
       first := first + 1
    end
    from
    until
       data.item (second) <= pivot_element
    loop
       second := second - 1
    end
    from
    until
       first >= second
    loop
       temp := data.item (second)
       data.put (data.item (first), second)
       data.put (temp, first)
       from
       until
          data.item (first) > pivot_element
       loop
          first := first + 1
       end
       from
       until
          data.item (second) <= pivot_element
       loop
```

```
            second := second - 1
         end
      end
      temp := data.item (second)
      data.put (data.item (low), second)
      data.put (temp, low)
      pivot_index := second
   ensure
      -- data.item (i) < data.item (pivot_index) for all i < pivot_index
      -- data.item (i) >= data.item (pivot_index) for all i > pivot_index
   end -- partition
```

The attribute *pivot_index* provides a query indicating which index element divides the subarray into two parts. Let us walk through a simple example to see how the partition algorithm works. Consider the following array of numbers: 6, 2, 8, 14, 3, 21, 19, 1

The *pivot_element* is set to the left-most value (index *low*), or 6. The value of index *first* is incremented until an element is found that exceeds the pivot element. This occurs for the above data set when *first* equals 3. The value of index *second* is decremented until an element is found whose value is equal or less than the pivot element. This occurs when *second* equals 8.

Next, the items in indices first and second are interchanged. This produces the revised array given as: 6, 2, 1, 14, 3, 21, 19, 8.

Index *first* is again incremented (from position 3) until an element is found that exceeds the pivot element. This occurs when *first* is at position 4. Index *second* is decremented until an element is found whose value is equal or less than the pivot element. This occurs when *second* equals 5.

The items in positions 4 and 5 are interchanged producing the new array: 6, 2, 1, 3, 14, 21, 19, 8.

Since first is still less than second, the process continues. Index *first*, starting at 4 is incremented to 5 and index *second*, starting at 5, is decremented to 4. Since first is now larger than second the main loop terminates. The final action is to interchange the item in index 1 with index second (items in index 1 and index 4).

The final partitioned array is: 3, 2, 1, 6, 14, 21, 19, 8. The value of *pivot_index* is 4.

The algorithm for quick-sort is given in Listing 3.9.

Listing 3.9   Quick-sort algorithm

```
Small: INTEGER is 16
    -- threshold for insertion_sort

quicksort (low: INTEGER; high: INTEGER) is
  do
    if (high - low) <= small then
      insertion_sort (low, high)
    else
      partition (low, high)
      quicksort (low, pivot_index - 1)
      quicksort (pivot_index + 1, high)
    end
  end  -- quicksort
```

When the size of the subarray (i.e., *high - low*) is less than the constant *Small* the subarray is sorted using *insertion_sort*.

Quick-sort performs according to O(nlogn) on the average. Ironically, if the data starts out sorted, the performance of quick-sort degrades to $O(n^2)$. You are asked to show this as an exercise.

How might one package the quick-sort algorithm? Listing 3.10 shows a class named QUICK_SORT that contains algorithms insertion-sort, partition and quick-sort.

Listing 3.10   Packaging of quick-sort

```
class QUICK_SORT [T -> COMPARABLE]

creation
  make

feature

  -- Queries
  pivot_index : INTEGER

  data: ARRAY [T]
      -- data being sorted

  size : INTEGER

  Small : INTEGER is 16
      -- threshold for insertion_sort
```

```
make (dta: ARRAY [T]; sz: INTEGER) is
  require
    sz > 0
  do
    !! data.make (1, sz)
    data.copy (dta)
    size := sz
  end  -- make

insertion_sort (low: INTEGER; high: INTEGER) is
  local
    index1, index2   : INTEGER
    x                : T
  do
    if low <= high then
      from
        index1 := low
      until
        index1 = high
      loop
        index1 := index1 + 1
        x := data.item (index1)
        index2 := index1 - 1
        from
        until
          index2 < 1 or x >= data.item (index2)
        loop
          data.put (data.item (index2), index2 + 1)
          index2 := index2 - 1
        end
        data.put (x, index2 + 1)
      end
    end
  end -- insertion_sort

partition (low: INTEGER; high: INTEGER) is
  require
    low <= high
  local
    first, second: INTEGER
    pivot_element: T
    temp: T
```

Sorting

```
do
  pivot_element := data.item (low)
  first := low
  second := high
  from
  until
    data.item (first) > pivot_element or first >= high
  loop
    first := first + 1
  end
  from
  until
    data.item (second) <= pivot_element
  loop
    second := second - 1
  end
  from
  until
    first >= second
  loop
    temp := data.item (second)
    data.put (data.item (first), second)
    data.put (temp, first)
    from
    until
      data.item (first) > pivot_element
    loop
      first := first + 1
    end
    from
    until
      data.item (second) <= pivot_element
    loop
      second := second - 1
    end
  end
  temp := data.item (second)
  data.put (data.item (low), second)
  data.put (temp, low)
  pivot_index := second
end  -- partition
```

```
quicksort (low: INTEGER; high: INTEGER) is
  do
    if (high - low) < small then
      insertion_sort (low, high)
    else
      partition (low, high)
      quicksort (low, pivot_index - 1)
      quicksort (pivot_index + 1, high)
    end
  ensure
    sorted: sorted (data)
  end  -- quicksort

sorted (dta: ARRAY [T]): BOOLEAN is
  local
    index: INTEGER
  do
    Result := true
    from
      index := 0
    until
      index = size - 1
    loop
      index := index + 1
      if dta.item (index) > dta.item (index + 1) then
        Result := false
      end
    end
  end  -- sorted

end -- class QUICK_SORT
```

Class QUICK_SORT is written so that any type that conforms to class COMPARABLE (i.e., has instances that can be compared with the usual comparison operators) can be sorted. This is established by using the constrained generic parameter, T -> COMPARABLE.

The attribute *data* holds the elements that are to be sorted. The constant *Small* defines the size threshold below which insertion_sort is used to sort a subarray.

The creation routine *make* takes the input array to be sorted and its size. The quicksort command has a postcondition, *sorted*. The query (function) *sorted* is invoked upon exit from quicksort to verify that *data* is actually sorted.

To show how one might typically invoke quicksort, portions of an APPLICATION class are shown in Listing 3.11.

Listing 3.11   Portions of APPLICATION class for testing quicksort

```
class APPLICATION
creation
  start
feature
  Size : INTEGER is 1000
  sort : QUICK_SORT [REAL]
  start is
    local
      index: INTEGER
      data: ARRAY [REAL]
    do
      !! data.make (1, Size)
      !! sort.make (data, Size)
      -- Array data is loaded with values
      sort.quicksort (1, Size)
      -- Other details not shown
    end
end -- class APPLICATION
```

An attribute *sort* is declared to be of type QUICK_SORT. An instance of this class is created by invoking the creation routine, *make*, and passing the local *data* array and its size as a parameter. The *quicksort* command is invoked through the object *sort*.

3.3 Strings

In the business of programming, a string is an array of characters, not something that you tie your shoes with or fasten a box with. These characters can be ordinary upper- and lower-case letters, numerals, or special symbols on the keyboard such as '$', '%', '&', etc. Even a blank space is a character. Examples of strings are:

(1) "My name is Richard Wiener"
(2) "Testing, testing, 1, 2, 3"
(3) "!@#$%^&*()-+"

One can think about a string such as "hello" as a single value. In reality, this single entity (the string "hello") consists of five more basic entities, namely the characters 'h', 'e', 'l', 'l', and 'o'. These individual characters can be accessed, like any elements of an array, by invoking the query *item* with parameter equal to the index whose character is desired.

Since strings are a basic and useful component of many programs, the Eiffel library provides a class STRING. This class provides a surprisingly large number of routines that define the behavioral characteristics of STRING objects. Clearly a great deal of effort has gone into the development of this powerful and reusable class. Only the most important functions in this class will be discussed.

The most basic operations that one usually needs to support a string type include: (1) creating a string of given size—an array of characters that can hold a predetermined number of characters, (2) inserting characters into the string at various index locations, (3) filling an entire string at once by using an assignment to a string literal (a set of characters delimited by quotation marks such as "hello" or "goodbye"), (4) accessing characters at specified index locations, (5) copying one string to another (the target string must already be initialized), and (6) returning the length of a string—the number of characters actually in the string, not its potential size.

Are there any additional operations that you might wish to add to this relatively short list of six operations? This is the question that a STRING class designer must ask herself when constructing this reusable software component.

Would it surprise you to learn that the STRING class contained in the ISE Eiffel library contains approximately 60 routines that define the behavior of a STRING object. This suggests that the STRING class is a mature and highly evolved class that has been developed and perfected over a long period of time and used in diverse applications.

In order to appreciate the workmanship that goes into the design of such an important reusable software component let us examine the functionality of the STRING class closely before looking at its formal interface and demonstrating its use through an application.

The STRING class is divided into several *feature* sections, each containing a logically related set of operations. In Table 3.4, the various feature sections are shown and a list of some of the routines in the feature sections are listed along with a brief description of their purpose.

Table 3.4 Examination of STRING Class

(1) Access queries	Used to obtain various parts of a STRING object
has	does STRING include a particular character
index_of	position of the first occurence of a character
item	character at specified index
item_code	numeric code of character at specified index
substring_index	position of first occurrence of another string contained within given string
infix "@"	character at specified index (alternative to item)
(2) Comparison queries	**Used to compare two strings**
is_equal	do two strings contain the same sequence of characters
infix "<"	is one string lexicographically smaller than another
(3) Conversion commands	**Used to convert string from one form to another**
mirror	reverse the order of characters in the string
mirrored	test to see whether another string is mirror of first
to_double	convert to type DOUBLE, if possible
to_integer	convert to type INTEGER, if possible
to_lower	convert all upper case characters to lower case
to_real	convert to type REAL, if possible
to_upper	convert all lower case characters to upper case
(4) Duplication command	**Used to copy parts of one string to another**
substring	copy of substring (string contained within a string) containing characters between one index and another

Table 3.4 Examination of STRING Class

(5) Element change commands	Used to modify parts of a given string
append	add a copy of one string to the end of another
copy	transfer characters from source string to target
extend	add a character to the end of a given string
fill_blank	fill a string with blank characters
head	remove all but the first n characters
insert	add a string to the left of specified index in given string
left_adjust	remove leading blanks in a string
precede	add a character in front of a given string
prepend	add a string in front of a given string
put	replace character at specified index by given character
replace_substring	copy characters of another string to specified positions of given string
replace_substring_all	replace every occurence of original with new
right_adjust	rmove trailing blank characters from given string
set	inappropriate to discuss here
share	make current string share the text of another string; any change to the text of the other string will affect original
tail	remove all characters except the last n from a given string
(6) Initialization	**Used to initialize a STRING object**
make	allocate space for at least n characters
(7) Measurement queries	**Used to obtain numerical features of string**
capacity	allocated space
count	Actual number of characters in string
occurrences	number of times a specified character appears in string

STRINGS

Table 3.4 Examination of STRING Class

(8) Output	**Used to output string**
out	creates printable representation
(9) Removal commands	**Used to remove parts of a string**
prune	remove first occurence of a specified character
prune_all	remove all occurences of a specified character
remove	remove i^{th} character
wipe_out	remove all characters
(10) Resizing commands	**Used to dynamically change the size of a string**
adapt_size	change the size to accommodate current number of characters
grow	ensure that the capacity is at least the specified integer
resize	reallocate space to accommodate a specified number of characters
(11) Status report queries	**Used to obtain some important characteristics of string**
consistent	can given string be the target of a copy operation
extendible	may new items be added to given string
prunable	may items be removed from given string
valid_index	is specified index within the range of allowable index values

A small portion of the interface to class STRING is presented in Listing 3.12.

Listing 3.12 Interface to class STRING

class *interface STRING*

creation
  make

feature

  has (c: CHARACTER): BOOLEAN
    -- Does string include 'c'?

  item (i: INTEGER): CHARACTER
    -- Character at position 'i'

  substring_index (other: STRING; start: INTEGER): INTEGER
    -- Position of first occurrence of 'other' at or after 'start';
    -- 0 if none.

  infix "@" (i: INTEGER): CHARACTER
    -- Character at position 'i'

  is_equal (other: like Current): BOOLEAN
    -- Is string made of same character sequence as 'other'
    -- (possibly with a different capacity)?

  infix "<" (other: STRING): BOOLEAN
    -- Is string lexicographically lower than 'other'?
    -- (False if 'other' is void)

  to_double: DOUBLE
    -- "Double" value;
    -- for example, when applied to "123.0", will yield 123.0 (double)

  to_integer: INTEGER
    -- Integer value;
    -- for example, when applied to "123", will yield 123

  to_lower
    -- Convert to lower case.

  to_real: REAL
    -- Real value;
    -- for example, when applied to "123.0", will yield 123.0

  to_upper
    -- Convert to upper case.

substring (n1, n2: INTEGER): like Current
    -- Copy of substring containing all characters at indices
    -- between 'n1' and 'n2'

append (s: STRING)
    -- Append a copy of 's' at end.

copy (other: like Current)
    -- Reinitialize by copying the characters of 'other'.
    -- (This is also used by 'clone'.)

fill_blank
    -- Fill with blanks.

insert (s: like Current; i: INTEGER)
    -- Add 's' to the left of position 'i' in current string.

put (c: CHARACTER; i: INTEGER)
    -- Replace character at position 'i' by 'c'.

capacity: INTEGER
    -- Allocated space

count: INTEGER
    -- Actual number of characters making up the string

occurrences (c: CHARACTER): INTEGER
    -- Number of times 'c' appears in the string

wipe_out
    -- Remove all characters.

end *-- class STRING*

Appendix A provides all of the information that is required to use the STRING class in a given application. As part of the learning process in becoming a competent client, the reader should carefully study the interface information in this Appendix.

One highly recommended strategy for becoming comfortable and familiar with the use of a class such as STRING is to create a test program that exercises some of its functions. Although this may take some time and even appear tedious, the payoff is potentially great. Once the programmer gains confidence in the proper use of a reusable class like STRING, then the real benefit of software reuse can come into play.

The test application given in Listing 3.13 is designed to exercise a small sample of the routines of class STRING. Comments throughout the routine indicate the purpose of each code segment. The reader is encour-

ARRAYS, SORTING AND STRINGS

aged to carefully review this listing and to make modifications and additions in order to gain additional insights into the behavior of a STRING object.

Listing 3.13   Test program for class STRING

```
class APPLICATION

creation
    start

feature

    start is
        local
            message     : STRING
            reverse     : STRING
            str1, str2  : STRING
            r           : REAL
        do
            message := "Testing, testing, 123, 1234"
            io.putstring ("message = ")
            io.putstring (message)
            io.new_line
            !! str1.make (50)
            str1.copy (message)
            if str1.is_equal (message) then
                io.putstring ("str1 = message")
            else
                io.putstring ("str1/= message")
            end
            io.new_line

            str1.put ('t', 1)
            if str1.is_equal (message) then
                io.putstring ("str1 = message")
            else
                io.putstring ("str1/= message")
            end
            io.new_line

            str1.mirror
            io.putstring ("str1 = ")
```

STRINGS

```
io.putstring (str1)
io.new_line
str1.mirror
str1.to_upper
io.putstring ("str1 = ")
io.putstring (str1)
io.new_line

io.putstring ("First occurrence of 'G%' = ")
io.putint (str1.index_of ('G', 1))
io.new_line

io.putstring ("First occurrence of 'ING%' = ")
io.putint (str1.substring_index ("ING", 1))
io.new_line

io.putstring (str1.true_constant)
io.new_line

str2 := str1.substring (24, 27)
io.putstring ("str2 = ")
io.putstring (str2)
io.new_line

r := str2.to_real
io.putstring ("r = ")
io.putreal (r)
io.new_line

message.append (". More testing ")
message.append_real (12345.6)
io.putstring ("message = ")
io.putstring (message)
io.new_line

str1.head (4)
io.putstring ("str1 = ")
io.putstring (str1)
io.new_line

str1.tail (2)
io.putstring ("str1 = ")
io.putstring (str1)
io.new_line
```

```
        message.prune_all ('T')
        io.putstring ("message = ")
        io.putstring (message)
        io.new_line

        io.putstring ("str2.capacity = ")
        io.putint (str2.capacity)
        io.new_line

        io.putstring ("str2.count = ")
        io.putint (str2.count)
        io.new_line

        str2.resize (100)
        io.putstring ("str2.capacity = ")
        io.putint (str2.capacity)
        io.new_line

        io.putstring ("str1.capacity = ")
        io.putint (str1.capacity)
        io.new_line

        io.putstring ("str1.count = ")
        io.putint (str1.count)
        io.new_line
    end

end -- class APPLICATION
```

The output of the program is:

```
message = Testing, testing, 123, 1234
str1 = message
str1/= message
str1 = 4321 ,321 ,gnitset ,gnitset
str1 = TESTING, TESTING, 123, 1234
First occurrence of 'G' = 7
First occurrence of 'ING' = 5
true
str2 = 1234
r = 1234
message = Testing, testing, 123, 1234. More testing 12345.6
str1 = TEST
str1 = ST
message = esting, testing, 123, 1234. More testing 12345.6
```

```
str2.capacity = 9
str2.count = 4
str2.capacity = 100
str1.capacity = 40
str1.count = 2
```

3.4 String searching—simple algorithm

Suppose that we wish to determine whether a substring (pattern) is present in a given string. Suppose the length of the pattern is m and the length of the string is n. We examine only the simplest string-searching algorithm in this chapter.

The algorithm for this simple string search is given in Listing 3.14, in command *simple_search*. This command is embedded in a class, STRING_SEARCH.

The string and pattern are sent into an instance of STRING_SEARCH when this object is created (as parameters to the creation routine *make*). The *make* routine can also be used to change either the pattern or string once an instance of STRING_SEARCH is created.

Listing 3.14 Algorithm for simple string search

class STRING_SEARCH

creation
   make

feature

   string: STRING

   pattern: STRING

   make (ptr: STRING; str: STRING) **is**
     require
       ptr /= void
       str /= void
     do
       string := str
       pattern := ptr
     ensure
       string = str

```
        pattern = ptr
    end

    -- Query for pattern matching
    simple_search : INTEGER is
        -- Returns starting index of location of pattern in string otherwise 0
    local
        str_pos, ptr_pos: INTEGER
        str_len, pat_len: INTEGER
    do
        str_len := string.count
        pat_len := pattern.count
        from
            str_pos := 1
            ptr_pos := 1
        until
            str_pos > str_len or ptr_pos > pat_len
        loop
            from
            until
                str_pos > str_len or else string.item (str_pos) = pattern.item (ptr_pos)
            loop
                str_pos := str_pos - ptr_pos + 2
                ptr_pos := 1
            end
            str_pos := str_pos + 1
            ptr_pos := ptr_pos + 1
        end
        if ptr_pos > pat_len then
            Result := str_pos - pat_len
        end
    ensure
        -- Result > 0 implies pattern is contained within string
        -- Result = 0 implies pattern is not contained within string
    end  -- simple search

end -- class STRING_SEARCH
```

The worst-case complexity of the command *simple_search* is O (mn), where m and n are the length of the search and sub-strings respectively. For string pattern searches, such as the ones done in a typical text editor, the average-case complexity is O(m + n).

SUMMARY

It is left as an exercise to "walk" through the algorithm for a simple test case.

For repetitive patterns in strings containing a small alphabet (e.g., binary strings), more efficient searching algorithms such as the Knuth-Pratt-Morris or Boyer-Moore algorithms have been devised. These will not be discussed in this book.

3.5 Summary

- A sorting **algorithm** is a formal sequence of instructions for performing a computation.
- The study of algorithms helps to justify the "science" in "computer science."
- The efficiency of an algorithm is related to the speed with which it performs its work and the memory that is required to do this work.
- A problem has many instances, usually an infinite number of instances.
- Various measures have been devised to indicate the computational efficiency of an algorithm. These include: worst-case asymptotic complexity and average-case asymptotic complexity.
- Asymptotic complexity refers to the growth in computation time as a function of the growth in problem size, as the problem size approaches infinity.
- The "big O" notation is often used to express the asymptotic complexity of an algorithm.
- Selection-sort, bubble-sort, and insertion-sort have worst-case and average-case complexities of $O(n^2)$.
- Quick-sort, a divide and conquer recursive algorithm, has an average-case complexity of $O(nlogn)$.
- The most basic operations that one usually needs to support a string type include: (1) creating a string of given size—an array of characters that can hold a predetermined number of characters, (2) inserting characters into the string at various index locations, (3) filling an entire string at once by using an assignment to a string literal (a set of characters delimited by quotation marks such as "hello" or "goodbye"), (4) accessing characters at specified index locations, (5) copying one string to another (the target string must already be initialized), and (6) return-

ing the length of a string—the number of characters actually in the string, not its potential size.

- The STRING class contained in the ISE Eiffel library contains approximately 60 routines that define the behavior of a STRING object. This suggests that the STRING class is a mature and highly evolved class that has been developed and perfected over a long period of time and used in diverse applications.

- The worst-case complexity of the command *simple_search* is O (mn). For string pattern searches, such as the ones done in a typical text editor, the average-case complexity is O(m + n).

3.6 Exercises

1. Describe three problems and for each problem state three instances.

2. Using semi-log paper, run and verify that when the shrink factor is close to 1.3, comb-sort performs according to O (nlogn).

3. Do the same for quick-sort. Use random numbers to generate data.

4. Explain why it is essential to assign *interchanged* to TRUE above the first *from-until* loop in the bubble-sort algorithm. What would happen if this statement were omitted?

5. Change the shrink_factor in the comb-sort algorithm and observe the effect it has on sorting time.

6. Show that when an input array is already sorted, the performance of the *quicksort* algorithm degenerates to O (n^2).

7. Show the steps in the *simple_search* string searching algorithm if the pattern is equal to "abac" and the string is "abccaaacabaaabacabca".

8. Discuss why you believe that the average-case complexity of the "brute-force" string-searching algorithm is O (m + n). (Hint: Choose a small alphabet and a repetitive pattern).

Chapter 4

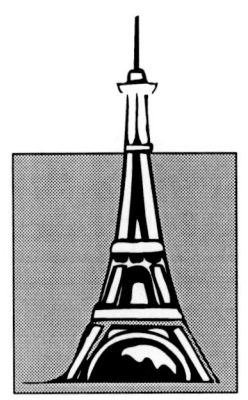

Stacks and Queues

4.1 Container classes

A box of paper clips, a stack of trays in a cafeteria, a room full of desks, chairs, lamps, and other furniture, an array of integers, a bag of groceries, a set of lottery tickets, a dictionary of words, and a database of patient records are all examples of container objects. Some of the container objects, such as the box of paper clips, stack of cafeteria trays, set of lottery tickets, and dictionary of words, consist of identical types of objects (i.e., paper clip, cafeteria trays, integers, lottery tickets, dictionary words), whereas the other container objects contain a diversity of objects (i.e., desks, chairs, lamps and other furniture in a room, groceries, and patient records).

It is important to make a distinction between the container object and the things that it contains. For example in the case of the cafeteria trays, we can distinguish the trays from the stack. This may seem quite artificial but it is actually a useful abstraction. We can visualize an empty stack as being the physical location where the trays are piled, one on top of another. We can identify an empty grocery sack (i.e., paper bag) as a legitimate object in its own right—one that becomes a useful artifact when it is filled with grocery or other objects. In short, containers have an existence separate from the things they contain.

This chapter examines two relatively simple types of containers: stacks and queues. Such classes, once perfected, can be used in many software applications and are therefore ideal candidates for software reuse.

More formally, a container class is one that holds zero or more elements, each formally declared to be of a particular class type. The actual type inserted in the container must conform to (be a descendant of) the formal type. This allows a container to hold either a homogeneous or heterogeneous collection of elements.

There are many types of container classes. If the capacity of a container object, specified at the time of its creation, cannot be later modified, it is a static container, otherwise it is a dynamic container. The number of elements that can be inserted into a dynamic container is limited only by the memory space of the computer running the program. The capacity of a static container class is specified by the user or programmer.

In Chapter 3, an important container class, the ARRAY, was introduced. In later chapters other more complex container classes are presented and discussed. These include DEQUE, UNORDERED_LIST, ORDERED_LIST, PRIORITY_QUEUE, and SEARCH_TREE.

A container class must specify protocol (a set of rules) for inserting, deleting and accessing elements. This is what differentiates one type of container from another.

Before a given class, container or otherwise, can be considered "reusable," it typically has to meet the following conditions: (1) each of its features have been extensively tested in many different applications over a reasonably long period of time, (2) it provides a range of services (commands and queries) sufficient to meet the varied needs of many clients (applications that use the component), and (3) each of the services are efficiently implemented.

The data structure libraries that are part of Eiffel provide definitions for the container types discussed in this and later chapters. It is highly recommended that one should utilize such highly tested and mature software components instead of writing one's own if one is building a commercial application. An important goal of this chapter is to explore some of the fundamental issues associated with the construction of "reusable" container classes. Therefore for some container classes we will construct our own whereas for others we will use and examine those present in the standard Eiffel library.

4.2 Stack

A stack is one of the simplest and, perhaps for this reason, most widely used abstract data type. Many software applications require the logical equivalent of piling objects on top of each other. The only object that can be accessed in such a pile or stack is the last object put on the pile or the top object (assuming that gravity prevails and the stack is built vertically). An interior object can be accessed only by first removing all the objects on top of it.

Figure 4.1 shows a typical stack.

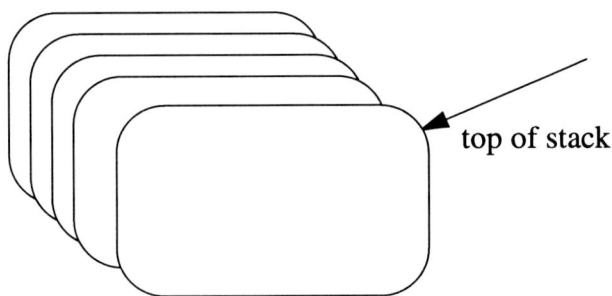

Figure 4.1 Stack of objects.

The protocol for insertion and deletion that defines the unique signature of a stack specifies that the last element inserted onto a stack is the first element that can be deleted from the stack. This is called a "last-in-first-out" (LIFO) protocol. If one inserts a sequence of objects onto a stack and then removes all of the objects, the sequence in which the objects are removed will be the reverse of the sequence in which they were inserted. Therefore, stacks are useful containers for reversing the order of a collection of entities.

It is not legal to violate the strict LIFO protocol of a stack by, for example, accessing the next to the last item inserted before accessing the last item inserted. If this capability were needed, a container type other than a stack would have to be used.

The operations with their interface that define the behavior of a STACK class are:

- *push (item : T)*—add item to stack (command)

- *pop*—remove item from stack (command)

- *top* : T—access top element (query)

- *empty : BOOLEAN*—True if no elements contained in stack (query)
- *capacity : INTEGER*—The number of elements that can be held in stack (query)
- *num_elements : INTEGER*—The actual number of elements on the stack (query)

As a reminder, use verbs to name commands and use nouns to name queries.

The commands that change the configuration of the stack are *push* and *pop*. The queries that return information about the stack but do not change its configuration are *top, capacity, num_elements* and *empty*. Some of these queries may be implemented through storage (as attributes) rather than as routines.

4.2.1 Static implementation of STACK

Listing 4.1 presents a static implementation of the container class STACK.

Listing 4.1 Static implementation of STACK

class FIXED_STACK [T]

creation
   initialize

feature

   capacity: INTEGER

   num_elements: INTEGER

   push (item: T) **is**
     require
       under_capacity: num_elements < capacity
     local
       new_item : T
     do
       num_elements := num_elements + 1
       new_item := clone (item)
       data.put (new_item, num_elements)
     ensure
       num_elements = **old** num_elements + 1

      not *empty*
      top_element = item
    end

  pop **is**
    require
      non_empty: **not** *empty*
    do
      num_elements := num_elements - 1
    ensure
      num_elements = **old** *num_elements - 1*
    end

  top : T **is**
    require
      non_empty: **not** *empty*
    do
      Result := data.item (num_elements)
    end

  at_capacity : BOOLEAN **is**
    do
      Result := num_elements = capacity
    ensure
      Result = **true implies** *num_elements = capacity*
    end

  empty : BOOLEAN **is**
    do
      Result := num_elements = 0
    ensure
      Result = **true implies** *num_elements = 0*
    end

feature *{NONE} -- Protected section for internal use only*

  data: ARRAY [T]

  initialize (size: INTEGER) **is**
    require
      positive_size: size > 0
    do
      capacity := size
      !! data.make (1, size)

STACK

> **ensure**
>   capacity = size
>   num_elements = 0
> **end**
>
> **invariant**
>   num_elements <= capacity
>   num_elements >= 0
>
> **end** -- class FIXED_STACK

In Listing 4.1, the creation routine *initialize* is implemented in the protected section of the class (*feature { NONE }*). This is to ensure that *initialize* can be used *only for creation* and not used as a mutator routine. We do not want to allow an existing STACK object to have its capacity changed once it is created.

The two attributes of STACK are *capacity* and *num_elements*. This latter attribute stores the last element to be removed from the STACK, if any.

Command *push* requires that the attribute *num_elements* be less than the attribute *capacity* (see the precondition), otherwise an overflow condition will result. The attribute *num_elements* is incremented by 1. The command *put* sets *item* at index *num_elements* in the internal attribute *data*. The postcondition specifies that when the routine exits, the *num_elements* equals the old value plus 1. Figure 4.2 shows the mechanism for routine *push*.

The object is inserted at index *num_elements* + 1. The *clone* function that creates storage for *new_item* is essential. If separate storage is not created, serious aliasing problems may occur if nonsimple items are pushed onto the stack. See exercise 4.8.

Command *pop* requires as a precondition that the stack is not empty. It is the client's responsibility to test for this condition using the query *empty*. The only change to the internal state of the fixed stack is that the attribute *num_elements* is decremented by 1. This does not remove the item being popped from the array but allows the cell to be reused the next time a *push* command occurs.

The query *top*, implemented through computation (as opposed as through storage as an attribute) returns the datum at index *num_elements*.

STACKS AND QUEUES

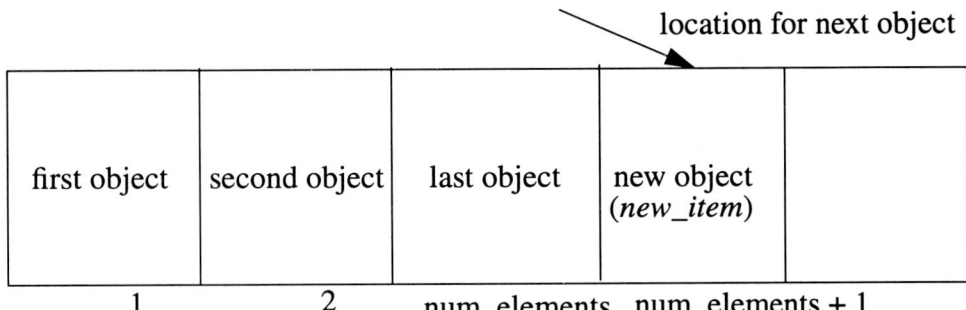

Figure 4.2 Mechanism of push for static stack.

A class invariant is specified in the last section of the class. The conditions *num_elements <= capacity* and *num_elements >= 0* are given. This indicates that upon exit from any routine of the class this condition must hold as well as on entry to every public routine except initialize.

Listing 4.2 presents a short form of the class. From this documentation all of the relevant module interface information is given.

Listing 4.2 Short form for class FIXED_STACK

class interface FIXED_STACK [T]

creation
  initialize

feature

  at_capacity: BOOLEAN

  capacity: INTEGER

  empty: BOOLEAN

  num_elements: INTEGER

  pop
    require
      non_empty: not empty
    ensure
      num_elements = old num_elements - 1

  push (item: T)
    require
      under_capacity: num_elements < capacity

```
    ensure
      num_elements = old num_elements + 1
      not empty
      top_element = item
  top : T
    require
      non_empty: not empty
invariant
  num_elements <= capacity
  num_elements > 0

end -- class FIXED_STACK
```

Listing 4.3 presents a test program that exercises a fixed stack.

Listing 4.3   Test program for fixed stack

```
class APPLICATION

creation
  start

feature

  start is
    local
      my_stack  : FIXED_STACK [INTEGER]
      index     : INTEGER
    do
      !! my_stack.initialize (500)
      from
        index := 0
      until
        index = 1000
      loop
        index := index + 1
        if not my_stack.at_capacity then
          my_stack.push (index)
        end
      end
      from
        index := 0
```

```
    until
      index = 1000
    loop
      index := index + 1
      if not my_stack.empty then
        my_stack.pop
        if index <= 20 then
          io.putint (my_stack.top_element)
          io.new_line
        end
      end
    end
  end

end -- class APPLICATION
```

The code in Listing 4.3 is protected against violating any of the preconditions of the stack commands. Before attempting to *push* onto *my_stack* a test is performed using *my_stack.at_capacity*. Before attempting to *pop* from *my_stack* a test is performed using *my_stack.empty*.

4.2.2 Dynamic implementation

In exchange for efficient access, the FIXED_STACK presented in Listing 4.1 imposes an artificial constraint on the user, namely a fixed and predetermined limit (the capacity) on the number of items that can be pushed onto the stack. This limitation is removed in another stack class, DYNAMIC_STACK presented in Listing 4.4.

Listing 4.4   Class DYNAMIC_STACK

```
class DYNAMIC_STACK [T]

feature

  num_elements: INTEGER

  push (item: T) is
    local
      new_node: NODE [T]
    do
      !! new_node.make (item, first)
      first := new_node
      num_elements := num_elements + 1
```

STACK

```
      ensure
        num_elements = old num_elements + 1
        not empty
      end

    pop is
      require
        non_empty: not empty
      do
        first := first.next
        num_elements := num_elements - 1
      ensure
        num_elements = old num_elements - 1
      end

    top: T is
      require
        non_empty: not empty
      do
        Result := first.item
      end

    empty: BOOLEAN is
      do
        Result := num_elements = 0
      ensure
        Result = (num_elements = 0)
      end

  feature {NONE}

    first: NODE [T]

invariant
  num_elements >= 0

end -- class DYNAMIC_STACK
```

Listing 4.5 presents the details of class NODE.

Listing 4.5   Class NODE

```
class NODE [T]
```

creation *{DYNAMIC_STACK}*
  make

feature *{DYNAMIC_STACK}* -- Limited export scope

  item: T

  next: NODE [T]

  make (value: T; link: NODE [T]) **is**
    do
      item := clone (value)   -- separate storage is created for item
      next := link
    end

end -- class NODE

As shown in Listing 4.4, a DYNAMIC_STACK has the attribute *num_elements* exported everywhere and the attribute *first* in a protected section. A client of DYNAMIC_STACK need not know about *first* but only the two public attributes.

Let us examine the three lines of code in routine *push*. Figure 4.3 shows an existing DYNAMIC_STACK containing two elements. Attribute *first* points to the NODE object containing *item1*. This NODE object points to (is linked to) the NODE object containing *item2*.

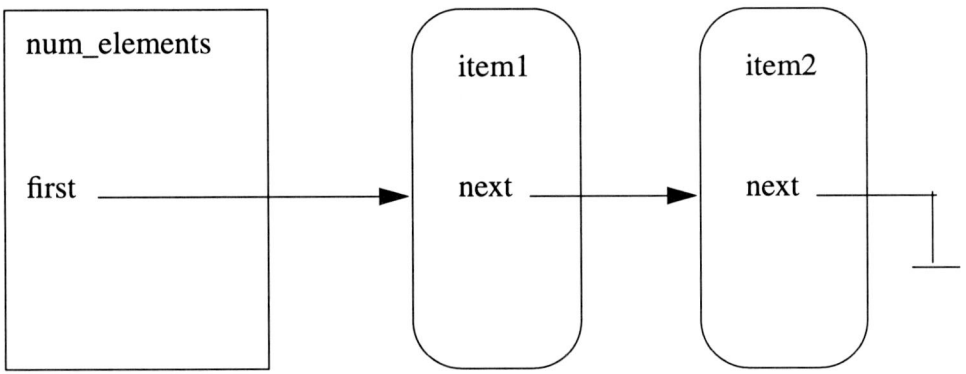

Figure 4.3 Initial dynamic stack.

The first line of code creates and initializes a NODE object, *new_node*, with value equal to *item* and *next* equal to *first*.

Figure 4.4 shows the results of this first line of code.

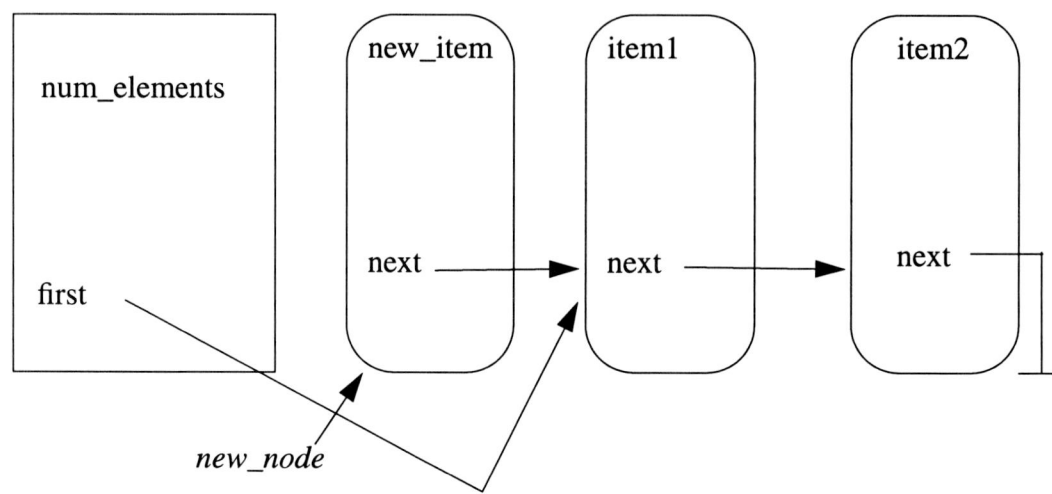

Figure 4.4 Dynamic stack after new node.

Figure 4.5 shows the results after the second line of code, *first := new_node*.

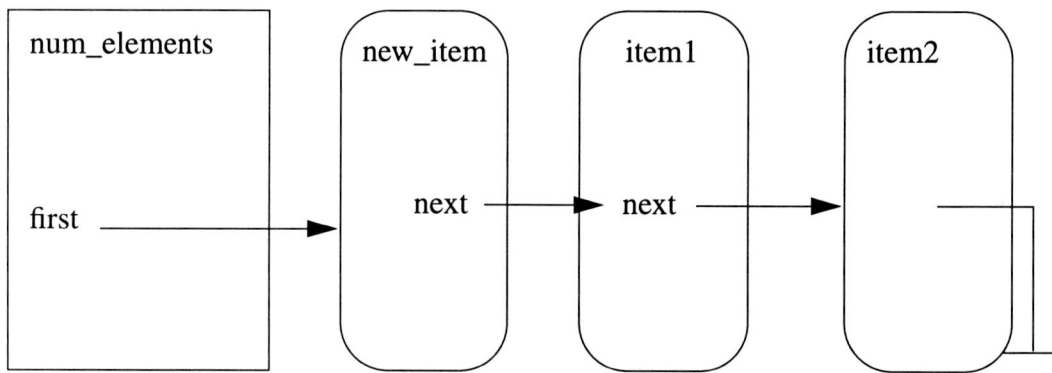

Figure 4.5 Completed push operation.

4.3 Queue

A queue is a close cousin of a stack; it's a container class that stores elements in the order first-in-first-out. It is an abstraction of a waiting line. A common variant of a queue is a priority queue. For this data abstraction, elements are ordered (inserted into the queue) according to some metric or priority value. Elements are positioned in the queue according to their priority value rather than their time of entry. Priority queues are considered in the next chapter.

Queues can be implemented either statically or dynamically. We will consider only a dynamic implementation in this section. As an exercise, the reader is invited to implement a static queue.

The basic operations that define the queue abstraction are listed below:

- *insert (item : T)*—add item to queue (command)
- *remove*—remove item from queue (command)
- *front : T*—access next item that can be removed from queue (query)
- *empty : BOOLEAN*—True if no elements contained in queue (query)
- *num_elements : INTEGER*—The actual number of elements in the queue (query)

An implementation of a dynamic queue is given in Listing 4.6.

Listing 4.6 Class DYNAMIC_QUEUE

```
class DYNAMIC_QUEUE [T]

feature

  number_elements: INTEGER;

  insert (item: T) is
    do
      insert_back (item);
      number_elements := number_elements + 1
    ensure
      number_elements = old number_elements + 1
    end;

  remove is
    require
      non_empty: not empty
    do
      front_node := front_node.next;
      number_elements := number_elements - 1
    ensure
```

QUEUE

```
      number_elements = old number_elements - 1
    end;

  front: T is
    require
      non_empty: number_elements > 0
    do
      Result := front_node.value
    end;

  empty: BOOLEAN is
    do
      Result := number_elements = 0
    end;

feature {NONE}

  front_node: NODE [T];

  back_node: NODE [T];

  insert_back (item: T) is
      -- Add item to the back of the list
    local
      new_node: NODE [T]
    do
      if number_elements = 0 then
        !! back_node.make (item, void);
        front_node := back_node
      else
        !! new_node.make (item, void);
        back_node.link (new_node);
        back_node := new_node
      end;
      number_elements := number_elements + 1
    ensure
      number_elements = old number_elements + 1
    end;

invariant
  number_elements >= 0;

end -- class DYNAMIC_QUEUE
```

The export lists of class NODE must be changed to include DYNAMIC_QUEUE in order for the above code to work.

The data structure used for this implementation of the queue contains two protected attributes, *front_node* and *back_node*. These are for internal use only. The reason for including the additional attribute *back_node* (compared to the stack implementation) is that insertion is to the back of the structure. Maintaining a "pointer" to the back of the structure avoids the need to traverse the linked set of nodes.

Figure 4.6 shows a typical queue structure, with 2 elements.

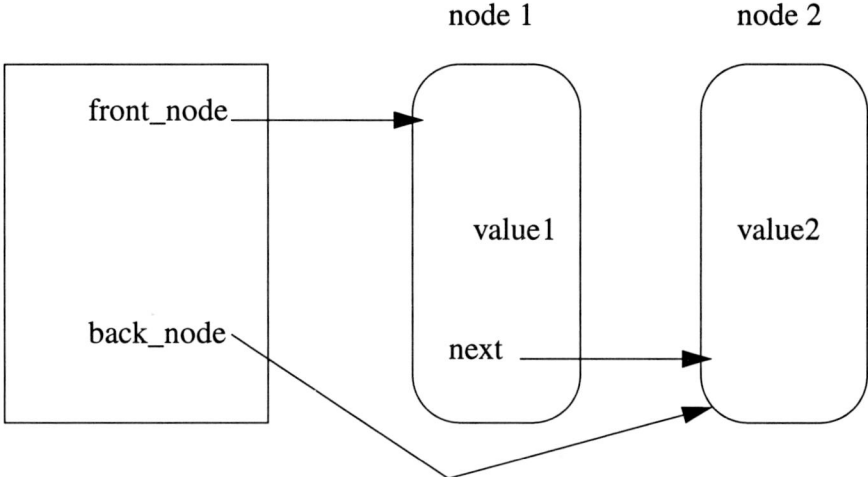

Figure 4.6 Queue with two elements.

The *remove* command has the same implementation as the *pop* command for a stack. The *front_node* is replaced by the node that it is linked to.

The *insert* command invokes the protected command *insert_back* with *item* as a parameter. The *insert_back* logic is divided into two cases: insertion into an empty queue and insertion into an existing queue.

In the first case, insertion into an empty queue, a *back_node* is created and then *front_node* is assigned to *back_node*.

In the second case, insertion into an existing queue, a new node is created. The node *back_node* is linked to the new node. Finally, *back_node* is assigned to the new node.

4.4 Summary

- It is important to make a distinction between the container object and the things that it contains.

- A container class is one that holds zero or more elements, each formally declared to be of a particular class type. The actual type inserted in the container must conform to (be a descendant of) the formal type. This allows a container to hold either a homogeneous or heterogeneous collection of elements.

- If the capacity of a container object, specified at the time of its creation, cannot be later modified, it is a static container; otherwise, it is a dynamic container. The number of elements that can be inserted into a dynamic container is limited only by the memory space of the computer running the program. The capacity of a static container class is specified by the user or programmer.

- Before a given class, container or otherwise, can be considered "reusable", it typically has to meet the following conditions: (1) each of its features has been extensively tested in many different applications over a reasonably long period of time, (2) it provides a range of services (commands and queries) sufficient to meet the varied needs of many clients (applications that use the component), and (3) each of the services is efficiently implemented.

- The protocol for insertion and deletion that defines the unique signature of a stack specifies that the last element inserted onto a stack is the first element that can be deleted from the stack. This is called a "last-in-first-out" (LIFO) protocol.

- A queue is a close cousin of a stack—it's a container class that stores elements in the order first-in-first-out. It is an abstraction of a waiting line.

4.5 Exercises

1. Write a static implementation of a queue. Write a short test class that exercises all of the commands and queries of the queue. Show and discuss your output.

2. Write a test class that exercises all of the commands and queries of the dynamic stack and dynamic queue implemented in this chapter. Show and discuss your output.

3. Write an application class that uses a stack to reverse the sequence of characters in a string. Write a short test class that allows the user to input an arbitrary string. Your test class should output the reverse sequence for each string input by the user.

4. Write an implementation of command insert for a dynamic queue if only one attribute, *front_node* is defined.

5. Write a test class that defines a dynamic stack that can contain objects of any class (Hint: Consider the possibility of using ANY as the base type for the stack).

6. Write a test class that constructs a queue of stacks.

7. Write a test class that constructs a stack of queues.

8. Explain in detail the consequences of pushing *item* directly onto the stack, rather than using clone as in Listing 4.1.

Chapter 5

Lists

The list abstraction is more complex and general than either the stack or the queue. As we will see later in this chapter, a stack or queue can easily be implemented using a list. Other important data abstractions, including priority queues and deques, can also be implemented using a list.

Lists are important in their own right. A list is a container class that provides sequential access to arbitrary elements. It is a linear data structure because it has a well defined beginning and well defined end. One can traverse through a list, element by element, from the beginning to the end.

5.1 Types of lists

A LIST can be specified in many ways. The basic questions that help define the specifications of a LIST include the following:

- Does the list allow duplicates (i.e., can the same value appear more than once)?

- Are the elements ordered (i.e., is the first element smaller than the second which is smaller than the third, …, which is smaller than the last)?

- Is the list static or dynamic (i.e., does the number of elements need to be specified in advance or does the size of the list grow on demand)?

- Can the list be traversed in one direction or two directions (i.e., can one traverse the list from end location to beginning location in addition to the usual capability of traversing the list from beginning location to end location)?

The answers to the above questions determine the implementation details of the list and, more importantly, its potential use. In the next several sections, several LIST implementations are presented and discussed.

5.2 Dynamic unordered list without duplicates

The container class examined in this section is an unordered list with duplicates not allowed. The size of the list can grow on demand.

In designing the data abstraction UNORDERED_LIST we must identify its commands and queries. We must ask ourselves the questions, "What do we wish to find out about a list?" and "What do we wish to do to a list?"

In designing an abstract data type as complex as an unordered list, it is useful to formulate the interface before worrying about implementation details. The interface precisely specifies the "behavior" of a list. Because of the protection associated with encapsulation, only the commands and queries that are specified in the class interface can be used to modify or access information about a list.

5.2.1 The UNORDERED_LIST data abstraction

We answer the questions, "What do we wish to find out about a list?" and "What do we wish to do to a list?"

Queries ("What do we wish to find out about a list?")

- What is the first item on the list, if any?
- What is the last item on the list, if any?
- What is the last item removed from the list, if any?
- How many elements are in the list?
- Is a given item present in the list?
- What is the element just after a given item?
- What is the element just before a given item?

- Is the list empty?
- Is there an element directly to the right of the current element that a cursor points to?
- What is the element being pointed to by the cursor?

   Commands ("What do we wish to do with a list?")

- Insert an item into the front of the list
- Insert an item into the back of the list
- Insert an item just after a given item on the list
- Insert an item just before a given item on the list
- Remove a given item from the list
- Remove an item from the front of the list
- Remove an item from the back of the list
- Remove an item just after a given item on the list
- Remove an item just before a given item on the list
- Move a cursor so it points to the first element in the list
- Move the cursor forward so it points to the next element in the list

The notion of a *cursor* is mentioned in two queries and two commands. Conceptually, this is a pointer that enables client code to iterate through the elements of a list (i.e., access each element in sequence from the front to back) and perform some appropriate operation on each successive list element. Often this operation merely consists of displaying the element. Client code cannot directly access this cursor, but can only manipulate it using the two commands associated with the cursor (the last two bullets given above).

5.2.2 Interface to UNORDERED_LIST

From the queries and commands given in Section 5.2.1, the interface to class UNORDERED_LIST is constructed. This interface contains the external view of the class—the features that comprise the public data model of the class including queries implemented as attributes, queries implemented as functions and commands implemented as routines.

For each routine, its parameters (if any) and return type (if any) are given. In addition, the semantics (desired behavior) of the routine are

DYNAMIC UNORDERED LIST WITHOUT DUPLICATES

more completely specified if preconditions and postconditions (if any) are given. It should be evident that the short form of the class comprises its formal interface.

Listing 5.1 presents the short form for class UNORDERED_LIST. The features that are normally presented in alphabetical order have been rearranged into the categories of queries and commands.

Listing 5.1 Interface to class UNORDERED_LIST (short form)

class interface UNORDERED_LIST [T]

feature

    -- Queries implemented as attributes
    front_node   : T
    back_item   : T
    last_removed   : T
    number_elements : INTEGER

    -- Queries implemented as functions
    item_after (item: T): T
        -- Return the element just after item in the list
    require
      sufficient_elements: number_elements >= 2
      not_last_item: item /= back_item
      item_present: present (item)

    item_before (item: T): T
        -- Return the element just before item in the list
    require
      sufficient_elements: number_elements >= 2
      not_first_item: item /= front_item
      item_present: present (item)

    present (item: T): BOOLEAN
        -- Return TRUE if item is in list, otherwise FALSE

    empty: BOOLEAN
        -- Return TRUE if no elements in list, otherwise FALSE

    can_move: BOOLEAN
        -- Returns TRUE if cursor can move forward otherwise false

    item_at_cursor: T
        -- Return the item under cursor

-- Commands
insert_front (item: T)
    -- Add item to the front of the list
  require
    no_duplicate: not present (item)
  ensure
    number_elements = old number_elements + 1
    front_item = item
    number_elements = 1 implies back_item = item

insert_back (item: T)
    -- Add item to the back of the list
  require
    no_duplicate: not present (item)
  ensure
    number_elements = old number_elements + 1
    back_item = item
    number_elements = 1 implies front_item =

insert_after (item: T; value: T)
    -- Add item after element item in list
  require
    item_present: present (item)
    no_duplicate: not present (value)
  ensure
    number_elements = old number_elements + 1 and number_elements >= 2

insert_before (item: T; value: T)
    -- Add item before element item in list
  require
    item_present: present (item)
    no_duplicate: not present (value)
  ensure
    number_elements = old number_elements + 1 and number_elements >= 2

remove (item: T)
    -- Remove the item from the list
  require
    item_present: present (item)
  ensure

number_elements = old number_elements - 1
number_elements = 1 implies front_item = back_item

remove_front
-- Remove the first item in list
require
sufficient_elements: number_elements > 0
ensure
number_elements = old number_elements - 1
number_elements = 1 implies front_item = back_item

remove_back
-- Remove the last item in list
require
sufficient_elements: number_elements > 0
ensure
number_elements = old number_elements - 1
number_elements = 1 implies front_item = back_item

remove_after (item: T)
-- Remove the element after item on list
require
sufficient_elements: number_elements >= 2
item_present: present (item)
item_not_last: item /= back_item
ensure
number_elements = old number_elements - 1
number_elements = 1 implies front_item = back_item

remove_before (item: T)
-- Remove the element before item on list
require
sufficient_elements: number_elements >= 2
item_present: present (item)
item_not_first: item /= front_item
ensure
number_elements = old number_elements - 1
number_elements = 1 implies front_item = back_item

start
-- Move cursor to the first element in list
require
not_empty: number_elements > 0

```
    move_forward
        -- Move the cursor to the right one element
    require
        can_move_forward: move

invariant
    number_elements >= 0

end -- class UNORDERED_LIST
```

We discuss several of the routine specifications given in Listing 5.1.

The interface to the query routine *item_after* is:

```
item_after (item: T): T
    -- Return the element just after item in the list
    require
        sufficient_elements: number_elements >= 2
        not_last_item: item /= back_item
        item_present: present (item)
```

A client must verify before making this query on a list object that: (1) the number of elements currently contained within the list object is at least two, (2) the *item* is not the last item in the list, and (3) the *item* is present in the list. If any of these conditions are violated the *item_after* routine cannot do its job and an exception will be raised by the routine. If all of the conditions are met the three postconditions will be satisfied.

The interface to routine *remove_before* is:

```
remove_before (item: T)
    -- Remove the element before item on list
    require
        sufficient_elements: number_elements >= 2
        item_present: present (item)
        item_not_first: item /= front_item
    ensure
        number_elements = old number_elements - 1
        number_elements = 1 implies front_item = back_item
```

Before invoking this routine on a list object the client must verify that: (1) the number of elements contained within the object is at least two, (2) the *item* is present in the object, and (3) the *item* is not the first object in the list. If the three preconditions are met, the two postconditions will be satisfied.

The reader is encouraged to carefully study the remaining details of the interface before moving on to Section 5.2.3. From this interface, it should be clear how to use an UNORDERED_LIST.

5.2.3 Implementation of class UNORDERED_LIST

The implementation details for UNORDERED_LIST, are given in Listings 5.2, 5.3, and 5.4. It is important that you understand every detail.

First, the details of class NODE are given in Listing 5.2. An UNORDERED_LIST is constructed by linking instances of class NODE in a linear manner.

Listing 5.2   Class NODE

```
class NODE [T]

creation {LIST_TYPE}
  make

feature {LIST_TYPE}

  value: T

  next: NODE [T]

  link (to: NODE [T]) is
    do
      next := to
    end

feature {NONE}

  make (item: T; connected_to: NODE [T]) is
    do
      value := clone (item) -- separate storage for value is created
      next := connected_to
    end

end -- class NODE
```

There are no public features of class NODE. The creation routine and most of the features are available only in class LIST_TYPE and its descendants. This abstract class contains queries and commands that are common to all LIST classes and can be captured through inheritance. Class UNORDERED_LIST is defined as a subclass of LIST_TYPE. Other specialized list types are also defined as descendants of LIST_TYPE later in the chapter.

The queries of NODE, both implemented as attributes, are *value* and *next*.

Figure 5.1 shows two typical nodes linked together. It may seem strange that class NODE [T] has an attribute of type NODE [T]. This suggests that a node has knowledge of another node. The *next* query is called a link. The data structure shown in Figure 5.1 is referred to as a linked list.

Figure 5.1 Two nodes linked together.

Some of the protocol (queries and commands) of UNORDERED_LIST are embedded in the abstract root class LIST_TYPE. This class is presented in Listing 5.3.

The queries *item_after* and *item_before* are deferred. They are implemented in subclasses of LIST_TYPE, such as UNORDERED_LIST. Although no implementation details are shown, preconditions are specified for each of these important queries. The preconditions were presented earlier as part of the class interface to UNORDERED_LIST. Recall that the preconditions of a parent class routine are combined with the preconditions of the effective or redefined routine in a descendant class through the logical "or" operation. If the descendant class routine (e.g., routine *item_after* in class UNORDERED_LIST) does not impose further preconditions, then the preconditions of the parent class routine prevail. This is in fact what is done with classes LIST_TYPE and UNORDERED_LIST. No additional preconditions are introduced in the subclass.

Clearly the query *item_after* requires that there be at least two elements in the list, that the item not be the last item and that the item be present in the list. The particular implementation details of this query should not affect these logical requirements.

Listing 5.3 presents the details of abstract class LIST_TYPE. A detailed discussion of some of the details is presented after this Listing 5.3.

Listing 5.3   Class LIST_TYPE

deferred class LIST_TYPE [T]

feature -- public section
-- Queries implemented as attributes

  front_item: T

  back_item: T

  last_removed: T

  number_elements: INTEGER

  item_after (item: T): T **is**
    -- Return the element just after item in the list
    require
      sufficient_elements: number_elements >= 2
      not_last_item: item /= back_item
      item_present: present (item)
    deferred
    end

  item_before (item: T): T **is**
    -- Return the item just before the first occurrence of item in the list
    require
      sufficient_elements: number_elements >= 2
      not_first_item: item /= front_item
      item_present: present (item)
    deferred
    end

  present (item: T): BOOLEAN **is**
    -- Return TRUE if item is in list, otherwise FALSE
    local
      item_node: NODE [T]
    do
      item_node := find (item)
      Result := item_node /= void
    end

  empty: BOOLEAN **is**
    -- Return TRUE if no elements in list, otherwise FALSE
    do
      Result := number_elements = 0
    end

can_move: BOOLEAN is
   -- Returns TRUE if cursor can move forward otherwise false
do
  Result := cursor /= void
end

item_at_cursor: T is
   -- Return the item under cursor
do
  Result := cursor.value
end

remove (item: T) is
   -- Remove the item from the list
require
  item_present: present (item)
local
  curr, previous: NODE [T]
do
  previous := void
  from
    curr := front_node
  until
    curr.value = item
  loop
    previous := curr
    curr := curr.next
  end
  if *previous = void* **then**
    front_node := front_node.next
    if *front_node = void* **then**
      back_node := front_node
    else
      front_item := front_node.value
    end
  elseif *curr = back_node* **then**
    back_node := previous
    back_item := previous.value
    previous.link (void)
  else
    previous.link (curr.next)
  end

Dynamic unordered list without duplicates

```
        last_removed := curr.value
        number_elements := number_elements - 1
    ensure
        number_elements = old number_elements - 1
        number_elements = 1 implies front_item = back_item
    end

remove_front is
        -- Remove the first item in list
    require
        sufficient_elements: number_elements > 0
    do
        remove (front_item)
    ensure
        number_elements = old number_elements - 1
        number_elements = 1 implies front_item = back_item
    end

remove_back is
        -- Remove the last item in list
    require
        sufficient_elements: number_elements > 0
    do
        remove (back_item)
    ensure
        number_elements = old number_elements - 1
        number_elements = 1 implies front_item = back_item
    end

remove_after (item: T) is
        -- Remove the element after item on list
    require
        sufficient_elements: number_elements >= 2
        item_present: present (item)
        item_not_last: item /= back_item
    deferred
    ensure
        number_elements = old number_elements - 1
        number_elements = 1 implies front_item = back_item
    end

remove_before (item: T) is
        -- Remove the element before item on list
```

        require
          sufficient_elements: number_elements >= 2
          item_present: present (item)
          item_not_first: item /= front_item
        deferred
        ensure
          number_elements = **old** *number_elements - 1*
          number_elements = 1 **implies** *front_item = back_item*
        end

    start **is**
        -- Move cursor to the first element in list
        require
          not_empty: number_elements > 0
        do
          cursor := front_node
        ensure
          cursor = front_node
        end

    move_forward **is**
        -- Move the cursor to the right one element
        require
          can_move_forward: can_move
        do
          cursor := cursor.next
        end

  feature *{NONE} -- Protected section for internal use*

    front_node: NODE [T]

    back_node: NODE [T]

    cursor: NODE [T]

    find (item: T): NODE [T] **is**
        -- Return the node containing item, if present \
        local
          item_node: NODE [T]
        do
          from
            item_node := front_node
          until

Dynamic Unordered List Without Duplicates

```
              item_node = void or else item_node.value = item
         loop
              item_node := item_node.next
         end
         Result := item_node
    end

invariant
    number_elements >= 0

end -- class LIST_TYPE
```

5.2.3.1 Discussion of class LIST_TYPE

The four queries, *front_item*, *back_item*, *last_removed*, and *number_elements* are implemented as attributes in the public section of LIST_TYPE. It is useful to have knowledge of this information for all list types.

The query *present* invokes the internal routine *find* (defined in feature section NONE). If the *item_node* returned is not Void, then *present* returns the value TRUE; otherwise, it returns the value FALSE. The internal query *find* traverses the list starting at *front_node*, until the end of the list is reached or the value field of one of its nodes equals the item being sought.

The query *empty* returns TRUE if *number_elements* is zero; otherwise, it returns FALSE.

The query *can_move* returns TRUE if the internal attribute *cursor* is not Void (the *cursor* is an internal query that points to the next element that can be accessed).

The query *item_at_cursor* returns the *value* field of the internal feature cursor.

We examine the *remove* command carefully: The first loop advances the local NODE objects *curr* and *previous* until *curr* contains the value being removed and *previous* is the node just "in front" of *curr*.

If the node being removed is the *front_node* then *previous* will still equal Void and *front_node* is assigned to *front_node.next*. If *front_node* is Void, then *back_node* is assigned to *front_node*. If *front_node* is not Void (the *else* clause), then *front_item* is assigned *front_node.value*.

If the node being removed is the last node (*back_node*), *back_node* is assigned to *previous*, *back_item* is assigned to *previous.value*, and *previous* is linked to Void.

If the node being removed is neither the first node nor the last node, then *previous* node is linked to *curr.next*.

This last and typical case is depicted in Figure 5.2.

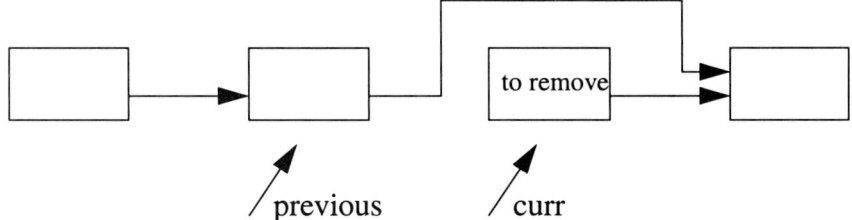

Figure 5.2 Removing node from linked list.

The commands *remove_front* and *remove_back* are implemented by invoking *remove* with parameters *front_item* and *back_item* respectively.

The commands *remove_after* and *remove_before* are deferred (their implementation depends on whether duplicates are allowed).

The internal queries, implemented as attributes, are *front_node, back_node,* and *cursor*.

5.2.4 Details of UNORDERED_LIST

Listing 5.4 presents the details of the subclass UNORDERED_LIST.

Listing 5.4   Class UNORDERED_LIST

class UNORDERED_LIST [T]

inherit
  LIST_TYPE [T]

feature -- Queries implemented as functions

  item_after (item: T): T *is*
    -- Return the element just after item in the list
  local
    item_node: NODE [T]
  do
    item_node := find (item)
    Result := item_node.next.value
  end

  item_before (item: T): T *is*
    -- Return the element just before item in the list
  local
    previous, curr: NODE [T]

Dynamic unordered list without duplicates

```
  do
    previous := front_node
  from
    curr := previous.next
  until
    curr.value = item
  loop
    previous := curr
    curr := curr.next
  end
  Result := previous.value
end

insert_front (item: T) is
    -- Add item to the front of the list
  require
    no_duplicate: not present (item)
  local
    old_front: NODE [T]
  do
    if front_node = void then
      !! front_node.make (item, void)
    else
      old_front := front_node
      !! front_node.make (item, old_front)
    end
    front_item := item
    if number_elements = 0 then
      back_node := front_node
      back_item := item
    end
    number_elements := number_elements + 1
  ensure
    number_elements = old number_elements + 1
    front_item = item
    number_elements = 1 implies back_item = item
  end

insert_back (item: T) is
    -- Add item to the back of the list
  require
    no_duplicate: not present (item)
```

```
   local
      new_node: NODE [T]
   do
      back_item := item
      if number_elements = 0 then
         !! back_node.make (item, void)
         front_node := back_node
         front_item := item
      else
         !! new_node.make (item, void)
         back_node.link (new_node)
         back_node := new_node
      end
      number_elements := number_elements + 1
   ensure
      number_elements = old number_elements + 1
      back_item = item
      number_elements = 1 implies front_item = item
   end

insert_after (item: T; value: T) is
      -- Add value after item in list
   require
      item_present: present (item)
      no_duplicate: not present (value)
   local
      item_node: NODE [T]
      new_node: NODE [T]
   do
      item_node := find (item)
      !! new_node.make (value, item_node.next)
      item_node.link (new_node)
      if new_node.next = void then
         back_node := new_node
         back_item := value
      end
      number_elements := number_elements + 1
   ensure
      number_elements = old number_elements + 1 and number_elements >= 2
   end
```

Dynamic unordered list without duplicates

```
insert_before (item: T; value: T) is
    -- Add value before item in list
  require
    item_present: present (item)
    no_duplicate: not present (value)
  local
    curr, previous: NODE [T]
    new_node: NODE [T]
  do
    previous := void
    from
      curr := front_node
    until
      curr.value = item
    loop
      previous := curr
      curr := curr.next
    end
    !! new_node.make (value, curr)
    if previous = void then
      front_node := new_node
      front_item := value
    else
      previous.link (new_node)
    end
    number_elements := number_elements + 1
  ensure
    number_elements = old number_elements + 1 and
 number_elements >= 2
  end

remove_after (item: T) is
    -- Remove the element after item on list
  local
    value: T
  do
    value := item_after (item)
    remove (value)
  end

remove_before (item: T) is
    -- Remove the element before item on list
```

```
local
    value: T
do
    value := item_before (item)
    remove (value)
end
```

end -- *class UNORDERED_LIST*

5.2.4.1 Discussion of UNORDERED_LIST

The query *item_after* is implemented by first invoking the internal query, *find*, which returns *item_node*, and then returning *item_node.next.value*. The preconditions (specified in the parent class LIST_TYPE) guarantee that *item_node* is not Void and has a non-Void link (*next*).

The implementation of query *item_before* is more complicated. The loop moves local nodes *previous* and *curr* until *curr* points to the node containing *item* and *previous* is the node "in front" of *curr*. The value returned is *previous.value*.

The implementation of the command *insert_front* imposes the precondition *not present (item)*.

If the element being inserted is the first element (*front_node = Void*), then a *front_node* is created with *value* equal to *item* and *next* equal to Void.

If the element being inserted is not the first element (*else* clause), then *front_node* is created with *value* equal to *item* and *next* equal to the old front node.

The other details of this routine are straightforward and not discussed.

Perhaps the most complex implementation of all the commands is *insert_before*. We discuss this command in detail.

The preconditions require that the *item* is present and the *value* being inserted before the *item* is not present.

Local nodes *previous* and *curr* are set as before (*curr* pointing to *item* and *previous* pointing to the node "in front" of *curr*). The node *new_node* is created with fields *value* and *curr* (for *next*).

If *previous* is Void, then *front_node* and *front_item* are updated; otherwise, *previous* is linked to *new_node*.

Finally, the *number_elements* is incremented by one.

The analyses of the remaining commands are left as exercises.

5.3 Unordered list with duplicates

In this section, we examine the effect of relaxing the requirement that no duplicate values are allowed in an unordered list. We shall call the new class UNORDERED_LIST_D, the suffix "_D" meaning with duplicates allowed.

What are the meaning of the commands *insert_before, insert_after, remove_before,* and *remove_after* if more than one of the item being inserted or removed are in the list? What are the meaning of the queries *item_before* and *item_after* if item appears more than once in the list?

There are several ways of handling this issue. The simplest way is to eliminate these commands and queries from class UNORDERED_LIST_D. Another approach is to add the constraint that the commands and queries given above operate on the first occurrence of the given item if more than one item is present. A third approach is to allow the user to specify which occurrence of the item the command or query should operate on. For example, the command *insert_after* might be called as follows: *insert_after (my_item, 3)*. This would imply that *my_item* would be added directly after the third occurrence of *my_item* in the list.

Clearly, the first approach provides the least functionality among the three approaches. It might be unsatisfactory in many applications. The second approach also falls short in cases where it is desirable to insert, remove, or access an item in front of or after a particular occurrence of an item in a list. Therefore, it is the most complex third option that we choose.

Each of the commands and queries given above have one parameter, *item* (see Listings 5.3. and 5.4). These commands and queries must be blocked in our new class and replaced with commands and queries that take 2 parameters. The signature of one such typical command would be: *insert_after_occurence (item : T; occurrence : INTEGER)*.

The details of class UNORDERED_LIST_D are given in Listing 5.5.

Listing 5.5   Class UNORDERED_LIST_D

class UNORDERED_LIST_D [T]

inherit
  LIST_TYPE [T]
    export
      {NONE} item_before, item_after, remove, remove_before, remove_after
        redefine

        remove_back
    end

feature -- *Null implementations to make class effective (non-deferred)*

   item_before (item: T): T **is**
     do
     end

   item_after (item: T): T **is**
     do
     end

   remove_before (item: T) **is**
     do
     end

   remove_after (item: T) **is**
     do
     end

   number_occurences (item: T): INTEGER **is**
     local
       curr: NODE [T]
     do
       from
         curr := front_node
       until
         curr = void
       loop
         if *curr.value = item* **then**
           Result := Result + 1
         end
         curr := curr.next
       end
     end

   item_before_occurence (item: T; occurence: INTEGER): T **is**
     require
       item_present_occurence_times: number_occurences (item) >= occurence
       not_first_item: occurence > 1 **or** *item /= front_item*
       sufficient_elements: number_elements >= occurence + 1
     local
       prev_curr: ARRAY [NODE [T]]

Unordered list with duplicates

```
    do
      prev_curr := find_occurence (item, occurence)
      Result := prev_curr.item (1).value
    end

  item_after_occurence (item: T; occurence: INTEGER): T is
    require
      item_present_occurence_times: number_occurences (item) >= occurence
      item_not_last: occurence < number_occurences (item) or item /= back_item
      sufficient_elements: number_elements >= occurence + 1
    local
      prev_curr: ARRAY [NODE [T]]
    do
      prev_curr := find_occurence (item, occurence)
      Result := prev_curr.item (2).next.value
    end

  remove_back is
      -- Remove the last item on list
    local
      prev_curr: ARRAY [NODE [T]]
    do
      prev_curr := find_occurence (back_item, number_occurences (back_item))
      back_node := prev_curr.item (1)
      if back_node /= void then
        back_item := prev_curr.item (1).value
        prev_curr.item (1).link (void)
      end
      last_removed := prev_curr.item (2).value
      if number_elements = 2 then
        front_item := back_item
        front_node := back_node
      elseif number_elements = 1 then
        front_node := void
      end
      number_elements := number_elements - 1
    end

  insert_front (item: T) is
      -- Add item to front of list
    local
      old_front: NODE [T]
```

```
    do
      if front_node = void then
        !! front_node.make (item, void)
      else
        old_front := front_node
        !! front_node.make (item, old_front)
      end
      front_item := item
      if number_elements = 0 then
        back_node := front_node
        back_item := item
      end
      number_elements := number_elements + 1
    ensure
      number_elements = old number_elements + 1
      front_item = item
      number_elements = 1 implies back_item = item
    end

  insert_back (item: T) is
    local
      new_node: NODE [T]
    do
      back_item := item
      if number_elements = 0 then
        !! back_node.make (item, void)
        front_node := back_node
        front_item := item
      else
        !! new_node.make (item, void)
        back_node.link (new_node)
        back_node := new_node
      end
      number_elements := number_elements + 1
    ensure
      number_elements = old number_elements + 1
      back_item = item
      number_elements = 1 implies front_item = item
    end

  insert_before_occurence (item: T; occurence: INTEGER; value: T) is
```

Unordered list with duplicates

    require
      item_present_occurence_times: number_occurences (item) >= occurence
    local
      prev_curr: ARRAY [NODE [T]]
      new_node: NODE [T]
    do
      prev_curr := find_occurence (item, occurence)
      !! new_node.make (value, prev_curr.item (2))
      if prev_curr.item (1) = void **then**
        front_node := new_node
        front_item := value
      else
        prev_curr.item (1).link (new_node)
      end
      number_elements := number_elements + 1
    ensure
      number_elements = **old** number_elements + 1 **and** number_elements >= 2
    end

insert_after_occurence (item: T; occurence: INTEGER; value: T) **is**
    require
      item_present_occurence_times: number_occurences (item) >= occurence
    local
      prev_curr: ARRAY [NODE [T]]
      item_node: NODE [T]
      new_node: NODE [T]
    do
      prev_curr := find_occurence (item, occurence)
      item_node := prev_curr.item (2)
      !! new_node.make (value, item_node.next)
      item_node.link (new_node)
      if new_node.next = void **then**
        back_node := new_node
        back_item := value
      end
      number_elements := number_elements + 1
    end

remove_after_occurence (item: T; occurence: INTEGER) **is**
    require
      item_present_occurence_times: number_occurences (item) >= occurence
      item_not_last: occurence < number_occurences (item) **or** item /= back_item

        sufficient_elements: number_elements >= occurence + 1
      do
      end

    remove_before_occurence (item: T; occurence: INTEGER) **is**
      do
      end

  feature {NONE}

    find_occurence (item: T; occurence: INTEGER): ARRAY [NODE [T]] **is**
      local
        prev, curr: NODE [T]
        index: INTEGER
      do
        !! Result.make (1, 2)
        from
          curr := front_node
        until
          curr = void **or else** curr.value = item
        loop
          prev := curr
          curr := curr.next
        end
        if curr.value = item **then**
          from
            index := 1
          until
            curr = void **or else** index = occurence
          loop
            index := index + 1
            from
              prev := curr
              curr := curr.next
            until
              curr = void **or else** curr.value = item
            loop
              prev := curr
              curr := curr.next
            end
          end
        end

```
            Result.put (prev, 1)
            Result.put (curr, 2)
        end

    end -- class UNORDERED_LIST_D
```

5.3.1 Discussion of class UNORDERED_LIST_D

The inheritance clause is interesting and important. In the *export {NONE}* subclause, the queries *item_before* and *item_after* are listed. In addition, the commands *remove, remove_before,* and *remove_after* are given in this subclause. As a result, these queries and commands are inaccessible to any client of UNORDERED_LIST_D. The *redefine* clause indicates that command *remove_back* will be modified.

The null implementations of queries *item_before* and *item_after* and commands *remove_before* and *remove_after* are required. If these features were not made effective (given some implementation, even null implementation) class UNORDERED_LIST_D would be a deferred class.

The query *number_occurences* traverses through the list and returns the number of occurrences of item.

The query *item_before_occurence* uses the internal query *find_occurence*. The details of this query should be studied closely. The list is traversed until the end is encountered or the *item* being sought is located *occurrence* times. Two nodes are returned in an array of base type NODE [T]. The first element in this array is the node just "in front" of the item being sought. The second element in this array is the node being sought. Once this array is obtained, the remaining line of code sets the result to the value field of the previous node.

The query *item_after_occurence* also uses the internal query *find_occurence*. The result returned is the value field of the node just after the item node.

The remaining commands are left as exercises for the reader to discuss.

5.4 Ordered list

Another useful abstraction is an ordered list. Such a list type maintains a strict ordering relationship among its elements from smallest to largest. It is therefore inappropriate to allow the insertion commands: *insert_front, insert_back, insert_after,* and *insert_before*. These commands allow for the possibility of destroying the ordering relationship among the elements. Only a single insertion command, *insert*, is appropriate. The element being inserted must be placed after the element just smaller than it and before the element just larger than it. All of the other routines are identical to those of either class UNORDERED_LIST or UNORDERED_LIST_D, depending on whether one wishes the ordered list to deny or allow duplicate elements.

Because of the tremendous similarity in the protocol of ordered and unordered lists, code inheritance is the best way of capturing the protocol of class UNORDERED_LIST or UNORDERD_LIST_D in class ORDERED_LIST. With code inheritance, the logical relationship "is kind of" does not have to strictly satisfied. What does it mean to say that an ORDERED_LIST "is a kind of" UNORDERED_LIST?

Suppose we wish to construct class ORDERED_LIST so that it allows duplicate elements. Listing 5.6 shows the entire class ORDERED_LIST. Are you surprised that the listing is so short? This is because of the power afforded by code reuse and the shared protocol between classes ORDERED_LIST and UNORDERED_LIST_D.

Listing 5.6   Class ORDERED_LIST

```
class ORDERED_LIST [T -> COMPARABLE]

inherit
  UNORDERED_LIST_D [T]
    export
      {NONE}
        insert_front,insert_back, insert_before_occurence,insert_after_occurence
    end

feature

  insert (item: T) is
    local
      curr: NODE [T]
    do
      if number_elements = 0 then
        insert_front (item)
      elseif item > back_item then
        insert_back (item)
      else
        from
          curr := front_node
        until
```

```
                item <= curr.value
            loop
                curr := curr.next
            end
            insert_before_occurence (curr.value, 1, item)
        end
    ensure
        number_elements = old number_elements + 1
    end

end -- class ORDERED_LIST
```

The first observation concerning class ORDERED_LIST is that the generic parameter, T, is constrained by the expression, T -> COMPARABLE. This is required because the implementation details of the *insert* routine require that the inserted *item* be compared to the *value* fields of some elements. In order to assure that such a comparison is possible, it is necessary to guarantee that all elements of type T respond to the '<' operator. This is achieved if the actual type of *item* conforms to class COMPARABLE.

The inherit clause indicates that ORDERED_LIST is a child of UNORDERED_LIST_D. But the commands *insert_front*, *insert_back*, *insert_before*, and *insert_after*, blocked to all clients, are available for use within routine *insert*.

If upon insertion the list is empty, the *insert_front (item)* command assures that *item* will be the first (and only) element in the list. If the *item* being inserted is greater than *back_item*, the *insert_back (item)* command assures that *item* will be the last element in the list. Otherwise a loop is executed until *item* is equal or less than the *value* field of *curr*. When this occurs, the *insert_before (curr.value, item)* command assures that *item* will be inserted just before *curr.value*.

It should be evident that significant leverage is afforded by the protocol in class UNORDERED_LIST_D. This protocol is useful within routine *insert* and to clients that simply inherit the nonblocked features.

In class ORDERED_LIST, it was not necessary to reinvent the wheel.

5.5 Doubly-linked list

All of the list implementations so far have used a singly-linked list. Each node in the list points only to its successor. One can also link each node, except the front node, to its predecessor in addition to its successor. Such a linked list is called doubly-linked.

LISTS

An example of such a doubly-linked node is shown in Figure 5.3.

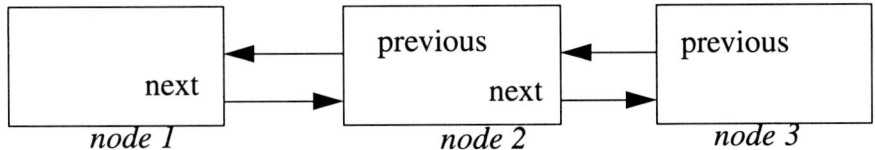

Figure 5.3 Doubly-linked node.

The implementation of many of the commands and queries would need to be modified if a doubly-linked implementation were used. Two such examples will be shown. You will be invited to modify other commands and queries as exercises.

The revised doubly-linked class NODE is shown in Listing 5.7.

Listing 5.7   Doubly-linked class NODE

    class NODE [T]

    creation
      make

    feature

      value: T

      next: NODE [T]

      previous: NODE [T]

      link (to: NODE [T]) **is**
        do
          next := to
        end

      link_back (to: NODE [T]) **is**
        do
          previous := to
        end

    feature {NONE}

      make (item: T; connected_to: NODE [T]; back_to: NODE [T]) **is**
        do
          value := clone(item) -- separate storage for value is created
          next := connected_to

```
        previous := back_to
      end

end -- class NODE
```

Listing 5.8 presents a revised version of command *insert_after*, and Listing 5.9 a revised version of command *insert_before*, each using a doubly-linked implementation.

Listing 5.8   Doubly-linked version of command insert_after

```
insert_after (item: T; value: T) is
    -- Add value after item in list
  require
    item_present: present (item)
    no_duplicate: not present (value)
  local
    item_node: NODE [T]
    new_node: NODE [T]
  do
    item_node := find (item)
    !! new_node.make (value, item_node.next, item_node)
    item_node.link (new_node)
    if new_node.next = void then
      back_node := new_node
      back_item := value
    else
      new_node.next.link_back (new_node)
    end
    number_elements := number_elements + 1
  ensure
    number_elements = old number_elements + 1 and number_elements >= 2
end
```

Listing 5.9   Doubly-linked version of command insert_before

```
insert_before (item: T; value: T) is
    -- Add value before item in list
  require
    item_present: present (item)
    no_duplicate: not present (value)
  local
```

```
    item_node: NODE [T]
    prev_node: NODE[T]
    new_node: NODE [T]
do
  item_node := find (item)
  prev_node := item_node.previous
  !! new_node.make (value, item_node, prev_node)
  item_node.link_back (new_node)
  if prev_node = void then
    front_node := new_node
    front_item := value
  else
    prev_node.link (new_node)
  end
  number_elements := number_elements + 1
ensure
  number_elements = old number_elements + 1 and number_elements >= 2
end
```

5.6 Stack revisited

In Chapter 4, the stack container class was presented and implemented both statically and dynamically. In this section, we revisit the stack abstraction and once again take advantage of code reuse. Specifically, the code from class UNORDERED_LIST_D (an unordered list with duplicates allowed) is used to implement a stack.

The principle of composition is used in this case to reuse the code of the unordered list abstraction. The new DYNAMIC_STACK class contains an instance of an UNORDERED_LIST_D. The implementation of this revised stack class is presented in Listing 5.10.

The layering of abstractions given by the DYNAMIC_STACK being composed of an UNORDERED_LIST_D allows only a few routines of the list to be used by the stack. Clients of the stack have access only to the public features of the stack and do not have access to the list.

A significant advantage of using composition in this design is that if the implementation of the list should be changed in the future, then as long as the interface to the two routines *insert_front* and *remove_front* remain unchanged, the stack class is unaffected. This would not be true if inheritance were used. In that case any changes made in the implementation of list would directly affect the stack.

Listing 5.10 Revised DYNAMIC_STACK class

```
class DYNAMIC_STACK [T]

creation
  make

feature {NONE} -- Protected section

  list: UNORDERED_LIST_D [T]

feature

  number_elements: INTEGER

  make is
    do
      !! list
    end

  push (item: T) is
    do
      list.insert_front (item)
      number_elements := number_elements + 1
    ensure
      number_elements = old number_elements + 1
    end

  pop is
    require
      non_empty: number_elements > 0
    do
      list.remove_front
      number_elements := number_elements - 1
    ensure
      number_elements = old number_elements - 1
    end

  top: T is
    require
      non_empty: number_elements > 0
    do
      Result := list.front_item
    end
```

```
  empty: BOOLEAN is
    do
      Result := number_elements = 0
    end

invariant
  number_elements >= 0

end -- class DYNAMIC_STACK
```

5.7 The queue revisited

Using the same approach as in section 5.6, the QUEUE is implemented in terms of an UNORDERED_LIST_D. The same principle of composition is used. Listing 5.11 presents the revised DYNAMIC_QUEUE implemented in terms of UNORDERED_LIST_D.

Listing 5.11   Class DYNAMIC_QUEUE

```
class DYNAMIC_QUEUE [T]

creation
  make

feature

  number_elements: INTEGER

  make is
    do
      !! list
    end

  insert (item: T) is
    do
      list.insert_back (item)
      number_elements := number_elements + 1
    ensure
      number_elements = old number_elements + 1
      number_elements = 1 implies first_element = item
    end

  remove is
    require
```

The Deque

```
      non_empty: number_elements > 0
    do
      list.remove_front
      number_elements := number_elements - 1
    ensure
      number_elements = old number_elements - 1
    end

  first_element: T is
    require
      non_empty: number_elements > 0
    do
      Result := list.front_item
    end

  empty: BOOLEAN is
    do
      Result := number_elements = 0
    ensure
      Result = true implies number_elements = 0
    end

feature {NONE}

  list: UNORDERED_LIST_D [T]

invariant

  number_elements >= 0

end -- class DYNAMIC_QUEUE
```

The list routines *insert_back* and *remove_front* are internally called by the queue routines *insert* and *remove*.

5.8 The Deque

A deque (pronounced "deck") is a container abstraction that allows insertion and removal from the front and back of the structure. Specifically, the operations that form the external interface to a deque are:

Queries

- number_elements : INTEGER (obtained through storage)
- front_element : T (obtained through computation)

LISTS

- back_element : T (obtained through computation)
- empty : BOOLEAN (obtained through computation)

Commands

- make
- insert_front (item : T)
- insert_back (item : T)
- remove_front
- remove_back

Using the class UNORDERED_LIST_WITH_D, Listing 5.12 presents an implementation of class DEQUE.

Listing 5.12   Class DEQUE

```
class DEQUE [T]
creation
  make
feature {NONE}
  list: UNORDERED_LIST_D [T]
feature
  -- Queries
  number_elements: INTEGER is
    do
      Result := list.number_elements
    end

  front_element: T is
    require
      non_empty: number_elements > 0
    do
      Result := list.front_item
    end

  back_element: T is
    require
      non_empty: number_elements > 0
    do
```

```
        Result := list.back_item
      end

    -- Commands
    make is
      do
        !! list
      end

    insert_front (item: T) is
      do
        list.insert_front (item)
      end

    insert_back (item: T) is
      do
        list.insert_back (item)
      end

    remove_front is
      require
        non_empty: number_elements > 0
      do
        list.remove_front
      end

    remove_back is
      require
        non_empty: number_elements > 0
      do
        list.remove_back
      end

end -- class DEQUE
```

Once again the protocol of class UNORDERED_LIST_D is used to implement the commands and queries of DEQUE. All of the queries of DEQUE are implemented as functions.

5.9 Priority queue

The final data abstraction to be implemented in this chapter is a priority queue. Each element in a priority queue has a *priority_value*, a real number. The first element in the priority queue has a *priority_value* smaller than the second, which is smaller than the third, ..., which is smaller than the last.

The ORDERED_LIST can be reused to implement a priority queue. An implementation of class PRIORITY_QUEUE is shown in Listing 5.13.

Listing 5.13   Class PRIORITY_QUEUE

class DYNAMIC_PRIORITY_QUEUE [T -> COMPARABLE]

creation
  make

feature {NONE}

  list: ORDERED_LIST [T]

feature

  number_elements: INTEGER **is**
    do
      Result := list.number_elements
    end

  first_element: T **is**
    require
      non_empty: number_elements > 0
    do
      Result := list.front_item
    end

  empty: BOOLEAN **is**
    do
      Result := number_elements > 0
    end

  make **is**
    do
      !! list
    end

  insert (item: T) **is**
    do
      list.insert (item)
    end

```
    remove is
      do
        list.remove_front
      end

end -- class DYNAMIC_PRIORITY_QUEUE
```

5.10 Summary

- It is useful to make a distinction between a container object and the things that it contains.

- A container class is one that holds zero or more elements, each formally declared to be of a particular class type.

- The actual type inserted in a container must conform (be a descendant of) to the formal type. This allows a container to hold either a homogeneous or heterogeneous collection of elements.

- A container class must specify protocol (a set of rules) for inserting, deleting, and accessing elements. This is what differentiates one type of container from another.

- The queries and commands defined for an UNORDERED_LIST are:
  Queries ("What do we wish to find out about a list?")
  What is the first item on the list, if any?
  What is the last item on the list, if any?
  What is the last item removed from the list, if any?
  How many elements are in the list?
  Is a given item present in the list?
  What is the element just after a given item?
  What is the element just before a given item?
  Is the list empty?
  Is there an element directly to the right of the current element that a cursor points to?
  What is the element being pointed to by the cursor?
  Commands ("What do we wish to do with a list?")
  Insert an item into the front of the list
  Insert an item into the back of the list
  Insert an item just after a given item on the list
  Insert an item just before a given item on the list
  Remove a given item from the list

Remove an item from the front of the list
Remove an item from the back of the list
Remove an item just after a given item on the list
Remove an item just before a given item on the list
Move a cursor so it points to the first element in the list
Move the cursor forward so it points to the next element in the list

- For an ORDERED_LIST, only a single insertion command, *insert*, is appropriate. The element being inserted must be placed after the element just smaller than it and before the element just larger than it.

- In an ORDERED_LIST, the generic parameter T is constrained by the expression, *T -> COMPARABLE*. This is required because the implementation details of the *insert* routine require that the inserted *item* be compared to the *value* fields of some elements.

- Several important classes, including STACK, QUEUE, DEQUE, and PRIORITY_QUEUE can be implemented in terms of a list. Each of these classes contains a list type as a protected attribute.

5.11 Exercises

1. Cite several examples of an UNORDERED_LIST that exist in the "real world."

2. Cite several examples of an UNORDERED_LIST_D that exist in the "real world."

3. Cite several examples of an ORDERED_LIST that exist in the "real world."

4. Write a test program that exercises all of the queries and commands of the UNORDERED_LIST given in Listing 5.4.

5. Explain in words and with diagrams, if appropriate, the commands in Listing 5.4 that are not discussed in the book.

6. Implement class UNORDERED_LIST statically. Discuss the advantages and disadvantages of the static versus dynamic implementation presented in the book.

7. Explain why it is not desirable to include a method display in any of the container classes presented in this chapter.

EXERCISES

8. Specify the details of command *remove_after* for class UNORDERED_LIST_D as presented in Listing 5.5.

9. Specify the details of the postconditions for *remove_after* in Listing 5.5.

10. Specify the details of the preconditions for *remove_before* in Listing 5.5.

11. Specify the details of the command *remove_before* in Listing 5.5

12. Specify the details of the postconditions of *remove_before* in Listing 5.5.

13. Explain the details of the command *insert_before_occurence* in Listing 5.5

14. Explain the details of the command *insert_after_occurence* in Listing 5.5.

15. Modify, if appropriate, all the commands of UNORDERED_LIST so that the list is doubly-linked.

16. Modify, if appropriate, all the queries of UNORDERED_LIST so that the list is doubly-linked.

17. Do problem 15 for the ORDERED_LIST.

18. Do problem 16 for the ORDERED_LIST.

Chapter 6

Recursion

An Eiffel routine can invoke itself. This capability, supported by most modern programming languages, is called **recursion**. Although the capability of recursion might seem quite innocent, and make you wonder why an entire chapter of this book is dedicated to the subject, recursion is a powerful and important design principle. Many important algorithms can be expressed recursively. Some of these will be explored in this chapter and many in later chapters. Some material of this chapter is taken with permission from the publisher from *An Object-Oriented Introduction to Computer Science* by Richard Wiener (Prentice Hall, 1996).

6.1 The mechanics of recursion

6.1.1 First example of recursion

As the first example of recursion, consider the routine *do_it_recursively* given in Listing 6.1. Assume that this routine is embedded in class APPLICATION, and that from its creation routine the function *do_it_recursively* ("Eiffel is a wonderful language", 5) is invoked. One would not normally perform a recursion to accomplish the five-time output of a string but would use a simple loop structure. This example is just a warm-up example, and is not intended as a role-model for recursion.

THE MECHANICS OF RECURSION

Listing 6.1   First example of recursion

```
do_it_recursively (str : STRING; number_times : INTEGER) is
  do
    if number_times > 0 then
      io.putstring (str)
      io.new_line
      do_it_recursively (str, number_times - 1) -- recursive call
    end
  end -- do_it_recursively
```

The program output is:

Eiffel is a wonderful language
Eiffel is a wonderful language
Eiffel is a wonderful language
Eiffel is a wonderful language
Eiffel is a wonderful language

As you might have expected, the input string, "Eiffel is a wonderful language" is output five times. Before we explain the mechanics of this routine, let us add one more simple specification to the problem. Suppose we wish the routine to number the five lines consecutively so that the output becomes:

1. Eiffel is a wonderful language
2. Eiffel is a wonderful language
3. Eiffel is a wonderful language
4. Eiffel is a wonderful language
5. Eiffel is a wonderful language

Listing 6.2 shows our first try at this; a modified version of Listing 6.1.

Listing 6.2   Modified version of Listing 6.1

```
do_it_recursively (str : STRING; number_times : INTEGER) is
  do
    if number_times > 0 then
      io.putint (number_times)
      io.putstring (". ")
      io.putstring (str)
      io.new_line
```

```
        do_it_recursively (str, number_times - 1) -- recursive call
     end
   end -- do_it_recursively
```

In Listing 6.2 two extra lines of code are inserted in front of the output statement for the string, *str*. Unfortunately, the modified *do_it_recursively* routine fails. Its output is:

5. Eiffel is a wonderful language
4. Eiffel is a wonderful language
3. Eiffel is a wonderful language
2. Eiffel is a wonderful language
1. Eiffel is a wonderful language

Oh well, at least the third line of output is correct!

Upon entry to the routine the first time, the test, *number_times* > 0, is passed. The value of *number_times*, namely 5, is output followed by a dot and space. Then the routine invokes itself (i.e., recursion) sending the value 4 as input. The same thing happens again, and the routine is recursively invoked with input 3, then later input 2, then later input 1, and finally input 0. When the input is 0, the test *number_times* > 0 fails and control is passed back to the previous level of recursion (when *value* = 1). The location within the *do_it_recursively* routine at which control is passed back is one line under the call to *do_it_recursively*. But this line is the "end" of the *if-then* control structure. Nothing further needs to be done. Control is then passed back to the call to the routine when *value* = 2. Again, nothing further needs to be done. In this same way control is passed back to the recursive call when *value* = 3, then *value* = 4, and finally *value* = 5. In each case no further output or processing occurs. The routine terminates.

Suppose we change the first line of code in Listing 6.2 to the following: *io.putint (6 - number_times)*. Now we have it. Now the output will be the desired output given above. Unfortunately, this routine works only if called initially to print exactly 5 times. This solution therefore is unacceptable.

Suppose we perform one final modification on *do_it_recursively*. This is shown in Listing 6.3 as a complete application.

Listing 6.3   Final version of do_it_recursively

```
class APPLICATION

creation
   start
```

The Mechanics of Recursion

```
feature

  start is
    do
      do_it_recursively ("Eiffel is a wonderful language", 5)
    end

  do_it_recursively (str: STRING; number_times: INTEGER) is
    do
      if number_times > 0 then
        do_it_recursively (str, number_times - 1)
        io.putint (number_times)
        io.putstring (". ")
        io.putstring (str)
        io.new_line
      end
    end

end -- class APPLICATION
```

Let us dissect the recursion of Listing 6.3.

The first recursive call, *do_it_recursively (str, 5)* is pushed onto the run-time stack (the parameter *number_times* has the value 5). This is followed by five additional calls to *do_it_recursively* that are pushed onto the run-time stack with *number_times* equal to 4, 3, 2, 1, and 0 respectively.

When the last recursive call is invoked, with *number_times* equal to 0 the *if number_times > 0* expression fails, causing the run-time stack to be popped. Control is transferred automatically to the *io.putint (number_times)* command with *number_times* equal to 1. This produces the first line of output: **1. Eiffel is a wonderful language**.

The run-time stack is again popped, control again transferred to the *io.putint (number_times)* command and the parameter *number_times* equal to 2. This produces the second line of output: **2. Eiffel is a wonderful language**.

This pattern is continued until all of the desired output is produced. It is noted that if the user wishes n numbered output lines this final version of the routine allows this by invoking the routine with the appropriate *number_times*.

6.1.2 Second example of recursion

Let us reinforce our understanding of the mechanics by considering another relatively simple recursive routine. This is given in Listing 6.4.

Listing 6.4   Another relatively simple recursive routine

```
print_recursively (value : REAL) is
   local
      temporary : REAL
   do
      temporary := 10 * value
      if value > 0.0 then
         io.putreal (value)
         io.new_line
         print_recursively (value - 0.1) -- recursive call
         io.putstring ("%Ntemporary = ")
         io.putreal (temporary)
         io.new_line
      end
   end -- print_recursively
```

Suppose the routine is invoked from the creation routine of the application class as *print_recursively (1.0)*. This routine is more challenging to understand because there are 3 lines of code below the recursive call.

Let us walk through the recursion and trace the details to uncover the mechanics.

During the first call of the routine, the value of *temporary* is set to 10.0. The first output to occur is *value*, 1.0. Before any of the last three lines of output occur, the recursive call inputs 0.9 and we return to the beginning of *print_recursively*. The value of temporary is set to 9.0. The next output of 0.9 occurs. The successive recursive calls cause the output 0.8, 0.7, 0.6, 0.5, 0.4, 0.3, 0.2, and 0.1 to occur. When the recursive call is made with input 0.0, *temporary* is set to 0.0 but the entire block of code nested in the *if-then* structure is bypassed. The last recursive execution of the routine actually reaches its end statement.

Following this event, control is returned to the recursively called routine in the program statement one line below the recursive call statement that has just been completed. The values of all local objects and input parameters are restored to the state that existed just before the recursive call was made. This information is automatically stored on a stack called the run-time stack. When the recursive call (the one just completed) had been made in the first place, the values of all local objects and input parameters had been automatically pushed onto this run-time stack.

Now the last 3 lines of the routine are executed and "Temporary = 1.0" is output.

THE MECHANICS OF RECURSION

When the end of the routine is reached, the recursive stack is again popped and control is returned, as before, to the previous call to *print_recursively* when *temporary* is equal to 2.0. This pattern continues until all recursive calls have been popped from the run-time stack. This leads to the following output for Listing 6.4:

1.0
0.9
0.8
0.7
0.6
0.5
0.4
0.3
0.2
0.1

Temporary = 1.0
Temporary = 2.0
...
Temporary = 10.0

The actual mechanics of recursion are summarized below.

6.1.2.1 Mechanics of recursion

Each time a recursive call occurs, the values of all local objects and input parameters are pushed onto a run-time stack. Upon hitting the "end" statement of a recursive routine the previous recursive call (activation record), if any, is popped from the run-time stack. All the local variables and input parameters are restored to the values that were in place just before the recursive call was executed. Program control returns to the statement that is one line below the recursive call that was just completed.

6.1.3 Third example of recursion

Consider the recursive routine in Listing 6.5. Suppose that it is invoked as: *print_recursively (10)*.

Listing 6.5   More recursion to solidify mechanics

```
print_recursively (value : INTEGER) is
    do
```

>   **if** *value /= 0* **then**
>   *print_recursively (value // 2)*
>   *io.new_line*
>   *io.putint (value)*
>   *print_recursively (value // 2)*
>   **end**
> **end** -- *print_recursively*

Some of the events that occur in Listing 6.5 when the initial value of 10 is passed to *print_recursively* are explained below.

1. Enter the routine with value = 10.

2. The system pushes this input parameter (10) onto the run-time stack before the next recursive call with value = 5 occurs.

3. The system pushes this input parameter (5) onto the run-time stack before the next recursive call with value = 2 occurs.

4. The system pushes this input parameter (2) onto the run-time stack before the next recursive call with value = 1 occurs.

5. The system pushes this input parameter (1) onto the run-time stack before the next recursive call with value = 0 occurs.

6. The routine by-passes the code in the *if-then* clause and hits its end statement.

7. The system returns control to the statements, *io.new_line, io.putint (value)* (output statements) and pops the run-time stack so that value is restored to 1. The value 1 is output.

8. Another recursive call is made with value = 0.

9. The code in the *if-then* statement is bypassed and the end statement is reached.

10. The system returns control to the line below this recursive call (the end statement).

11. The system again returns control to one line below the previous recursive call (the first line of output) and restores the input parameter value to 2. This value is output.

12. The routine is called recursively with value = 1.

13. A recursive call is made with value = 0.

THE MECHANICS OF RECURSION

14. The code in the *if-then* statement is bypassed and the end statement is reached.

15. The system returns control to the line below this recursive call (the end statement).

16. The system again returns control to the output statements and restores the input parameter to 5. This value is output.

17. A recursive call with value = 2 occurs.

It is left as an exercise for you to explain all the remaining events associated with this recursion. The final output is:

1
2
1
5
1
2
1
10
1
2
1
5
1
2
1

6.1.4 Final example of recursion—permutation group

The last example provided in this section to illustrate the mechanics of recursion is more complex, but also more practical than the previous examples. Suppose one wishes to generate and output all possible permutations of a set of entities.

Several years ago I had to efficiently generate several million misspelled words that would be used to test a special purpose hashing algorithm (the subject of hashing is covered later in this book). The words needed to be at least 10 characters in length. The solution that I used was to generate the first several million permutations of the group of characters 'a', 'b', 'c', 'd', 'e', 'f', 'g', 'h', 'i', and 'j'. The total number of such permutations is 10!, or 3,628,800.

First, an algorithm for generating all permutations of a group of distinct elements of arbitrary size will be presented and discussed. Then the algorithm will be used to output the 4! permutations of the letters 'a' through 'd'. The reader is free to modify the application program and generate the 10! permutations of the letters "a' through 'j'. This may take a while.

Listing 6.6 presents the details of class PERMUTATIONS. The command *permutations* invokes the protected command *permute*. The structure of the recursion is more complex because two recursive calls are embedded in command *permute;* one at the beginning of the routine and one in the middle of a loop in the middle of the routine.

Listing 6.6   Class PERMUTATIONS

```
class PERMUTATIONS [T]

creation
  make

feature {NONE}

  permute (n: INTEGER) is
    local
      i, j : INTEGER
      temp: T
    do
      if n > 1 then
        permute (n - 1)
        from i := n
        until i = 1
        loop
          i := i - 1
          temp := data.item (n)
          data.put (data.item (i), n)
          data.put (temp, i)
          permute (n - 1)
          temp := data.item (n)
          data.put (data.item (i), n)
          data.put (temp, i)
        end
      else
        from
```

The Mechanics of Recursion

```
          j := 0
        until
          j = size
        loop
          j := j + 1
          print (data.item (j))
        end
        io.new_line
      end
    end  -- permute

feature

  size: INTEGER
      -- number of elements in permutation group
      -- permutation group

  data: ARRAY [T]

  make (input: ARRAY [T]; sz: INTEGER) is
      -- input contains the permutation group
      -- sz represents the number of elements in this group
    require
      sz > 0
    do
      data := clone (input)
      size := sz
    end  -- make

  output_permutations is
    do
      permute (size)
    end  -- output_permutations

end -- class PERMUTATIONS
```

    Let us walk through a simple example. We will find the permutations of the letters 'a', 'b', and 'c'.

    As soon as *permute (3)* is called, a recursive call is made to *permute (2)*. This leads to another recursive call to *permute (1)*. This causes control in routine *permute* to transfer to the *else* clause and the output "abc" followed by a carriage return to occur.

    Upon hitting the *end* statement of *permute*, the recursive stack is popped and the value $n = 2$ is restored. The local variable i is set to 1 in the loop and the values in index positions 1 and 2 of *data* are interchanged. A recursive call is made to *permute (1)*. This causes the output "bac" followed by a carriage return to occur. Control resumes in the middle of the loop with $n = 2$. The items in index positions 1 and 2 are again interchanged. The array data now contains the sequence "abc." Upon hitting the *end* statement of the loop and the *end* statement to *permute*, the first recursive call to *permute (2)* is completed.

The value of n is restored to 3. Control passes to the loop and the value of i is set to 2. The items in positions 2 and 3 are interchanged leaving *data* in the state "acb". A recursive call is made to *permute (2)*. Following the same path of reasoning as before, this causes the output "acb" and "cab" to occur. Following the recursive call the items are interchanged so that data again contains "abc". The value of i in the loop is decremented and is set to 1. The items in position 1 and 3 are interchanged, leaving data in the state "cba". A recursive call is made to *permute (2)*. This causes the output "cba" and "bca." Following the recursive call, the items are interchanged so that data again contains "abc." The recursion terminates. The sequence of output is:

abc
bac
acb
cab
cba
bca

The reader is invited to walk through the algorithm when the letters are 'a' and 'b.'

Listing 6.7 shows a simple application class that creates an instance of PERMUTATIONS.

Listing 6.7   Application class to test permutations

```
class APPLICATION

creation
   start

feature

   start is
      local
         data : ARRAY [CHARACTER];
```

```
        permute : PERMUTATIONS [CHARACTER]
    do
        !! data.make (1, 10);
        data.put ('a', 1);
        data.put ('b', 2);
        data.put ('c', 3);
        data.put ('d', 4);
        !! permute.make (data, 4);
        permute.output_permutations
    end;

end -- class APPLICATION
```

6.2 Recursion used in design

In the previous section, the focus was on mechanics—what actually happens during a recursion. Understanding the mechanics of recursion, although important, provides little clue as to its real importance in program development. Recursion, although supported by many programming languages, is not a language feature. Recursion is a design methodology. Thus, the title of this chapter.

There are problems or systems that can naturally be modeled recursively. We describe several of these in this section. Many of the algorithms in later sections of the book are expressed recursively.

6.2.1 Binary Search of Sorted Arrays

Suppose we have built an array containing sorted data in ascending order (we will assume without loss of generality that the index locations of the data range from 1 to *size*). The datum in index 1 is given as smaller than the datum in index 2, which is smaller than the datum in index 3, etc.

We wish to construct an algorithm that efficiently determines whether a particular value is present in this sorted array.

A simple but inefficient method for doing this would be to visit each and every index location of the array and compare its value to the input value. If all of the index values fail to turn up the input value, the function returns FALSE, otherwise it returns TRUE. The asymptotic efficiency of this linear search algorithm would be $O(n)$. Doubling the size of the array would, on the average, double the search time.

Can we do better? The answer is yes!

RECURSION

Let us consider the following example that searches an array containing 10 data items, each an integer.

1   3   5   7   9   11   13   15   17   19

Suppose we wish to search for the value 3.

We start by considering the element in index *(1 + size) // 2*, or the element in index 5, and comparing it to the input value. The input value 3 is less than the value at index 5 (which is 9). We can therefore eliminate from consideration the values from index 5 to index 10 and concentrate our search on the first 4 index locations. We continue by considering the element at index *(1 + 4) // 2* or the element at index 2. Bingo! We have found a match.

Okay, so this was fairly simple. Let us search for the presence of element 20, which is not present in the array.

We begin again by comparing the input value to the value in index *(1 + 10) // 2* or index 5. Since 9 is less than 20 we can eliminate from further consideration the array indices 1 to 5 and focus our search on indices 6 to 10. We take the midpoint index again in the remaining range, namely index (6 + 10) // 2, or index 8. The value 20 is greater than 15. Now we know that if the value 20 is present in the array it must be in either index 9 or 10. We choose the midpoint of the range once again, namely index (9 + 10) // 2 or index 9. Since 20 is greater than 17, we choose the midpoint of (10 + 10) // 2 or index 10. The value 20 is greater than 19 so we know for sure now that 20 is not present in the array.

After each comparison, roughly half of the index range being searched can be eliminated. This suggests that the total number of comparison operations, on the average, would be $O(\log_2 n)$, where n is the size of the array. The algorithm that we have informally used is called the *binary search* algorithm.

Listing 6.8 presents a recursive implementation of this algorithm.

Listing 6.8   Recursive implementation of binary search algorithm

```
present (data : ARRAY[ INTEGER ]; first_index : INTEGER;
         second_index : INTEGER; value : INTEGER) : BOOLEAN is
   require
     data_sorted: sorted (data)
   local
     index : INTEGER
   do
     if first_index <= second_index then
```

```
            index := (first_index + second_index) // 2
            if data.item (index) = value then
               Result := TRUE
            elseif value > data.item (index) then
               Result := present (data, index + 1, second_index, value)
            else
               Result := present (data, first_index, index - 1, value)
            end
         else
            Result := FALSE
         end
      ensure
         --Result = TRUE implies value is present in data
      end -- present
```

The precondition with tag *sorted_data* is very important. As with all preconditions, it is the responsibility of the client (user) to ensure that the input array is already sorted before attempting a binary search of the array. A function, *sorted*, is invoked to evaluate the precondition. See the *quick_sort* routine in Chapter 3 for a definition of the query *sorted*.

The recursive binary search algorithm of Listing 6.8 does the following: if the *first_index* is equal or less than the *second_index* (if it is not, the algorithm concludes that the input *value* is not present), the local variable *index* is set to the midpoint of the range. The array is tested for the presence of this input *value* at location *index*. If *value* is greater than the information at *index*, the routine is called recursively but with *first_index* set to *index* + 1. Otherwise the routine is called recursively but with *second_index* set to *index* - 1.

To illustrate the workings of this algorithm, we trace the values of *first_index* and *second_index* when we search an array of 10,000 integers loaded with values equal to 10 times their index location (i.e., the value at index 1 is 10, the value at index 2 is 20, etc.) for the input value equal to 795 (not present in the array). The trace is the following:

```
first_index = 1  second_index = 10000
first_index = 1  second_index = 4999
first_index = 1  second_index = 2499
first_index = 1  second_index = 1249
first_index = 1  second_index = 624
first_index = 1  second_index = 311
first_index = 1  second_index = 155
first_index = 79 second_index = 155
```

first_index = 79 second_index = 116
first_index = 79 second_index = 96
first_index = 79 second_index = 86
first_index = 79 second_index = 81
first_index = 79 second_index = 79
first_index = 80 second_index = 79
795 not present in sorted_data

We trace the algorithm with the same set of 10,000 integers as before for the value 9000 (which is present):

first_index = 1 second_index = 10000
first_index = 1 second_index = 4999
first_index = 1 second_index = 2499
first_index = 1 second_index = 1249
first_index = 626 second_index = 1249
first_index = 626 second_index = 936
first_index = 782 second_index = 936
first_index = 860 second_index = 936
first_index = 899 second_index = 936
first_index = 899 second_index = 916
first_index = 899 second_index = 906
first_index = 899 second_index = 901
9000 present in sorted_data

Finally, using the same array of 10,000 integers, we trace for the value 100,001, which lies just beyond the range present in the array. The trace is the following:

first_index = 1 second_index = 10000
first_index = 5001 second_index = 10000
first_index = 7501 second_index = 10000
first_index = 8751 second_index = 10000
first_index = 9376 second_index = 10000
first_index = 9689 second_index = 10000
first_index = 9845 second_index = 10000
first_index = 9923 second_index = 10000
first_index = 9962 second_index = 10000
first_index = 9982 second_index = 10000
first_index = 9992 second_index = 10000
first_index = 9997 second_index = 10000
first_index = 9999 second_index = 10000
first_index = 10000 second_index = 10000

first_index = 10001 second_index = 10000
100001 not present in sorted_data

The efficiency of the binary search algorithm should be evident from these traces.

What would happen if the programmer forgot the test *if first_index <= second_index* ?

What might happen if the precondition were removed from routine *present* in Listing 6.8 and the data were not sorted?

6.3 Summary

- An Eiffel routine can invoke itself. This capability, also supported by most modern programming languages, is called **recursion**.
- Recursion is a powerful and sometimes subtle design principle.
- Each time a recursive call occurs, the values of all local objects and input parameters are pushed onto a run-time stack. Upon hitting the "end" statement of a recursive routine the previous recursive call, if any, is popped from the run-time stack. All the local variables and input parameters are restored to the values that were in place just before the recursive call was executed. Program control returns to the statement one line below the recursive call that was just completed.

6.4 Exercises

1. Explain why the line of code, *io.putint (6 - number_times)*, corrects the routine given in Listing 6.2 but is a poor solution to the problem.

2. What would be output if the routine given in Listing 6.3 were modified as follows:

    print_recursively (value : REAL) **is**
       local
          temporary : REAL
       do
          *temporary := 10 * value*
          if *value >= 0.0* **then**
             io.putreal (value)
             io.new_line
             io.putstring ("Temporary = ")
             io.putreal (temporary)

```
            io.new_line
            print_recursively (value - 0.1) -- recursive call
            io.putstring ("%Ntemporary = ")
            io.putreal (temporary)
            io.new_line
        end
    end -- print_recursively
```

3. How would the routine in Listing 6.1 have to be modified in order to produce the following output (4 spaces of additional indentation for each new line):

    Eiffel is a wonderful language.
        Eiffel is a wonderful language.
            Eiffel is a wonderful language.
                Eiffel is a wonderful language.
                    Eiffel is a wonderful language.

4. Carefully explain all of the recursive events that lead to the output shown for Listing 6.4.

5. What would happen if the test, *if first_index <= second_index*, were removed from the binary search algorithm of Listing 6.7?

6. If the command *output_permutations* were invoked on an array of size 26 with all letters of the alphabet included, is there much chance that the computer you are running the program on would run out of memory?

7. If the machine you are running the program of problem 6 (permutations of the 26 letters of the alphabet) were able to output 1 million lines per second (no machine in this universe can put ink onto paper this fast), how long would it take for all of the output to be generated?

8. Write and test a recursive function that computes the sum of the integers in an array of integers.

9. One staple example, which has been avoided in this book, is the computation of the factorial function using recursion. It is usually presented as the first example of recursion in many data structure books. Design and implement a function that takes an integer as input and outputs the factorial value of the number (e.g., $3! = 3 \times 2 \times 1 = 6$).

Chapter 7

Applications of Stacks

Part 3 of this book, containing Chapters 7, 8, and 9, shows the use of stacks, queues, and lists in applications. This chapter focuses on the applications of stacks. These include the conversion of a recursive routine to an iterative routine, the conversion of an infix mathematical expression to postfix, a calculator, and an implementation of solitaire poker.

7.1 Permutation iterator

In Listing 6.5, a recursive routine, *permute*, is presented. This routine generates all permutations of a group of elements stored in the protected attribute, *data*. This routine is given again in Listing 7.1 for your convenience.

Listing 7.1 Recursive implementation of routine permute

```
permute (n: INTEGER) is
   local
      i, j : INTEGER
      temp: T
   do
      if n > 1 then
         permute (n - 1)
         from i := n
```

```
        until i = 1
        loop
          i := i - 1
          temp := data.item (n)
          data.put (data.item (i), n)
          data.put (temp, i)
          permute (n - 1)
          temp := data.item (n)
          data.put (data.item (i), n)
          data.put (temp, i)
        end
      else
        from
          j := 0
        until
          j = size
        loop
          j := j + 1
          print (data.item (j))
        end
        io.new_line
      end
    end -- permute
```

Suppose we wish to construct a permutation iterator. This would allow a user to control the generation of each permutation, one at a time. The user might wish to perform some operation other than output on each permutation. Although the *permute* command given in Listing 7.1 efficiently generates and outputs all permutations, it provides the user no control over accessing each permutation individually.

In order to construct a permutation iterator, it is necessary to remove the recursion from the logic of routine *permute*. This turns out not to be a trivial task. There are three benefits that make this task worthwhile: (1) a better understanding of recursion may be obtained while converting the recursion to an iteration, (2) an important application of the stack abstraction is shown, (3) a useful software component, class PERMUTE_ITERATOR, is produced.

Let us briefly review the key concepts associated with the two recursive calls to *permute* in Listing 7.1. Prior to each of the two recursive calls, the values of the parameter n and the local variables i, j, and *temp* are pushed onto the system stack. Of the four variables pushed onto the system stack, only the values of *n* and *i* are needed. A return location (i.e., the line just below the recursive call) is also pushed onto the stack. This enables control to flow to the appropriate place following a return from the recursive call.

In converting the recursive structure to an iterative structure we must manually simulate the system stack. There are four pieces of information that must be pushed and popped from our stack: *n*, *i*, and two variables that represent the two return locations. We shall call these two Boolean variables *after_first* and *in_loop* (indicating that control returns to the line just below the "first" recursive call or after the recursive call inside the loop).

A class INFORMATION is created to encapsulate the four variables that must be maintained on our stack. This class is shown in Listing 7.2.

Listing 7.2   Class INFORMATION

class *INFORMATION*

creation
  make

feature

  n: INTEGER

  i: INTEGER

  in_loop: BOOLEAN

  after_first: BOOLEAN

  make (n_value: INTEGER; i_value: INTEGER; in_loop_value: BOOLEAN;
      after_first_value: BOOLEAN) **is**
    do
      n := n_value
      i := i_value
      in_loop := in_loop_value
      after_first := after_first_value
    end

end -- *class INFORMATION*

The stack that shall be used for this occasion is the FIXED_STACK presented in Listing 4.1. Its size is known before it is used and it therefore qualifies nicely for this assignment.

PERMUTATION ITERATOR

A main control loop is used to determine when an iteration is completed (i.e., when the next permutation has been generated). This corresponds to the case $n = 1$ given in the recursive version of Listing 7.1. Following this case, the loop must be terminated. The attribute *data*, an array of elements, must be available in read-only form to the user. Since the $n = 1$ case in the recursive version results in reaching the end of the routine, this requires that we *pop* the stack that we are using to simulate the system stack.

The beginning of the loop structure including the $n = 1$ case is shown below:

```
from end_loop := False
until stack.empty or else end_loop = True
loop
    if n = 1 then
        info := stack.top
        stack.pop
        n := info.n
        i := info.i
        in_loop := info.in_loop
        after_first := info.after_first
        end_loop := True
    end
    -- Other conditions to follow
end -- loop
```

If the value of n is greater than 1, there are three major cases to consider. The first of these cases occurs when *in_loop* and *after_first* have the value false. This corresponds to entering the beginning of the recursive version in Listing 7.1.

The first line of code in this recursive version makes a call to *permute* with parameter $n - 1$. This requires us to push the current values of n, i, *in_loop*, and *after_first* onto our stack. The code for this case is given below.

```
from end_loop := False
until stack.empty or else end_loop = True
loop
    if n = 1 then
        -- Details not repeated
    end
    if not end_loop and in_loop = false and after_first = False then
        info.make (n, i, false, true)
```

```
        stack.push (info)
        n := n - 1
    end
    -- Other conditions to follow
end -- loop
```

The second case occurs when *in_loop* is false and *after_first* is true. This corresponds to a return from the first recursive call. In this case, we must simulate the entry into the loop given in Listing 7.1. The value of *i* must be set to $n - 1$. We must then interchange the elements in index locations *i* and *n* (a command *interchange* is defined for this purpose). Then we must push the current information onto our stack to simulate the entry into the recursive call *permute* that occurs in the middle of this loop. The code for this second case is shown below.

```
from end_loop := False
until stack.empty or else end_loop = True
loop
    if n = 1 then
        -- Details not repeated
    end
    if not end_loop and in_loop = false and after_first = False then
        -- Details not repeated
    end
    if not end_loop and in_loop = False and after_first = True then
        i := n - 1
        interchange (i, n)
        info.make (n, i, True, False)
        stack.push (info)
        n := n - 1
        in_loop := False
        after_first := False
    end
    -- Other conditions to follow
end -- loop
```

Note that the values of *in_loop* and *after_first* are set to false before leaving this branch (the value of *in_loop* is set to true before pushing information onto the stack—this is to ensure the correct return position). This forces control to return to the beginning of the *permute* routine.

The final case occurs when *in_loop* is true. This corresponds to a return from a recursive call to *permute* (in Listing 7.1) in the middle of the loop. The first task is to again interchange the elements in index positions *i* and *n*. Next the value of *i* is decremented by 1. Two subcases must be considered. The first is the case when *i* equals 0. This corresponds to ending the loop. In this case, the stack must be popped because the *permute* routine reaches its end. In the other case, corresponding to reentering the loop in Listing 7.1, the values in index locations *i* and *n* must be interchanged. Then the information must be pushed onto the stack to simulate the recursive call to *permute*. The values of *in_loop* and *after_first* must be set to false to force control back to the beginning of the routine.

The code for this final case is given below.

```
from end_loop := False
until stack.empty or else end_loop = True
loop
    if n = 1 then
        -- Details not repeated
    end
    if not end_loop and in_loop = false and after_first = False then
        -- Details not repeated
    end
    if not end_loop and in_loop = False and after_first = True then
        details not repeated
    end
    if not end_loop and in_loop = True then
        interchange (i, n)
        i := i - 1
        if i = 0 then
            info := stack.top
            stack.pop
            n := info.n
            i := info.i
            in_loop := info.in_loop
            after_first := info.after_first
        else
            interchange (i, n)
            info.make (n, i, True, False)
            stack.push (info)
            n := n - 1
            in_loop := False
            after_first := False
        end
```

end -- loop

The class PERMUTE_ITERATOR that contains the revised command *permute* is shown in Listing 7.3.

Listing 7.3 Class PERMUTE_ITERATOR

```
class PERMUTE_ITERATOR [T]
creation
  make
feature {NONE}
  size: INTEGER
  stack: FIXED_STACK [INFORMATION]
  info: INFORMATION
  n: INTEGER
  i: INTEGER
  in_loop: BOOLEAN
  after_first: BOOLEAN
  make (input: ARRAY [T]; sz: INTEGER) is
    require
      sz > 1
    do
      data := clone (input)
      size := sz
      !! stack.make (size + 1)
      n := size
      in_loop := false
      i := 0
      after_first := false
      !! info.make (n, 0, false, false)
      stack.push (info)
    ensure
      data.is_equal (input)
      stack.capacity = sz + 1
      stack.num_elements = 1
    end  -- make
```

```
interchange (index1: INTEGER; index2: INTEGER) is
  local
    temp: T
  do
    temp := data.item (index2)
    data.put (data.item (index1), index2)
    data.put (temp, index1)
  end

feature

  data: ARRAY [T]

  done: BOOLEAN is
    do
      Result := stack.empty
    end

  permute is
    require
      stack_not_empty: not done
    local
      end_loop: BOOLEAN
    do
      from
        end_loop := false
      until
        done = true or else end_loop = true
      loop
        if n = 1 then
          info := stack.top
          stack.pop
          n := info.n
          i := info.i
          in_loop := info.in_loop
          after_first := info.after_first
          end_loop := true
        end
        if not end_loop and in_loop = false and after_first = false then
          info.make (n, i, false, true)
          stack.push (info)
          n := n - 1
        end
```

```
            if not end_loop and in_loop = false and after_first = true then
                i := n - 1
                interchange (i, n)
                info.make (n, i, true, false)
                stack.push (info)
                n := n - 1
                in_loop := false
                after_first := false
            end
            if not end_loop and in_loop = true then
                interchange (i, n)
                i := i - 1
                if i = 0 then
                    info := stack.top
                    stack.pop
                    n := info.n
                    i := info.i
                    in_loop := info.in_loop
                    after_first := info.after_first
                else
                    interchange (i, n)
                    info.make (n, i, true, false)
                    stack.push (info)
                    n := n - 1
                    in_loop := false
                    after_first := false
                end
            end
        end
    ensure
        -- a new permutation of data is generated
    end  -- permute

end -- class PERMUTE_ITERATOR
```

The creation routine, *make*, creates and initializes *data* using a *clone* of *input*. The *stack* is initialized and set to size *sz* + 1. The object *info* is created and initialized. This object is pushed onto the stack.

In order to get a feel of how the routine *permute* works, a simple test program is constructed. The first three letters of the alphabet, 'A', 'B', and 'C' are loaded into an array, *group*. Then all 6 permutations of these letters

Permutation iterator

are generated. The values of the INFORMATION object are output after each *push* or *pop* from our stack. The test program is given in Listing 7.4.

The output to the program is given below the program. The reader is encouraged to study this output carefully. It should be clear how central the stack is to the successful operation of this program.

Listing 7.4 First test program for permutation iterator

```
class APPLICATION

creation
  start

feature

  group: ARRAY [CHARACTER]
  iterator: PERMUTE_ITERATOR [CHARACTER]

  start is
    local
      count: INTEGER
    do
      !! group.make (1, 3)
      group.put ('A', 1)
      group.put ('B', 2)
      group.put ('C', 3)
      !! iterator.make (group, 3)
      from count := 0
      until terator.done
      loop
        if count > 0 then
          output (count)
        end
        count := count + 1
        iterator.permute
      end
    end  -- start

  output (count: INTEGER) is
    local
      index: INTEGER
    do
      io.putint (count)
```

APPLICATIONS OF STACKS

```
      io.putstring (". ")
      from index := 0
      until index = 3
      loop
         index := index + 1
         io.putchar (iterator.data.item (index))
      end
      io.new_line
   end -- output

end -- class APPLICATION
```

The output of Listing 7.4 is the following:

Initial push onto stack: n = 3 i = 0 in_loop = False after_first = False
Push the stack, first call to permute: n = 3 i = 0 in_loop = False after_first = True
Push the stack, first call to permute: n = 2 i = 0 in_loop = False after_first = True
Pop the stack because n = 1: n = 2 i = 0 in_loop = False after_first = True
1. ABC
Push the stack, first loop call to permute: n = 2 i = 1 in_loop = True after_first = False
Pop the stack because n = 1: n = 2 i = 1 in_loop = True after_first = False
2. BAC
Pop the stack because i = 0: n = 3 i = 0 in_loop = False after_first = True
Push the stack, first loop call to permute: n = 3 i = 2 in_loop = True after_first = False
Push the stack, first call to permute: n = 2 i = 2 in_loop = False after_first = True
Pop the stack because n = 1: n = 2 i = 2 in_loop = False after_first = True
3. ACB
Push the stack, first loop call to permute: n = 2 i = 1 in_loop = True after_first = False
Pop the stack because n = 1: n = 2 i = 1 in_loop = True after_first = False
4. CAB
Pop the stack because i = 0: n = 3 i = 2 in_loop = True after_first = False
Push the stack, second loop call to permute: n = 3 i = 1 in_loop = True after_first = False
Push the stack, first call to permute: n = 2 i = 1 in_loop = False after_first = True
Pop the stack because n = 1: n = 2 i = 1 in_loop = False after_first = True
5. CBA
Push the stack, first loop call to permute: n = 2 i = 1 in_loop = True after_first = False
Pop the stack because n = 1: n = 2 i = 1 in_loop = True after_first = False
6. BCA
Pop the stack because i = 0: n = 3 i = 1 in_loop = True after_first = False
Pop the stack because i = 0: n = 3 i = 0 in_loop = False after_first = False

PERMUTATION ITERATOR

A more interesting test program is shown in Listing 7.5. Its output is shown below the program. In this final test program, three iterators are constructed and used together.

Listing 7.5   Final test program for permutation iterator

class APPLICATION

creation
  start

feature

  group1: ARRAY [CHARACTER]

  group2: ARRAY [INTEGER]

  group3: ARRAY [STRING]

  iterator1: PERMUTE_ITERATOR [CHARACTER]

  iterator2: PERMUTE_ITERATOR [INTEGER]

  iterator3: PERMUTE_ITERATOR [STRING]

  start **is**
    local
      count: INTEGER
    do
      !! group1.make (1, 3)
      group1.put ('A', 1)
      group1.put ('B', 2)
      group1.put ('C', 3)
      !! group2.make (1, 4)
      group2.put (1, 1)
      group2.put (2, 2)
      group2.put (3, 3)
      group2.put (4, 3)
      !! group3.make (1, 3)
      group3.put ("Hanne", 1)
      group3.put ("Richard", 2)
      group3.put ("Henrik", 3)
      !! iterator1.make (group1, 3)
      !! iterator2.make (group2, 4)
      !! iterator3.make (group3, 3)

```
     from
        count := 0
     until
        iterator2.done
     loop
        if count > 0 and not iterator1.done then
           output1 (iterator1, count, 3)
        end
        if count > 0 then
           output2 (iterator2, count, 4)
        end
        if count > 0 and not iterator3.done then
           output3 (iterator3, count, 3)
        end
        count := count + 1
        if not iterator1.done then
           iterator1.permute
        end
        iterator2.permute
        if not iterator3.done then
           iterator3.permute
        end
     end
  end

output1 (iterator: PERMUTE_ITERATOR [CHARACTER];
      count: INTEGER; sz: INTEGER) is
   local
      index: INTEGER
   do
      io.putint (count)
      io.putstring (". ")
      from index := 0
      until index = sz
      loop
         index := index + 1
         io.putchar (iterator.data.item (index))
      end
      io.new_line
   end
```

Permutation iterator

```
output2 (iterator: PERMUTE_ITERATOR [INTEGER];
        count: INTEGER; sz: INTEGER) is
  local
    index: INTEGER
  do
    io.putint (count)
    io.putstring (". ")
    from index := 0
    until index = sz
    loop
      index := index + 1
      io.putint (iterator.data.item (index))
    end
    io.new_line
  end

output3 (iterator: PERMUTE_ITERATOR [STRING];
        count: INTEGER; sz: INTEGER) is
  local
    index: INTEGER
  do
    io.putint (count)
    io.putstring (". ")
    from index := 0
    until index = sz
    loop
      index := index + 1
      io.putstring (iterator.data.item (index))
      io.putstring (" ")
    end
    io.new_line
  end

end -- class APPLICATION
```

The output of Listing 7.5 is the following:

1. ABC
1. 1240
1. Hanne Richard Henrik
2. BAC
2. 2140
2. Richard Hanne Henrik

3. ACB
3. 1420
3. Hanne Henrik Richard
4. CAB
4. 4120
4. Henrik Hanne Richard
5. CBA
5. 4210
5. Henrik Richard Hanne
6. BCA
6. 2410
6. Richard Henrik Hanne
7. 1204
8. 2104
9. 1024
10. 0124
11. 0214
12. 2014
13. 1042
14. 0142
15. 1402
16. 4102
17. 4012
18. 0412
19. 0241
20. 2041
21. 0421
22. 4021
23. 4201
24. 2401

7.2 Infix to postfix conversion and function evaluation

A basic problem in computer science is the evaluation of algebraic expressions. Such algebraic expressions are ordinarily expressed in a form called **infix**. In this standard form, operators are sandwiched between operands (are fixed *in* between operands—hence, the name, infix).

An example of a typical infix expression is the following: (a * b + c) / d, where a, b, c, and d are operands and "*", "+", and "/" are operators.

INFIX TO POSTFIX CONVERSION AND FUNCTION EVALUATION

Software to evaluate algebraic expressions is often needed in such applications as statistical packages, graphics and plotting programs, and spreadsheets.

We will limit our discussion in this section to only binary operators; operators that have two operands. These include "+," "-," "*," and "/."

Table 7.1 shows several expressions in infix form and their equivalent in postfix and prefix form.

Table 7.1 Infix, postfix, and prefix expressions.

Infix	Postfix	Prefix
a + b	ab+	+ab
a + b * c	abc*+	+a*bc
(a + b) * c	ab+c*	*+abc
a + b * c - d / e	abc*+de/-	+a-*bc/de

The postfix and infix expressions do not contain parentheses. They are unambiguous without ever requiring parentheses.

7.2.1 Evaluation of postfix expressions

Suppose we have converted an infix expression to its postfix equivalent (that is the subject of Section 7.2.2). We now demonstrate that using the stack abstraction (who would have guessed!), it is quite easy to evaluate the postfix expression.

We note that in a postfix expression, each operator performs its operation on the two previous operands. For example, let us evaluate the postfix expression $abc*+d/$. The steps are the following (the expression is scanned from left to right):

- Push the value of a onto the stack (push all operands from left to right onto the stack)

- Push the value of b onto the stack

- Push the value of c onto the stack

- Pop the stack twice and compute the product of the two operands ($b*c$)

- Push this product ($b*c$) onto the stack

- Pop the stack twice and add the two operands ($a + b*c$)

- Push this result onto the stack $e = (a + b*c)$

- Push the operand *d* onto the stack
- Pop the stack twice and divide the two operands producing the result: $f = (a + b*c)/d$
- Push the result onto the stack

The steps are illustrated in Figure 7.1.

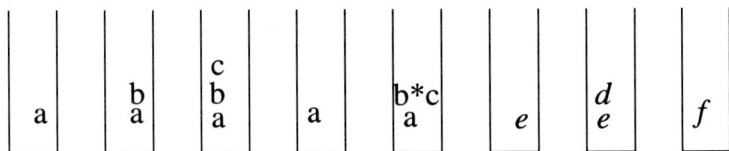

Figure 7.1 Evaluating a postfix expression.

A pseudo-code algorithm for evaluating a postfix expression is given as follows:

```
scan a symbol
if the symbol is an operand then
    push its value onto a stack
else
    pop operand2 from the stack
    pop operand1 from the stack
    perform the operation specified by the current operator symbol
    push the result onto the stack
end
the value of the expression is the single value remaining on the stack
```

In Section 7.2.3 an Eiffel implementation of this algorithm is presented as part of an overall software system for evaluating arithmetic expressions.

7.2.2 Conversion from infix to postfix

In the previous section we have seen how we can use a stack to evaluate a postfix expression. In this section we explain an algorithm that can convert an arbitrary infix expression possibly containing parentheses to its postfix equivalent. Our objective is to convert an infix expression that may contain parentheses to a postfix expression in one pass from left to right.

As we scan the infix expression (we assume that it is represented as a string), we immediately pass all operands that we encounter to the output string (the postfix string). As each operator or parenthesis is encountered it is either placed onto a stack (another surprise!) or passed directly to the

INFIX TO POSTFIX CONVERSION AND FUNCTION EVALUATION

postfix string. The choice depends on the precedence of the current operator symbol with the operator symbol on the top of the stack. Specifically, if the precedence of the operator on the top of the stack is greater than the current operator symbol, we pop the operator at the top of the stack and send it to the postfix string. We continue to compare the current operator symbol with the operator symbol on the top of the stack until the stack is empty or the precedence of the operator on the top of the stack is less than our current operator symbol. In either case, we push the current operator symbol onto the stack. When we reach the end of the infix expression, we pop the remaining operators off the stack and add them to the postfix string.

A pseudo-code representation of this algorithm follows.

```
scan an input symbol from the infix string
if the symbol is an operand then
    add the symbol to the postfix string
else
    while the operator stack is not empty and the precedence of the top of the
        symbol on the top of the stack is greater than the current symbol
    loop
        pop the operator stack and add the operator symbol to the postfix string
    end loop
    push current symbol
end
while the operator stack is not empty
loop
    pop the operator stack and add the symbol to the postfix string
end
```

Let us walk through an example. Suppose we wish to convert the infix expression $a + b *c$ to a postfix expression using the algorithm given above.

- We pass the operand symbol a directly to the postfix string (a).

- We push the operator symbol + onto the operator stack.

- We pass the operand symbol b directly to the postfix string (ab).

- We compare the precedence of the symbol on the top of the stack, "+", with the current symbol, "*." Since the "+" has a lower precedence than the "*," we push the "*" symbol onto the stack.

Applications of Stacks

- We pass the operand symbol c directly onto the postfix string (abc).
- We pop the operator stack until its empty and add the operators directly to the postfix string producing the result *abc*+*.

Let us do this problem again for the case *a * b + c*.

- The symbol *a* is passed directly to the postfix string (*a*).
- The operator symbol "*" is pushed onto the stack.
- The symbol *b* is passed directly to the postfix string (*ab*).
- We compare the precedence of the symbol on the top of the stack, "*" with the current symbol, "+." Since the "*" has a higher precedence, we pop it from the stack and pass it directly to the postfix string (*ab**).
- We add the symbol *c* directly to the postfix string (*ab*c*).
- We pop the operator stack until it is empty and add the final operator, "+" to the postfix string producing the result *ab*c+*.

The two infix expressions that we have converted so far do not contain parentheses. The presence of parentheses is handled by defining the appropriate precedence between parentheses and other operator symbols.

A query *precedence* is defined below that handles parentheses.

```
precedence (op1 : CHARACTER; op2: CHARACTER) : BOOLEAN is
do
    Result := True
    if ((op1 = '+' or (op1 = '-')) and ((op2 = '*') or (op2 = '/') then
        Result := False
    end
    if ((op1 = '(' ) and (op2 /= ')') or (op2 = '(') then
        Result := False
    end
end
```

To illustrate this query, we walk through another conversion process. Let us convert the expression *(a + b) * c*. Compare the steps to those in the first example.

- The left parenthesis, "(," is pushed onto the stack.
- The symbol *a* is passed directly to the postfix string.
- The precedence of the symbol "(" is compared to the current symbol, "+." According to the query *precedence*, defined above, "(" has a lower

precedence than the current symbol "+." We therefore push the "+" onto the stack.

- The symbol *b* is passed directly to the postfix string.

- We compare the precedence of the top of the stack symbol "+" with the current symbol ")." According to the *precedence* function defined above, the "(" symbol has a higher precedence. We pop it from the stack and add it to the postfix string. We next compare the top of the stack symbol "(" with the current symbol ")." It also has a higher precedence than the current symbol. We pop the "(" from the stack and discard it (we do not allow parentheses in the postfix string). We finally add the symbol ")" to the stack.

- We compare the precedence of the top of the stack symbol ")" with the operator "*." Since the top of the stack symbol is higher in precedence (according to the query precedence given above), we pop it from the stack and discard it. We push the symbol "*" onto the stack.

- We pass the symbol "c" directly to the postfix string.

- Finally we pop the remaining operator symbol "*" from the stack and add it to the postfix string producing the result *ab+c**.

The stack has played a central role in converting an infix expression to its postfix equivalent and, as seen in the previous section, evaluating a postfix expression. In the next section, we explore an Eiffel implementation of a system that evaluates algebraic expressions through infix to postfix conversion.

7.2.3 Implementation of system that evaluates algebraic expressions

An ELEMENT type is constructed to hold character symbols (both operands and operators) and their associated value (in the case of operands). Class ELEMENT is shown in Listing 7.6.

Listing 7.6 Class ELEMENT used to encapsulate character symbols and values

class ELEMENT

creation
  make,
  init

feature

  symbol: CHARACTER

  value: REAL

  init **is**
    do
      symbol := ' '
      value := 0.0
    end

  make (sym: CHARACTER; val: REAL) **is**
    do
      symbol := sym
      value := val
    end

  sentinel: ELEMENT **is**
    -- Used to terminate infix expression and postfix expression
    once
      !! Result.make ('&', 0.0)
    end

end -- class ELEMENT

    Class EXPRESSION_EVALUATOR contains only one public command and two queries. The *make* command is a creation routine that takes as input an array of type ELEMENT (the infix expression with values associated with each operand. The two public queries are *operator* which returns a Boolean value based on whether its input symbol is either "+," "-," "*," or "/," and *evaluate*, which returns a real number. The real number returned by *evaluate* represents the solution to our problem—the value of the infix expression.

    Included among the protected attributes of class EXPRESSION_EVALUATOR are two stacks: *operator_stack* holds ELEMENT and *operand_stack* holds REAL. The *operator_stack* is used to convert an infix expression to postfix. The *operand_stack* is used in the evaluation of the postfix expression.

    The protected query, *convert*, implements the algorithm discussed earlier for converting an infix expression to postfix. A special value of

ELEMENT, *sentinel,* is used to detect when the end of the input array has been reached. This same value is used to terminate the postfix array.

Two additional protected attributes are *infix_expr* and *postfix*. Each of these are arrays of type ELEMENT.

Two important protected queries are *precedence* and *computation_-result*. The first of these is used to determine which of two operators has the higher algebraic precedence. The second is used to produce a real value from two operands based on the type of operator that is input.

The code for class EXPRESSION_EVALUATOR is presented in Listing 7.7. The reader is urged to study each of the public and protected routines carefully.

Listing 7.7   Class EXPRESSION_EVALUATOR

```
class EXPRESSION_EVALUATOR

creation
  make

feature

  make (input_expr: ARRAY [ELEMENT]) is
    do
      infix_expr := clone (input_expr)
      !! operator_stack
      !! operand_stack
      !! postfix.make (1, infix_expr.count)
      !! elmn.init
      convert
    end

  operator (symbol: CHARACTER): BOOLEAN is
      -- Returns True if symbol is an operator
    do
      Result := symbol = '*' or symbol = '/' or symbol = '+' or symbol = '-'
              or symbol = '(' or symbol = ')'
    end

  evaluate: REAL is
      -- Evaluates the postfix expression
    local
      elem: ELEMENT
      symbol: CHARACTER
```

```
      opnd1, opnd2: REAL
      index: INTEGER
   do
     from
       index := 1
     until
       postfix.item (index) = elmn.sentinel
     loop
       elem := postfix.item (index)
       symbol := elem.symbol
       if operator (symbol) then
         opnd1 := operand_stack.top
         operand_stack.pop
         opnd2 := operand_stack.top
         operand_stack.pop
         operand_stack.push (computation_result (symbol, opnd1, opnd2))
       else
         operand_stack.push (elem.value)
       end
       index := index + 1
     end
     Result := operand_stack.top
     operand_stack.pop
   end

feature {NONE}

   operator_stack: DYNAMIC_STACK [ELEMENT]

   operand_stack: DYNAMIC_STACK [REAL]

   infix_expr: ARRAY [ELEMENT]

   postfix: ARRAY [ELEMENT]

   elmn: ELEMENT

   convert is
     require
       infix_string_exists: infix_expr /= void
     local
       infix_index: INTEGER
       post_index: INTEGER
       symbol: CHARACTER
```

```
            top_symbol: CHARACTER
            top_elem: ELEMENT
            elem: ELEMENT
        do
          from
            infix_index := 1
          until
            infix_expr.item (infix_index) = elmn.sentinel
          loop
            elem := infix_expr.item (infix_index)
            symbol := elem.symbol
            if symbol /= ' ' then
              if not operator (symbol) then
                post_index := post_index + 1
                postfix.put (elem, post_index)
              else
                if not operator_stack.empty then
                  from
                    top_elem := operator_stack.top
                    top_symbol := top_elem.symbol
                  until
                    operator_stack.empty or else not
                        precedence (top_symbol, symbol)
                  loop
                    if top_symbol /= '(' then
                      post_index := post_index + 1
                      postfix.put (top_elem, post_index)
                    end
                    operator_stack.pop
                    if not operator_stack.empty then
                      top_elem := operator_stack.top
                      top_symbol := top_elem.symbol
                    end
                  end
                end
                if symbol /= ')' then
                  operator_stack.push (elem)
                end
              end
            end
            infix_index := infix_index + 1
```

```
          end
        from
        until
          operator_stack.empty
        loop
          post_index := post_index + 1
          postfix.put (operator_stack.top, post_index)
          operator_stack.pop
        end
        post_index := post_index + 1
        postfix.put (elmn.sentinel, post_index)
      ensure
        -- postfix array contains the postfix equivalent of infix_expr
      end

    precedence (op1: CHARACTER; op2: CHARACTER): BOOLEAN is
        -- Returns True if op1 has a higher algebraic precedence compared
with op2
      require
        legal_operators: operator (op1) and operator (op2)
      do
        Result := true
        if ((op1 = '+') or (op1 = '-')) and ((op2 = '*') or (op2 = '/')) then
          Result := false
        end
        if ((op1 = '(') and (op2 /= ')') or (op2 = '(')) then
          Result := false
        end
      ensure
        -- Result = True implies op1 has a higher precedence than op2
      end

    computation_result (symbol: CHARACTER; opnd1: REAL; opnd2:
REAL): REAL is
        -- Returns the result of symbol operating on opnd1 and opnd2
      require
        legal_symbol: operator (symbol)
      do
        if symbol = '+' then
          Result := opnd1 + opnd2
        elseif symbol = '-' then
          Result := opnd1 - opnd2
```

Infix to Postfix Conversion and Function Evaluation

```
      elseif symbol = '*' then
        Result := opnd1 * opnd2
      elseif symbol = '/' then
        Result := opnd1 / opnd2
      end
    end

  end -- class EXPRESSION_EVALUATOR
```

Listing 7.8 presents a simple application test that exercises the routines of class EXPRESSION_EVALUATOR.

Listing 7.8   Test program for class EXPRESSION_EVALUATOR

```
class APPLICATION

creation
  start

feature

  start is
    local
      eval: EXPRESSION_EVALUATOR
      elem: ELEMENT
      expr: ARRAY [ELEMENT]
    do
      -- Creating the expression (2 + 3) + 4
      !! expr.make (1, 50)
      !! elem.make ('(', 0.0)
      expr.put (elem, 1)
      !! elem.make ('A', 2.0)
      expr.put (elem, 2)
      !! elem.make ('+', 0.0)
      expr.put (elem, 3)
      !! elem.make ('B', 3.0)
      expr.put (elem, 4)
      !! elem.make (')', 0.0)
      expr.put (elem, 5)
      !! elem.make ('*', 0.0)
      expr.put (elem, 6)
      !! elem.make ('C', 4.0)
      expr.put (elem, 7)
```

expr.put (elem.sentinel, 8)
!! eval.make (expr)
io.putstring ("The value of the expression = ")
io.putreal (eval.evaluate)
io.new_line

*-- Creating the expression 2 + 3 * 4*
!! elem.make ('A', 2.0)
expr.put (elem, 1)
!! elem.make ('+', 0.0)
expr.put (elem, 2)
!! elem.make ('B', 3.0)
expr.put (elem, 3)
!! elem.make ('', 0.0)*
expr.put (elem, 4)
!! elem.make ('C', 4.0)
expr.put (elem, 5)
expr.put (elem.sentinel, 6)

!! eval.make (expr)
io.putstring ("The value of the expression = ")
io.putreal (eval.evaluate)
io.new_line

*-- Creating the expression 3 * (3 + 4)*
!! elem.make ('A', 3.0)
expr.put (elem, 1)
!! elem.make ('', 0.0)*
expr.put (elem, 2)
!! elem.make ('(', 0.0)
expr.put (elem, 3)
!! elem.make ('B', 3.0)
expr.put (elem, 4)
!! elem.make ('+', 0.0)
expr.put (elem, 5)
!! elem.make ('C', 4.0)
expr.put (elem, 6)
!! elem.make (')', 0.0)
expr.put (elem, 7)
expr.put (elem.sentinel, 8)

!! eval.make (expr)
io.putstring ("The value of the expression = ")

```
            io.putreal (eval.evaluate)
            io.new_line
        end

    end -- class APPLICATION
```

7.3 Las Vegas Solitaire

For the final stack application in this chapter, we consider a simulation of a real game: Las Vegas Solitaire. This is one of many variants of the card game solitaire.

7.3.1 Specifications

One of the attractive features of Las Vegas Solitaire is that a game ends after only a relatively short number of moves. The rules of the game are given in Table 7.2 below.

Table 7.2 Specifications for LasVegas Solitaire

1. Cut and shuffle a deck of 52 cards until they are mixed.
2. Deal cards to the **tableau** (layout on a table) as follows:
One card face up in column 1, then 6 cards face down in the same row to the right.
Deal one card face-up in column 2, then five cards face down in the same row to the right.
Continue this pattern until a face-up card is dealt to column 7. The top card in each tableau pile is face-up; the remaining cards are face-down.
3. After the tableau cards are dealt, the remaining cards form the **card pile**.
4. Play involves taking one card at a time from the card pile and placing it face-up on the **talon** (a stack of cards taken from the card pile; only the top card of the talon is visible). Each card taken from the card pile is available for placement on the tableau or **foundation**.
5. Each foundation pile contains cards of one suit (clubs, hearts, diamonds, or spades). Each pile begins with an ace followed by two, three, ..., ten, jack, queen, and king of the given suit. These cards are face-up. A card once placed on the foundation may not thereafter be removed.

Table 7.2 Specifications for LasVegas Solitaire (continued)

6. The face-up card in each tableau pile is the highest-ranking card in the pile (rankings go from king high to ace low). Other face-up cards can be placed below the top card if they are of next lower rank and opposite color. For example, if the top card in a tableau pile is the ten of clubs, then either the nine of diamonds or nine of hearts can be placed, face-up, below the ten of clubs.

7. All face-up cards on a tableau pile can be moved as a unit onto a card of next higher rank and opposite color in another tableau pile. When such a transfer occurs, the top face-down card of the pile that is transferred from is turned face-up and becomes available. The top card of the talon is always available to be placed on the tableau.

8. If a tableau pile is completely transferred to another tableau pile and a space is created, this space can be filled with a king.

9. On every play, an attempt is made to place the bottom tableau card from a tableau pile onto a foundation pile (foundation cards provide the payoff). Also an attempt is made to move the face-up cards from one tableau pile to another, thus uncovering the top card of the pile. Finally, an attempt is made to place the top talon card onto a tableau pile. These attempts are made repeatedly until none of the above events are possible. Then, as a last resort, a card is taken from the card pile. If the card from the card pile cannot be put on the foundation or the bottom of some tableau pile, it is placed on top of the talon pile face-up. The game ends when the card pile is empty and there are no available cards that can be moved to the foundation, to a tableau pile, or transferred from one tableau pile to another.

10. The final score of a game is determined by multiplying the number of cards on the foundation by 5. A score of 260 is considered a perfect game. When this game is played in Las Vegas, a player must pay $60 to enter each game. The player receives back an amount equal to his or her score.

7.3.2 Analysis and Implementation

The nouns that are shown in boldfaced type in Table 7.2 are natural candidates for the basic problem domain classes. These classes are the following: PLAYING_CARD, CARD_PILE, TABLEAU, FOUNDATION, and GAME. In addition, a class CARD_DECK represents the initial set of cards from which the CARD_PILE and TABLEAU are initialized.

Because of the relative simplicity of this application, the only additional support classes that are needed are FIXED_STACK (this *is* a chapter about stacks) and RANDOM_NUMBER.

Listing 7.9 shows the details of class PLAYING_CARD. The four public attributes *Club*, *Diamond*, *Heart*, and *Spade* are defined as constant integers. This gives them unique values that can be called by descriptive names. The additional public attributes of PLAYING_CARD are *suit*, *value*, *code*, and *black*. The first three of these are of type INTEGER and the last of type BOOLEAN.

LAS VEGAS SOLITAIRE

The comment under the *code* attribute indicates that each card is represented by a unique integer code.

The only public command is *display*. The creation routine, *make*, is in the protected section.

Listing 7.9   Class PLAYING_CARD

```
class PLAYING_CARD
creation
    make
feature
    Club: INTEGER is 1
    Diamond: INTEGER is 2
    Heart: INTEGER is 3
    Spade: INTEGER is 4
    suit: INTEGER
        -- Club = 1, Diamond = 2, Heart = 3, Spade = 4
    value: INTEGER
        -- Jack = 11, Queen = 12, King = 13
    black: BOOLEAN
        -- Club and Spade true, otherwise false
    code: INTEGER
        -- AC = 1, 2C = 2, .., KC = 13, AD = 14, ..., KD = 26,
        -- AH = 27, ..., KH = 39, AS = 40, ..., KS = 52
    display is
        do
            if value = 1 then
                io.putchar ('A')
            elseif value = 10 then
                io.putchar ('T')
            elseif value = 11 then
                io.putchar ('J')
            elseif value = 12 then
                io.putchar ('Q')
            elseif value = 13 then
                io.putchar ('K')
```

```
      else
         io.putint (value)
      end
      if suit = 1 then
         io.putchar ('C')
      elseif suit = 2 then
         io.putchar ('D')
      elseif suit = 3 then
         io.putchar ('H')
      else
         io.putchar ('S')
      end
   end

feature {NONE}

   make (new_code: INTEGER) is
      require
         valid_code: new_code >= 1 and new_code <= 52
      do
         suit := (new_code - 1) // 13 + 1
         value := (new_code - 1) \\ 13 + 1
         black := suit = club or suit = spade
         code := new_code
      end

invariant
   suit = club or suit = spade implies black = true
   suit = heart or suit = diamond implies black = false

end -- class PLAYING_CARD
```

The next abstraction that we consider is class CARD_DECK. The code for this class is presented in Listing 7.10.

CARD_DECK is shown as a subclass of FIXED_STACK, with base type PLAYING_CARD. A CARD_DECK is "a kind of" FIXED_STACK. The number of cards is known, namely 52.

The two public commands of this class are the creation routine, *deal_shuffle_new_deck,* and *show.* A protected command, *shuffle,* actually simulates the shuffling of the cards. The code has many comments to assist in understanding its details.

LAS VEGAS SOLITAIRE

Listing 7.10   Class CARD_DECK

```
class CARD_DECK
inherit
  FIXED_STACK [PLAYING_CARD]
creation
  deal_shuffle_new_deck
feature
  deal_shuffle_new_deck is
      -- A new deck from top to bottom consists of:
      -- AH, 2H, ..., KH, AC, .., KC, AD, ..., KD, AS, ..., KS
    local
      index: INTEGER
      new_card: PLAYING_CARD
    do
      !! rnd.initialize
      !! card.make (1, 52)
      -- Deal the hearts
      from
        index := 0
      until
        index = 13
      loop
        index := index + 1
        !! new_card.make (index + 26)
        card.put (new_card, index)
      end
      -- Deal the clubs and diamonds
      from
        index := 13
      until
        index = 39
      loop
        index := index + 1
        !! new_card.make (index - 13)
        card.put (new_card, index)
      end
      from
        index := 39
```

```
      until
        index = 52
      loop
        index := index + 1
        !! new_card.make (index)
        card.put (new_card, index)
      end
      -- Shuffle the deck 8 times
      from
        index := 0
      until
        index = 8
      loop
        index := index + 1
        shuffle
      end
      capacity := 52
      !! data.make (1, 52)
      from
        index := 53
      until
        index = 1
      loop
        index := index - 1
        push (card.item (index))
      end
    end

  show is
      -- Cards from top to bottom
    local
      index: INTEGER
    do
      from
        index := 0
      until
        index = 52
      loop
        index := index + 1
        card.item (index).display
        io.new_line
```

                end
            end

        feature *{NONE}* -- *Protected section*

            rnd: RANDOM_NUMBER

            card: ARRAY [PLAYING_CARD]
                -- *Cards from top to bottom*

            shuffle **is**
                local
                    size1, size2: INTEGER
                    index1, index2: INTEGER
                    index: INTEGER
                    pile1, pile2: ARRAY [PLAYING_CARD]
                    deck_index: INTEGER
                    number_cards: INTEGER
                    count: INTEGER
                do
                    -- *Choose size of each pile randomly*
                    rnd.next
                    size1 := rnd.value_between (18, 40)
                    size2 := 52 - size1
                    !! pile1.make (1, size1)
                    !! pile2.make (1, size2)
                    -- *Load pile1 with cards from deck*
                    from
                        index := 0
                    until
                        index = size1
                    loop
                        index := index + 1
                        pile1.put (card.item (index), index)
                    end
                    -- *Load pile2 with cards from deck*
                    from
                        index := 0
                    until
                        index = size2
                    loop
                        index := index + 1
                        pile2.put (card.item (size1 + index), index)

```
    end
    -- Shuffle the two piles together
    -- Take from 1 to 5 cards from pile1 and put into deck
    -- Take from 1 to 5 cards from pile2 and put into deck
    -- Continue this pattern until each pile runs out
    from
        index1 := 0
        index2 := 0
        deck_index := 0
    until
        index1 = size1 and index2 = size2
    loop
        rnd.next
        number_cards := rnd.value_between (1, 5)
        from count := 0
        until index2 = size2 or count = number_cards
        loop
            count := count + 1
            index2 := index2 + 1
            deck_index := deck_index + 1
            card.put (pile2.item (index2), deck_index)
        end
        rnd.next
        number_cards := rnd.value_between (1, 5)
        from
            count := 0
        until
            index1 = size1 or count = number_cards
        loop
            count := count + 1
            index1 := index1 + 1
            deck_index := deck_index + 1
            card.put (pile1.item (index1), deck_index)
        end
    end
end

end -- class CARD_DECK
```

The next class to be presented is CARD_PILE. Its details are presented in Listing 7.11.

CARD_PILE also inherits from FIXED_STACK, with base type PLAYING_CARD. The protected attribute *data* (from FIXED_STACK) is exported to CARD_PILE and TABLEAU since each of these classes needs to directly access data (in class CARD_PILE this occurs in command *add_pile*.

The public queries of CARD_PILE are: *top_visible*, *cards_under_top_visible*, and *top_visible_index*. The first query, *top_visible*, returns the top card that is visible in the pile of cards. The second query, *cards_under_top_visible*, returns True if there are 1 or more cards under the top visible card. The final query *top_visible_index*, returns the index (in the protected attribute data) of the top visible card, or 0 if none exists.

The public commands are: *set_top, add_pile*, and *decrement_number_elements*. It should be clear that CARD_PILE is not just a stack but a specialized kind of stack. This justifies the use of inheritance.

The implementation details of these commands are straightforward and may be studied in Listing 7.11.

Listing 7.11   Class CARD_PILE

class CARD_PILE

inherit
  FIXED_STACK [PLAYING_CARD]
    export
      {CARD_PILE, TABLEAU} data
    end

creation
  make

feature

  top_visible: PLAYING_CARD

  set_top (top_card: PLAYING_CARD) **is**
    do
      top_visible := top_card
    end

  cards_under_top_visible: BOOLEAN **is**
      -- Determine whether 1 or more cards are under the top_visible card
    do
      Result := top_visible_index > 1

```
    end
add_pile (another_pile: CARD_PILE) is
  require
    not_empty: not another_pile.empty
  local
    index: INTEGER
  do
    if empty then
      top_visible := another_pile.top_visible
    end
    from index := another_pile.top_visible_index - 1
    until ndex = another_pile.num_elements
    loop
      index := index + 1
      push (another_pile.data.item (index))
    end
    another_pile.decrement_number_elements (another_pile.num_elements -
      another_pile.top_visible_index + 1)
    if not another_pile.empty then
      another_pile.set_top (another_pile.top)
    end
  end

top_visible_index: INTEGER is
    -- Returns the index of the top_visible card in data
    -- Returns 0 if there is no visible card
  local
    index: INTEGER
  do
    from index := 1
    until data.item (index) = top_visible or index = capacity
    loop
      index := index + 1
    end;
    if data.item (index) = top_visible then
      Result := index
    else
      Result := 0
    end
  end
```

```
    decrement_number_elements (by: INTEGER) is
      do
        pos_last := pos_last - by
        num_elements := num_elements - by
        if num_elements = 0 then
          top_visible := void
        end
      end

  end -- class CARD_PILE
```

Class TABLEAU, presented in Listing 7.12, encapsulates the queries and commands associated with the physical layout of cards that are central to the solitaire game.

A public attribute of TABLEAU is *pile* of type ARRAY [CARD_PILE]. This makes sense because the physical layout consists of seven physical piles of cards, each of potentially different size. The only public command, the creation routine *make*, shows the details of how an initial tableau is constructed.

The use of concatenated query/commands such as *pile.item (index1).push (from_pile.top)* is fairly typical. This command accesses the *pile* in location *index1* (using the query *item* from class ARRAY) then sends the command *push* (from class FIXED_STACK) to this *pile* with parameter *from_pile.top* (a query of FIXED_STACK).

Listing 7.12 Class TABLEAU

```
class TABLEAU

creation
  make

feature

  pile: ARRAY [CARD_PILE]

  make (from_pile: CARD_DECK) is
    local
      index1: INTEGER
      index: INTEGER
      card_pl: CARD_PILE
    do
      !! pile.make (1, 7)
      from
```

```
        index := 0
      until
        index = 7
      loop
        index := index + 1
        !! card_pl.make (20)
        pile.put (card_pl, index)
      end
      from
        index1 := 0
      until
        index1 = 7
      loop
        index1 := index1 + 1
        pile.item (index1).push (from_pile.top)
        pile.item (index1).set_top (from_pile.top)
        from_pile.pop
        from
          index := index1
        until
          index = 7
        loop
          index := index + 1
          pile.item (index).push (from_pile.top)
          from_pile.pop
        end
      end
    end

  display is
    local
      pile_number: INTEGER
      index: INTEGER
      card_pl: CARD_PILE
    do
      from
        index := 0
      until
        index = 18
      loop
        index := index + 1
```

LAS VEGAS SOLITAIRE

```
            io.new_line
            from
              pile_number := 0
            until
              pile_number = 7
            loop
              pile_number := pile_number + 1
              if index <= pile.item (pile_number).num_elements then
                pile.item (pile_number).data.item (index).display
                if pile.item (pile_number).top_visible_index = index then
                  io.putstring ("* ")
                else
                  io.putstring (" ")
                end
              else
                io.putstring (" ")
              end
            end
            io.new_line
          end
```

end -- *class TABLEAU*

Class FOUNDATION, presented in Listing 7.13, contains three public attributes: *next_card*, *suit*, and *num_cards*. The attribute *next_card* indicates the next card that can legally be placed on the particular pile associated with a given suit. The attribute *suit* of type ARRAY [INTEGER], stores the number of foundation cards in each of the four piles. Finally, the attribute *num_cards* keeps track of the total number of foundation cards.

Listing 7.13   Class FOUNDATION

class FOUNDATION

creation
  make

feature

  next_card: ARRAY [PLAYING_CARD]

  suit: ARRAY [INTEGER]

APPLICATIONS OF STACKS

num_cards: INTEGER

make **is**
  local
    card: PLAYING_CARD
  do
    !! suit.make (1, 4)
    !! next_card.make (1, 4)
    !! card.make (1)
    next_card.put (card, 1)
    !! card.make (14)
    next_card.put (card, 2)
    !! card.make (27)
    next_card.put (card, 3)
    !! card.make (40)
    next_card.put (card, 4)
  end

add_card (index: INTEGER) **is**
  do
    num_cards := num_cards + 1
    suit.put (suit.item (index) + 1, index)
    increment_next_card (index)
  end

score: INTEGER **is**
  do
    *Result := 5 * num_cards*
  end

display **is**
  do
    io.putstring ("Clubs: ")
    io.putint (suit.item (1))
    io.putstring (" Diamonds: ")
    io.putint (suit.item (2))
    io.putstring (" Hearts: ")
    io.putint (suit.item (3))
    io.putstring (" Spades: ")
    io.putint (suit.item (4))
    io.putstring (" Value of foundation: $")
    *io.putint (5 * num_cards)*

```
      io.new_line
   end

feature {NONE}

   increment_next_card (index: INTEGER) is
      local
         card: PLAYING_CARD
         new_card: PLAYING_CARD
      do
         card := next_card.item (index)
         if card.code \\ 13 /= 0 then
            !! new_card.make (card.code + 1)
            next_card.put (new_card, index)
         end
      end

end -- class FOUNDATION
```

The GAME class, given in Listing 7.14, contains instances of CARD_DECK, TABLEAU, FOUNDATION, FIXED_STACK, and PLAYING_CARD. The creation routine *play* orchestrates several support commands and queries that are implemented in the protected section of the class.

A simple loop contains the command *get_new_talon_card* followed by *make_play*. This loop continues until the deck is empty. The command *make_play*, implemented in the protected section, consists of the following loop:

from
until not add_tableau_card_to_foundation **and then not**
      transfer_tableau_pile **and then not**
      add_talon_to_foundation **and then not** transfer_talon_to_tableau

Here is a rare example of combining commands and queries. Consider the first such command/query, *add_tableau_card_to_foundation*. If it is possible to perform this operation, then the operation is performed and the value *True* is returned; otherwise, no operation is performed, and the value *False* is returned. The sequence of these command/queries is important. The stack abstraction is central to the implementation of all of these operations. It is instructive to carefully study each of the command/queries given in this loop. The exercises at the end of this chapter encourage you to explore this class in more detail.

Listing 7.14 Class GAME

```
class GAME
creation
  play
feature
  deck: CARD_DECK
  tableau: TABLEAU
  foundation: FOUNDATION
  talon: FIXED_STACK [PLAYING_CARD]
  talon_card: PLAYING_CARD
  cum_score: REAL
  Num_games: INTEGER is 1000
  perfect_games: INTEGER
  play is
    local
      game_number: INTEGER
    do
      from
        game_number := 0
      until
        game_number = num_games
      loop
        game_number := game_number + 1
        !! deck.deal_shuffle_new_deck
        !! foundation.make
        !! tableau.make (deck)
        !! talon.make (52)
        from
        until
          deck.empty
        loop
          get_new_talon_card
          make_play
        end
```

```
        if foundation.score = 260 then
          perfect_games := perfect_games + 1
        end
        cum_score := cum_score + foundation.score
        io.putstring ("Game: ")
        io.putreal (game_number)
        io.putstring (" Score: ")
        io.putint (foundation.score)
        io.putstring (" Average score: ")
        io.putreal (cum_score / game_number)
        io.putstring (" Number perfect games = ")
        io.putreal (perfect_games)
        io.new_line
      end
    end

  feature {NONE}

    make_play is
      do
        from
        until
          not add_tableau_card_to_foundation and then not
            transfer_tableau_pile and then not
            add_talon_to_foundation and then not transfer_talon_to_tableau
        loop
        end
      end

    get_new_talon_card is
      require
        deck_not_empty: not deck.empty
      do
        talon_card := deck.top
        deck.pop
        talon.push (talon_card)
      end

    add_talon_to_foundation: BOOLEAN is
          -- See whether talon card can be added to foundation
      local
        index: INTEGER
      do
```

```
       if talon_card /= void then
         Result := false
         from
           index := 0
         until
           Result = true or else index = 4
         loop
           index := index + 1
           if talon_card.code = foundation.next_card.item (index).code then
             Result := true
             talon.pop
             foundation.add_card (index)
             if not talon.empty then
               talon_card := talon.top
             elseif not deck.empty then
               get_new_talon_card
             else
               talon_card := void
             end
           end
         end
       end
     end

    add_tableau_card_to_foundation: BOOLEAN is
         -- See whether a tableau card can be added to foundation
       local
         pile_number: INTEGER
         index: INTEGER
       do
         Result := false
         from pile_number := 0
         until Result = true or else pile_number = 7
         loop
           pile_number := pile_number + 1
           from
             index := 0
           until
             Result = true or else index = 4
           loop
             index := index + 1
```

```
        if not tableau.pile.item (pile_number).empty then
          if tableau.pile.item (pile_number).top.code =
              foundation.next_card.item (index).code then
            Result := true
            foundation.add_card (index)
            tableau.pile.item (pile_number).
              decrement_number_elements (1)
            if not tableau.pile.item (pile_number).empty then
              tableau.pile.item (pile_number).
              set_top (tableau.pile.item (pile_number).top)
            end
          end
        end
      end
    end
  end

  can_transfer (card1: PLAYING_CARD; card2: PLAYING_CARD): BOOLEAN is
      -- Determines whether card1 can be placed beneath card 2
    do
      if card1 = void or card2 = void then
        Result := false
      else
        Result := (card1.black = not card2.black) and (card1.value =
                card2.value - 1)
      end
    end

  transfer_tableau_pile: BOOLEAN is
      -- See whether one tableau pile can be transferred to another
    local
      pile_number: INTEGER
      index: INTEGER
      card1, card2: PLAYING_CARD
    do
      Result := false
      from
        pile_number := 0
      until
        Result = true or else pile_number = 7
      loop
        pile_number := pile_number + 1
```

```
        card1 := void
        card2 := void
        if not tableau.pile.item (pile_number).empty then
          card1 := tableau.pile.item (pile_number).top_visible
          from
            index := 0
          until
            Result = true or else index = 7
          loop
            index := index + 1
            if not tableau.pile.item (index).empty then
              card2 := tableau.pile.item (index).top
              if can_transfer (card1, card2) then
                Result := true
                tableau.pile.item (index).
                  add_pile (tableau.pile.item (pile_number))
              end
            else
              if card1.value = 13 and tableau.pile.
                  item (pile_number).cards_under_top_visible then
                Result := true
                tableau.pile.item (index).
                  add_pile (tableau.pile.item (pile_number))
              end
            end
          end
        end
      end
    end
  end

transfer_talon_to_tableau: BOOLEAN is
    -- See whether talon can be transferred to tableau
  local
    index: INTEGER
    card2: PLAYING_CARD
  do
    if talon_card /= void then
      Result := false
      from index := 0
      until Result = true or else index = 7
      loop
```

```
            index := index + 1
            if not tableau.pile.item (index).empty then
               card2 := tableau.pile.item (index).top
               if can_transfer (talon_card, card2) then
                  Result := true
                  tableau.pile.item (index).push (talon.top)
                  talon.pop
                  if not talon.empty then
                     talon_card := talon.top
                  elseif not deck.empty then
                     get_new_talon_card
                  else
                     talon_card := void
                  end
               end
            else
               if talon_card.value = 13 then
                  Result := true
                  tableau.pile.item (index).push (talon.top)
                  tableau.pile.item (index).set_top (talon.top)
                  talon.pop
                  if not talon.empty then
                     talon_card := talon.top
                  elseif not deck.empty then
                     get_new_talon_card
                  else
                     talon_card := void
                  end
               end
            end
         end
      end
   end

display_game is
   do
      io.putstring ("Size of deck: ")
      io.putint (deck.num_elements)
      io.putstring ("%NFoundation score: ")
      foundation.display
      io.putstring ("Talon: ")
```

```
        if talon_card /= void then
          talon_card.display
        end
        io.putstring ("%NTableau:%N")
        tableau.display
      end

    end -- class GAME
```

Some typical statistics resulting from running the application for 1000 games are:

Average score: 42.67   Number of Perfect Games: 7

It is clear from these statistics why the odds are with the house in Las Vegas Solitaire.

7.4 Summary

Three applications of the stack abstraction were presented in this chapter. In the first application, a stack abstraction was used to convert a recursive algorithm into an iterative equivalent. A permutation iterator is constructed with the stack serving as the central computation engine. In the second application, the stack abstraction was used to convert an algebraic expression from infix form to postfix form. A stack was used again to help in the evaluation of the postfix expression when numerical values are provided for each operand. In the third application, a stack is used in several places in simulating a game of Las Vegas Solitaire.

The stack finds its way naturally into a diversity of applications and is a staple data abstraction.

7.5 Exercises

1. Convert the following infix expressions to their equivalent postfix form:
   (a) ((a + b) * c + d)/ e
   (b) a * (b - c * d) / e
   (c) a / (b + c) * d

2. Convert the following postfix expressions to their equivalent infix form:
   (a) abcd-/+
   (b) abc*d*e-+
   (c) ab + ac-ad*ae/+*/

EXERCISES

3. Write and test an algorithm for converting from postfix form to fully parenthesized infix form. For example, the expression abc*+ would be converted to (a + (b*c)).

4. Implement an iterative equivalent of the recursive routine given in Listing 6.3

5. Implement an iterative equivalent of the recursive routine given in Listing 6.4.

6. In class GAME in Listing 7.14, enumerate all commands and queries that are associated with class FIXED_STACK.

7. Discuss the role played by class FIXED_STACK in the overall Las Vegas Solitaire application. In doing this, examine each of the classes in detail and show what role the FIXED_STACK plays in the operation of the class.

8. Based on your work in problem 9, would you say that the stack plays an incidental role in the Las Vegas Solitaire application or a central role?

Chapter 8

Application of Queues

This chapter presents an important application of queues: a discrete event simulation of a simple waiting line.

8.1 Queuing theory

Queuing theory is an important application area in applied mathematics. In a typical queuing application, customers arrive at a service facility (e.g., a toll booth, an airline check-in counter, a bank teller) and wait on a line until it is their turn to be served. It is normally assumed that the interarrival time between successive customers can be modeled by a specified probability density function—the interarrival probability density function. It is also assumed that the service time can be modeled by a specified probability density function—the service time probability density function. The line that forms is stable only if the average interarrival time is larger than the average service time.

Queuing theory explores the probabilistic behavior of such systems by computing such statistics as the average line length and the average customer wait-time.

In this chapter, we bypass the mathematical details and theory and go directly to a discrete-event simulation of a well known waiting line—one whose interarrival and service density functions are particularly simple exponential probability density functions.

In order to generate the time between customer arrivals or the service time, the following pseudo-random number generator is employed:

$$random\_time := - average\_interval * \ln(r)$$

where r is a uniformly distributed random number between 0.0 and 1.0 and *random_time* represents either a service time or a customer interarrival time. It can be shown that the above formula for *random_time* produces a sequence of real numbers with exponentially distributed statistics.

The generation of random numbers is of fundamental importance in simulating queuing systems. Many algorithms have been developed for producing a random number stream, a sequence of pseudo-random numbers whose statistical properties are governed by a particular probability density function. The technique that will be used in this book is to use a well known C language random number function available on many UNIX systems. If the reader is using an Eiffel system running under some other operating system or a version of UNIX that does not support this C function, another C function for generating random numbers must be found or generated.

8.2   Random number generator

The details of a general purpose pseudo-random number generator that is generally considered to have good statistical characteristics is presented in this section. Listing 8.1 shows the details of class RANDOM_NUMBER.

Listing 8.1   Class RANDOM_NUMBER

class *RANDOM_NUMBER*
-- Generates uniformly distributed random numbers

creation
  initialize

feature *-- public*

  -- Queries
  next_value: REAL
    -- Set by command next

  value_between (low: INTEGER; high: INTEGER): INTEGER **is**
  -- Returns uniformly distributed random number between low and high

```
    local
      t: REAL
    do
      t := (high - low + 1) * next_value
      Result := low + t.truncated_to_integer
    end

  -- Commands
  initialize is
  -- Creation routine
    do
      initialize_and_warm_up_generator
    end

  next is
  -- Advance to next random number
    do
      next_value := uniform
    end

feature {NONE} -- For internal use only

  c_init is
      -- C function seeds random number generator using current clock time
    external "C"
    alias
      "initial"
    end

  c_uniform: REAL is
    external
      "C"
    alias
      "rrandom"
    end

  initialize_and_warm_up_generator is
    local
      index: INTEGER
      value: INTEGER
    once
      c_init
      from
        index := 0
```

RANDOM NUMBER GENERATOR

```
        until
          index = 500
        loop
          index := index + 1
          next
        end
      end

    uniform: REAL is
        -- Returns a uniform random real number between 0.0 and 1.0
      do
        Result := c_uniform
      end

end -- class RANDOM_NUMBER
```

There are two commands and two queries.

The *initialize* command uses the current system clock time to provide an initial seed and then generates 500 random numbers to "warm-up" the generator. The *next* command is used to generate the next random number.

The *next_value* query holds a uniformly distributed real number between 0 and 1 resulting from the last *next* command. The *value_between* query holds a uniformly distributed integer between *low* and *high*.

Most of the implementation details are found in the C language functions that are referenced in the Eiffel routines. These C functions are given in Listing 8.2.

The user must compile the C file containing the functions shown and then include a reference to the object file in the system Ace file that is used. Such an Ace file is shown in Listing 8.3. Observe, in particular, the *external* section that is included; it makes reference to the object file, *rand.o*. The procedure for linking to an external object file might be different under different versions of Eiffel.

Listing 8.2 C functions used for class RANDOM_NUMBER

```c
#include <time.h>
#include <stdlib.h>

double drand48();

void initial()
{
    long seed;
```

```
      time_t t;
      time( &t );
      seed = ( long ) t;
      seed *= seed;
      seed = abs( seed );
      srand48( seed );
   }
   float rrandom()
   {
      return drand48();
   }
```

Listing 8.3   Typical Ace file (ISE Version under UNIX)

    system test

    root application (ROOT_CLUSTER): "start"

    default
      assertion (all);
      precompiled ("$EIFFEL3/precomp/spec/$PLATFORM/base")

    cluster

      ROOT_CLUSTER: "/disk2/EIFFELWORK3/WORK";

    external
      Object: "/disk2/EIFFELWORK3/WORK/rand.o"

    end

    Using inheritance, a more specialized random number class, RANDOM_EXPONENTIAL, is constructed. This class adds the additional query *exponential*, which returns an exponentially distributed real number. The details of this class are shown in Listing 8.4.

Listing 8.4   Class RANDOM_EXPONENTIAL

    class *RANDOM_EXPONENTIAL*

    inherit
      RANDOM_NUMBER

    creation
      initialize

```
feature

    exponential (av_interval: REAL): REAL is
        -- Returns a exponential pseudo random variable
    do
        Result := - av_interval * math.log (next_value)
    end

feature {NONE}

    math: expanded SINGLE_MATH  -- for the log function

end -- class RANDOM_EXPONENTIAL
```

The creation routine *initialize*, inherited from the ancestor class RANDOM_NUMBER, is redeclared as the creation routine of class RANDOM_EXPONENTIAL.

A simple test program that exercises some of the protocol of classes RANDOM_NUMBER and RANDOM_EXPONENTIAL is presented in Listing 8.5.

Listing 8.5   Simple test program for random numbers

```
class APPLICATION

creation
  start

feature

  N: INTEGER is 1000

  rnd: RANDOM_NUMBER

  exp: RANDOM_EXPONENTIAL

  start is
    local
      sum: REAL
      index: INTEGER
    do
      !! rnd.initialize
      from
        index := 0
      until
        index = n
      loop
```

```
            index := index + 1
            rnd.next
            sum := sum + rnd.next_value
        end
        io.putstring ("average = ")
        io.putreal (sum / n)
        io.new_line
        !! exp.initialize
        sum := 0.0
        from
            index := 0
        until
            index = n
        loop
            index := index + 1
            exp.next
            sum := sum + exp.exponential (10.0)
        end
        io.putstring ("average = ")
        io.putreal (sum / n)
        io.new_line
     end
```

end -- class APPLICATION

The application program initializes and generates 1000 uniformly distributed random numbers, each between 0 and 1, and outputs the average value. It then initializes and generates 1000 exponentially distributed random numbers with an average value of 10 and outputs the average value. Values very close to 0.5 in the first case and 10.0 in the second case are consistently obtained.

8.3 Simple queuing application

Consider the modeling of a single waiting line if customers arrive and are served according to an exponential interarrival/interservice distribution. As you will see shortly, two separate queues, an ordinary queue and a priority queue, are useful in the design of the system.

Class CUSTOMER_GENERATOR is constructed to produce customers for the waiting line. Class LINE, a subclass of a more general class

SERVICE_FACILITY, is constructed to model the actual waiting line that we wish to simulate.

We use the general model of a discrete-event simulation to accomplish our task. In this model, time advances according to the next critical event rather than uniformly. For this simple application, the two types of critical events are customer arrival and customer departure. Class SCHEDULER takes responsibility for scheduling and dispatching the next event that occurs in the system.

An interesting triad of classes exist: classes SCHEDULER, CUSTOMER_GENERATOR, and LINE. An instance of class SCHEDULER must dispatch next event commands to instances of classes CUSTOMER_GENEATOR and LINE.

Classes CUSTOMER_GENERATOR and LINE are descendants of a more general abstract class, TIMABLE, that responds to the general command *take_action*, issued by an instance of class SCHEDULER. The command *take_action* for class LINE causes a customer departure, whereas *take_action* for class CUSTOMER_GENERATOR produces a new customer.

Whenever an instance of LINE or CUSTOMER_GENERATOR receives the command *take_action* (customer completing service or being produced), it must compute its next critical event (next completion of service or next time of customer arrival) and "register" itself (along with its next event time) with the scheduler. The scheduler, using an internal priority queue as its key data structure, assigns the object that has "registered" with it to a position in its priority queue based on the relative value of its next event time—smaller next event times get processed first. When the scheduler is sent the command *next_event* it removes the TIMABLE object (either an instance of class LINE or CUSTOMER_GENERATOR) from its internal priority queue and sends it the *take_action* command. The TIMABLE object responds appropriately based on whether it is of type LINE or CUSTOMER_GENERATOR.

To see the highest level organization of the system, class QUEUING_SIMULATION, the main application class, is shown first in Listing 8.6. The main "players" in this application class are: *server* of type LINE, *schedule* of type SCHEDULER, *new_customers* of type CUSTOMER_GENERATOR, *rnd* of type RANDOM_EXPONENTIAL and the three control parameters *Average_service_time*, *Average_arrival_time*, and *Ending_time*. This latter parameter determines the last legal time that a customer can be generated. This corresponds to the time at which the "door" to the service facility is closed.

Listing 8.6   Class QUEUING_SIMULATION

class QUEUING_SIMULATION
-- Main application class that organizes the entire simulation

creation
  start

feature

  server: LINE

  schedule: SCHEDULER

  new_customers: CUSTOMER_GENERATOR

  rnd: RANDOM_EXPONENTIAL

  Average_service_time: REAL

  Average_arrival_time: REAL **is** 10.0

  Ending_time: REAL **is** 3600.0

  start **is**
    do
      !! rnd.initialize
      !! schedule.make
      from
        Average_service_time := 4.5
      until
        Average_service_time = 9.5
      loop
        Average_service_time := Average_service_time + 0.5
        !! server.make (rnd, schedule, Average_service_time)
        !!new_customers.make (rnd, server, schedule,
                  Average_arrival_time, Ending_time)
        from
        until
          schedule.empty
        loop
          schedule.next_event
        end
        output_stats
      end
    end

SIMPLE QUEUING APPLICATION

```
       output_stats is
       do
          io.new_line
          io.new_line
          io.putstring ("Load factor: ")
          io.putreal (average_service_time / average_arrival_time)
          io.new_line
          io.putstring ("Maximum line length: ")
          io.putint (server.maximum_line_size)
          io.new_line
          io.putstring ("Average line length: ")
          io.putreal (server.average_line_length)
          io.new_line
          io.putstring ("Fraction idle time: ")
          io.putreal (server.fraction_idle_time)
          io.new_line
          io.putstring ("Average customer time to wait for service: ")
          io.putreal (server.av_cust_time_to_service)
          io.new_line
          io.putstring ("Average customer wait time: ")
          io.putreal (server.av_cust_wait_time)
          io.new_line
          io.putstring ("Total customers generated: ")
          io.putint (new_customers.customers_generated)
          io.putstring (" Total customers served: ")
          io.putint (server.cust_served)
          io.new_line
          io.new_line
       end

end -- class QUEUING_SIMULATION
```

The simulation is run several times as the control parameter *Average_service_time* is varied from 5.0 to 9.5. In all cases, its value is smaller than the *Average_arrival_time* of 10.0. The **load factor** is defined as the ratio of *Average_service_time* and *Average_arrival_time* and must be kept less than 1 in order for the queuing statistics to remain stable.

Before each successive run of the simulation, the LINE and CUSTOMER_GENERATOR objects must be initialized using the code:

Application of Queues

```
!! server.make (rnd, schedule, Average_service_time)
!new_customers.make (rnd, server, schedule,
                    Average_arrival_time, Ending_time)
```

The *server* object must receive a reference to the *schedule* and the *new_customers* object must receive a reference to the *server* and *schedule*. The *new_customers* object needs a reference to the *server* so that it knows where to send new customers once they are generated.

Listing 8.7 shows the details of abstract class TIMABLE, the parent of classes CUSTOMER_GENERATOR and SERVICE_FACILITY.

Listing 8.7   Class TIMABLE

```
deferred class
-- Ancestor of all classes that want to register with a scheduler
   TIMABLE

feature

   schedule: SCHEDULER

   register (event_time: REAL) is
       -- Tell scheduler to schedule next event at event_time
   require
       pos_event_time: event_time > 0
       schedule_exists: schedule /= Void
   do
       schedule.register (Current, event_time)
   end

   take_action (event_time: REAL) is
       -- Action to be performed when scheduler sends "wake-up" call at event_time
   deferred
   end

end -- class TIMABLE
```

The *register* command requires *schedule /= Void* as one of its preconditions. This assures that registration is possible. The creation routine of each of the subclasses of TIMABLE is responsible for setting the value of the *schedule* attribute.

Listing 8.8 presents the code of class CUSTOMER_GENERATOR.

Listing 8.8   Class CUSTOMER_GENERATOR

```
class CUSTOMER_GENERATOR

inherit
  TIMABLE
    rename
      take_action as generate_customer
    end

creation
  make

feature

  server              : SERVICE_FACILITY
  av_arrival_time     : REAL
  ending_time         : REAL
  done                : BOOLEAN
  customers_generated : INTEGER
      -- Total number of customers generated

  generate_customer (event_time: REAL) is
    require
      pos_event_time: event_time > 0.0
    local
      customer: CUSTOMER
    do
      if event_time < ending_time then
        customers_generated := customers_generated + 1
        !! customer.make (event_time)
        server.enter (customer, event_time)
        rnd.next
        register (event_time + rnd.exponential (av_arrival_time))
      else
        done := true
      end
    end

feature {NONE}

  rnd: RANDOM_EXPONENTIAL
```

APPLICATION OF QUEUES

```
  make (rnd_exp: RANDOM_EXPONENTIAL; service: SERVICE_FACILITY;
      scheduler: SCHEDULER; av_interarrival_time: REAL; quit_time: REAL) is
  require
    pos_arrival_time: av_interarrival_time > 0.0
  do
    rnd := rnd_exp
    schedule := scheduler
    server := service
    ending_time := quit_time
    av_arrival_time := av_interarrival_time
    rnd.next
    register (rnd.exponential (av_arrival_time))
  end

end -- class CUSTOMER_GENERATOR
```

The command *take_action* is renamed *generate_customer*.

The five public attributes of class CUSTOMER_GENERATOR are: *server, av_arrival_time, ending_time, done,* and *customers_generated*.

The public command *generate_customer* with parameter *event_time* first determines whether the *event_time* is less than *ending_time*. If not, the Boolean attribute *done* is set to *True*. If so, the attribute *customers_generated* is incremented by 1. A *customer* object is created with parameter *event_time*. This new customer is passed as a parameter to the *enter* command of class SERVICE_FACILITY. The *register* command (inherited from class TIMABLE) is invoked with parameter *event_time* + *rnd.exponential (av_arrival_time)*. Recall from Listing 8.7 that this causes the command *schedule.register (Current, event_time)* to be invoked (*schedule* is an inherited attribute of class TIMABLE). This causes the schedule object to send another *generate_customer* command at *event_time* + *rnd.exponential (av_arrival_time)*.

The other subclass of TIMABLE, namely SERVICE_FACIULITY, is presented in Listing 8.9.

Listing 8.9   Class SERVICE_FACILITY

```
deferred class SERVICE_FACILITY

inherit
  TIMABLE
    rename
```

SIMPLE QUEUING APPLICATION

```
        take_action as depart
    end

feature

    av_service_time: REAL

    enter (a_customer: CUSTOMER; event_time: REAL) is
        deferred
    end

end -- class SERVICE_FACILITY
```

This abstract class renames *take_action* as *depart*. The *enter* command is deferred.

The one subclass of SERVICE_FACILITY used in this application, namely LINE, is presented in Listing 8.10.

Listing 8.10 Class LINE

```
class LINE

inherit
    SERVICE_FACILITY

creation
    make

feature -- Line statistics queries

    average_line_length        : REAL
    fraction_idle_time         : REAL
    av_cust_time_to_service    : REAL
    av_cust_wait_time          : REAL
    cust_served                : INTEGER
    maximum_line_size          : INTEGER

    enter (a_customer: CUSTOMER; event_time: REAL) is
        do
            if queue.number_elements = 0 then
                a_customer.set_enter_service_time (event_time)
                register (event_time + rnd.exponential (av_service_time))
                total_empty_time := total_empty_time + (event_time - line_change_time)
            end
            total_line_length_time := total_line_length_time +
```

Application of Queues

```
                queue.number_elements * (event_time - line_change_time)
            update_average_line_length (event_time)
            update_fraction_idle_time (event_time)
            line_change_time := event_time
            queue.insert (a_customer)
            if queue.number_elements > maximum_line_size then
                maximum_line_size := queue.number_elements
            end
        end

    depart (event_time: REAL) is
        require
            pos_event_time: event_time > 0.0
        local
            customer: CUSTOMER
        do
            total_line_length_time := total_line_length_time +
                queue.number_elements * (event_time - line_change_time)
            update_average_line_length (event_time)
            update_fraction_idle_time (event_time)
            line_change_time := event_time
            customer := queue.front
            customer.set_finish_time (event_time)
            total_cust_time_to_service := total_cust_time_to_service +
                (customer.enter_service_time - customer.start_time)
            total_cust_wait_time := total_cust_wait_time +
                (customer.finish_time - customer.start_time)
            cust_served := cust_served + 1
            update_av_cust_time_to_service
            update_av_cust_wait_time
            queue.remove
            if queue.number_elements > 0 then
                customer := queue.front
                customer.set_enter_service_time (event_time)
                register (event_time + rnd.exponential (av_service_time))
            end
        end

feature {NONE}

    queue: DYNAMIC_QUEUE [CUSTOMER]
```

```
rnd: RANDOM_EXPONENTIAL
    -- Queries for maintaining statistics

line_change_time: REAL

total_empty_time: REAL

total_line_length_time: REAL

total_cust_time_to_service: REAL

total_cust_wait_time: REAL

make (rnd_exp: RANDOM_EXPONENTIAL; scheduler: SCHEDULER;
      service_time: REAL) is
  do
    !! queue
    rnd := rnd_exp
    schedule := scheduler
    av_service_time := service_time
  end

update_average_line_length (event_time: REAL) is
  do
    average_line_length := total_line_length_time / event_time
  end

update_fraction_idle_time (event_time: REAL) is
  do
    fraction_idle_time := total_empty_time / event_time
  end

update_av_cust_time_to_service is
  do
    av_cust_time_to_service := total_cust_time_to_service / cust_served
  end

update_av_cust_wait_time is
  do
    av_cust_wait_time := total_cust_wait_time / cust_served
  end

end -- class LINE
```

The public attributes include queries for line statistics: *average_line_length*, *fraction_idle_time*, *av_cust_time_to_service*, *av_cust_wait_time*, *cust_served*, and *maximum_line_size*.

In the protected section of the class an attribute *queue* is declared to be of type DYNAMIC_QUEUE [CUSTOMER].

The *enter* command, deferred in the abstract ancestor class, SERVICE_FACILITY, first tests to see whether the *queue* is empty.

If the *queue* is empty the *event_time* is recorded for the *customer* using the *set_enter_service_time* command of class CUSTOMER. The time of the service completion is generated and registered with the *schedule*. The protected statistical attribute *total_empty_time* is updated.

Next, the protected statistical attribute *total_line_length_time* is updated. The following few lines of code update other statistical attributes. The customer is inserted into the queue. Finally, the statistical attribute *maximum_line_size* is updated, if appropriate.

The command *depart* (the renamed version of *take_action*) first updates statistical attributes. The *remove* command is sent to the *queue*. If the queue still contains one or more elements, the service completion time of the front customer is registered with the *schedule*.

The details of class SCHEDULER are shown in Listing 8.11.

Listing 8.11   Class SCHEDULER

```
class SCHEDULER
  -- Provides service to any TIMABLE objects that register with it

creation
  make

feature

  empty: BOOLEAN is
    do
      Result := sleepers.number_elements = 0
    end

  make is
    do
      !! sleepers.make
    end

  register (sleeper: TIMABLE; event_time: REAL) is
    -- Register sleeper so that it will be awakened at event_time
```

SIMPLE QUEUING APPLICATION

```
    require
      pos_event_time: event_time > 0.0
    local
      com_pair: COMPARABLE_2_TUPLE [TIMABLE, REAL]
    do
      !! com_pair.set_x_y (sleeper, event_time)
      sleepers.insert (com_pair)
    end

  next_event is
      -- Wake up first sleeper and trigger next event
    do
      sleepers.first.x.take_action (sleepers.first.y)
      sleepers.remove
    end

feature {NONE}

  sleepers:
  DYNAMIC_PRIORITY_QUEUE [COMPARABLE_2_TUPLE [TIMABLE, REAL]]

end -- class SCHEDULER
```

In the protected section of SCHEDULER, the attribute *sleepers* is declared to be of type DYNAMIC_PRIORITY_QUEUE with base type COMPARABLE_2_TUPLE of base types TIMABLE and REAL.

The interface to class COMPARABLE_2_TUPLE is given in Listing 8.12.

Listing 8.12   Interface to class COMPARABLE_2_TUPLE

```
class interface COMPARABLE_2_TUPLE [X, Y -> COMPARABLE]

creation
  set_x_y

feature

  infix "<" (other: like Current): BOOLEAN
    ensure
      Result = (y < other.y)

end -- class COMPARABLE_2_TUPLE
```

The *sleepers* attribute of SCHEDULER holds COMPARABLE_2_TUPLE objects (these objects consist of a TIMABLE object and its event time). The COMPARABLE_2_TUPLE objects are stored in the *sleepers* queue in the order of their critical event times.

Now examine the first line of *next_event*, *sleepers.first.x.take_action (sleepers.first.y)*. The *take_action* command is sent to the TIMABLE object stored in the COMPARBLE_2_TUPLE that is at the front of the *sleepers* priority queue. The query *sleepers.first* accesses the first COMPARABLE_2_TUPLE. The query *x* accesses the TIMABLE object portion of this 2-tuple. Finally, the command *take_action* is resolved through late-binding on either a LINE object or a CUSTOMER_GENERATOR object. The query *sleepers.first.y* accesses the critical event time associated with the first TIMABLE object. After sending the "wake-up" call to the first COMPARABLE_2_TUPLE object in the *sleepers* queue, this object is removed from the queue.

Recall from Listing 8.6 that the main simulation loop is:

from

until

  schedule.empty

loop

  schedule.next_event

end

This event loop assures that processing takes place only at an ascending sequence of critical event times (a new customer joining the line or a customer completing service).

The details of class CUSTOMER are given in Listing 8.13.

Listing 8.13 Class CUSTOMER

class CUSTOMER
-- *Maintains individual customer specific information*

creation
  make

feature

  make (event_time: REAL) **is**
    do

Simple queuing application

```
            start_time := event_time
        end

    start_time: REAL
        -- Time when this customer completes service

    enter_service_time: REAL
        -- Time at which customer enters service

    finish_time: REAL
        -- Time when this customer completes service

    set_enter_service_time (t: REAL) is
        require
            enter_service_time: t >= start_time
        do
            enter_service_time := t
        end

    set_finish_time (t: REAL) is
        require
            finish_time: t >= enter_service_time
        do
            finish_time := t
        end

end -- class CUSTOMER
```

The output of the simulation (see Listing 8.6 for the application class that drives the simulation) is given in Table 8.1.

Table 8.1 Simulation output

Load factor: 0.5
Maximum line length: 5
Average line length: 1.00443
Fraction idle time: 0.33838
Average customer time to wait for service: 3.38987
Average customer wait time: 9.93229
Total customers generated: 365   Total customers served: 365

Load factor: 0.55
Maximum line length: 7
Average line length: 1.50003
Fraction idle time: 0.226516
Average customer time to wait for service: 6.96546
Average customer wait time: 14.3809
Total customers generated: 376   Total customers served: 376

Table 8.1 Simulation output (continued)

Load factor: 0.6
Maximum line length: 9
Average line length: 2.00122
Fraction idle time: 0.196522
Average customer time to wait for service: 12.7897
Average customer wait time: 21.3693
Total customers generated: 337   Total customers served: 337

Load factor: 0.65
Maximum line length: 7
Average line length: 2.41877
Fraction idle time: 0.0962306
Average customer time to wait for service: 15.7047
Average customer wait time: 25.0732
Total customers generated: 352   Total customers served: 352

Load factor: 0.7
Maximum line length: 27
Average line length: 16.081
Fraction idle time: 0.0239766
Average customer time to wait for service: 158.016
Average customer wait time: 168.227
Total customers generated: 357   Total customers served: 357

Load factor: 0.75
Maximum line length: 64
Average line length: 31.0272
Fraction idle time: 0.0106979
Average customer time to wait for service: 355.893
Average customer wait time: 367.614
Total customers generated: 346   Total customers served: 346

Load factor: 0.8
Maximum line length: 58
Average line length: 32.5911
Fraction idle time: 0.00582323
Average customer time to wait for service: 356.126
Average customer wait time: 367.332
Total customers generated: 369   Total customers served: 369

Load factor: 0.85
Maximum line length: 70
Average line length: 33.6425
Fraction idle time: 0.00530795
Average customer time to wait for service: 383.19
Average customer wait time: 394.865
Total customers generated: 351   Total customers served: 351

SUMMARY

Table 8.1 Simulation output (continued)

Load factor: 0.9
Maximum line length: 92
Average line length: 48.4136
Fraction idle time: 0.00933695
Average customer time to wait for service: 647.46
Average customer wait time: 660.986
Total customers generated: 355   Total customers served: 355

Load factor: 0.95
Maximum line length: 107
Average line length: 51.3519
Fraction idle time: 0.00339429
Average customer time to wait for service: 686.943
Average customer wait time: 700.538
Total customers generated: 343   Total customers served: 343

The reader should note the dramatic jump in line length and wait time when the load factor increases from 0.65 to 0.7. Clearly the relationship between these statistics and load factor is highly nonlinear.

8.4 Summary

Two types of queues are used in the internal model of a discrete-event queuing simulation—an ordinary dynamic queue and a priority queue. The power of each of these abstract types is evident. The ordinary queue is used to model a service facility waiting line. The priority queue is used to schedule the next critical event that occurs in the system. Both of these queues are central to the function of the discrete-event simulation.

8.5 Exercises

1. Modify the discrete-event model by replacing the exponential interarrival time with a constant interarrival time of 10.0 seconds. Display the new simulation output.

2. Modify the discrete-event model by replacing the exponential service time with constant service times of 5.5, 6.0, 6.5, 7.0, 7.5, 8.0, 8.5, 9.0, and 9.5 seconds. Display the new simulation output.

3. Suppose the single server is replaced with two servers. Each has a distinct service time, exponentially distributed with the same mean value. Arriving customers choose one of the two servers randomly. Show the changes in the simulation model. Display new simulation output when the average service time for each of the two servers ranges from 5.5 to 18.0 seconds.

4. Repeat problem 3, but with 4 servers. Allow the range of service times to range from 15.0 to 36.0 seconds in increments of one second.

Chapter 9

Applications of Lists

This chapter presents two mathematical applications of lists: long integers and polynomials. Perhaps because there is no obvious connection between the LIST abstract data type and these mathematical applications, you will find these applications interesting and useful.

9.1 Long integers

There are many applications that require integer precision in excess of that provided by the primitive integer type. The precision of primitive integer types is usually dictated by the word size of the underlying compiler. For example, using a 32-bit compiler, the range of integers is from -2,147,483,648 to 2,147,483,647. If integers of size greater than 10 digits are required, the primitive integer type will not suffice. In many cryptology applications (creating secure encoding schemes for protecting and transmitting data) integers with precision of size greater than 100 digits are common.

This section presents an application of lists that allow integers of arbitrary precision to be represented and manipulated. A class LONG_INTEGER is constructed. Because the main purpose of this application is to show the applicability of the LIST abstraction in representing long integers, the class that is presented encapsulates only a tiny subset of the important operations normally associated with an integer type. Specifically, only the addi-

LONG INTEGERS

tion operation is shown in detail. The operations of subtraction, multiplication and division are left as exercises. An *as_string* command is provided to allow long integers to be displayed using the normal *putstring* command.

The initial interface to our desired class is presented in Listing 9.1. This interface will change as we study the problem more closely.

Listing 9.1   **Initial interface to class LONG_INTEGER**

```
class interface LONG_INTEGER
creation
   make
feature
   as_string: STRING
      -- Converts the long integer to a string that can be output
   make (long: STRING)
      -- Creates a long integer
   infix "+" (operand2: LONG_INTEGER): LONG_INTEGER
      -- Adds operand2 to the receiver
end -- class LONG_INTEGER
```

The internal data structure used to represent the long integer (the main point of this application) is not present in the Eiffel short form. This is the subject of the next subsection.

9.1.1 The internal representation of LONG_INTEGER

Suppose we wish to represent the long integer 123,456,789,012,345,678,901. Figure 9.1 shows one possible way to do this

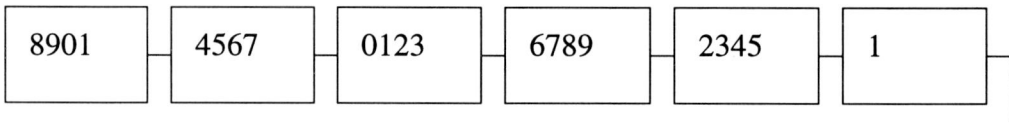

Figure 9.1 A linked list representation of a long integer.

Starting from the least significant digit and working to the left (the most significant digit), groups of four digits are formed into a list using the *insert_back* command. In this example a list containing six nodes is constructed. Each node contains up to a four-digit integer.

The reason for limiting the range to four digits is to ensure that when two long integers are multiplied, the integer resulting from the product of the integers contained in two nodes is representable in the 32-bit range given above.

The list is constructed from least significant to most significant integers to expedite the implementation of the arithmetic operators (i.e., arithmetic processing proceeds from least significant to most significant digits). The implementation of addition is discussed in the next section.

The unnatural representation of a long integer adds a small amount of complexity to the *as_string* command, which converts the long integer to a string. We discuss this operation in a later section.

9.1.2 Addition of long integers

It is instructive to consider a sample problem that we work by hand. Suppose we wish to add the long integers $n_1 = 99{,}998{,}888$ and $n_2 = 7777$. The number n_1 is shown in Figure 9.2. The number n_2 is shown in Figure 9.3.

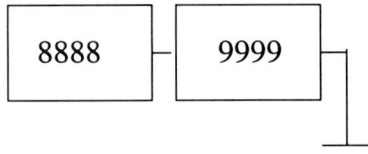

Figure 9.2 The long integer 99,998,888.

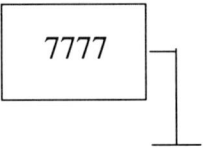

Figure 9.3 The long integer 7777.

To add the long integers of Figures 9.2 and 9.3, we begin by adding the four-digit integers in the first node of each list. This produces the sum 16,665. We truncate the result to 6665 and note that we must "carry" a 1 to the next place (the 10,000th place).

Next we add the 9999 (the four-digit number in the second node of the first list) to the carry digit of 1 to produce 10,000. Again we truncate the result to 0000 and note the carry digit of 1. Finally, the carry digit of 1 is

LONG INTEGERS

added as the most significant digit, producing the sum, 100,006,665. This sum is shown in Figure 9.4.

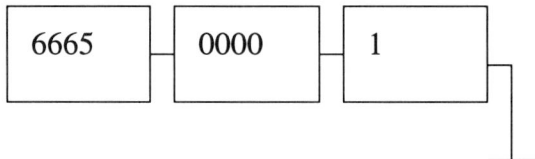

Figure 9.4 The sum 99,998,888 + 7777.

An informal algorithm for adding long integers is the following:

1. Traverse the lists representing each long integer operand until the end of one of the lists is encountered.

2. Add the integers in corresponding nodes of each list, truncating each result to four digits and storing a "carry" digit, if appropriate. Insert the truncated sum into a resultant list.

3. When the shorter list is exhausted, continue this process with the longer list (the list with more nodes) until it is exhausted.

9.1.3 Construction of class LONG_INTEGER

Using the concepts presented in sections 9.1.1 and 9.1.2, we discuss the details of class LONG_INTEGER. This class is shown in Listing 9.2.

Listing 9.2   Class LONG_INTEGER

```
class LONG_INTEGER

creation
    make,
    initialize

feature

    make (long: STRING) is
        -- Creates a LONG_INTEGER from the input string
        require
            valid_input: long.is_integer
        local
            length: INTEGER
            index: INTEGER
```

```
      group: STRING
      group_value: INTEGER
    do
      !! list
      length := long.count
      from
        index := length - 3
      until
        index <= 0
      loop
        group := long.substring (index, index + 3)
        group_value := group.to_integer
        list.insert_back (group_value)
        index := index - 4
      end
      if index /= 1 and index /= - 3 then
        index := index + 4
        group := long.substring (1, index - 1)
        group_value := group.to_integer
        list.insert_back (group_value)
      end
    end

  initialize is
    do
      !! list
    end

  exists: BOOLEAN is
      -- Returns True if LONG_INTEGER has been created
    do
      Result := list.number_elements > 0
    end

  number_groups: INTEGER is
      -- Returns the number of 4 digit groups
    do
      Result := list.number_elements
    end

  infix "+" (operand2: LONG_INTEGER): LONG_INTEGER is
      -- Adds operand2 to receiver and returns result
    require
```

```
      number_exists: exists
      op2_exits: operand2.exists
   local
      carry, sum: INTEGER
      num1, num2: INTEGER
      list2: UNORDERED_LIST_D [INTEGER]
      list3: UNORDERED_LIST_D [INTEGER]
   do
      !! Result.initialize
      list2 := operand2.list
      from
         list.start
         list2.start
         num1 := list.item_at_cursor
         num2 := list2.item_at_cursor
         sum := (num1 + num2 + carry) \\ 10000
         if num1 + num2 >= 10000 then
            carry := 1
         else
            carry := 0
         end
         Result.list.insert_back (sum)
         list.move_forward
         list2.move_forward
      until
         (not list.can_move) or (not list2.can_move)
      loop
         num1 := list.item_at_cursor
         num2 := list2.item_at_cursor
         sum := (num1 + num2 + carry) \\ 10000
         if num1 + num2 >= 10000 then
            carry := 1
         else
            carry := 0
         end
         Result.list.insert_back (sum)
         list.move_forward
         list2.move_forward
      end
      if not list.can_move then
         list3 := list2
```

```
    else
       list3 := list
    end
    from
    until
       not list3.can_move
    loop
       num1 := list3.item_at_cursor
       sum := (num1 + carry) \\ 10000
       if num1 + num2 >= 10000 then
          carry := 1
       else
          carry := 0
       end
       Result.list.insert_back (sum)
       list3.move_forward
    end
    if carry = 1 then
       Result.list.insert_back (1)
    end
  end

as_string: STRING is
    -- Converts the long integer to a string that can be output
  require
    long_exists: exists
  local
    group_value: INTEGER
    str: STRING
    list1: UNORDERED_LIST_D [INTEGER]
  do
    !! list1
    from
       list.start
       group_value := list.item_at_cursor
       list1.insert_front (group_value)
       list.move_forward
    until
       not list.can_move
    loop
       group_value := list.item_at_cursor
```

```
        list1.insert_front (group_value)
        list.move_forward
      end
      !! Result.make (number_groups * 4)
      Result.fill_blank
      list1.start
      from
        group_value := list1.item_at_cursor
        Result.append_integer (group_value)
        list1.move_forward
      until
        not list1.can_move
      loop
        group_value := list1.item_at_cursor
        if group_value < 1000 then
          Result.append ("0")
        end
        if group_value < 100 then
          Result.append ("0")
        end
        if group_value < 10 then
          Result.append ("0")
        end
        if group_value = 0 then
          Result.append ("0")
        else
          Result.append_integer (group_value)
        end
        list1.move_forward
      end
    end

feature {LONG_INTEGER}

  list: UNORDERED_LIST_D [INTEGER]

end -- class LONG_INTEGER
```

9.1.3.1 Implementation of creation routine *make*

This routine creates a LONG_INTEGER from the given input string. The precondition requires that the input string is of integer format. The query *is_integer*, from class STRING, is used to confirm this.

APPLICATIONS OF LISTS

The first step is to create an internal list. Using the string *group* and the integer *group_value*, digits from the right-most portion of the string are fetched, converted to an integer and inserted using the *insert_back* command.

9.1.3.2 Implementation of the addition operation

The precondition requires each of the operand long integers to exist. The first step is to create the resultant long integer *Result*. The local variable *list2* is assigned to *operand2.list*. This is made possible by placing this protected attribute in an export section LONG_INTEGER (see the end of Listing 9.2).

Each list is reset using the *start* command. The integer values at each of the corresponding nodes is obtained using the list query, *item_at_cursor*. The truncated sum is obtained using *sum := (num1 + num2 + carry) \\ 10000*. This sum is added to the long integer *Result* using *Result.list.insert_back (sum)*. The cursor is advanced in each list. This continues until the end of one (or both) of the lists occurs.

The local variable *list3* is assigned to the list that is not exhausted. The same processing is repeated until *list3* is exhausted.

Finally, if the carry digit is 1 upon the completion of the loop that processes *list3*, the value 1 is inserted as the final node in the resultant.

9.1.3.3 Implementation of *as_string* command

A new list, *list1*, is constructed with the reverse sequence of elements of the *list* associated with the long integer we are converting to a string. This is accomplished by employing the *insert_front* command on *list1* while using the sequence of elements in *list*.

The resultant string, *Result*, is formed by using the *append_integer* command to the integers found while traversing *list1*. This is accomplished using *Result.append_integer (group_value)*.

Several *if-then* statements take care of appending the appropriate number of zeros to each intermediate value as the resultant string is built, to assure that each is a four-digit number.

9.2 Polynomials

A polynomial of degree n can generally be expressed as: $p(x) = a_n x^n + a_{n-1} x^{n-1} + ... + a_1 x + a_0$. If many of the coefficients are zero, the polynomial is said to be sparse.

POLYNOMIALS

Consider the sparse polynomial $p(x) = 3x^6 + 2x^3 - 5$. We could represent this polynomial as a list. Each node contains the coefficient corresponding to the term in the polynomial. The polynomial given above would be represented by the list shown in Figure 9.5.

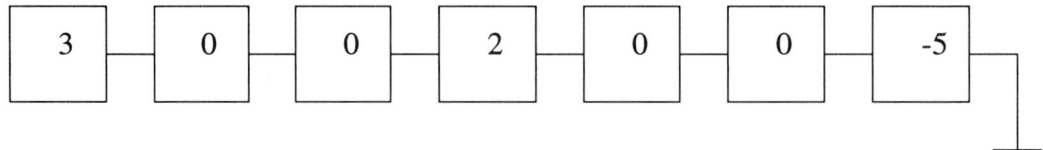

Figure 9.5 Linked-list representation of $p(x) = 3x^6 + 2x^3 - 5$.

Most of the nodes contain the value 0 (corresponding to the absence of a term). A more efficient representation would include only terms with non-zero coefficient. Each node would contain the coefficient and the degree of the term associated with the coefficient. The polynomial represented in Figure 9.5 would be represented by the list shown in Figure 9.6.

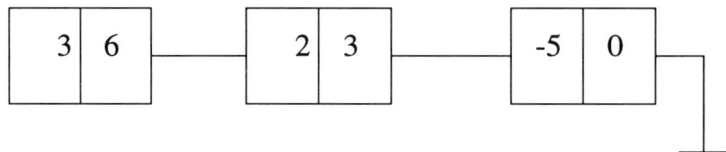

Figure 9.6 More efficient linked-list representation of $p(x) = 3x^6 + 2x^3 - 5$.

The representation shown in Figure 9.6 is more appropriate when the polynomial is sparse.

The choice of representation affects the complexity of the implementation for the operations defined for polynomials. These operations might typically include: addition, subtraction, multiplication, division, differentiation, and integration.

We consider here the operations of addition, differentiation, and integration. The other operations are left as exercises.

9.2.1 Class POLYNOMIAL

We choose the representation that includes all terms of the polynomial (with zero coefficients to represent missing terms), such as the representation given in Figure 9.5.

The partial implementation of class POLYNOMIAL is given in Listing 9.3. We explain this listing in the subsections that follow.

Listing 9.3 Class POLYNOMIAL

```
class POLYNOMIAL

creation
  make

feature

  degree: INTEGER

  make (coefficients: ARRAY [REAL]; the_degree: INTEGER) is
      -- The array of coefficients contains terms from the highest to lowest order
      -- i.e., 2x^2 + 3x + 4 would be stored as: <2, 3, 4>
    require
      array_exists: coefficients /= void
      non_negative_degree: the_degree >= 0
    local
      index: INTEGER
    do
      !! list
      from
        index := 0
      until
        index = the_degree + 1
      loop
        index := index + 1
        list.insert_back (coefficients.item (index))
      end
      degree := the_degree
    end

  display is
    local
      index: INTEGER
    do
      io.putstring ("<")
      from
        list.start
      until
        not list.can_move
      loop
        io.putreal (list.item_at_cursor)
```

POLYNOMIALS

```
      io.putstring (" ")
      list.move_forward
    end
    io.putstring (">")
    io.new_line
  end

  infix "+" (other_polynomial: POLYNOMIAL): POLYNOMIAL is
    require
      other_exists: other_polynomial /= void
    local
      coeff: ARRAY [REAL]
      degree_result: INTEGER
      smaller_degree: INTEGER
      other_bigger: BOOLEAN
      r_list, r_other: UNORDERED_LIST_D [REAL]
      index: INTEGER
    do
      if degree >= other_polynomial.degree then
        degree_result := degree
        smaller_degree := other_polynomial.degree
      else
        degree_result := other_polynomial.degree
        smaller_degree := degree
        other_bigger := true
      end
      !! coeff.make (1, degree_result + 1)
      r_list := list.reverse_list
      r_other := other_polynomial.list.reverse_list
      from
        r_list.start
        r_other.start
        index := 0
      until
        index = smaller_degree + 1
      loop
        index := index + 1
        coeff.put (r_list.item_at_cursor + r_other.item_at_cursor,
              degree_result + 2 - index)
        r_list.move_forward
        r_other.move_forward
```

```
      end
    from
    until
      index > degree_result
    loop
      index := index + 1
      if other_bigger then
        coeff.put (r_other.item_at_cursor, degree_result + 2 - index)
        r_other.move_forward
      else
        coeff.put (r_list.item_at_cursor, degree_result + 2 - index)
        r_list.move_forward
      end
    end
    !! Result.make (coeff, degree_result)
  end

differentiate: POLYNOMIAL is
    -- Returns the derivative of the receiver
  require
    degree_of_one_or_more: degree >= 1
  local
    coeff: ARRAY [REAL]
    index1: INTEGER
    index2: INTEGER
  do
    !! coeff.make (1, degree)
    from
      list.start
      index1 := degree + 1
      index2 := 0
    until
      index1 = 1
    loop
      index2 := index2 + 1
      index1 := index1 - 1
      coeff.put (list.item_at_cursor * index1, index2)
      list.move_forward
    end
    !! Result.make (coeff, degree - 1)
  end
```

POLYNOMIALS

```
    integrate: POLYNOMIAL is
        -- Returns the integral of the receiver
      local
        coeff: ARRAY [REAL]
        index1: INTEGER
        index2: INTEGER
      do
        !! coeff.make (1, degree + 2)
        from
          list.start
          index1 := degree + 1
          index2 := 0
        until
          index2 = degree + 1
        loop
          index2 := index2 + 1
          index1 := index1 - 1
          coeff.put (list.item_at_cursor / (index1 + 1), index2)
          list.move_forward
        end
        coeff.put (0, degree + 2)
        !! Result.make (coeff, degree + 1)
      end

  feature {POLYNOMIAL}

    list: UNORDERED_LIST_D [REAL]

  end -- class POLYNOMIAL
```

9.2.2 Creation routine for POLYNOMIAL

In the protected section of the class, an unordered list allowing duplicates is declared (protected attribute *list* of type UNORDERED_LIST_D). This internal data structure supports all of the polynomial operations.

Using the LIST command *insert_back*, an internal list containing *the_degree + 1* elements is constructed. The first element in this list represents the highest order term of the polynomial, with subsequent list elements representing terms of decreasing degree. The preconditions require that the client supply a non-Void array of coefficients and that the degree be equal or greater than zero.

9.2.3 The "+" query

The "+" query requires that *other_polynomial* exist. The first *if-then-else* construct establishes the values of *degree_result, smaller_degree,* and *other_bigger.* Next the array, *coeff,* is initialized to be of size *degree_result + 1* (the extra 1 is used to hold the 0th order coefficient). The lists r_list and r_other are returned by the query *reverse_list,* added to class UNORDERED_LIST_D. This new list query is presented in Listing 9.4.

The reason for reversing the internal list is to allow the addition to be performed from lowest order to highest order terms, the way arithmetic is normally performed by hand.

The first loop traverses each of the reversed lists and adds the contents term by term. The loop terminates when the smaller of the two lists is exhausted. As each sum, representing a term in the resultant polynomial, is computed it is inserted into the *coeff* array.

The second loop traverses only the larger of the two lists and inserts the contents into the *coeff* array.

Finally the *Result* is constructed by using the creation routine with *coeff* and *degree_result* as parameters.

Listing 9.4   New query reverse_list from class UNORDERED_LIST_D

```
reverse_list: UNORDERED_LIST_D [T] is
    -- Return a new list with the sequence of elements the reverse of the receiver
  require
    non_empty: number_elements > 0
  do
    !! Result
    from
      start
    until
      not can_move
    loop
      Result.insert_front (item_at_cursor)
      move_forward
    end
  end
```

9.2.4 The differentiate query

The *differentiate* query requires that the *degree* of the given polynomial be of order equal or greater than 1.

An array *coeff* is initialized to be of size *degree*. This accounts for the fact that the polynomial representing the derivative is of degree one lower than the given polynomial.

The loop traverses the internal list and accesses each coefficient from highest order to lowest order and inserts the values *list.item_at_cursor* * *index1* into the *coeff* array. These represent the derivative terms.

Finally, the *Result* is constructed using the creation routine.

9.2.5 The integrate query

This query is implemented in a manner quite similar to the derivative query. A *coeff* array of size *degree* + 2 is constructed. This accounts for the fact that the polynomial representing the integral is of degree one greater than the given polynomial.

The loop traverses the internal list and accesses each coefficient, as before, from highest order to lowest order. The values *list.item_at_cursor* / *(index1 + 1)* are inserted into the *coeff* array.

Finally, the *Result* is constructed using the creation routine, as before.

9.3 Conclusions

The list abstraction is effectively used as the internal data structure in two applications that do not appear on the surface to be related to lists: long integers and polynomials. The list's ability to store and access a sequence of items proves to be applicable in these two applications.

We have seen that such data abstractions as STACK, QUEUE, and the various LIST types can be used as basic building blocks in solving larger problems. Each of these linear structures has well defined beginning and end locations.

9.4 Exercises

1. Add the operation of subtraction to class LONG_INTEGER.
2. Add the operation of multiplication to class LONG_INTEGER.
3. Add the operation of division to class LONG_INTEGER.
4. Add the operation subtraction to class POLYNOMIAL.
5. Add the operation of multiplication to class POLYNOMIAL.

APPLICATIONS OF LISTS

6. Write an electronic phone directory using some type (you choose) of LIST as the underlying internal data structure. Your electronic phone directory should allow users to: (1) add a new record to the book, (2) delete an existing record from the book, (3) access and display an existing record by keying on some data field (e.g., last name or last name/first name).
7. Implement all of the operations of class POLYNOMIAL given in Listing 9.3 (addition, differentiation, and integration) by using the more memory-efficient list implementation given in Figure 9.6.

Chapter 10

Binary Trees

A binary tree is one of the most important nonlinear data structures used for information storage and retrieval in computer science. Applications of binary trees include syntax checking, expression evaluation, database management, searching, sorting, and game algorithms. Extremely efficient storage and retrieval algorithms may be designed for specialized kinds of binary trees. Some of these specialized tree types are discussed in Chapter 11.

10.1 What is a binary tree?

In the following discussion, important key words are shown in boldface the first time they are used.

Formally, a **binary tree** is a finite set of one or more nodes with the properties that:

1. There is a special **node**, the **root node**, that provides an entry-way into the structure.

2. The remaining nodes, if any, are partitioned into two disjoint sets, each of which is a binary tree. The disjoint sets are called the **left subtree** and **right subtree** of the root. Each node in a binary tree has either zero, one or two **children**.

WHAT IS A BINARY TREE?

This formal definition is recursive since a binary tree is defined in terms of a binary tree (see statement 2 above). As we will later see, the recursive nature of the binary tree definition makes it quite natural to express many important tree algorithms recursively.

A typical binary tree is shown in Figure 10.1

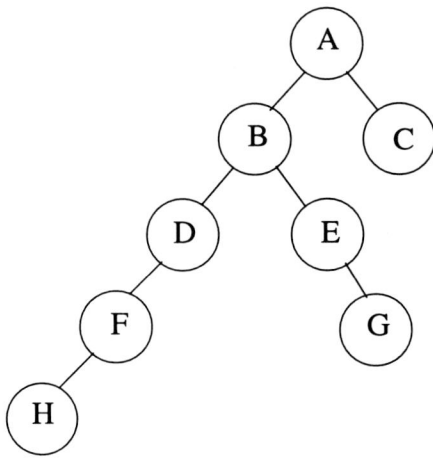

Figure 10.1 A binary tree.

The root node of the binary tree of Figure 10.1 is node A. It has two children, nodes B and C. Each of these child nodes is the root of a subtree. The **right child**, node C, has no children. It is called a **leaf node**. The **left child**, node B, is the root of the **subtree** shown in Figure 10.2.

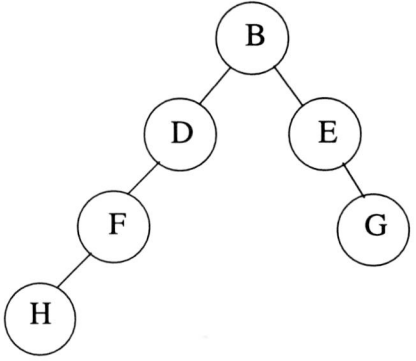

Figure 10.2 A subtree.

Binary Trees

The recursive nature of a binary tree should be evident by comparing Figures 10.1 and 10.2. Each looks like a separate binary tree even though the tree of Figure 10.2 rooted at node B is actually a subtree embedded in the tree of Figure 10.1 rooted at node A.

Additional leaf nodes in Figure 10.1 include nodes H and G. Each of these nodes have no children. Nodes A and B each have two children whereas nodes D, E, and F have one child each.

The entry node of a binary tree (or subtree) is its root node (i.e., node A in Figure 10.1 and node B in Figure 10.2). The exit nodes are the leaf nodes (i.e., nodes C, H, and G of Figure 10.1). Because there is no single path from entry to exit, the binary tree is classified as a nonlinear data structure.

The labels associated with each node provide a convenient reference for identifying each node. In practice, information is associated with each node of a tree.

Each node of a binary tree is situated at a particular **level**. The root node is defined as being at level 1. Its children, if any, are at level 2. Their children, if any, are at level 3.

In Figure 10.3 the levels in the tree of Figure 10.1 are labelled. Node A, the root node, is at level 1. Nodes B and C are at level 2, nodes D and E at level 3, nodes F and G at level 4, and node H at level 5.

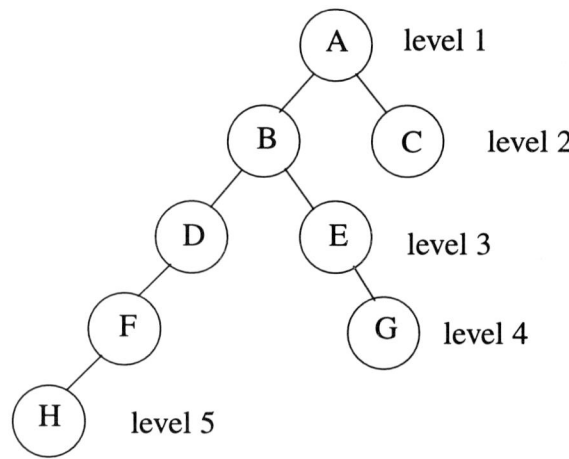

Figure 10.3 Levels in a binary tree.

You have probably asked yourself why the diagrams in Figures 10.1, 10.2, and 10.3 are called trees. What resemblance do these trees have to the ordinary variety of trees that nature provides us?

Consider the appearance of any of these figures if they are turned upside down. Figure 10.4 shows Figure 10.1 turned upside down.

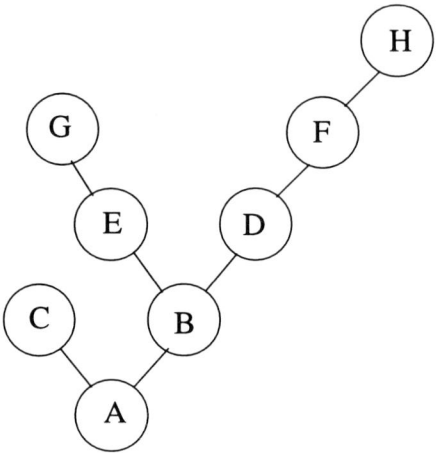

Figure 10.4 Figure 10.1 upside down.

Perhaps now in Figure 10.4 you see a general resemblance to a natural tree? (Use your imagination!) In nature, the root of a tree is at its bottom and its leaves are near the top. The trees of computer science are inverted.

10.2 Tree traversal

Given the nonlinear nature of a binary tree, how can one iterate through each of the nodes of a tree? This is important, for example, if one wishes to display the information contained in each node or perform some operation on each tree node. Where does one begin such a **traversal** of the tree? How does the traversal proceed? And when does it end? The goal is to "visit" each node of the tree exactly once.

The algorithms for traversing the nodes of a binary tree are recursive. There are three basic algorithms called **preorder, inorder** and **postorder traversal**. Each of these are given below.

Assume that the "visit" operation (e.g., displaying the node or performing some other useful command) is given by the command *node.visit*.

Algorithm preorder (node)—Assume that node is initially the root node:

```
if (node /= Void)
    node.visit -- perform some command on node
    preorder (node.left)
    preorder (node.right)
end
```

Algorithm inorder (node)—Assume that node is initially the root node:

```
if (node /= Void)
    inorder (node.left)
    node.visit -- perform some command on node
    inorder (node.right)
end
```

Algorithm postorder (node)—Assume that node is initially the root node:

```
if (node /= Void)
    postorder (node.left)
    postorder (node.right)
    node.visit -- perform some command on node
end
```

We illustrate each of the three traversal algorithms by considering their application to the tree of Figure 10.1. For each of the algorithms we list the order of node visitation.

The *preorder* algorithm visits the root node first. Next a recursive call is made with node equal to B. Node B is then visited. This pattern of recursive calls continues with the nodes D, F, and H being visited. Since H is a leaf node, the calls to *preorder (node.left)* and *preorder (node.right)* cause the test *if (node /= Void)* to fail, bringing these recursive calls to an end. The recursive process then backtracks to node equal to F. A call *preorder (node.right)* reaches its end because node F's right child is Void. The recursive process backtracks to node D. The call preorder (node.right) again reaches its end because node D's right child is Void. The recursive process then backtracks to node B. The recursive call *preorder (node.right)* causes node E to be visited. The recursive call *preorder (node.left)* ends (because node E's left child is Void. The recursive call *preorder (node.right)* causes node G to be visited next. The recursive process then backtracks to node E, then B, then A. Then with node equal to A a recursive call *preorder (node.right)* causes node C to be visited. The recursion then backtracks again to node A and the program ends. The sequence of nodes visited is A, B, D, F, H, E, G, C.

For the algorithm *inorder*, a series of recursive calls (following node equal to A) occur with node equal to B, D, F, and H occur. Since the left child of H is Void, the first node to be visited is node H. Since its right child is Void, the recursive process backtracks to node F. This becomes the second node to be visited. The algorithm then backtracks to node D. This node gets visited. The algorithm then backtracks to node B. This node gets visited. Following this a recursive call to *inorder (node.right)* occurs. Since the left child of E is Void, node E gets visited next. The recursive call *inorder (node.right)* causes node to equal G. Since G's left child is Void, node G is the next to be visited. Following this, backtracking through nodes E, B, and A followed by a recursive call *inorder (node.right)* from node A causes node C to be the last node visited. The sequence of nodes visited is H, F, D, B, E, G, A, C.

It is left as an exercise for the reader to confirm that the sequence of nodes visited using the postorder traversal is H, F, D, G, E, B, C, A.

It is important to observe that each of the traversal algorithms visits each node exactly once.

10.3 Path length

If a binary tree is being used as an information structure we would like to be able to compute some measure of its shape and size. Generally, the deeper the tree (i.e., the higher the largest level for some leaf node) the longer the search time. Information stored in leaf nodes many levels down from the root take longer to access than information stored near the "top" (i.e., near the root) of the tree.

We define the average internal path length of a binary tree as follows:

$$averageInternalPathLength = \frac{\sum_{k=1}^{numberOfLevels} k \times numberNodesAtLevel(k)}{numberNodes}$$

The numerator represents a weighted sum of the number of nodes at a given level weighted by the level number. The denominator represents the total number of nodes in the tree. The ratio, the average internal path length, represents the average level of the tree. As we shall see in the later section on search trees, the average level of the tree is directly related to the search time for locating a random node in the tree. Therefore, the average internal path length provides a quantitative measure of the relative average search performance of a given tree.

We illustrate the computation of average internal path length by considering three binary trees, each containing seven nodes.

The tree in Figure 10.5, is a **perfectly balanced** tree. That is, each level contains the maximum number of nodes that is possible. Such a tree should provide for highly efficient searching since the depth is minimum. As a quick exercise, you should verify that the required number of nodes in a perfectly balanced tree equals two raised to an integer power minus one. In this case, two raised to the third power is eight. Our tree has exactly seven nodes.

The tree in Figure 10.6 is a worst-case tree from the perspective of balance. In fact, it resembles a linked-list. All seven nodes are contained within a single branch (it does not matter whether the branch is to the left or to the right of the root node).

Figure 10.7 contains a tree between the two extremes of Figures 10.5 and 10.6.

In Figures 10.5, 10.6, and 10.7, only the structure of each tree is shown, not the values associated with the nodes.

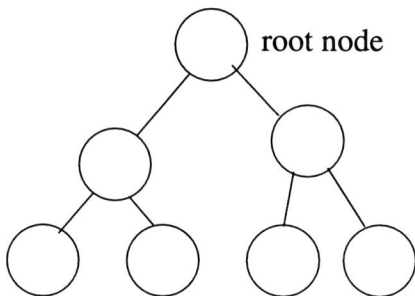

Figure 10.5 A balanced tree.

PATH LENGTH

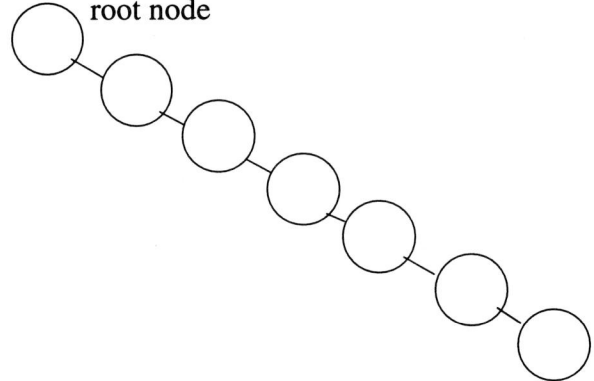

Figure 10.6 An unbalanced tree.

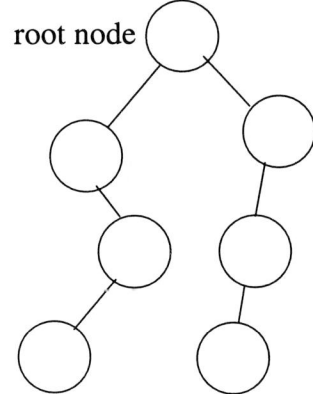

Figure 10.7 Partially balanced tree.

For the balanced tree of Figure 10.5, the computation is:
$(1 + (2)(2) + (4)(3)) / 7 = 2.43$.

For the unbalanced tree of Figure 10.6, the computation is:
$(1 + 2 + 3 + 4 + 5 + 6 + 7) / 7 = 3.71$.

Finally, for the partially balanced tree of Figure 10.7, the computation is:
$(1 + (2)(2) + (2)(3) + (2)(4)) / 7 = 2.71$.

The smaller the average internal path length, the more balanced the tree is, relatively speaking, and the faster its average search-time performance.

10.4 Implementation of binary tree

The behavior of a binary tree is defined by its queries and commands. In previous sections we have discussed the following commands: *preorder traversal, inorder traversal, postorder traversal*; and the following query: *average internal path length*. In addition, we need the commands *insert* and *delete* in order to be able to add and remove nodes in a binary tree. The implementation of these last two commands are deferred to the more specialized types of binary trees discussed later.

We first present the interface to class BINARY_TREE. It is important in formulating this interface to specify the pre- and postconditions of each routine. This interface is presented in Listing 10.1.

Listing 10.1 Interface to class BINARY_T

> **deferred class interface** *BINARY_T [T -> COMPARABLE]*
> **feature**
>   -- *Queries*
>   *average_internal_path_length: REAL*
>
>   *is_present (item: T): BOOLEAN*
>   **require**
>   *valid_item: item /= void*
>   *not_empty: not_empty*
>
>   *not_empty: BOOLEAN*
>
>   -- *Commands*
>   *postorder*
>
>   *preorder*
>
>   *inorder*
>
>   *delete (item: T)*
>   **require**
>   *item_exists: item /= void*
>   **ensure**
>   *item_not_present:* **not** *is_present (item)*
>
>   *insert (item: T)*
>   **require**
>   *item_exists: item /= void*
>   *item_not_present:* **not** *is_present (item)*

Implementation of Binary Tree

    ensure
        item_is_present: is_present (item)

end -- class BINARY_T

    The command *insert* requires that the item not be present in the given tree and then guarantees that after its execution is completed that the item is present. The command *delete* requires the item be present in the given tree and guarantees that after it is completed that the item is not present.

    Before discussing each of the features of class BINARY_T, we list the entire implementation in Listing 10.2.

Listing 10.2 Class BINARY_T

deferred class BINARY_T [T -> COMPARABLE]

feature {NONE}

  root_node: NODE [T]

  pre_order (node: NODE [T]) **is**
    -- Supports preorder
  do
    if node /= void **then**
      node.visit
      pre_order (node.left)
      pre_order (node.right)
    end
  end

  in_order (node: NODE [T]) **is**
    -- Support inorder
  do
    if node /= void **then**
      in_order (node.left)
      node.visit
      in_order (node.right)
    end
  end

  post_order (node: NODE [T]) **is**
    -- Supports postorder
  do
    if node /= void **then**

```
            post_order (node.left)
            post_order (node.right)
            node.visit
         end
      end

   sum     :     INTEGER
   num_nodes: INTEGER
   compute (node: NODE [T]; depth: INTEGER) is
         -- Supports average_internal_path_length
      do
         if node /= void then
            sum := sum + depth
            num_nodes := num_nodes + 1
            compute (node.left, depth + 1)
            compute (node.right, depth + 1)
         end
      end

feature

   -- Queries
   not_empty: BOOLEAN is
      do
         Result := root_node /= void
      end

   is_present (item: T): BOOLEAN is
      require
         valid_item: item /= void
      deferred
      end

   average_internal_path_length: REAL is
      do
         sum := 0
         num_nodes := 0
         compute (root_node, 1)
         Result := sum.to_real / num_nodes.to_real
      end

   -- Commands
   preorder is
      do
```

```
      pre_order (root_node)
   end
inorder is
   do
      in_order (root_node)
   end
postorder is
   do
      post_order (root_node)
   end
insert (item: T) is
   require
      item_exists: item /= void
      item_not_present: not is_present (item)
   deferred
   ensure
      item_is_present: is_present (item)
   end
delete (item: T) is
   require
      item_exists: item /= void
      item_present: is_present (item)
   deferred
   ensure
      item_not_present: not is_present (item)
   end
end -- class BINARY_T
```

10.4.1 The constrained generic parameter in BINARY_T

The generic parameter, T -> COMPARABLE, indicates that only base types that conform (are proper descendants) to class COMPARABLE are allowed. This guarantees that the base type element can respond to the operators ">" and "<" and "=." Although this requirement is not necessary for ordinary binary trees, it is essential for the more specialized types of binary trees discussed later. These specialized types of binary tree are proper descendants of BINARY_T. For these specialized types of binary trees, the operations of *insert* and *delete* require that the information stored in tree nodes can be compared.

10.4.2 Implementation of commands preorder, inorder, and postorder

We consider only one of these commands, *inorder*, as typical of all three. Its implementation involves the public routine *inorder* and the protected routine *in_order*. These are shown in Listing 10.3. The recursive code of *in_order* is identical in appearance to the algorithm presented in Section 10.2. The same is true of commands *preorder* and *postorder*.

Listing 10.3 Routines that support the inorder command

```
inorder is
  do
    in_order (root_node)
  end

in_order (node: NODE [T]) is
    -- Supports inorder traversal
  do
    if node /= void then
      in_order (node.left)
      node.visit
      in_order (node.right)
  end
```

10.4.3 Implementation of average_internal_path_length

The routines that support the query average_internal_path_length are shown in Listing 10.4.

Listing 10.4 Routines that support average_internal_path_length

```
sum:   INTEGER
num_nodes: INTEGER

compute (node: NODE [T]; depth: INTEGER) is
    -- Supports average_internal_path_length
  do
    if node /= void then
      sum := sum + depth
      num_nodes := num_nodes + 1
      compute (node.left, depth + 1)
      compute (node.right, depth + 1)
```

```
        end
    end
  average_internal_path_length: REAL is
    do
      sum := 0
      num_nodes := 0
      compute (root_node, 1)
      Result := sum.to_real / num_nodes.to_real
    end
```

The protected variables *sum* and *num_nodes* are first initialized to zero. The recursive routine compute is invoked. Its structure is that of a preorder traversal. Its "visit" operation consists of incrementing the *sum* by *depth*. This latter value is stored on the stack because of the recursion. When the recursion ends the value stored in variable *sum* equals the numerator of the mathematical expression presented earlier for internal path length.

The command *to_real* converts the integer values *sum* and *num_nodes* to type real.

10.5 Search trees

Binary search-trees are a widely used information structure. When they are reasonably balanced they provide efficient access to data.

What is a search tree? **A search tree is a binary tree in which each node has a relative "value" that is greater than all its left descendants and smaller than all its right descendants.** This is a recursive definition since it applies to each node of a search tree. Clearly we must be able to compare the value of nodes. Therefore the base type must be of a type that conforms to COMPARABLE.

Figure 10.8 shows a search tree in which the values are integers.

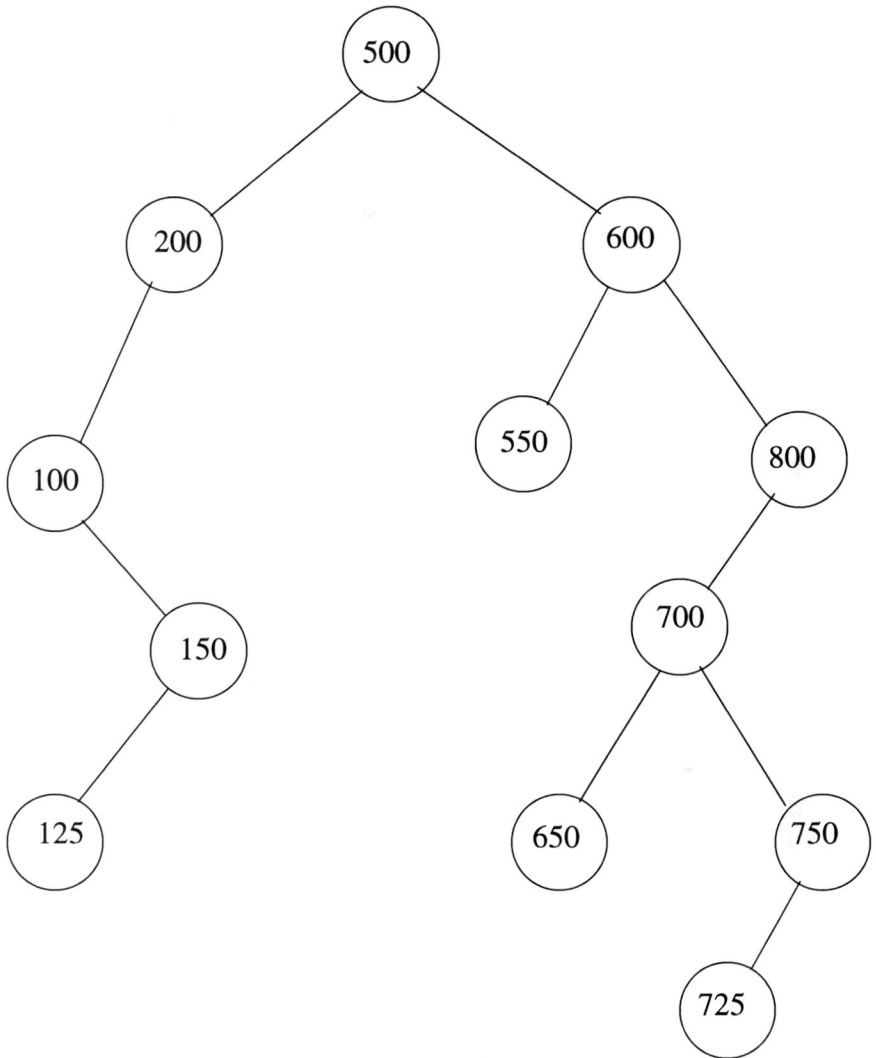

Figure 10.8 Binary search tree.

You should verify that each node satisfies the search-tree property stated above.

Let us examine the output of the search tree given in Figure 10.8 when a preorder traversal of the tree is performed. Verify that the preorder traversal visits the nodes in the order: 100, 125, 150, 200, 500, 550, 600, 650,

700, 725, 750, 800. This is an ordered sequence of output. This in fact explains why this algorithm is called an inorder traversal.

How might one search for the element 725? We shall call the 725 *item*. We first compare item to the root node. Since item is greater than the root node we eliminate roughly half of the tree from further consideration (i.e., the left subtree under the root).

We next compare *item* to node 600. Since *item* is again larger, we eliminate the left subtree of node 600 (in this case only a single node).

We next compare *item* to node 800. Since *item* is smaller, we eliminate the right subtree of 800 (in this case there are no nodes to eliminate).

We next compare *item* to node 700. Since *item* is larger, we eliminate the left subtree of 700 (i.e., node 650).

We next compare *item* to node 750. Since *item* is smaller, we eliminate the right subtree of 750, which in this case is empty.

Finally we compare item to node 725. A match up is found. In this worst-case scenario, the number of comparison operations equals the maximum depth of the tree along the search path shown in Figure 10.9.

We now examine the query *is_present* for search trees. The query returns True if the parameter *item* is stored in the binary tree and False otherwise. The routines that support its implementation are shown in Listing 10.5.

Listing 10.5 Routines that support the query is_present for class SEARCH_TREE

```
is_present (item: T): BOOLEAN is
  do
    Result := present (root_node, item)
  end

present (node: NODE [T]; item: T): BOOLEAN is
  do
    if node = Void then
      Result := False
    else
      if item = node.information then
        Result := true
      elseif item < node.information then
        Result := present (node.left, item)
      elseif item > node.information then
        Result := present (node.right, item)
      end
```

        end
    end

The recursive routine, in the form of a preorder traversal *present*, moves down the tree as we did in the example above until a node with value *Void* is hit or until *item* is equal to *node.information*. This query is quite important because it is used in several of the pre- and postconditions.

An iterative version of *is_present* is given in Listing 10.6.

Listing 10.6 Support routines for iterative version of query is_present

```
present (item: T): BOOLEAN is
  local
    current_node: NODE [T]
  do
    from
      current_node := root_node
    until
      Result = true or current_node = Void
    loop
      if item = current_node.information then
        Result := true
      elseif item < current_node.information then
        current_node := current_node.left
      else
        current_node := current_node.right
      end
    end
  end

is_present (item: T): BOOLEAN is
  do
    Result := present (item)
  end
```

It is important for the loop to terminate when either a match up has been found (i.e., *Result* = *True*) or the current_node has hit the bottom of the tree (i.e., *current_node* = *Void*). The iterative version might be faster on some machines. You ought to consider performing careful timing analyses to determine which version is faster.

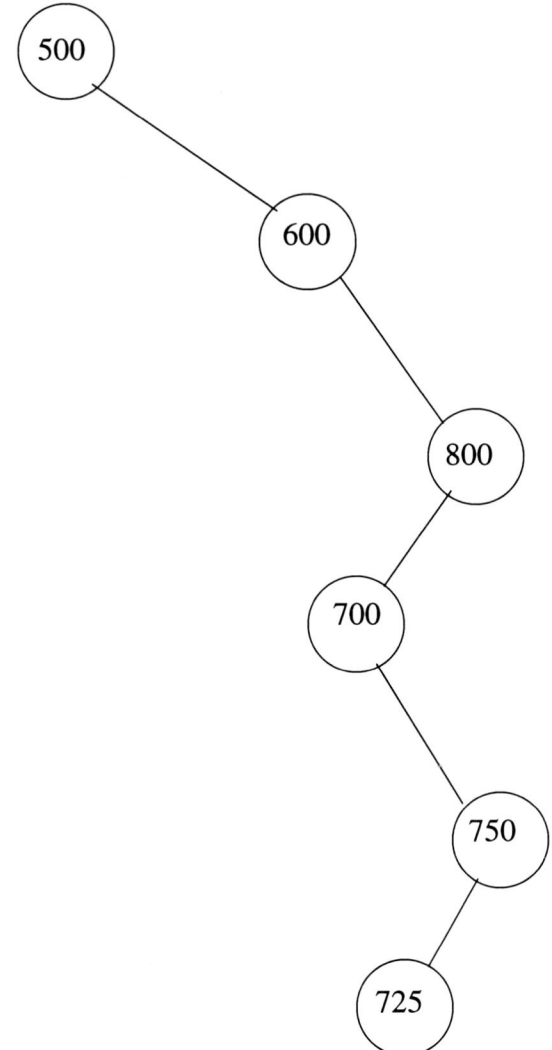

Figure 10.9 Search path for finding 725.

10.5.1 Insertion

How can we insert an item into a search tree?

Consider the task of inserting the node with value 175 into the search tree shown in Figure 10.8. The approach is to first search for the element

175. Using the search logic given earlier, the search path from the root node down the tree is 500, 200, 100, 150. But the node 175 is not found! Clearly, if node 175 were present, it would be the right child of node 150. So this is where we put it. Figure 10.10 shows the insertion process.

This leads to the recursive insert routine given in Listing 10.7.

Listing 10.7 Support routines for insert in class SEARCH_TREE

```
leaf_node (node: NODE [T]; parent: NODE [T]; item: T): NODE [T] is
  local
    return_node: NODE [T]
  do
    if node /= void then
      if item < node.information then
        return_node := leaf_node (node.left, node, item)
      elseif item > node.information then
        return_node := leaf_node (node.right, node, item)
      end
    else
      return_node := parent
    end
    Result := return_node
  end

insert (item: T) is
  local
    insert_under: NODE [T]
    new_node: NODE [T]
  do
    if root_node = void then
      !! root_node.make (item)
    else
      insert_under := leaf_node (root_node, root_node, item)
      !! new_node.make (item)
      if item < insert_under.information then
        insert_under.link_left (new_node)
      else
        insert_under.link_right (new_node)
      end
    end
  end
```

SEARCH TREES

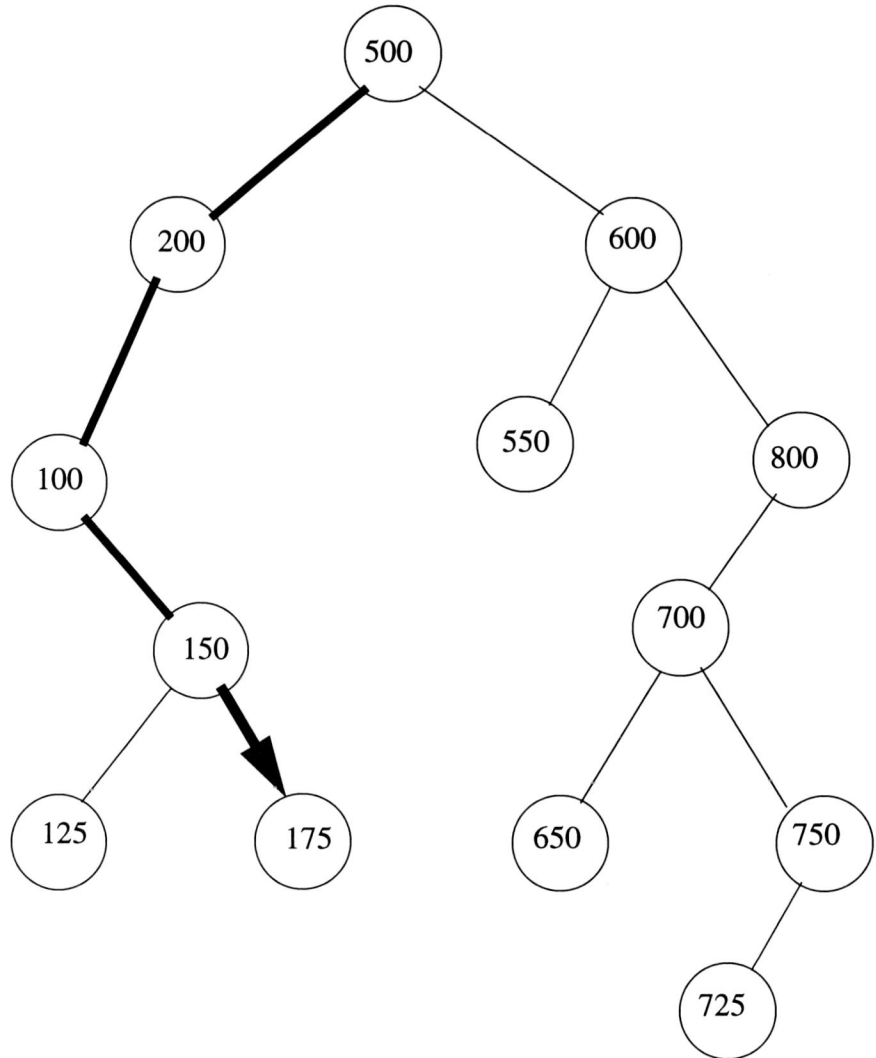

Figure 10.10 Insertion of node 175.

The routine *insert*, in Listing 10.7, first determines whether the root node is Void. If it is, it creates a root node and assigns *item* to it.

If a root node already exists, the protected function *leaf_node* is invoked. This recursive function recursively descends down the tree each time sending in as the second parameter the parent node. When the bottom of the tree is eventually encountered, the parent node is returned.

The insert command creates a new node and assigns *item* to it. It then compares *item* to the parent node. If *item* is greater than the parent node the new node is linked to the right of the parent node, otherwise to the left of the parent node.

An iterative version of the insert command is shown in Listing 10.8.

Listing 10.8 An iterative version of the insert command for SEARCH_TREE

```
leaf_node (item: T): NODE [T] is
    -- Returns the leaf node just above the new_node being inserted
  local
    return_node: NODE [T]
    current_node: NODE [T]
  do
    from
      current_node := root_node
    until
      current_node = void
    loop
      return_node := current_node
      if item < current_node.information then
        current_node := current_node.left
      else
        current_node := current_node.right
      end
    end
    Result := return_node
  ensure
    Result /= void
  end

insert (item: T) is
  local
    insert_under: NODE [T]
    new_node: NODE [T]
  do
    if root_node = void then
      !! root_node.make (item)
```

```
      else
        insert_under := leaf_node (item)
        !! new_node.make (item)
        if item < insert_under.information then
          insert_under.link_left (new_node)
        else
          insert_under.link_right (new_node)
        end
      end
    end
```

The basic difference between the recursive version and iterative version is in the protected function *leaf_node*. In the iterative version, a loop is used to descend down the search path to the bottom of the tree.

On some systems, the iterative version might be less stressful to the underlying compiler since it does not require the same stack space as the recursive version. If the tree is reasonably balanced, then the depth of the recursion would be approximately equal to the log to the base 2 of the number of nodes in the tree.

10.5.2 Deletion

How does one delete a node from a search tree? This is a more difficult problem then insertion. There are three separate cases: (1) deleted node has no children, (2) deleted node has one child, and (3) deleted node has two children.

We consider each of these subproblems and illustrate their solutions by again using the search tree in Figure 10.8. The situations are shown in Figures 10.11, 10.12, and 10.13.

BINARY TREES

Problem 1: We wish to delete node 650

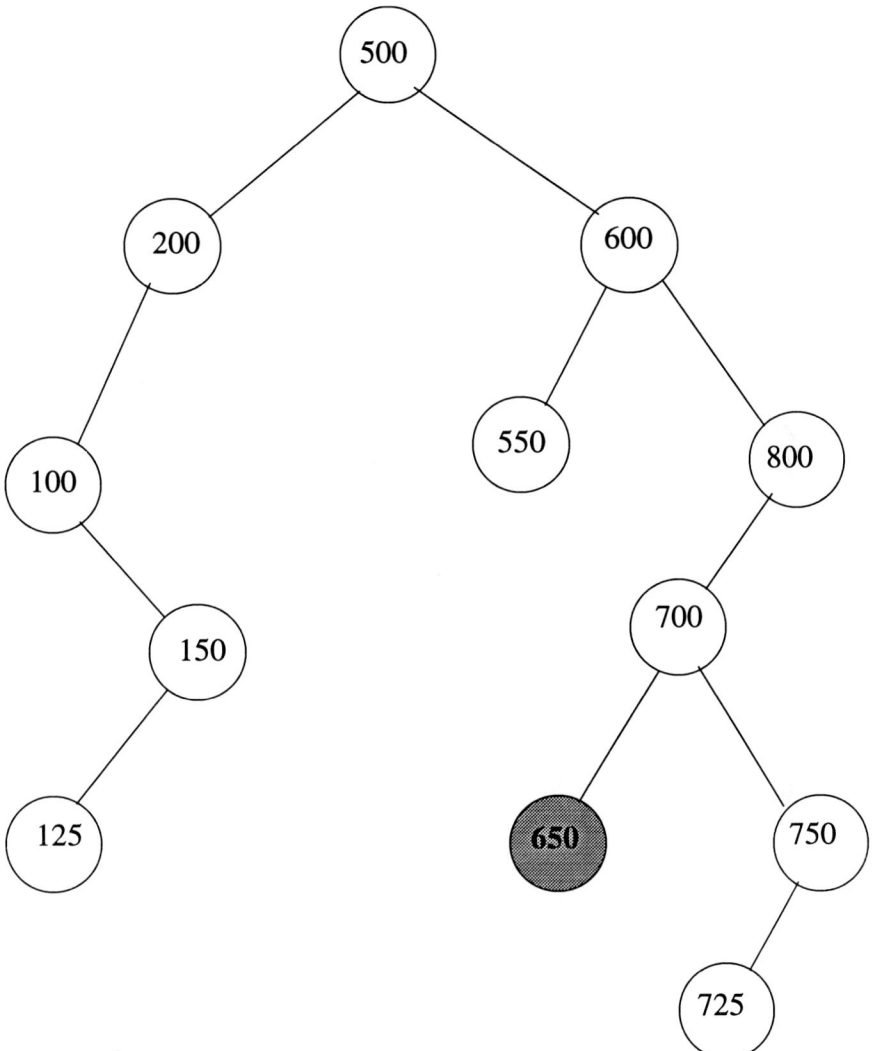

Figure 10.11 Delete node 650.

The procedure for this simple deletion is to search for the node to be deleted and then simply remove it by linking its parent left reference to Void. Listing 10.9 shows the general solution for delete. We examine the code for this special case.

Listing 10.9 Deletion

```
delete (item: T) is
  local
    parent, previous, item_node, replace, replace_left: NODE [T]
  do
    previous := void
    from
      item_node := root_node
    until
      item = item_node.information
    loop
      previous := item_node
      if item < item_node.information then
        item_node := item_node.left
      else
        item_node := item_node.right
      end
    end
    if item_node.left = void then
      replace := item_node.right
    elseif item_node.right = void then
      replace := item_node.left
    else
      parent := item_node
      replace := item_node.right
      replace_left := replace.left
      from
      until
        replace_left = void
      loop
        parent := replace
        replace := replace_left
        replace_left := replace.left
      end
      if parent /= item_node then
        parent.link_left (replace.right)
        replace.link_right (item_node.right)
      end
      replace.link_left (item_node.left)
    end
```

```
        if previous = void then
          root_node := replace
        else
          if item_node = previous.left then
            previous.link_left (replace)
          else
            previous.link_right (replace)
          end
        end
      end
```

The first loop terminates when a match occurs between *item* and *item_node.information*. This is guaranteed because one of the preconditions requires *item* to be in the tree. When the loop terminates, *previous* is the parent of *item_node* and *item_node* contains *item*.

The next branch statement determines our course of action in this simple case. Since for the node containing 650, *item_node.left = Void*, the node *replace* is assigned to equal *item_node.right*, which is Void.

The final branch statement takes control to *if item_node = previous.left*, and the assignment *previous.link_left (replace)* occurs. This has the effect of bypassing node 650 and having the left reference of node 700 be Void.

SEARCH TREES

Problem 2: We wish to delete node 100

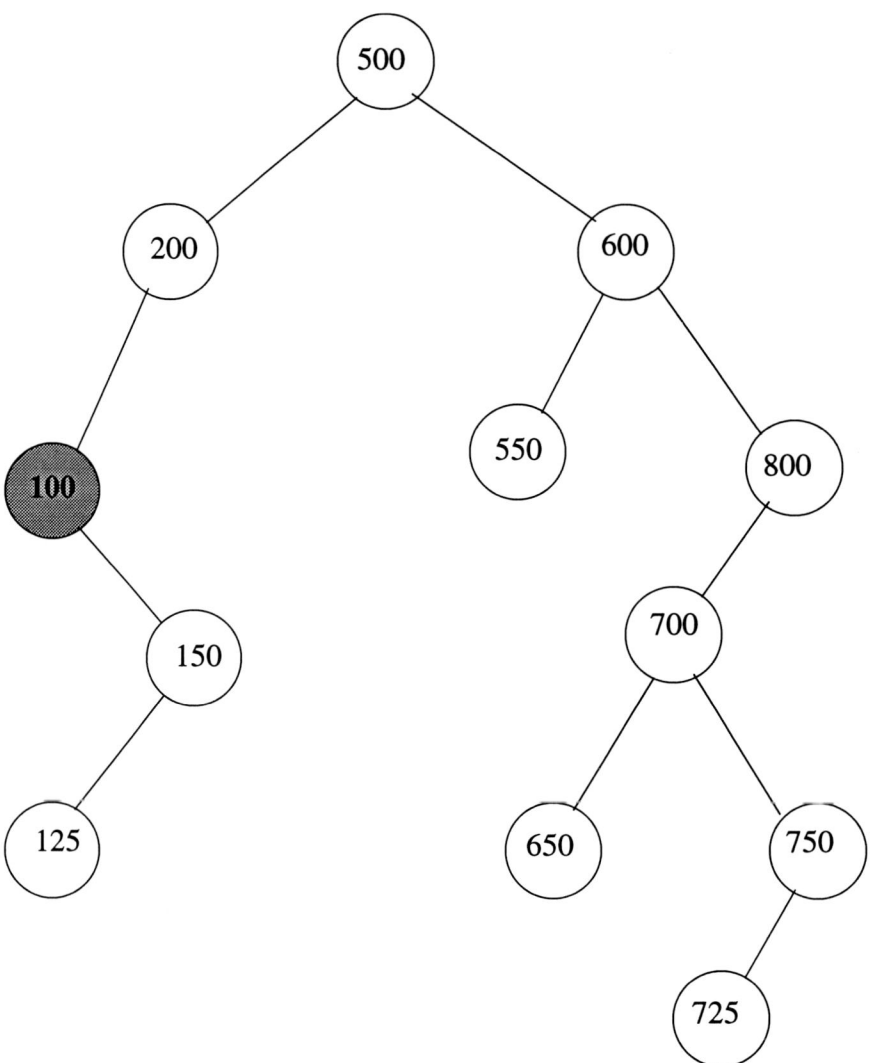

Figure 10.12 Delete node 100.

This second case might be called the "linked-list" case, since the removal of node 100 follows a procedure quite similar to a linked-list deletion, as we shall soon see.

Following the algorithm in Listing 10.9, we return to the first branch statement. In this case the node *replace* is set to node 150 (the right child of node 100). Then in the second branch statement the parent node 200 is left-linked to *replace* (node 150). Do you see the similarity to a linked-list deletion?

Problem 3: We wish to delete node 600

The final deletion example is the most difficult. The node 600 has two children. The tree is shown in Figure 10.13.

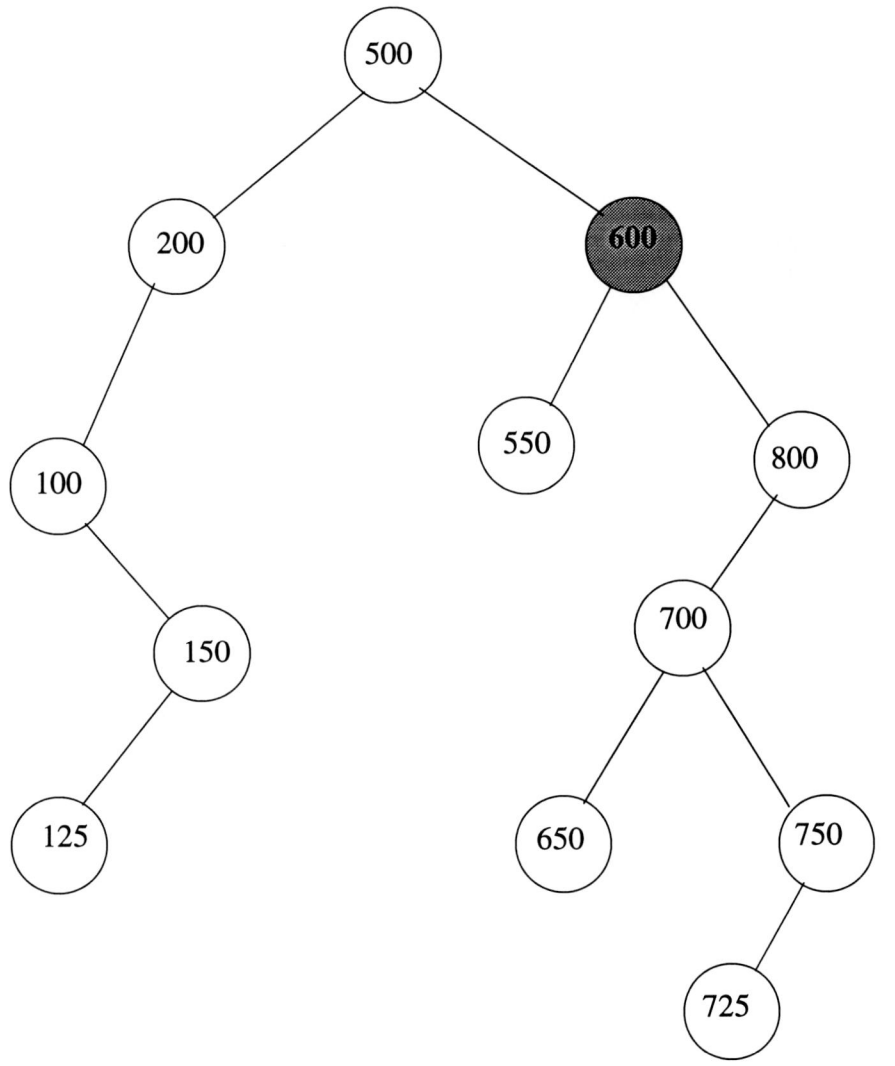

Figure 10.13 Deletion of node 600.

Again following the algorithm of Listing 10.9, the first branch statement takes control to the *else* clause. The node *parent* is assigned to 600, *replace* is assigned to 800 and *replace_left* is assigned to 700. The loop advances the variables *parent, replace* and *replace_left* until *replace_left* is Void, *replace* is 650 and *parent* is 700.

Following the loop, but still in the else clause since *parent /= item*, *parent* (node 700) is left-linked to Void (*replace.right*). Node *replace* is right-linked to *item_node.right* or node 800. Finally *replace* is left-linked to node *item_node.left* (node 550).

Effectively, node 650 has been linked in to replace node 600. This replacement node (600) is called the **inorder successor**. Verify that if an inorder traversal has just visited node 600, the next node that would be visited would be node 650.

We may now state in words the procedure for deleting a node that contains two children. That procedure is: replace the node to be deleted by its inorder successor and then delete the inorder successor. Can you prove that the inorder successor can never have more than one child? Therefore, its deletion is relatively simple.

10.5.3 Search tree implementation

Putting all of the algorithms of Section 10.5 together, we present the full implementation of class SEARCH_TREE in Listings 10.10 and 10.11. Listing 10.10 presents a recursive solution, whereas Listing 10.11 presents an iterative version.

Listing 10.10 Class SEARCH_TREE—Recursive version

class SEARCH_TREE [T -> COMPARABLE]
-- Recursive version

inherit
  BINARY_T [T]

feature {NONE}

  leaf_node (node: NODE [T]; parent: NODE [T]; item: T): NODE [T] *is*
    local
      return_node: NODE [T]
    do
      if node /= void *then*
        if item < node.information *then*
          return_node := leaf_node (node.left, node, item)

```
      elseif item > node.information then
        return_node := leaf_node (node.right, node, item)
      end
    else
      return_node := parent
    end
    Result := return_node
  ensure
    Result /= void
  end

present (node: NODE [T]; item: T): BOOLEAN is
  do
    if node = void then
      Result := false
    else
      if item = node.information then
        Result := true
      elseif item < node.information then
        Result := present (node.left, item)
      elseif item > node.information then
        Result := present (node.right, item)
      end
    end
  end

feature

  -- Queries
  is_present (item: T): BOOLEAN is
    do
      Result := present (root_node, item)
    end

  -- Commands
  insert (item: T) is
    local
      insert_under: NODE [T]
      new_node: NODE [T]
    do
      if root_node = void then
        !! root_node.make (item)
      else
```

```
      insert_under := leaf_node (root_node, root_node, item)
      !! new_node.make (item)
      if item < insert_under.information then
         insert_under.link_left (new_node)
      else
         insert_under.link_right (new_node)
      end
    end
  end

  delete (item: T) is
    local
      parent, previous, item_node, replace, replace_left: NODE [T]
    do
      previous := void
      from
        item_node := root_node
      until
        item = item_node.information
      loop
        previous := item_node
        if item < item_node.information then
           item_node := item_node.left
        else
           item_node := item_node.right
        end
      end
      if item_node.left = void then
         replace := item_node.right
      elseif item_node.right = void then
         replace := item_node.left
      else
         parent := item_node
         replace := item_node.right
         replace_left := replace.left
         from
         until
           replace_left = void
         loop
           parent := replace
           replace := replace_left
```

```
        replace_left := replace.left
      end
      if parent /= item_node then
        parent.link_left (replace.right)
        replace.link_right (item_node.right)
      end
      replace.link_left (item_node.left)
    end
    if previous = void then
      root_node := replace
    else
      if item_node = previous.left then
        previous.link_left (replace)
      else
        previous.link_right (replace)
      end
    end
  end

end -- class SEARCH_TREE
```

Listing 10.11 Class SEARCH_TREE—Iterative Version

```
class SEARCH_TREE [T -> COMPARABLE]
  -- Iterative version

inherit
  BINARY_T [T]

feature {NONE}

  leaf_node (item: T): NODE [T] is
      -- Returns the leaf node just above the new_node being inserted
    local
      return_node: NODE [T]
      current_node: NODE [T]
    do
      from
        current_node := root_node
      until
        current_node = void
      loop
        return_node := current_node
```

```
          if item < current_node.information then
            current_node := current_node.left
          else
            current_node := current_node.right
          end
        end
        Result := return_node
      ensure
        Result /= void
      end

    present (item: T): BOOLEAN is
      local
        current_node: NODE [T]
      do
        from
          current_node := root_node
        until
          Result = true or current_node = void
        loop
          if item = current_node.information then
            Result := true
          elseif item < current_node.information then
            current_node := current_node.left
          else
            current_node := current_node.right
          end
        end
      end

  feature -- Queries

    is_present (item: T): BOOLEAN is
      do
        Result := present (item)
      end

    insert (item: T) is
      local
        insert_under: NODE [T]
        new_node: NODE [T]
      do
        if root_node = void then
```

```
      !! root_node.make (item)
    else
      insert_under := leaf_node (item)
      !! new_node.make (item)
      if item < insert_under.information then
        insert_under.link_left (new_node)
      else
        insert_under.link_right (new_node)
      end
    end
  end

  delete (item: T) is
    -- Same details as in Listing 10.10
    end

end -- class SEARCH_TREE
```

10.6 The need for tree balancing

Figure 10.15 shows a perfectly balanced tree with 15 nodes ($2^4 - 1$).

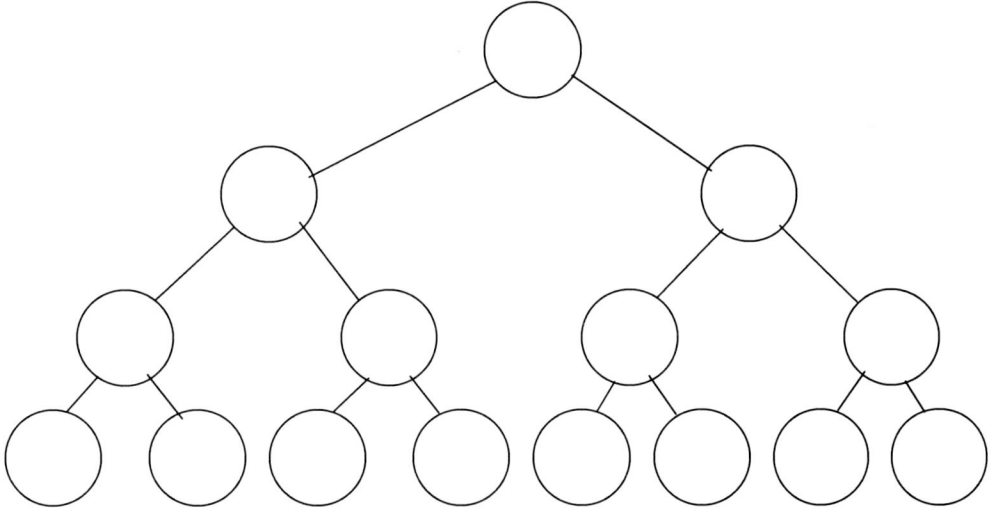

Figure 10.14 A balanced binary tree.

The number of levels in the balanced tree of Figure 10.15 is 4. The number of nodes is 15. The relationship between the number of nodes and

The Need for Tree Balancing

the number of levels is approximately: *number_levels* = $\log_2$ (*number_nodes*). Let us consider the implication of this. Suppose we construct a roughly balanced binary search tree with 1 million nodes. The number of levels would be approximately 20 (since 2^{20} is slightly more than 1 million). To search such a large but balanced binary tree would require no more than 20 comparison operations. In contrast, if a linked-list were used to hold the 1 million nodes, then the largest number of comparison operations would equal the number of nodes, namely, 1 million. The improvement in search-time efficiency between the roughly balanced search tree of 1 million nodes and the linked-list of 1 million nodes is quite dramatic.

You might well be asking yourself (or perhaps should be asking yourself) "but wait a minute—what assurance do I have that my large search tree would be approximately balanced?" Glad you asked! This is an important question.

Clearly the answer is dependent on the sequence of input data and the sequence of insert and delete operations that are performed in producing the large search tree.

Before we continue, let us design a simple game. We will prompt the user to input exactly 15 distinct integers. We will insert these into a search tree and compare the average internal path length of the resulting tree to that of a perfectly balanced tree with 15 nodes. It might be interesting to compare the percentage difference between the two average path lengths.

A simple application class that plays this game is given in Listing 10.12.

Listing 10.12 A game of trees

```
class APPLICATION

creation
   start

feature

   tree: SEARCH_TREE [INTEGER]

   start is
      local
         index: INTEGER
      do
         io.putstring ("You will be asked to enter 15 distinct integer values%N")
         !! tree
         from
```

```
            index := 0
        until
            index = 15
        loop
            index := index + 1
            io.putstring ("Enter a distinct integer: ")
            io.read_integer
            tree.insert (io.lastint)
            io.new_line
        end
        io.putstring ("The average internal path length of your tree of integers = ")
        io.putreal (tree.average_internal_path_length)
        io.new_line
        io.putstring ("A perfectly balanced tree of 15 nodes has a path length = ")
        io.putreal ((1 + 2 * 2 + 4 * 3 + 8 * 4) / 15.0)
        io.new_line
        io.putstring ("Your tree is ")
        io.putreal (100.0 * (tree.average_internal_path_length - 3.27) / 3.27)
        io.putstring (" percent larger than the perfectly balanced tree%N%N")
    end

end -- class APPLICATION
```

The transactions for a typical game are:

You will be asked to enter 15 distinct integer values

Enter a distinct integer: 113

Enter a distinct integer: 115

Enter a distinct integer: 12

Enter a distinct integer: 19

Enter a distinct integer: 34

Enter a distinct integer: 36

Enter a distinct integer: 13

Enter a distinct integer: 15

Enter a distinct integer: 29

Enter a distinct integer: 1

Enter a distinct integer: 104

Enter a distinct integer: 106

Enter a distinct integer: 125

Enter a distinct integer: 132

Enter a distinct integer: 17

The average internal path length of your tree of integers = 4
A perfectly balanced tree of 15 nodes has a path length = 3.26667
Your tree is 22.3242 percent larger than the perfectly balanced tree

Of course the results of this game can vary greatly depending on the set of input values.

Let us do another experiment. Suppose we construct a search tree containing 2047 nodes. Verify that the average internal path length of a perfectly balanced tree of this size is 10.0 (the answer is slightly greater than 10, but equals 10.00 with two digits of precision). No, we will not ask you or anyone else to enter 2047 numbers from the keyboard. We will load up this tree with randomly generated real numbers (a random number generator class will serve us well here). The question to ponder is how favorably will this tree compare to a perfectly balanced tree. Before we perform this experiment, let us compute the worst case average internal path length (apl), namely that associated with a linked-list like tree containing 2047 nodes. That value may be computed as: 1 + 2 * 2 + 4 * 3 + 8 * 4 + 16 * 5 + ... = 1024. So the continuum of possible values for apl (average internal path length) is:

10.0   1024.0

Where do you suppose the apl of the randomly generated search tree will sit on this line (near the left side, somewhere in the middle, or near the right side)?

We design a simulation program to determine this. Since the results of one tree may be misleading, we generate 100 independent search trees, each of size 2047 nodes. For each tree constructed, we output its apl. We also monitor the largest and smallest apl over the set of 100 runs and output the average of these 100 apls and the largest and smallest values. This will give us an indication regarding the statistical stability of our answer.

Listing 10.13 presents an application class that performs this experiment.

Listing 10.13 Computation of apl for randomly generated search trees

```
class APPLICATION

creation
  start

feature

  my_tree: SEARCH_TREE [REAL]

  rnd: RANDOM_NUMBER

  Size: INTEGER is 2047

  Num: INTEGER is 100

  start is
    local
      index: INTEGER
      expr: INTEGER
      value: REAL
      total: REAL
      max: REAL
      min: REAL
      apl: REAL
    do
      max := 0.0
      min := 1000.0
      !! rnd.initialize
      from
        expr := 0
      until
        expr = num
      loop
        expr := expr + 1
        !! my_tree
        from
          index := 0
        until
          index = size
        loop
          index := index + 1
          rnd.next
```

```
            value := 100.0 * rnd.next_value
            if not my_tree.is_present (value) then
               my_tree.insert (value)
            end
         end
         apl := my_tree.average_internal_path_length
         io.putint (expr)
         io.putstring (". ")
         io.putstring ("The APL of the random search tree = ")
         io.putreal (apl)
         io.new_line
         total := total + apl
         if max < apl then
            max := apl
         end
         if apl < min then
            min := apl
         end
      end
      io.new_line
      io.putstring ("Number of trees constructed = ")
      io.putint (num)
      io.new_line
      io.putstring ("Average internal path length = ")
      io.putreal (total / num)
      io.new_line
      io.putstring ("Maximum internal path length = ")
      io.putreal (max)
      io.new_line
      io.putstring ("Minimum internal path length = ")
      io.putreal (min)
      io.new_line
      io.read_line
   end

end -- class APPLICATION
```

The output of the program is given in Table 10.1.

Table 10.1 Output of simulation of 100 random search trees

1. The APL of the random search tree = 13.4353
2. The APL of the random search tree = 12.7372
3. The APL of the random search tree = 13.0132
4. The APL of the random search tree = 13.4358
5. The APL of the random search tree = 12.4958
6. The APL of the random search tree = 13.4314
7. The APL of the random search tree = 13.5305
8. The APL of the random search tree = 13.1979
9. The APL of the random search tree = 12.5398
10. The APL of the random search tree = 13.1975
11. The APL of the random search tree = 13.6615
12. The APL of the random search tree = 13.9375
13. The APL of the random search tree = 13.5452
14. The APL of the random search tree = 14.0298
15. The APL of the random search tree = 13.2941
16. The APL of the random search tree = 13.3835
17. The APL of the random search tree = 13.3048
18. The APL of the random search tree = 13.5638
19. The APL of the random search tree = 12.7655
20. The APL of the random search tree = 13.3864
21. The APL of the random search tree = 13.0415
22. The APL of the random search tree = 14.107
23. The APL of the random search tree = 13.8803
24. The APL of the random search tree = 13.9502
25. The APL of the random search tree = 13.0484
26. The APL of the random search tree = 13.0728

The Need for Tree Balancing

Table 10.1 Output of simulation of 100 random search trees (continued)

27. The APL of the random search tree = 12.7382

28. The APL of the random search tree = 12.9428

29. The APL of the random search tree = 13.7826

30. The APL of the random search tree = 13.4519

31. The APL of the random search tree = 13.5154

32. The APL of the random search tree = 14.0845

33. The APL of the random search tree = 14.0616

34. The APL of the random search tree = 13.4392

35. The APL of the random search tree = 12.892

36. The APL of the random search tree = 14.1104

37. The APL of the random search tree = 12.3659

38. The APL of the random search tree = 13.6507

39. The APL of the random search tree = 13.681

40. The APL of the random search tree = 12.9091

41. The APL of the random search tree = 13.7885

42. The APL of the random search tree = 13.6561

43. The APL of the random search tree = 12.9326

44. The APL of the random search tree = 12.9223

45. The APL of the random search tree = 13.5843

46. The APL of the random search tree = 13.1602

47. The APL of the random search tree = 13.1299

48. The APL of the random search tree = 13.001

49. The APL of the random search tree = 13.0713

50. The APL of the random search tree = 12.917

51. The APL of the random search tree = 12.7313

52. The APL of the random search tree = 13.9248

53. The APL of the random search tree = 12.7396

Table 10.1 Output of simulation of 100 random search trees (continued)

54. The APL of the random search tree = 12.7245
55. The APL of the random search tree = 13.6492
56. The APL of the random search tree = 13.6937
57. The APL of the random search tree = 12.5061
58. The APL of the random search tree = 13.2452
59. The APL of the random search tree = 12.7108
60. The APL of the random search tree = 12.7963
61. The APL of the random search tree = 14.0493
62. The APL of the random search tree = 12.7274
63. The APL of the random search tree = 13.1089
64. The APL of the random search tree = 12.5374
65. The APL of the random search tree = 13.0655
66. The APL of the random search tree = 12.5725
67. The APL of the random search tree = 13.2946
68. The APL of the random search tree = 13.2374
69. The APL of the random search tree = 13.5975
70. The APL of the random search tree = 12.5603
71. The APL of the random search tree = 14.3092
72. The APL of the random search tree = 12.9722
73. The APL of the random search tree = 13.1983
74. The APL of the random search tree = 13.5838
75. The APL of the random search tree = 12.5579
76. The APL of the random search tree = 13.9604
77. The APL of the random search tree = 12.3425
78. The APL of the random search tree = 12.7126
79. The APL of the random search tree = 13.1871
80. The APL of the random search tree = 13.873

The Need for Tree Balancing

Table 10.1 Output of simulation of 100 random search trees (continued)

81. The APL of the random search tree = 14.0874
82. The APL of the random search tree = 15.1588
83. The APL of the random search tree = 13.618
84. The APL of the random search tree = 12.9091
85. The APL of the random search tree = 12.594
86. The APL of the random search tree = 14.478
87. The APL of the random search tree = 13.0459
88. The APL of the random search tree = 13.3224
89. The APL of the random search tree = 12.8183
90. The APL of the random search tree = 12.5315
91. The APL of the random search tree = 13.0166
92. The APL of the random search tree = 12.6297
93. The APL of the random search tree = 13.2257
94. The APL of the random search tree = 12.7499
95. The APL of the random search tree = 13.7509
96. The APL of the random search tree = 12.7782
97. The APL of the random search tree = 14.1915
98. The APL of the random search tree = 13.1808
99. The APL of the random search tree = 14.7841
100. The APL of the random search tree = 13.0352

Number of trees constructed = 100

Average internal path length = 13.2885

Maximum internal path length = 15.1588

Minimum internal path length = 12.3425

From Table 10.1, it is evident that the average internal path length for the random search trees is about 32 percent higher than a perfectly balanced tree. That implies that the search-time performance of a randomly generated search-tree would be about 32 percent worse than that of a perfectly balanced tree. The apl is very close to the left side of the range of values shown above. It can be theoretically shown that the apl of a random search tree is 1.386 times the apl of a perfectly balanced tree. This simulation has produced excellent results. It should also be clear from the simulation results that the variance around this mean is quite small. That indicates that the mean value computed by this simulation is a good predictor of apl for any random search-tree.

What about nonrandom search trees—the kind that we encounter in practice? That important issue is the subject of Exercise 10.11. Suffice it to say here that if the pattern of input values departs, even so slightly from total randomness, the apl of the resulting search-tree increases significantly compared to the apl of a random search-tree. This motivates the work of Chapter 11. In this next chapter we investigate procedures for assuring that a search-tree remains balanced after both insertion and deletion.

10.7 Summary

- A binary tree is one of the most important nonlinear data structures used for information storage and retrieval in computer science.

- Extremely efficient storage and retrieval algorithms may be designed for specialized kinds of binary trees.

- Formally, a binary tree is a finite set of one or more nodes with properties such that: (1) There is a special node, the root node, that provides an entryway into the structure. (2) The remaining nodes, if any, are partitioned into two disjoint sets, each of which is a binary tree. The disjoint sets are called the left subtree and right subtree of the root. Each node in a binary tree has either zero, one or two children.

- The algorithms for traversing the nodes of a binary tree are recursive. There are three basic algorithms called preorder, inorder, and postorder traversal.

Summary

- We define the average internal path length of a binary tree as follows:

$$averageInternalPathLength = \frac{\sum_{k=1}^{numberOfLevels} k \times numberNodesAtLevel(k)}{numberNodes}$$

- The behavior of a binary tree is defined by its queries and commands.
- The command *insert* requires that the item not be present in the given tree and then guarantees that after its execution is completed that the item is present.
- The command *delete* requires the item be present in the given tree and guarantees that after it is completed that the item is not present.
- Binary search trees are widely used information structures. When they are reasonably balanced they provide efficient access to data.
- A search tree is a binary tree in which each node has a relative "value" that is greater than all its left descendants and smaller than all its right descendants.

10.8 Exercises

1. Compute the average internal path length of the following tree:

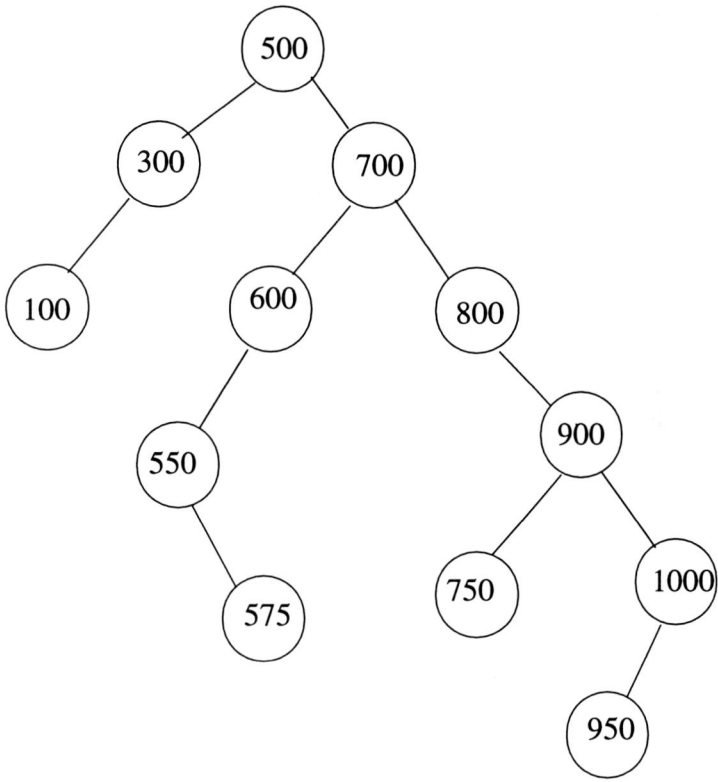

2. For the tree shown in Exercise 1, determine whether this tree is a search tree. State your reasons.

3. Using the tree of Exercise 1, show the output if the nodes are visited using a postorder traversal.

4. Using the tree of Exercise 1, show the output if the nodes are visited using a preorder traversal.

5. Using the tree of Exercise 1, show the output if the nodes are visited using a inorder traversal.

6. Write a function query (in class SEARCH_TREE) that takes an item as input and returns the level of that item in the tree (if the item is present).

EXERCISES

7. Write a function query (in class SEARCH_TREE) that determines whether the tree is perfectly balanced.

8. Do the leaf nodes in a binary tree occur in the same order for preorder, inorder and postorder traversals? Why?

9. Write and test a recursive version of delete for a search tree.

10. Perform a simulation experiment in which you generate 20 random search trees, each with 511 nodes. Compute the minimum and maximum depths of each search tree (you should output 20 minimum depths and 20 maximum depths). The minimum depth is defined as the level of the highest leaf node. The maximum depth is defined as the level of the lowest leaf node (measured from the top of the tree).

11. This simulation project investigates the affect of ordering input data on the apl of the search tree produced by the input data. Suppose we load an array of 1000 real numbers with random real values between 0.0 and 1.0. We construct a search tree using this random sequence as input. We compute and record the apl of this random search tree. Next, we perform one iteration of bubble-sort on the input array and using this partially sorted array, rebuild the search tree from scratch and again compute and record the apl. (Note: one iteration of bubble-sort involves comparing all of the numbers, two at a time, in sequence, and interchanging their order if the first number is larger than the second number and doing nothing if the first number is smaller than the second number.) We continue performing additional iterations of bubble-sort, each time constructing a search tree from the resulting sequence and computing and recording the apl. We do this until the array is completely sorted. Your simulation should output a table with apl in one column and number of iterations of bubble-sort in the second column. Clearly, the values of apl will increase as the number of iterations increases. It is the goal of your simulation experiment to estimate how fast this increase occurs.

Chapter 11

Balanced Search Trees

In this chapter, we investigate two methods for constructing and maintaining balanced search trees. Two distinct types of balanced trees are considered: height-balanced and weight-balanced. It is not realistic to maintain perfectly balanced trees. Such trees require that the number of nodes equals two raised to an integer power minus 1 (e.g., 15 nodes, 31 nodes, 63 nodes, etc.).

The challenge in defining the notion of balance is that we must be able to design commands for insertion and deletion that leave the tree balanced using whatever definition we have established for balance. That is, if we assume that our tree is balanced before performing an insertion of a new element or the deletion of an existing element, the tree must also be balanced after either of these operations.

In 1962 the Russian mathematicians G.M. Adelson-Velskii and E.M. Landis defined a workable definition of balance for binary search trees and described procedures for insertion and deletion that maintain balance. The trees that are produced using their methods have been called AVL trees in honor of their important accomplishment. A remarkable result is that usually the average internal path length of an AVL tree approximates the average internal path length of a perfectly balanced tree when the number of nodes is appropriate. As we will see, the balancing criteria for AVL trees is based on height considerations, so therefore they are considered height-balanced trees.

ROTATIONS

More recent work by Gaston Gonnet of the University of Waterloo (1983) defines an alternative definition of balance based on the weights of nodes. The insertion and deletion algorithms for such weight-balanced trees provide outstanding average internal path lengths, generally even slightly smaller than AVL trees. We examine such trees later in this chapter.

11.1 Rotations

Before we consider either AVL or weight-balanced trees we examine a technique that is common to both types of tree balancing—tree rotation. Consider the simple tree configuration given in Figure 11.1

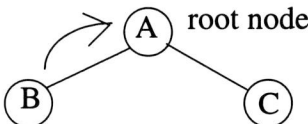

Figure 11.1 (a) Before rotation.

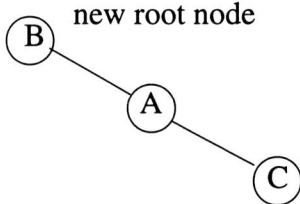

Figure 11.1 (b) After right rotation.

The right rotation may be visualized as applying a right torque (force) to the root node A. This causes node A to move down to the right and node B to move up to the right. Node B becomes the new root node.

In Figure 11.2, we consider a slightly more complicated rotation, this time a left rotation.

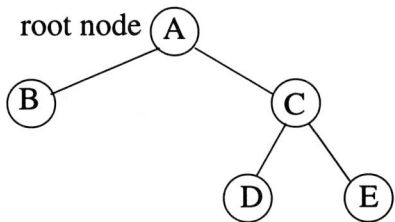

Figure 11.2 (a) Before rotation.

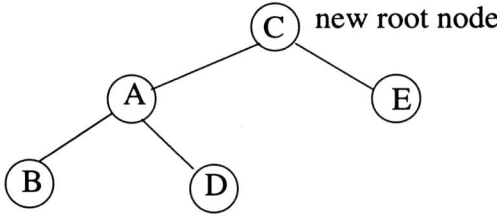

Figure 11.2 (b) After left rotation.

As described before, we envision a torque applied in the counterclockwise direction to node A. This causes node A to rotate down to the left and node C to rotate up to the left. Node C becomes the new root node. Its new left child is node A (a consequence of the twisting force to the left). Its right child continues to be node E. Node A's left child continues to be node B. But what about the location of node D? It can no longer be the left child of node C because as indicated above, node C has the new left child, node A. Since the tree after a rotation must continue to be a search tree, node D must be in the left subtree under node C since its value is smaller than that of node C (it used to be the left child of node C). Its value is also larger than that of node A (it used to be in the right subtree from A). The perfect home for node D is the right child of node A. This assures that its value is larger than node A's and smaller than node C's.

ROTATIONS

The two examples given above both involve rotations with respect to the root node. Rotations may be performed on any node in a tree. We illustrate this concept with the example shown in Figure 11.3.

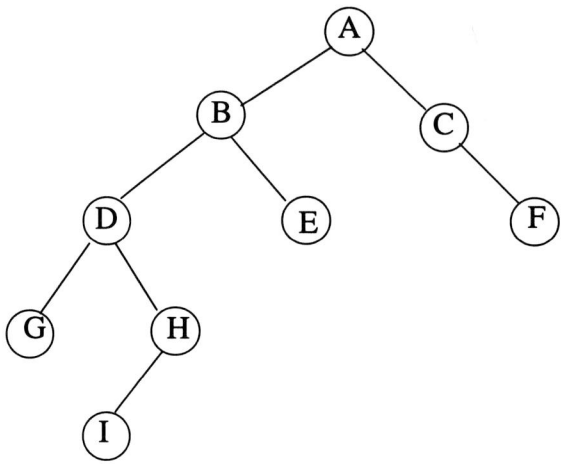

Figure 11.3 (a) Before rotations.

Suppose that we wish to perform the following sequence of rotations: left rotation on node D, followed by a right rotation on node B. We show the resulting trees in Figures 11.3 (b) and 11.3 (c)

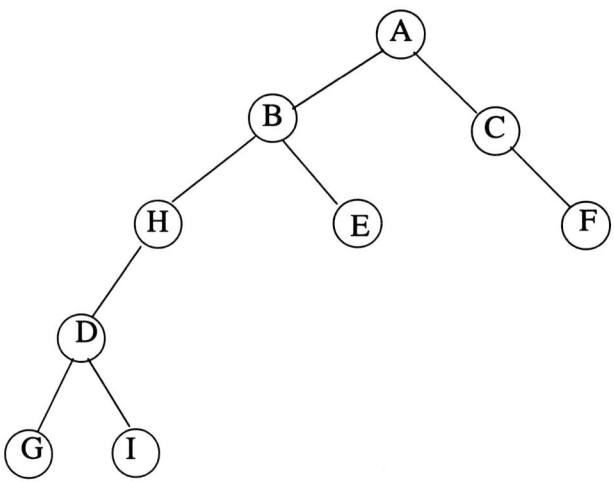

Figure 11.3 (b) After left rotation on node D.

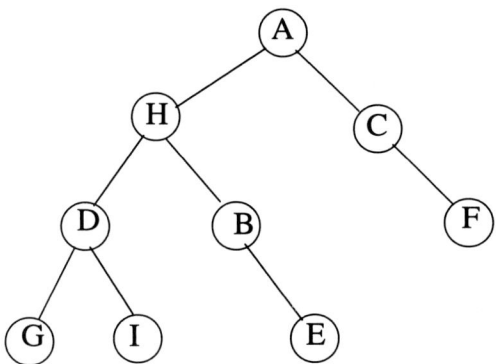

Figure 11.3 (c) After right rotation on node B.

It turns out that the tree resulting from the pair of rotations is more balanced than the original tree of Figure 11.3 (a). This serves as a preview of the fact that if done in the appropriate sequence, rotations about certain nodes have the potential to lower the internal path of the overall tree.

Listings 11.1 and 11.2 show code for implementing leftrotate and rightrotate respectively.

Listing 11.1 Code for leftrotate

```
leftrotate (t: NODE [T]): NODE [T] is
    -- Rotates the subtree about node t and returns a new subroot
  local
    temp: NODE [T]
  do
    temp := t
    Result := t.right
    temp.link_right (Result.left)
    Result.link_left (temp)
  end
```

Listing 11.2 Code for rightrotate

```
rightrotate (t: NODE [T]): NODE [T] is
    -- Rotates the subtree about node t and returns a new subroot
  local
```

ROTATIONS

```
    temp: NODE [T]
do
    temp := t
    Result := t.left
    temp.link_left (Result.right)
    Result.link_right (temp)
end
```

We examine the details of *leftrotate* by considering a left rotation on the search tree shown in Figure 11.4: rotate to the left on node 600.

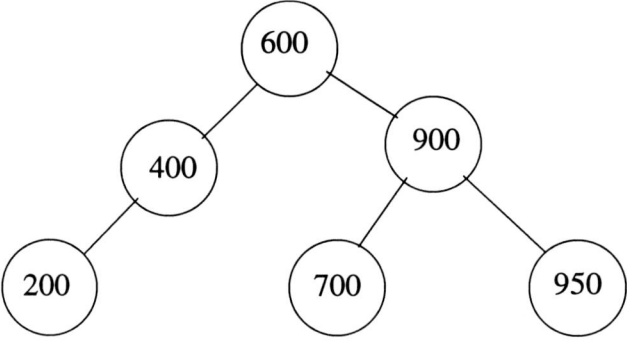

Figure 11.4 Search tree to illustrate *leftrotate*.

As shown in Figure 11.5, *temp* "points" to node 600. *Result* "points" to node 900. Two new links are forged: the right child of *temp* is set to 700 (*Result.left*) and the left child of 900 is set to 600 (*temp*). The function returns node 900 as the new subroot of the rotated subtree.

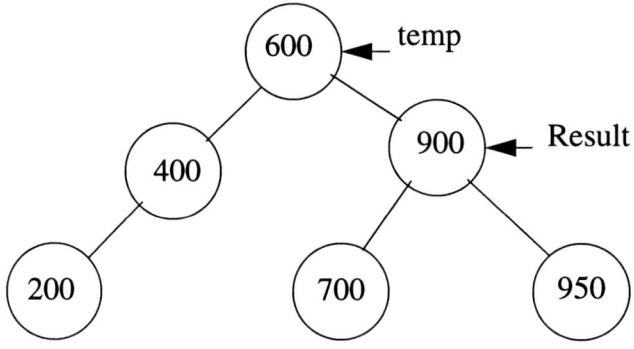

Figure 11.5 Details of *leftrotate*.

BALANCED SEARCH TREES

The rotated tree is shown in Figure 11.6.

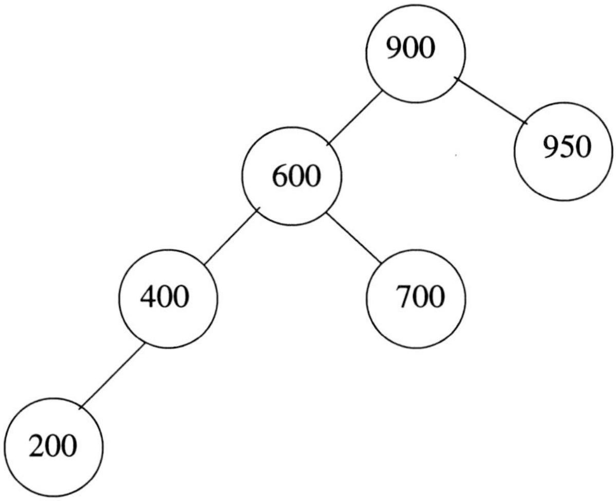

```
          900
         /   \
       600    950
      /   \
    400    700
   /
  200
```

Figure 11.6 Results of *leftrotate*.

It must be noted that the number of new links that must be set is always two, independent of the size of the subtree being rotated. Although the search tree of Figure 11.6 looks quite different from that of Figure 11.5, they differ in only two links. Therefore the computational complexity associated with subtree rotation is relatively modest (i.e., the CPU time associated with four assignment operations.

Can you show that a *leftrotate* and *rightrotate* preserve the search tree property?

11.2 AVL trees

Adelson-Velskii and E.M. Landis define balance as follows:

- Tree is a search tree.

- For each node, the height of its right subtree differs from the height of its left subtree by at most 1 (the height of a subtree is defined as its maximum depth from the node in question).

Figure 11.7 shows a binary search tree that is also an AVL tree. We define the balance of each node as the height of its right subtree minus the height of its left subtree (the opposite definition would of course also suffice but we will stick to this one). The balance of the nodes with nonzero balance are shown next to such nodes.

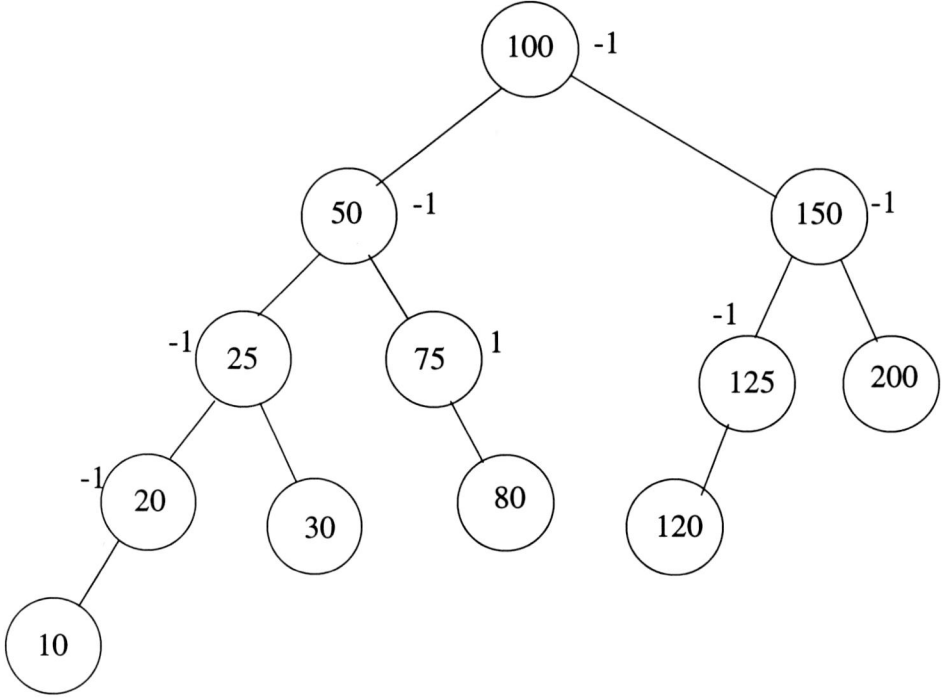

Figure 11.7 AVL tree.

Although there are several nodes that are teetering on the brink of violating the AVL condition, as long as the balance of all nodes is either -1, 0, or 1, the tree is an AVL tree (assuming that it is also a search tree). Therefore the tree in Figure 11.7 is an AVL tree. Its average internal path length compares favorably to the tree with 12 nodes that has minimal average internal path length (see Exercise 2).

To represent an AVL tree we need to augment our definition of tree NODE from that presented in Chapter 10 for ordinary search trees. Specifically, we need to add the integer field *balance*. The modified code for class NODE is shown in Listing 11.3.

Listing 11.3 Modified class NODE

class NODE [T -> COMPARABLE]

creation *{SEARCH_TREE}*
  make

feature *{BINARY_T}*
  information: T

  left: NODE [T]

  right: NODE [T]

  balance: INTEGER -- -1, 0, or 1

  make (item: T) **is**
    do
      information := item
      left := void
      right := void
      balance := 0
    end

  link_left (node: NODE [T]) **is**
    do
      left := node
    end

  link_right (node: NODE [T]) **is**
    do
      right := node
    end

  set_balance (balance_value: INTEGER) **is**
    do
      balance := balance_value
    end

  visit **is**
    do
      print (information)
      io.new_line
    end

end -- class NODE

How might we test whether a search tree is AVL? The query *is_avl* is added to class SEARCH_TREE. If you are wondering why this query is not part of class AVL_TREE the answer is that there is not much point test-

AVL TREES

ing to see whether an AVL tree is an AVL tree. There may be point testing to see whether a plain search tree is also an AVL tree.

The strategy that is used to determine whether a search tree is an AVL tree consists of the following steps:

- Invoke the command *set_balances* (this command computes and assigns each node in the search tree its balance)
- Invoke the query *is_avl* (this query visits each node and determines whether any node has a balance smaller than -1 or greater than 1)

To determine the balance of a given node, the height of its right subtree must be computed and then the height of its left subtree. The first height is subtracted from the second height and the difference assigned as the balance for the given node.

To compute the height of a subtree, a recursive routine is established that keeps track of the maximum level among all the nodes that are recursively visited.

It should be clear from this discussion that the task of determining whether a search tree is AVL involves considerable mechanics: computing heights of subtrees, assigning balances to every node, determining whether all the nodes have balances within the prescribed bounds.

Listing 11.4 presents all of the routines involved in the query *is_avl*.

Listing 11.4 Routines associated with the query is_avl

```
feature {NONE}

  avl: BOOLEAN
  depth: INTEGER

  test_avl (node: NODE [T]) is
    do
      if node /= void and avl then
        if node.balance > 1 or node.balance < - 1 then
          avl := false
        end
        test_avl (node.left)
        test_avl (node.right)
      end
    end

  compute_height (node: NODE [T]; level: INTEGER) is
    do
```

```
        if node /= void then
          if level > depth then
            depth := level
          end
          compute_height (node.left, level + 1)
          compute_height (node.right, level + 1)
        end
      end

    height (node: NODE [T]): INTEGER is
      do
        if node = void then
          Result := 0
        else
          depth := 0
          compute_height (node, 0)
          Result := 1 + depth
        end
      end

    balances (node: NODE [T]) is
      do
        if node /= void then
          node.set_balance (height (node.right) - height (node.left))
          balances (node.left)
          balances (node.right)
        end
      end

  feature

    is_avl: BOOLEAN is
        -- Returns True if search tree is an avl_tree
      do
        avl := true
        test_avl (root_node)
        Result := avl
      end

    assign_balances is
        -- Computes and assigns a balance to each node of the tree
      do
```

AVL TREES

```
        balances (root_node)
    end
```

In Exercise 3 you are asked to carefully explain each of the support routines.

11.2.1 AVL insertion

How is insertion performed on AVL trees?

We state and illustrate the algorithm put forth by Adelson-Velskii and Landis.

- Perform an ordinary search tree insertion.

- If after the ordinary insertion all nodes continue to have a balance of between -1 and 1 the insertion is completed.

- If one or more nodes have their balance changed as a consequence of the insertion to either -2 or 2, either a single rotational correction or sequence of two rotational corrections must be performed to correct the imbalance. There are two patterns of balances that were identified and must be recognized. The first pattern requires only a single rotational correction whereas the second pattern requires the sequence of two rotational corrections.

11.2.1.1 Pattern 1

The first pattern is characterized by a parent node with a balance of 2 or -2 and a child node with a balance of 1 or -1, but both balances of the same sign (i.e., positive or negative). In such a case, a single rotation must be performed on the parent node in a direction appropriate to restore balance. We illustrate pattern 1 and the AVL insertion algorithm in Figure 11.8(a). Suppose we insert the value 3 into the tree shown. The tree after the ordinary insertion of 3 is shown. The nonzero balances are shown next to the appropriate nodes.

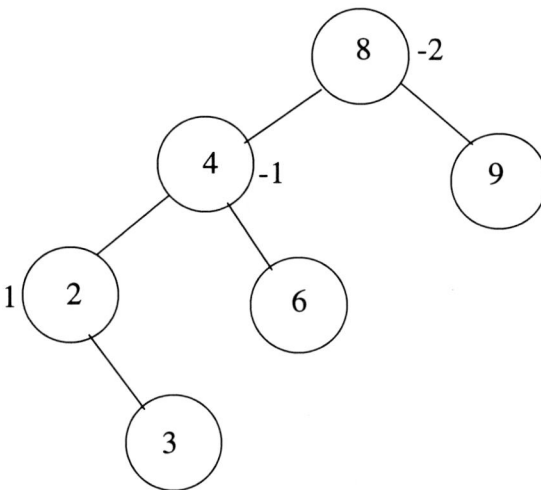

Figure 11.8 (a) Pattern 1 for AVL insertion

The parent node 8, with balance -2, and the child node 4, with balance -1, define this pattern as type 1. The AVL insertion algorithm requires that a single right rotation be performed on node 8. The results are shown in Figure 11.8 (b). Only one node has a nonzero balance. The AVL algorithm has worked as expected.

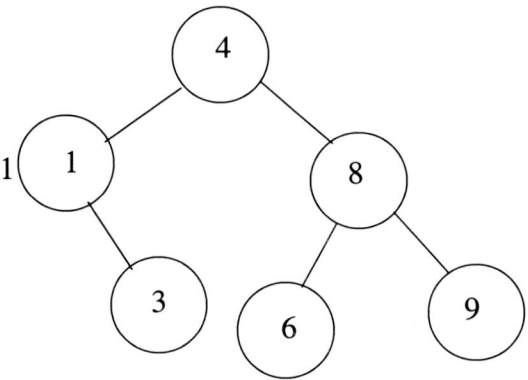

Figure 11.8 (b) Result of insertion.

AVL TREES

11.2.1.2 Pattern 2

The second pattern is characterized by a parent node with a balance of 2 or -2 and a child node with a balance of 1 or -1 but of opposite sign. We illustrate an insertion that leads to pattern 2 and demonstrate the action that must be taken in Figure 11.9. The tree shown in Figure 11.9 (a) represents the configuration after node 5 is inserted.

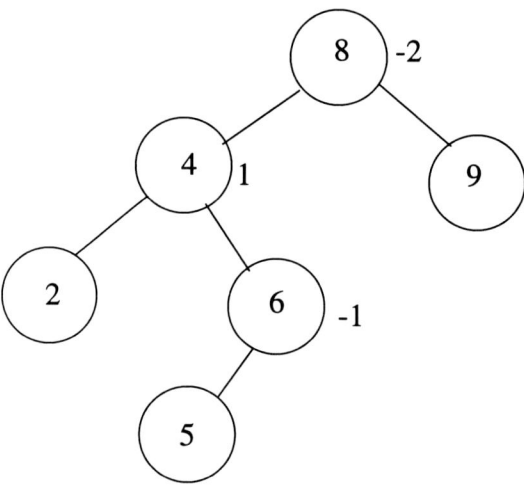

Figure 11.9 (a) Pattern 2 for AVL insertion.

The balances for each node are shown after this insertion. The balance of -2 for node 8, coupled with the balance of 1 in node 4, provides the signature of pattern 2.

The corrective action that is specified in the AVL insertion algorithm for correcting a pattern 2 situation works as follows: (1) perform a rotation on the node with the "1" value (either balance 1 or -1) in a direction to correct only that imbalance, (2) perform a rotation on the node with the "2" value (either 2 or -2) in a direction to correct only that imbalance. The sequence that has just been specified must be strictly adhered to.

In this case these rules translate to: (1) perform a left rotation on node 4 and then (2) perform a right rotation on node 8. The results of these two steps are shown in Figures 11.9 (b) and 11.9 (c).

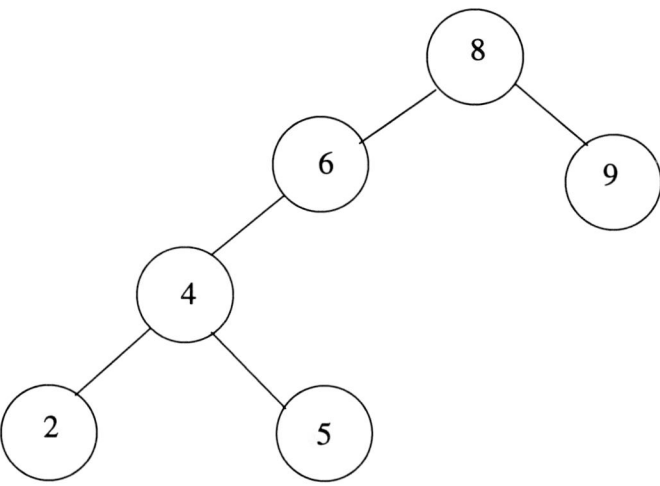

Figure 11.9 (b) Results of first rotation.

The first correctional rotation appears to make matters worse from the viewpoint of the overall tree. This is most typically the case. Certainly, the tree resulting from the first of the two rotations is not an AVL tree. But the tree following the second rotation is guaranteed to be an AVL tree. This we can see by examining Figure 11.9 (c). In this tree, only one of the six nodes has a balance different from 0.

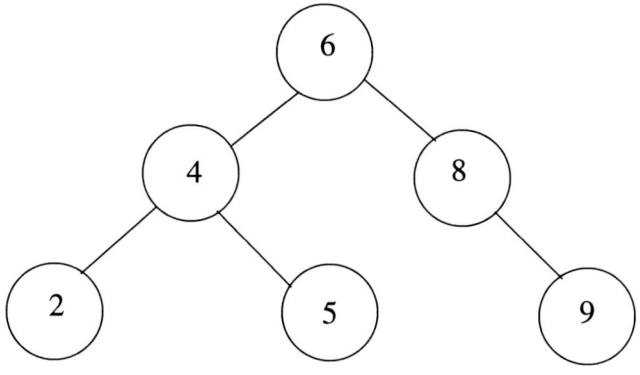

Figure 11.9 (c) Final results of pattern 2 insertion.

AVL TREES

As our final illustration of the AVL insertion algorithm, we consider the construction of an AVL tree with the sequence of values 1, 2, 3, 4, and 5. If one were to construct a search tree using the insertion algorithm presented in Chapter 10, a linked list of depth 5 would result. We trace the steps that are involved in performing 10 AVL insertions and display each of the 5 AVL trees along the way (Figre 11.10 (a) and (b)).

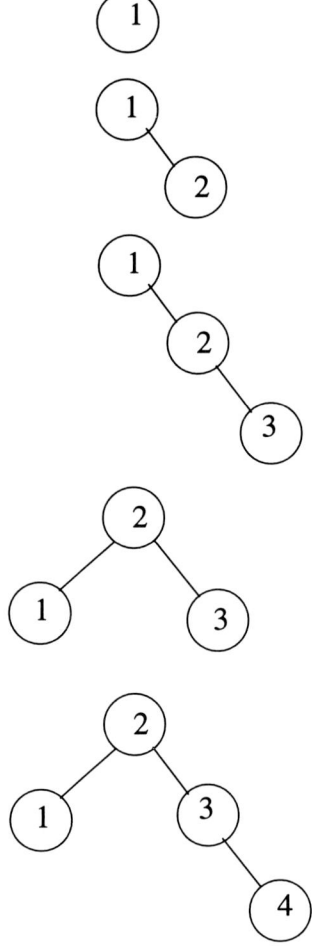

Figure 11.10 (a) Construction of a search tree.

BALANCED SEARCH TREES

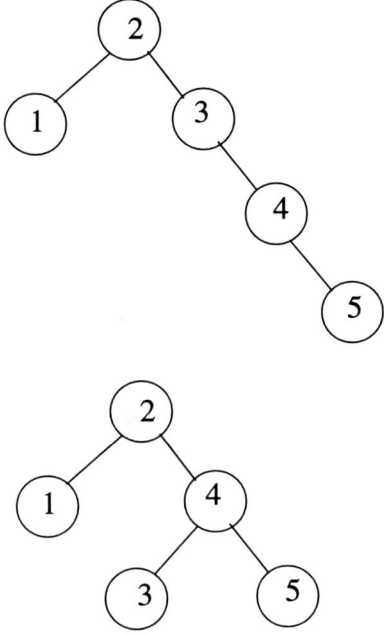

Figure 11.10 (b) Construction of a search tree.

11.2.2 Insertion algorithm

The AVL insertion algorithm is expressed using Eiffel code. This code is presented in Listing 11.5.

Listing 11.5   Class AVL_TREE

```
class AVL_TREE [T -> COMPARABLE]

inherit
  SEARCH_TREE [T]
    redefine
      insert
    end

feature

  insert (item: T) is
      -- Inserts new item into tree
```

AVL TREES

```
    require
        is_avl_tree: is_avl
    local
        return_node: NODE [T]
    do
        if root_node = void then
            !! root_node.make (item)
        else
            return_node := avl_insert (root_node, void, item)
        end
    ensure
        is_avl_tree: is_avl
    end

feature {NONE}

    stop_recursion: BOOLEAN
            -- Controls when the recursion terminates

    leftrotate (t: NODE [T]): NODE [T] is
            -- Rotates the tree about node t and returns a new subroot
        local
            temp: NODE [T]
        do
            temp := t
            Result := t.right
            temp.link_right (Result.left)
            Result.link_left (temp)
        end

    rightrotate (t: NODE [T]): NODE [T] is
        local
            temp: NODE [T]
        do
            temp := t
            Result := t.left
            temp.link_left (Result.right)
            Result.link_right (temp)
        end

    avl_insert (node: NODE [T]; parent: NODE [T]; item: T): NODE [T] is
        local
            p1, p2: NODE [T]
```

```
        return_node: NODE [T]
        new_node: NODE [T]
        res1, res2: NODE [T]
    do
      if node /= void then
        if item < node.information then
          return_node := avl_insert (node.left, node, item)
          if not stop_recursion then
            inspect return_node.balance
            when 1 then
              return_node.set_balance (0)
              stop_recursion := true
            when 0 then
              return_node.set_balance (- 1)
            when -1 then
              p1 := return_node.left
              if p1.balance = - 1 then
                return_node.set_balance (0)
                res2 := rightrotate (return_node)
                if parent /= void then
                  if res2.information < parent.information then
                    parent.link_left (res2)
                  else
                    parent.link_right (res2)
                  end
                else
                  root_node := res2
                end
              else
                p2 := p1.right
                if p2.balance = - 1 then
                  return_node.set_balance (1)
                else
                  return_node.set_balance (0)
                end
                if p2.balance = 1 then
                  p1.set_balance (- 1)
                else
                  p1.set_balance (0)
                end
                res1 := leftrotate (p1)
```

```
            return_node.link_left (res1)
            res2 := rightrotate (return_node)
            if parent /= void then
              if res2.information < parent.information then
                parent.link_left (res2)
              else
                parent.link_right (res2)
              end
            else
              root_node := res2
            end
          end
          res2.set_balance (0)
          stop_recursion := true
        end
      end
  elseif item > node.information then
    return_node := avl_insert (node.right, node, item)
    if not stop_recursion then
      inspect return_node.balance
      when -1 then
        return_node.set_balance (0)
        stop_recursion := true
      when 0 then
        return_node.set_balance (1)
      when 1 then
        p1 := return_node.right
        if p1.balance = 1 then
          return_node.set_balance (0)
          res2 := leftrotate (return_node)
          if parent /= void then
            if res2.information < parent.information then
              parent.link_left (res2)
            else
              parent.link_right (res2)
            end
          else
            root_node := res2
          end
        else
          p2 := p1.left
```

```
                    if p2.balance = 1 then
                        return_node.set_balance (- 1)
                    else
                        return_node.set_balance (0)
                    end
                    if p2.balance = - 1 then
                        p1.set_balance (1)
                    else
                        p1.set_balance (0)
                    end
                    res1 := rightrotate (p1)
                    return_node.link_right (res1)
                    res2 := leftrotate (return_node)
                    if parent /= void then
                        if res2.information < parent.information then
                            parent.link_left (res2)
                        else
                            parent.link_right (res2)
                        end
                    else
                        root_node := res2
                    end
                end
                res2.set_balance (0)
                stop_recursion := true
            end
          end
        end
      else
        stop_recursion := false
        !! new_node.make (item)
        if item < parent.information then
            parent.link_left (new_node)
        else
            parent.link_right (new_node)
        end
      end
      Result := parent
    end

end -- class AVL_TREE
```

11.2.2.1 Explanation of insertion algorithm

The algorithm for AVL insertion is certainly the most complex algorithm presented in this book thus far. It is a recursive algorithm. Both the pre- and postconditions for the *insert* command stipulate that the tree is an AVL tree. That is, the tree must be an AVL tree before the insertion begins and must be an AVL tree upon the conclusion of the insertion.

A protected attribute, *stop_recursion*, of type BOOLEAN, is used to control the recursion. Its scope covers all the routines of the class but, like all features in the NONE section of a class, is only available to all the routines only within the class.

The insert command creates a new *root_node* if the item being inserted is the first to be inserted in the tree otherwise it invokes the recursive procedure *avl_insert*. The first parameter in *avl_insert* represents the node being processed. The second parameter represents the immediate parent of the node being processed.

There are many branch paths that need to be explored if one is to fully understand this relatively complex algorithm. Many examples would have to be generated to cover each of these branch paths. I strongly encourage you to generate several additional examples and walk through the algorithm in a manner similar to the "walk" that we are about to take.

Consider the tree taken partially from Figure 11.9 (a) and reproduced below. We wish to insert an item of value 5 into the existing AVL tree. The only node with a non-zero balance is the root node. It has a balance of -1.

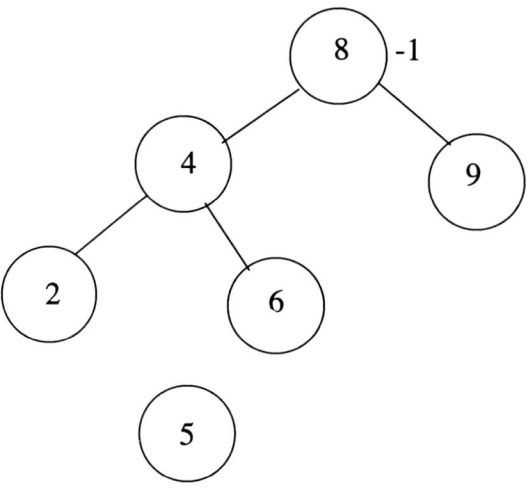

Figure 11.11 Adding node 5 to an existing AVL tree.

BALANCED SEARCH TREES

The *insert* command is invoked with *item* equal to 5. The command *avl_insert* is invoked. Since *item* is less than *node.information* (i.e., 5 is less than 8), the *avl_insert* command is recursively invoked with *node.left* as the first parameter and the result assigned to *return_node*.

Since in the recursive call, *node* "points" to node 4 and *item* is greater than *node.information*, another recursive call is made with node.right as the first parameter and the result assigned to *return_node*.

At this level of recursion, node "points" to node 6. One final recursive call is made to *avl_insert* with the first parameter *node.left* since *item* (5) is less than *node.information* (6).

At the innermost level of recursion, *node = Void* and control is transferred to the final *else* clause. In this block of code a new node, *new_node*, is created with *item*. Now the second parameter of the *avl_insert* command, *parent*, plays an important role. Since the item being inserted has a value smaller than *parent.information*, the command *parent.link_left (item)* is invoked. The result that is returned is *parent*. This returns control to the previous level of the recursion.

One line below *return_node := avl_insert (node.left, node, item)*, an *inspect* multiway branch is evaluated. Since the current balance of node 6 is 0, the balance of this node is set to -1. Control is transferred to the previous level of recursion with *return_node* equal to node 4.

One line below *return_node := avl_insert (node.right, node, item)*, another *inspect* multiway branch is evaluated. The balance equal to 0 branch causes the balance of node 4 to be set to 1. Control is transferred to the outermost level of the recursion with return_node equal to node 8.

One line below *return_node := avl_insert (node.left, node, item)*, an *inspect* multiway branch is evaluated one final time. The -1 case is the most involved. Let us examine all of its details:

The node *p1* is assigned to node 4 (*return_node.left*). Since the balance of node *p1* equals 1, *p2* is assigned to node 6 (*p1.right*). Since the balance of *p2* equals -1, the balance of node 8 is set to 1.

The command *leftrotate* is invoked on node 4 (*p1*) and the node returned is *res1*. Node 8 is linked to *res1* using *return_node.link_left (res1)*. The command *rightrotate* is invoked on node 8 (*return_node*).

Since parent equals *Void*, *root_node* is assigned to *res2*. The balance of *res2* is set to 0. The boolean variable *stop_recursion* is assigned to *true*.

The algorithm terminates, having correctly performed a left rotate on node 4 followed by a right rotate on node 8.

AVL TREES

11.2.3 Deletion algorithm

How is deletion performed on AVL trees?

We state and illustrate the algorithm put forth by Adelson-Velskii and Landis.

- Perform an ordinary search tree deletion.

- If after the ordinary deletion all nodes continue to have a balance of between -1 and 1 the deletion is completed.

- If one or more nodes have their balance changed as a consequence of the deletion to either -2 or 2, then it is possible that each node in the search path from root to the deleted node may require a single rotation or a pair of rotations using the same criteria as described in Section 11.2.1.

There are two basic differences in what may be required in deletion, compared to insertion. It may be necessary to perform one or two rotations with respect to some or all of the nodes in the search path from root to deleted node, whereas for insertion only a single or pair of rotations is required. This will be illustrated below. During deletion, one may encounter an interface between a parent node with a balance of 2 or -2 and a child node with a balance of 0. This 2, 0 or -2, 0 interface is not possible with insertion. If such an interface occurs, it must be handled using the same rules that apply to a "2, 1" interface (i.e., 2, 1, or 2, -1, or -2, 1, or -2, -1 interface), namely, a single rotational correction in a direction to restore balance. This will be illustrated below as well.

We consider several examples of deletion to illustrate the above rules.

In Figure 11.12 (a) we start with an AVL tree from which we wish to delete node 150.

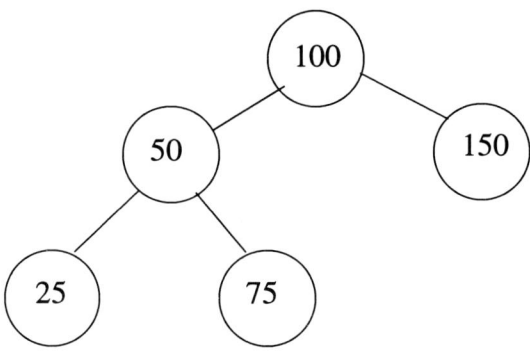

Figure 11.12 (a) AVL before deletion.

After performing an "ordinary" search tree-like deletion, the AVL tree, with balances shown, looks like Figure 11.12 (b).

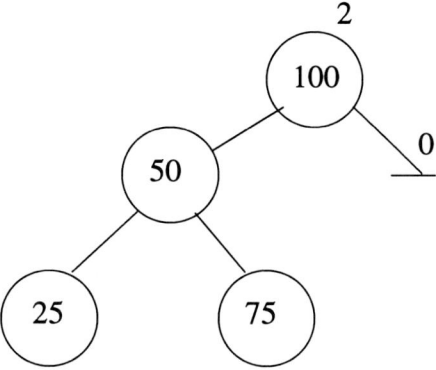

Figure 11.12 (b) AVL tree before rotations.

The "2, 0" combination of nodes discussed above appears in this example. The algorithm for deletion specifies that a rotation be performed on node 100 in a direction to restore balance (a right rotation in this case). The final result is shown in Figure 11.12 (c).

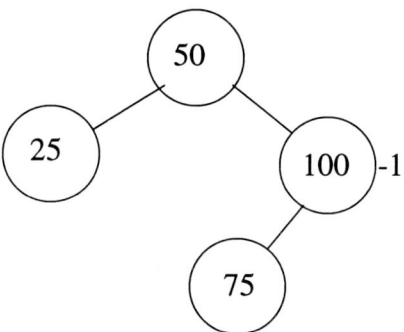

Figure 11.12 (c) AVL tree after rotations.

We next consider a more complex example. Consider the AVL tree shown in Figure 11.13 (a). This is the same tree as shown in Figure 11.7. We wish to delete node 200 from this tree.

AVL TREES

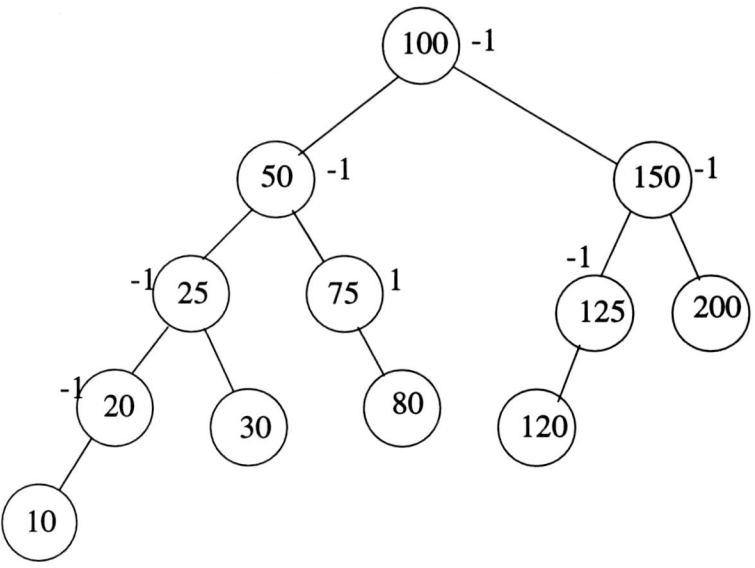

Figure 11.13 (a) AVL tree before deletion.

After performing an ordinary search-tree deletion, the resulting tree is:

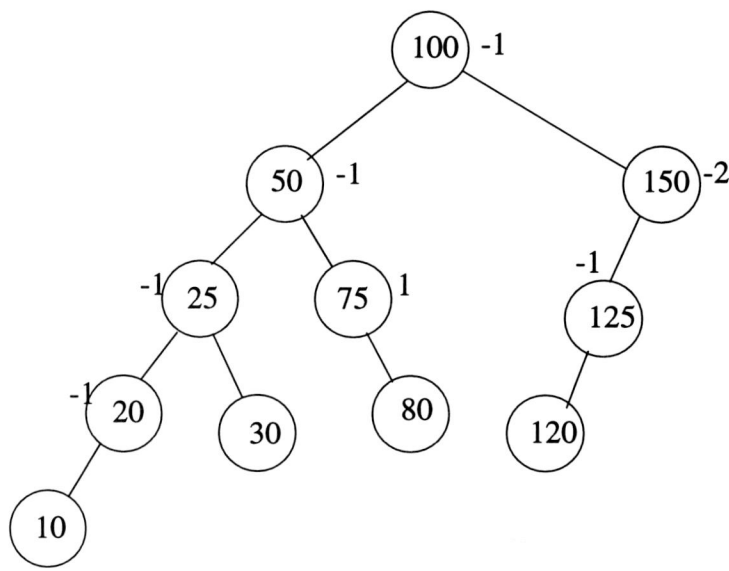

Figure 11.13 (b) AVL tree after ordinary deletion.

It would seem that our only requirement is to perform a single right rotation about node 150 (because of the -2, -1 interface). Figure 11.13 (c) shows the search tree resulting from this single rotation.

The consequence of this single right rotation about node 150 is to cause the root node, 100, to acquire a balance of -2. The -2, -1 combination necessitates a right rotation with respect to node 100.

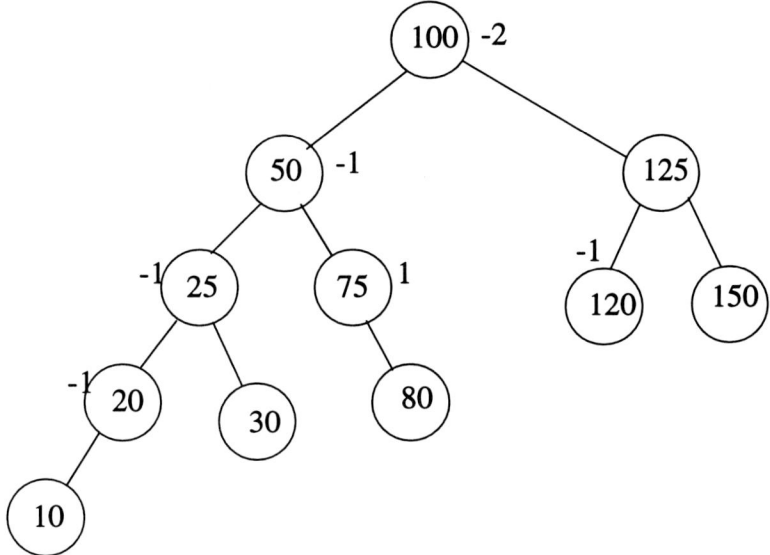

Figure 11.13 (c) AVL tree after first rotation.

Every node in the search path from root to deleted node has required a rotation. The final AVL tree is shown in Figure 11.13 (d). Few nodes have nonzero balances, as shown.

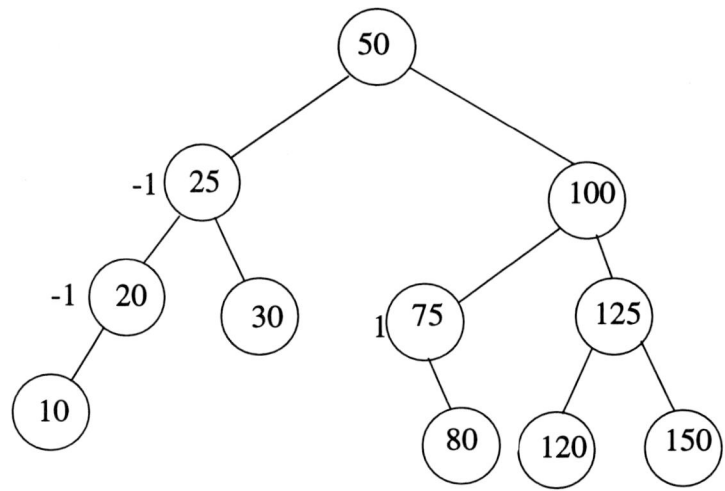

Figure 11.13 (d) Final AVL tree after deletion.

The implementation details for AVL deletion are quite involved. The interested reader may wish to consult Sincovec and Wiener[1] for the algorithmic details of AVL deletion implemented in another language.

11.3 Weight-balanced trees

Weight-balanced trees, proposed by Gaston Gonnet in 1983, require a single or double rotation on a node whenever such rotation can reduce the total internal path length of the subtree associated with the node. Gonnet shows that using such a strategy, the worst case internal path length is never more than 5 percent worse than optimal and the height never more than 44 percent taller than optimal. This compares favorably with AVL trees, for which a worst case of 28 percent worse than optimal internal path length and the same 44 percent taller than optimal constraints prevail.

A binary search tree is internal-path balanced (IPB) if no single or double rotation on any of its nodes will decrease its internal path length. When an insertion or deletion is performed on an IPB tree, the only nodes that may fail the balance conditions are those in the path from the root to the new or deleted node.

BALANCED SEARCH TREES

11.3.1 Conceptual framework

We define the weight of a node as the sum of the weights of its two children. If a node has only one child, its weight equals the weight of the child plus one. If a node has no children, its weight is two (i.e., each Void offspring is considered to have a weight of one).

Figure 11.14 shows a binary search tree that is IPB with the weight of each node shown next to the node. We will see shortly that this tree is weight balanced.

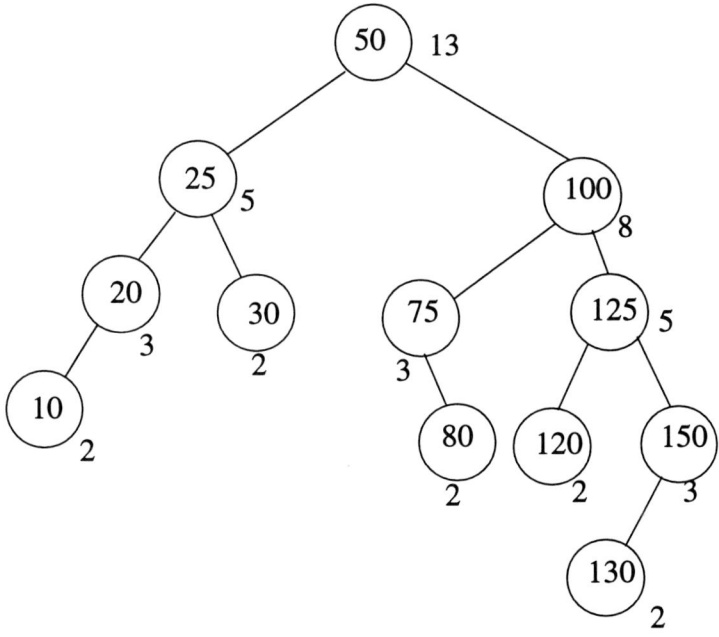

Figure 11.14 Search tree with weights shown.

Insertion into a weight-balanced tree consists of first performing an ordinary search-tree insertion and then testing each node to determine whether any rotation(s) are required. The algorithm for determining whether any rotations on a node are required is:

Algorithm check_rotations (t : NODE [T])

L := weight of left child
R := weight of right child
LL := weight of left node's left child
LR := weight of left node's right child

Weight-balanced trees

```
RR := weight of right node's right child
RL := weight of right node's left child
if R > L then
    if RR > L then
        leftrotate (t)
        check_rotations (t.left)
    elseif RL > L then
        rightrotate (t.right)
        leftrotate (t)
        check_rotations (t.left)
        check_rotations (t.right)
    end
elseif L > R then
    if LL > R then
        rightrotate (t)
        check_rotations (t.right)
    elseif LR > R then
        leftrotate (t.left)
        rightrotate (t)
        check_rotations (t.left)
        check_rotations (t.right)
    end
end
```

If we apply the *check_rotations* algorithm to every node shown in Figure 11.14, no rotations would be required. This implies that the tree of Figure 11.14 is a weight-balanced tree. Its internal path length could not be improved by performing any rotations on any of its nodes.

We consider an example, in Figure 11.15 (a), of performing an insertion into a weight-balanced tree that requires corrective rotations. We wish to insert node 600 into the tree shown.

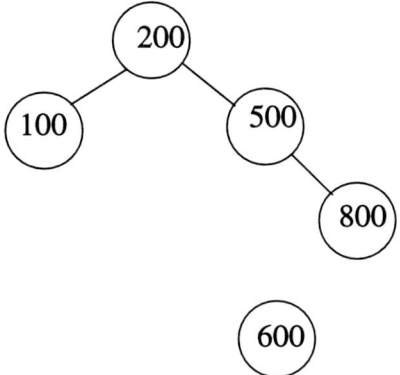

Figure 11.15 (a) Insertion into a weight-balanced tree.

After an ordinary search-tree insertion, the tree of Figure 11.15 (b) is obtained with the weights of each node shown.

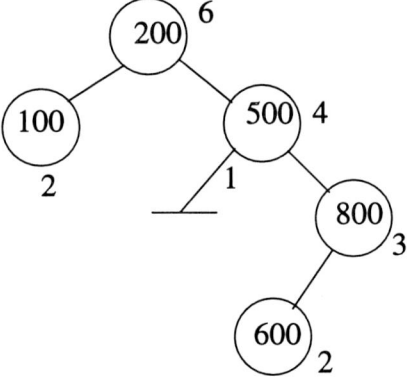

Figure 11.15 (b) After ordinary insertion.

There is a weight imbalance at node 500. This follows since R = 3, L = 1, RL = 2. The algorithm given above suggests a right rotation be performed on node 800, followed by a left rotation on node 500. The tree resulting from these rotations is given in Figure 11.15 (c).

WEIGHT-BALANCED TREES

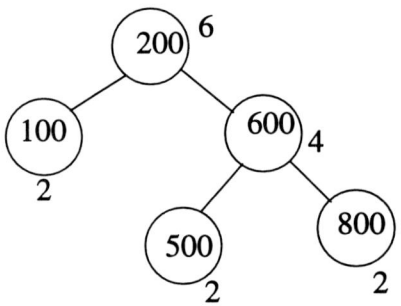

Figure 11.15 (c) Tree after 2 rotations.

There are no further rotations required. The same sequence of rotations would have been required if one were constructing an AVL tree. In general, of course, this will not be the case. Later we compare the properties of AVL and weight-balanced trees.

11.3.2 Implementation of insertion

Listing 11.6 shows the new details of NODE.

Listing 11.6 Modified class NODE

class NODE [T -> COMPARABLE]

creation {SEARCH_TREE}
  make

feature {BINARY_T}

  information: T

  left: NODE [T]

  right: NODE [T]

  balance: INTEGER
    -- -1, 0, or 1

  wt: INTEGER

  make (item: T) **is**
    do

```
      information := item
      left := void
      right := void
      balance := 0
      wt := 2
    end

  link_left (node: NODE [T]) is
    do
      left := node
    end

  link_right (node: NODE [T]) is
    do
      right := node
    end

  set_balance (balance_value: INTEGER) is
    do
      balance := balance_value
    end

  set_weight (weight_value: INTEGER) is
    do
      wt := weight_value
    end

  visit is
    do
      print (information)
      io.new_line
    end

end -- class NODE
```

Listing 11.7 shows the details of class WEIGHT_BALANCED.

Listing 11.7   Class WEIGHT_BALANCED

```
class WEIGHT_BALANCED [T -> COMPARABLE]

inherit
  SEARCH_TREE [T]
    redefine
```

WEIGHT-BALANCED TREES

```
      insert
   end

feature

   insert (item: T) is
      require else
         is_weight_balanced : is_wb
      do
         if root_node = void then
            !! root_node.make (item)
         else
            insert_weight (root_node, void, item)
         end
      ensure
         is_weight_balanced: is_wb
      end

feature {NONE}

   leftrotate (t: NODE [T]): NODE [T] is
         -- Rotates the tree about node t and returns a new subroot
      local
         temp: NODE [T]
      do
         temp := t
         Result := t.right
         temp.link_right (Result.left)
         Result.link_left (temp)
         Result.set_weight (temp.wt)
         temp.set_weight (weight (temp.left) + weight (temp.right))
      end

   rightrotate (t: NODE [T]): NODE [T] is
      local
         temp: NODE [T]
      do
         temp := t
         Result := t.left
         temp.link_left (Result.right)
         Result.link_right (temp)
         Result.set_weight (temp.wt)
```

```
      temp.set_weight (weight (temp.right) + weight (temp.left))
    end
  insert_weight (node: NODE [T]; parent: NODE [T]; item: T) is
    local
      new_node: NODE [T]
    do
      if node = void then
        !! new_node.make (item)
        if item < parent.information then
          parent.link_left (new_node)
        else
          parent.link_right (new_node)
        end
      else
        if item < node.information then
          insert_weight (node.left, node, item)
        else
          insert_weight (node.right, node, item)
        end
        node.set_weight (weight (node.right) + weight (node.left))
        check_rotations (node, parent)
      end
    end
  check_rotations (node: NODE [T]; parent: NODE [T]) is
    local
      wl, wr: INTEGER
      res1, res2: NODE [T]
    do
      if node /= void then
        wl := weight (node.left)
        wr := weight (node.right)
        if wr > wl then
          if weight (node.right.right) > wl then
            res1 := leftrotate (node)
            if parent /= void then
              if res1.information < parent.information then
                parent.link_left (res1)
              else
                parent.link_right (res1)
              end
```

```
        else
          root_node := res1
        end
        check_rotations (node.left, node)
      elseif weight (node.right.left) > wl then
        res1 := rightrotate (node.right)
        node.link_right (res1)
        res2 := leftrotate (node)
        if parent /= void then
          if res2.information < parent.information then
            parent.link_left (res2)
          else
            parent.link_right (res2)
          end
        else
          root_node := res2
        end
        check_rotations (node.left, node)
        check_rotations (node.right, node)
      end
    elseif wl > wr then
      if weight (node.left.left) > wr then
        res1 := rightrotate (node)
        if parent /= void then
          if res1.information < parent.information then
            parent.link_left (res1)
          else
            parent.link_right (res1)
          end
        else
          root_node := res1
        end
        check_rotations (node.right, node)
      elseif weight (node.left.right) > wr then
        res1 := leftrotate (node.left)
        node.link_left (res1)
        res2 := rightrotate (node)
        if parent /= void then
          if res2.information < parent.information then
            parent.link_left (res2)
          else
```

```
              parent.link_right (res2)
            end
         else
            root_node := res2
         end
         check_rotations (node.left, node)
         check_rotations (node.right, node)
       end
     end
   end
 end

weight (t: NODE [T]): INTEGER is
  do
    if t = void then
      Result := 1
    else
      Result := t.wt
    end
  end

end -- class WEIGHT_BALANCED
```

Exercises 11, 12, and 13 ask you to explore various aspects of the code given in Listing 11.7. The *leftrotate* and *rightrotate* commands are different from those of class AVL_TREE. Weights have to be adjusted during the rotation.

The protected query, *weight*, computes the weight of a node in terms of the weights of its children, if any.

Listing 11.8 permits us to compare the performance of AVL and weight-balanced trees. A random AVL tree containing 50,000 nodes is generated. Using the same set of random values, a weight-balanced tree of 50,000 nodes is generated. The time it takes to construct each tree are output. In addition, the average internal path length of each of the trees are output. Upon completing this, another AVL tree containing 50,000 nodes is constructed from the sequence of integers: 1, 2, 3, … ,50,000. Using this same sequence, another weight-balanced tree is constructed. Again the construction times as well as average internal path lengths are computed for each tree. The output is shown below Listing 11.8.

Listing 11.8 Application that compares performance of AVL and weight-balanced trees

```
class APPLICATION

creation
  start

feature

  Size: INTEGER is 50000

  start is
    local
      tm:              TIMER
      avl_tree, t1:    AVL_TREE [REAL]
      wb_tree, t2:     WEIGHT_BALANCED [REAL]
      rnd:             RANDOM_NUMBER
      data:            ARRAY [REAL]
      index:           INTEGER
    do
      !! tm
      !! rnd.initialize
      !! avl_tree
      !! wb_tree
      !! data.make (1, size)
      from
        index := 0
      until
        index = size
      loop
        index := index + 1
        rnd.next
        data.put (rnd.next_value, index)
      end
      tm.start_timing
      from
        index := 0
      until
        index = size
      loop
        index := index + 1
        wb_tree.insert (data.item (index))
```

```
end
tm.end_timing
io.putstring ("Weight-balanced timing results%N")
tm.report
tm.start_timing
from
   index := 0
until
   index = size
loop
   index := index + 1
   avl_tree.insert (data.item (index))
end
tm.end_timing
io.putstring ("AVL timing results%N")
tm.report
io.new_line
io.putstring ("APL (AVL) = ")
io.putreal (avl_tree.average_internal_path_length)
io.putstring (" APL (WB) = ")
io.putreal (wb_tree.average_internal_path_length)
io.new_line
io.new_line
!! t1
!! t2
tm.start_timing
from
   index := 0
until
   index = size
loop
   index := index + 1
   wb_tree.insert (index)
end
tm.end_timing
io.putstring ("Weight-balanced timing results%N")
tm.report
tm.start_timing
from
   index := 0
until
```

```
    index = size
loop
    index := index + 1
    avl_tree.insert (index)
end
tm.end_timing
io.putstring ("AVL timing results%N")
tm.report
io.putstring ("APL (AVL) = ")
io.putreal (avl_tree.average_internal_path_length)
io.putstring (" APL (WB) = ")
io.putreal (wb_tree.average_internal_path_length)
io.new_line
io.new_line
    end

end -- class APPLICATION
```

Table 11.1 Comparison of AVL and Weight-Balanced Trees (Data computed in Listing 11.8.)

On UNIX Workstation Using Finalized ISE Code		
AVL	Time to construct 50,000 random nodes: 21.0992 seconds APL: 14.9239	
	Time to construct 50,000 ordered nodes: 23.0824 seconds APL: 16.5373	
WB	Time to construct 50,000 random nodes: 24.699 seconds APL: 14.8666	
	Time to construct 50,000 ordered nodes: 28.8322 seconds APL: 15.7731	
On 133 MHz Pentium System on Windows'95 Using Finalized Tower Eiffel Code		
AVL	Time to construct 50,000 random nodes: 0.66 seconds APL: 13.9907	
	Time to construct 50,000 ordered nodes: 1.26 seconds APL: 16.1142	
WB	Time to construct 50,000 random nodes: 1.71 seconds APL: 14.8613	
	Time to construct 50,000 ordered nodes: 1.64 seconds APL: 15.8063	

The results suggest that there are no significant differences between the speed and internal path lengths of the trees constructed using AVL and weight-balanced insertion algorithms.

11.4 Summary

- The challenge in defining the notion of balance is that we must be able to design commands for insertion and deletion that leave the tree balanced using whatever definition we have established.

- In 1962, the Russian mathematicians G.M. Adelson-Velskii and E.M. Landis defined a workable definition of balance for binary search trees and described procedures for insertion and deletion that maintain balance.

- More recent work by Gaston Gonnet of the University of Waterloo in 1983 defines an alternative definition of balance based on the weights of nodes.

- Adelson-Velskii and E.M. Landis define balance as follows:

    Tree is a search tree.

    For each node, the height of its right subtree differs from the height of its left subtree by at most one (the height of a subtree is defined as its maximum depth from the node in question).

- If one or more nodes have their balance changed as a consequence of an AVL insertion to either -2 or 2, either a single rotational correction or sequence of two rotational corrections must be performed to correct the imbalance.

- In AVL deletion, it may be necessary to perform one or two rotations with respect to some or all of the nodes in the search path from root to deleted node, whereas for insertion only a single or pair of rotations is required.

- During deletion, one may encounter an interface between a parent node with a balance of 2 or -2 and a child node with a balance of 0.

- Weight-balanced trees, proposed by Gaston Gonnet in 1983, require a single or double rotation on a node whenever such rotation can reduce the total internal path length of the subtree associated with the node.

- A binary search tree is internal-path balanced (IPB) if no single or double rotation on any of its nodes will decrease its internal path length. When an insertion or deletion is performed on an IPB tree, the only nodes that may fail the balance conditions are those in the path from the root to the new or deleted node.

11.5 Exercises

1. Prove that the search tree property is preserved after either a right rotation or left rotation on any node in a search tree.

2. Compute the average internal path length of the AVL tree shown in Figure 11.7. Compare this number to the smallest average internal path length that is possible to achieve for a search tree with 12 nodes.

3. Carefully with explain with diagrams and words each of the support routines associated with the query *is_avl* given in Listing 11.4.

4. Perform a simulation that determines the fraction of insertions into a random AVL tree that requires at least one rotation.

5. Perform a simulation that determines the fraction of insertions into a random AVL tree that requires a single rotation and the fraction that require two rotations.

6. Implement a deletion command for an AVL tree. You may wish to consult Sincovec and Wiener[1] for help.

7. Verify that the search tree shown in Figure 11.14 is a weight-balanced tree.

8. Consider the tree shown below:

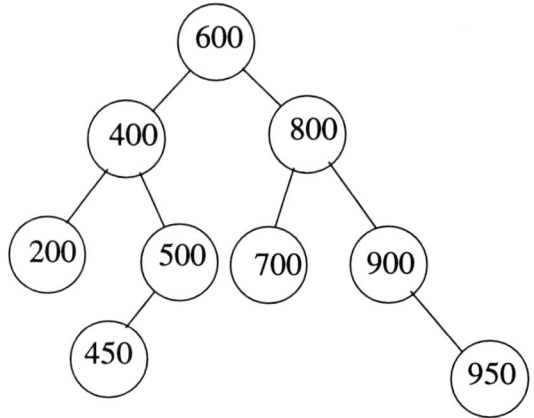

   (a) Show the steps involved in performing an AVL insertion of a node with value 425.
   (b) Show the steps involved in performing a weight-balanced insertion of 425.

9. Sketch the AVL resulting from the insertion of the following nodes: 27, 35, 10, 17, 86, 94, 11, 6, 12, 18, 23, 21, 29, 39, 77, 65, 50.

10. Sketch the weight-balanced tree resulting from the insertion of the same set of nodes given in problem 9.

11. Carefully explain the modified *leftrotate* and *rightrotate* commands in Listing 11.7.

12. Carefully explain the *insert, insert_weight,* and *check_rotations* commands of Listing 11.7.

13. Write the query *is_wb* in class SEARCH_TREE. This query is used in the precondition and postcondition of the insert command. Hint: You should write a *set_weights* command similar to the *set_balances* command. This would assign a weight to each node. After doing this, you should test each node for the same conditions as exist in *check_rotations*.

11.6 Reference

1. Sincovec, R, Wiener, R. *Data Structures Using Modula-2*. New York, John Wiley and Sons, 1986.

Chapter 12

Unordered Collections

This chapter examines two important collection classes in which the elements are not ordered: classes SET and HASH_TABLE. Each of these classes may be used to implement the DICTIONARY abstraction. This abstraction principally requires fast lookup of information to determine whether an item is present or not present in a DICTIONARY.

Applications that require a dictionary include parsers and spelling checkers. In a parser it is necessary to determine which words in the text of a program are reserved words in the underlying language. In a spelling checker, the principal task is to determine whether words found in the text are present or not present in the dictionary. Fast access to elements in a dictionary is typically required.

Before looking closely at the two unordered collection classes SET and HASH_TABLE we introduce another basic Eiffel type—the BIT data type. This data type permits low-level bit manipulations to be performed in system applications.

12.1 The BIT data type

A BIT data type requires the numerical specification of the number of bits associated with each element of this type. A typical declaration, *bit_pattern*, is shown below.

THE BIT DATA TYPE

bit_pattern : BIT 8

Each instance of *bit_pattern* requires an array of eight bits to represent it. Figure 12.1 shows the internal representation of *bit_pattern*.

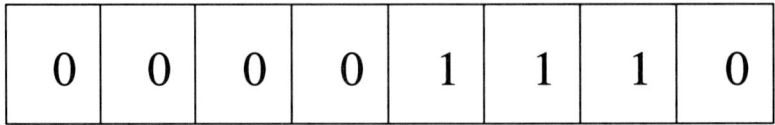

Figure 12.1 An 8-bit pattern.

The numerical value of bit_pattern is 13, the decimal value of the binary number 1110.

Listing 12.1 presents important portions of the interface to the Eiffel class BIT_REF.

Listing 12.1 Portions of the interface to class BIT_REF

```
class BIT_REF
feature -- Access
    item (i: INTEGER): BOOLEAN
        -- i-th bit
    require
        index_large_enough: i >= 1
        index_small_enough: i <= count

    infix "@" (i: INTEGER): BOOLEAN
        -- i-th bit
    require
        index_large_enough: i >= 1
        index_small_enough: i <= count

feature -- Element change
    put (value: BOOLEAN;  i: INTEGER)
        -- Set the i-th bit to 1 if value is True, 0 if False
    require
        index_large_enough: i >= 1
        index_small_enough: i <= count
    ensure
        value_inserted: item (i) = value
    end
```

feature -- Basic operations

  infix "^" (s: INTEGER): **like** Current
    -- Result of shifting bit sequence by s positions
    -- (Positive s shifts right, negative s shifts left
    -- bits falling off the sequence's bounds are lost.)

  infix "#" (s: INTEGER): **like** Current
    -- Result of rotating bit sequence by s positions
    -- (Positive s rotates right, negative s rotates left.)

  infix "and" (other: BIT_REF): BIT_REF
    -- Bit-by-bit boolean conjunction with other
  require
    other_exists: other /= void
    conformance: other.count <= count

  infix "or" (other: BIT_REF): BIT_REF
    -- Bit-by-bit boolean disjunction with other
  require
    other_exists: other /= void
    conformance: other.count <= count

  infix "xor" (other: BIT_REF): BIT_REF
    -- Bit-by-bit exclusive or with other
  require
    other_exists: other /= void
    conformance: other.count <= count

  prefix "not": **like** Current
    -- Bit-by-bit negation

feature -- Output

  out: STRING
    -- Tagged printable representation.

end -- class BIT_REF

12.1.1 Summary of BIT_REF features

The command *put (value : BOOLEAN; i : INTEGER)* allows one to enable a bit (set its value to 1) in the ith position. The first position corresponds to the most significant digit in the number (the first digit reading from left to right).

THE BIT DATA TYPE

The query *item (i : INTEGER) : BOOLEAN* (with infix form "@") allows one to determine whether the bit in the ith position is enabled (is a 1).

The command "#" allows one to rotate the bits to the right or left depending on whether the parameter following the "#" is positive or negative.

The command "^" allows one to shift the bits to the right or left depending on whether the parameter following the "^" is positive or negative.

The command *or* allows one to logically combine the bits of a binary number according to the logical "or" operation (i.e., $0 + 0 = 0$, $0 + 1 = 1$, $1 + 0 = 1$, $1 + 1 = 1$).

The command *and* allows one to logically combine the bits of a binary number according to the logical "and" operation (0 *and* $0 = 0$, 0 *and* $1 = 0$, 1 *and* $0 = 1$, 1 *and* $1 = 1$).

The prefix "not" operation allows one to reverse the bit pattern of a binary number (i.e., 1s become 0s and 0s become 1s).

We illustrate the workings of some of the bit commands and queries discussed above in the sample application given in Listing 12.2.

Listing 12.2 Application that exercises BIT_REF commands and queries

```
class APPLICATION
-- Illustrates the use of several important BIT_REF commands and queries

creation
  start

feature

  start is
    local
      bit_pattern: BIT 8
    do
      io.putstring ("Original bit pattern: ")
      bit_pattern := 00000101B
      output_pattern (bit_pattern)
      bit_pattern := bit_pattern # 4
      io.putstring ("After rotating pattern 4 to the left: ")
      output_pattern (bit_pattern)
      bit_pattern := bit_pattern # 4
      io.putstring ("After rotating pattern 4 more to the left: ")
      output_pattern (bit_pattern)
      bit_pattern := bit_pattern ^ 1
      io.putstring ("After shifting pattern 1 to the right: ")
```

```
            output_pattern (bit_pattern)
            bit_pattern.put (true, 1)
            bit_pattern.put (true, 2)
            io.putstring ("After enabling bits in positions 1 and 2: ")
            output_pattern (bit_pattern)
            bit_pattern := bit_pattern ^ - 1
            io.putstring ("After shifting pattern 1 to the left: ")
            output_pattern (bit_pattern)
            io.new_line
            io.read_line
         end

      output_pattern (pattern: BIT 8) is
         local
            str: STRING
         do
            str := pattern.out
            io.putstring (str)
            io.putstring (" value = ")
            io.putint (value (pattern))
            io.new_line
         end

      value (bit_pattern: BIT 8): INTEGER is
         local
            pos: INTEGER
            power: INTEGER
         do
            power := 1
            from
               pos := 9
            until
               pos = 1
            loop
               pos := pos - 1
               if bit_pattern @ pos then
                  Result := Result + power
               end
               power := power * 2
            end
         end
```

end *-- class APPLICATION*

The output of Listing 12.2 is the following:

Original bit pattern: 00000101 value = 5
After rotating pattern 4 to left: 01010000 value = 80
After rotating pattern 4 more to the left: 00000101 value = 5

After shifting pattern 1 to the right: 00000010 value = 2
After enabling bits in positions 1 and 2: 11000010 = 194
After shifting pattern 1 to the left6: 10000100 value = 132

It is left as an exercise for you to explain the output given above.

12.2 The Set abstraction

A set is a basic abstraction in mathematics and in computer science. It is an unordered collection of elements with no duplicate elements allowed. In addition to the operations of *insert* and *remove*, the most important operation on a set is the query *present (item : T) : BOOLEAN*, where T is the type stored in the set. This function returns True if *item* is in the set otherwise it returns False. As indicated earlier, we generally desire this function to perform its work quickly.

Other operations often associated with combining two sets include *union* and *intersection*. The union of two sets returns a set containing all of the elements that are in one or the other or both of the operand sets. The intersection of two sets returns only the elements that are common to both operand sets.

An UNORDERED_LIST can serve to support the set abstraction. This class contains a query *present* as part of its protocol. The problem with using an UNORDERED_LIST is its efficiency. To determine whether an element is present in the set, potentially every element in the structure must be searched. For large structures, this imposes considerable computational overhead, as will be seen later.

The implementation of SET that we shall pursue in this chapter relies on the low-level type BIT, described earlier.

12.3 Set of integers using BIT type

We shall represent a set of integers using an array whose base type is BIT 32. Each integer maps uniquely to a particular index location in this array and a particular bit location within the binary number contained within the index location.

The value of the array index is given by *element // 32* where *//* represents integer division with truncation (e.g., *3 // 2 = 1, 17 // 3 = 5, 5 // 12 = 0*).

The unique position within the BIT 32 pattern (the binary number stored at the index location in the array) is given by *element \\ 32*, where ** represents the remainder operator (e.g., *18 \\ 5 = 3, 23 \\ 7 = 2, 3 \\ 21 = 3*).

The 0th index location of the array used to represent the set of integers contains the integers 0 .. 31. The first index location contains the numbers 32 .. 63. Each subsequent index location contains the next 32 integers.

As an example, consider how the number 767 maps to this array. The value *767 // 32* produces the index 23. At this index location is stored a 32-bit binary number. The value *767 \\ 32* produces the position 31 (from right to left). This corresponds to the bit location one to the right of the most significant digit. This bit can be enabled (set to 1) by using the command *put (TRUE, 2)* on the element in the 23rd index location.

Figure 12.2 shows this mapping.

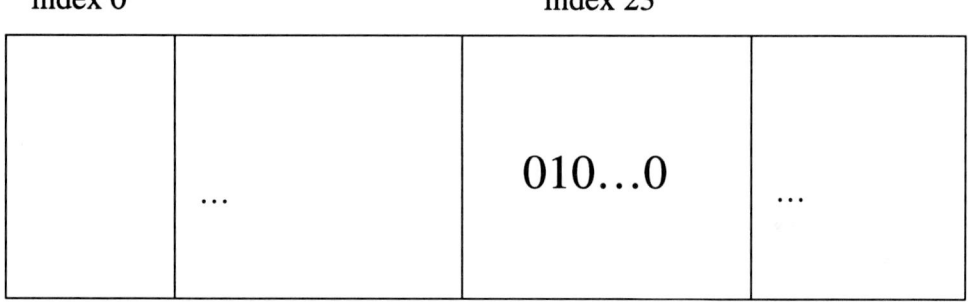

Figure 12.2 Mapping 767 to array.

Listing 12.3 shows an implementation of INTEGER_SET.

Listing 12.3   Class INTEGER_SET

class *INTEGER_SET*
   -- Implements the set abstraction for base type INTEGER

creation
   make

feature *{INTEGER_SET}*

   elements: ARRAY [BIT 32]

SET OF INTEGERS USING BIT TYPE

feature *{NONE}*

  num_zero: BIT 32

feature

  capacity: INTEGER

  number_elements: INTEGER

  make (highest_element: INTEGER) **is**
    require
      positive_number_elements: highest_element > 0
    local
      index: INTEGER
    do
      capacity := highest_element + 1
      !! elements.make (0, highest_element // 32)
      from
        index := - 1
      until
        index = highest_element // 32
      loop
        index := index + 1
        elements.put (num_zero, index)
      end
    end

  insert (element: INTEGER) **is**
    require
      non_negative_element: element >= 0
      within_range: element <= capacity - 1
      not_present: **not** present (element)
    local
      index: INTEGER
      bits: BIT 32
    do
      index := element // 32
      bits := elements.item (index)
      bits.put (**true**, 32 - (element \\ 32))
      elements.put (bits, index)
      number_elements := number_elements + 1
    ensure

```
      number_elements = old number_elements + 1
   end
remove (element: INTEGER) is
   require
      non_negative_element: element >= 0
      within_range: element <= capacity - 1
      is_present: present (element)
   local
      index: INTEGER
      bits: BIT 32
   do
      index := element // 32
      bits := elements.item (index)
      bits.put (false, 32 - (element \\ 32))
      elements.put (bits, index)
      number_elements := number_elements - 1
   ensure
      number_elements = old number_elements - 1
   end
present (element: INTEGER): BOOLEAN is
   require
      non_negative_element: element >= 0
      within_range: element <= capacity - 1
   local
      index: INTEGER
      bits: BIT 32
   do
      index := element // 32
      bits := elements.item (index)
      Result := bits.item (32 - (element \\ 32))
   end
union (another_set: INTEGER_SET): INTEGER_SET is
   require
      same_size: capacity = another_set.capacity
   local
      index: INTEGER
   do
      !! Result.make (capacity)
      from
```

SET OF INTEGERS USING BIT TYPE

```
      index := - 1
    until
      index = (capacity - 1) // 32
    loop
      index := index + 1
      Result.elements.put (elements.item (index) or
                  another_set.elements.item (index), index)
    end
  end

  intersection (another_set: INTEGER_SET): INTEGER_SET is
    require
      same_size: capacity = another_set.capacity
    local
      index: INTEGER
    do
      !! Result.make (capacity)
      from
        index := - 1
      until
        index = (capacity - 1) // 32
      loop
        index := index + 1
        Result.elements.put (elements.item (index) and
                    another_set.elements.item (index), index)
      end
    end

end -- class INTEGER_SET
```

12.3.1 Discussion of Listing 12.3

There are three feature sections in class INTEGER_SET. The first section, with export scope INTEGER_SET, declares an array, *elements*, with base type BIT 32 (binary number containing 32 bits for its internal representation). The export scope is INTEGER_SET because the routines union and intersection each have an INTEGER_SET parameter and need to be able to access the *elements* array from the input.

The second feature section, with export scope NONE, declares *num_zero* to be of type BIT 32. This object is used to initialize the *elements* array in the creation routine *make*.

The third feature section, with public export, declares the attributes *capacity* and *number_elements* as type INTEGER.

In the creation routine, *make*, the initial value of each binary number is set to 32 zeros.

In routine *insert*, the index is set to *element // 32*, as discussed earlier. The binary number, *bits*, contained in the array *elements* at *index* is fetched. The bit at position *32 - element \\ 32* is enabled. Then the binary number *bits* is reinserted into the array at *index*.

The routine *remove* works the same way as *insert*, only instead of enabling the bit at position *32 - element \\ 32*, the routine disables this bit (sets it to value 0).

The routines *union* and *intersection* take *another_set* as a parameter. The logical *or* is used to compute *union*, whereas the logical *and* is used to compute the *intersection* of the two sets.

Listing 12.4 demonstrates the much higher efficiency of the INTEGER_SET compared with the UNORDERED_LIST in implementing the query *present*.

A set of 100,000 integers is loaded into an INTEGER_SET, *my_set*, and an UNORDERD_LIST, *my_list*. The time that it takes to access all of the numbers, one at a time, is computed for each of the two structures. The results are dramatic.

Listing 12.4   Application that compares the efficiency of INTEGER_SET and UNORDERED_LIST

```
class APPLICATION
-- Compare the efficiency of INTEGER_SET and UNORDERED_LIST

creation
   start

feature

   Size: INTEGER is 100000

   my_set: INTEGER_SET

   my_list: UNORDERED_LIST [INTEGER]

   timer: TIMER

   start is
      local
         index: INTEGER
```

Set of integers using BIT type

```
        do
          !! timer
          !! my_set.make (size)
          !! my_list
          io.putstring ("Building my_set and my_list of size ")
          io.putint (size)
          io.new_line
          from
            index := - 1
          until
            index = size - 1
          loop
            index := index + 1
            my_set.insert (index)
            my_list.insert_front (index)
          end
          io.putstring ("Timing of access for every element in INTEGER_SET%N")
          timer.start_timing
          from
            index := - 1
          until
            index = size - 1
          loop
            index := index + 1
            if not my_set.present (index) then
              io.putstring ("Error in program%N")
            end
          end
          timer.end_timing
          timer.report
          io.putstring ("Timing of access for every element in UNORDERED_LIST%N")
          timer.start_timing
          from
            index := - 1
          until
            index = size - 1
          loop
            index := index + 1
            if not my_list.present (index) then
```

```
        io.putstring ("Error in program%N")
      end
    end
    timer.end_timing
    timer.report
  end

  end -- class APPLICATION
```

The output of Listing 12.4 is:

```
Building my_set and my_list of size 100000
Timing of access for every element in INTEGER_SET
Time duration = 0.06 seconds
Timing of access for every element in UNORDERED_LIST
Time duration = 742.64 seconds
```

The INTEGER_SET accessed all of its elements roughly 12,377 times faster. This dramatic result should come as no great surprise, since the INTEGER_SET data structure is specifically designed to provide fast access to its elements.

12.4 Hash functions and tables

A hash function maps an entity such as a string or some other data structure to an integer. This integer may be used as an index into a table called a hash table.

The word "hash" is often used to mean chop into fine and perhaps random sized pieces such as in hash brown potatoes. In the context of data structures, the word "hash" shall mean map an entity into what may appear to be a random index location in a table. Of course the index location is not truly random. It only appears to be, since the hash values of a collection of entities do not appear to follow any simple or easily recognizable pattern.

Suppose we wish to construct a dictionary for a spelling checker using a hash table. We wish to associate each string that represents a given word with an index in the hash table. If the hash function is properly constructed the hash indices associated with an arbitrary set of words will appear to be uniformly distributed (i.e., randomly distributed) across the range of values defined for the hash table. If the hash function is poorly designed then the distribution of hash indices will not be uniform and will

Hash Functions and Tables

exhibit clusters. Figure 12.3 shows the distribution of hash indices for both a good hash function and a poor hash function.

Distribution of values associated with good hash function

Distribution of values associated with a poor hash function

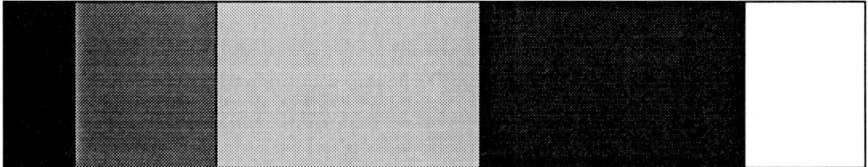

Figure 12.3 Distribution of values associated with hash functions.

The shaded rectangles in the bottom part of Figure 12.3 suggest an uneven distribution of hash indices produced by a poorly designed hash function.

It should be evident that a properly constructed hash function produces an unordered collection, since an ordering of elements has been removed by hashing (dicing) the elements so that they are randomly distributed.

We will continue our discussion about hashing using strings (ordinary words) as our example. The principles that we discuss apply to any set of entities that can be hashed into a table.

Can we expect each word to map to a unique hash index location? Generally, the answer is no. In a good hash function there should be no obvious relationship among the equivalence class of words that produce the same hash index for a specific hash function. But such equivalence classes produce a practical problem when constructing a hash table. Suppose two words symbolized as X and Y produce the same hash index. That is *hash_index* = *hash* (X) = *hash* (Y). We call such a situation a collision. Suppose that the word represented by symbol X is placed into the location given by *hash_index*. Where shall we place the word represented by symbol Y?

We must design a collision-resolution algorithm that provides a consistent mechanism for finding a home for Y or any other word that collides with a previously inserted word.

The two fundamental problems associated with constructing hash tables are:

- Designing a good hash function that randomly distributes indices across the hash table
- Designing a collision-resolution algorithm that finds a new index location for a word in the event that the hash index is currently occupied by another word

We consider each of these problems in the next two subsections.

12.4.1 Design of a good hash function

Most books on algorithm design present mathematical techniques for mapping strings to numbers. We consider in this section a variant on a common method that has been successfully used for mapping strings to hash indices. The technique is valid only for words that contain at least four characters.

Each character is mapped to a bit vector of size 5 (BIT 5). The mapping is the following:

A, a -> 00001b
B, b -> 00010b
C, c -> 00011b
D, d -> 00100b
E, e -> 00101b
...
Z, z -> 11010b

Groups of three characters are formed together to produce bit clusters of 15 bits. For example, the word "goodbye" is represented as follows (the vertical bars are placed for readability)

00111 | 01111 | 01111 | 00100 | 00010 | 11001 | 00101
  g   o   o   d   b   y   e

The three clusters that are formed for the word *goodbye* are:

Cluster 1:
000101100100101 - bye

Cluster 2:
011110111100100 - ood

Hash Functions and Tables

Cluster 3:
000000000000111 - g

The third cluster is padded with 12 zeros, since the letter "g" stands alone in this cluster. The 15-bit clusters are combined to form a resultant cluster as follows:

The second cluster is rotated (either way is fine) by one unit and then combined with the first cluster using the xor operator.

000101100100101
   xor
111101111001000

111000011101101

The third cluster is rotated by two units and then combined with the result of the first operation.

111000011101101
   xor
000000000011100

111000011110001 = 28913_{10}

The final decimal number, 28,913, is then folded to fit the size of the table using the remainder operator: *hash_index := number \\ table_size*.

The steps associated with this hash function are summarized below.

Steps associated with hash function
1. Break the string into groups of 5-bit vectors.
2. Form clusters of 15 bits from right to left.
3. Rotate the nth cluster by n - 1, beginning with n = 2.
4. Use the xor operator to combine successive clusters.
5. Convert the resultant 15-bit cluster to an integer.
6. Fold the integer to the size of the table using the remainder operator.

This algorithm, like others, attempts to scramble the internal bits to produce a random distribution of hash indices.

12.4.2 Implementation of hash function

We first design a support function, *to_bit_5 (ch : CHARACTER) : BIT 5*, that converts a character to a bit vector of size 5. The implementation details of this function are shown in Listing 12.5.

UNORDERED COLLECTIONS

Listing 12.5   Function to_bit_5

```
to_bit_5 (ch: CHARACTER): BIT 5 is
    -- Converts character to a bit vector of size 5
  do
    inspect ch
    when 'A','a' then
      Result := 00001B
    when 'B','b' then
      Result := 00010B
    when 'C','c' then
      Result := 00011B
    when 'D','d' then
      Result := 00100B
    when 'E','e' then
      Result := 00101B
    when 'F','f' then
      Result := 00110B
    when 'G','g' then
      Result := 00111B
    when 'H','h' then
      Result := 01000B
    when 'I','i' then
      Result := 01001B
    when 'J','j' then
      Result := 01010B
    when 'K','k' then
      Result := 01011B
    when 'L','l' then
      Result := 01100B
    when 'M','m' then
      Result := 01101B
    when 'N','n' then
      Result := 01110B
    when 'O','o' then
      Result := 01111B
    when 'P','p' then
      Result := 10000B
    when 'Q','q' then
      Result := 10001B
    when 'R','r' then
```

Hash Functions and Tables

```
        Result := 10010B
    when 'S','s' then
        Result := 10011B
    when 'T','t' then
        Result := 10100B
    when 'U','u' then
        Result := 10101B
    when 'V','v' then
        Result := 10110B
    when 'W','w' then
        Result := 10111B
    when 'X','x' then
        Result := 11000B
    when 'Y','y' then
        Result := 11001B
    when 'Z','z' then
        Result := 11010B
    else
        Result := 00000B
    end
end
```

We next show the details of the support function, *to_bit_15 (str3: STRING): BIT 15*, that converts a string of three characters to a bit vector of size 15. The details of this function are given in Listing 12.6. Many of the bit vector features discussed earlier are used here.

Listing 12.6 Function to_bit_15

```
to_bit_15 (str3: STRING): BIT 15 is
    -- Converts 3 character string to a bit vector of size 15
local
    bits: BIT 5
    index1, index2: INTEGER
do
    from
        index1 := 0
    until
        index1 = 3
    loop
        index1 := index1 + 1
```

Unordered Collections

```
      bits := to_bit_5 (str3 @ index1)
      from
        index2 := 0
      until
        index2 = 5
      loop
        index2 := index2 + 1
        Result.put (bits.item (index2), (index1 - 1) * 5 + index2)
      end
    end
  end
```

Each of the three 5-bit vectors is obtained by invoking *to_bit_5 (str3 @ index1)*. The individual bits in this bit vector are put into the Result using *Result.put (bits.item (index2), (index1 - 1) * 5 + index2)*.

Finally, class HASHING is constructed as shown in Listing 12.7. You are asked as an exercise to explain the details of this listing.

Listing 12.7 Class HASHING

```
class HASHING

creation
  make

feature

  size: INTEGER   -- size of hash table

  zero: BIT 15

  make (table_size: INTEGER) is
    local
      index: INTEGER
    do
      size := table_size
      from
        index := 0
      until
        index = 1
      loop
        index := index + 1
        zero.put (false, index)
```

```
      end
    end

  hash (word: STRING): INTEGER is
    require
      word_size_greater_than_three: word.count >= 4
    local
      length: INTEGER
      index: INTEGER
      index2: INTEGER
      str3: STRING
      remainder: INTEGER
      upper: INTEGER
      data: ARRAY [BIT 15]
      resultant: BIT 15
    do
      !! str3.make (3)
      str3.fill_blank
      length := word.count // 3
      remainder := word.count \\ 3
      if remainder > 0 then
        upper := length + 1
      else
        upper := length
      end
      !! data.make (1, upper)
      from
        index := 0
      until
        index = upper
      loop
        index := index + 1
        data.put (zero, index)
      end
      from
        index := 0
      until
        index = length
      loop
        index := index + 1
        from
```

```
        index2 := 0
    until
        index2 = 3
    loop
        index2 := index2 + 1
        str3.put (word @ ((index - 1) * 3 + index2), index2)
    end
    data.put (to_bit_15 (str3), index)
end
if remainder > 0 then
    from
        index2 := 0
    until
        index2 = 3
    loop
        index2 := index2 + 1
        if index * 3 + index2 <= word.count then
            str3.put (word @ (index * 3 + index2), index2)
        else
            str3.put (' ', index2)
        end
    end
    data.put (to_bit_15 (str3), index + 1)
end
resultant := data.item (1)
from
    index := 1
until
    index = upper
loop
    index := index + 1
    resultant := resultant xor (data.item (index) # (index - 1))
end
Result := 0
from
    index := 0
until
    index = 15
loop
    index := index + 1
    if resultant.item (16 - index) then
```

Hash functions and tables

```
            inspect index
            when 1 then
                Result := Result + 1
            when 2 then
                Result := Result + 2
            when 3 then
                Result := Result + 4
            when 4 then
                Result := Result + 8
            when 5 then
                Result := Result + 16
            when 6 then
                Result := Result + 32
            when 7 then
                Result := Result + 64
            when 8 then
                Result := Result + 128
            when 9 then
                Result := Result + 256
            when 10 then
                Result := Result + 512
            when 11 then
                Result := Result + 1024
            when 12 then
                Result := Result + 2048
            when 13 then
                Result := Result + 4096
            when 14 then
                Result := Result + 8192
            when 15 then
                Result := Result + 16384
            end
          end
        end
        Result := (Result \\ size) + 1
    end

feature {NONE}

    to_bit_15 (str3: STRING): BIT 15 is
        -- Converts 3 character string to a bit vector of size 15
```

            -- See Listing 12.5
        end

        to_bit_5 (ch: CHARACTER): BIT 5 **is**
            -- Converts character to a bit vector of size 5
            -- See Listing 12.6
        end

    end -- class HASHING

We exercise the hash function given in Listing 12.7 by using as input approximately 5000 English words and building a table of size 100 from these words. In particular, we wish to see how uniformly distributed the distribution of hash indices are in this small table. The root class that serves as our test program is given in Listing 12.8.

Listing 12.8 Test program for hash function

class APPLICATION

creation
    start

feature

    file: PLAIN_TEXT_FILE

    out_file: PLAIN_TEXT_FILE

    Table_size: INTEGER **is** 100

    start **is**
        local
            my_table: HASHING
            data: ARRAY [INTEGER]
            hash_index: INTEGER
            index: INTEGER
        do
            !! my_table.make (table_size)
            !! file.make_open_read ("words.txt")
            !! out_file.make_open_write ("output.txt")
            !! data.make (1, table_size)
            from
            until
                file.end_of_file

```
    loop
      file.readline
      if file.last_string.count > 3 then
        hash_index := my_table.hash (file.last_string)
        data.put (data.item (hash_index) + 1, hash_index)
      end
    end
    from
      index := 0
    until
      index = table_size
    loop
      index := index + 1
      out_file.putint (data.item (Index))
      out_file.new_line
    end
  end

end -- class APPLICATION
```

The output of the test program is shown below:

```
35
49
38
56
54
58
44
44
43
44
53
57
51
59
46
48
51
43
60
50
```

33
52
66
50
52
49
59
59
54
42
48
30
47
58
42
42
52
51
61
60
54
54
31
47
45
44
38
51
44
48
35
59
53
46
42
50
34
56
53
68
45

Hash functions and tables

34
57
53
43
53
49
61
50
56
55
52
56
66
44
59
45
43
42
52
57
60
58
50
37
52
51
40
43
47
56
46
46
43
68
56
48
51
54
56

It is clear from the output that the hash function has done quite well in distributing its indices uniformly across the table. Rigorous statistical tests (e.g., chi-square test) can be used to verify a uniform distribution.

12.4.3 Collision-resolution algorithms

Two well known collision-resolution algorithms are presented in this section. The first, **linear chaining**, is quite simple but inefficient. The second, coalesced chaining, is more complicated but much more efficient.

Linear chaining works as follows: If the space given by the hash index is occupied with another word, increment the index by one until an empty space is located or a match is found. In the latter case, discard the insertion, since we do not wish to allow duplicates in a hash table. When the end of the array is reached start at index location 1 at the beginning of the array.

This simple algorithm is illustrated in Figure 12.4.

```
word    ┌─────────────────────────────────────┐
        │     │     │     │  ▼  │     │     │
        │  X  │  X  │  X  │     │     │
        └─────────────────────────────────────┘
        hash_index
```

Figure 12.4 Linear chaining.

The word to be inserted would normally be assigned to the index location given by *hash_index*. The xs in Figure 12.4 indicate that an array location is occupied by another word. After chaining through *hash_index* + 1 and *hash_index* + 2, the first empty location is found at *hash_index* + 3. This is where the word is inserted. The number of **probes** associated with this collision-resolution event is four. The word being inserted needed to be compared with the contents of three table cells before doing the insertion into the fourth cell.

The minimum number of probes that must be performed during a hash table insertion equals one. The cost of insertion, and later hash-table lookup, equals the number of probes required for the insertion. When a hash table is relatively empty, the number of probes associated with a given word is usually one. Only rarely will a collision occur since the hash function distributes its indices uniformly across the table. As the table begins to fill, the probability of a collision increases. When the table is half full, the probability of a collision on the next insertion equals fifty percent.

The **load factor** of a hash table is defined as the ratio of the number of elements currently stored in the table, divided by the size of the table. As the load factor increases, a clustering phenomena begins to occur. Larger and larger collision chains begin to form. A collision chain is defined as a contiguous sequence of table cells that contain words. Such chains offer a bigger and bigger target for being hit (having a hash index collide with any of the index locations in the collision chain) when the next hash index is computed. If such a hit occurs, the collision chain grows bigger by one, since linear-chaining looks for the first available empty location. Since all cells have approximately the same probability as being hit (at least for a well designed hash function), the collision chains tend to grow larger. The only uncertainty is their location within the table.

The effect of large collision chains is to increase the average number of probes associated with insertions (and later lookup) in the table. It is interesting to investigate the growth of collision chains as the load factor increases. Exercise 10 in this chapter suggests a simulation experiment to accomplish this.

In the next section we compute, through simulation, the average number of probes as a function of load factor for linear chaining. The load factor must be kept below one, otherwise no empty space would be found for the next insertion.

The second collision resolution algorithm that we describe is called **coalesced chaining**. We illustrate its operation with a small example. Suppose that the following words are to be inserted in a table of size 10. The hash values for each word are shown next to the word (the symbols A, B, ... are used to represent the words to be inserted):

hash (A) = 2
hash (B) = 8
hash (C) = 3
hash (D) = 4
hash (E) = 8
hash (F) = 5
hash (G) = 3
hash (H) = 8

A link array of the same size as the hash table is initialized to 0 (each cell in the index array gets the initial value 0). A *link_index* is initialized to 10 (the size of the array). The word A (word represented by A) is inserted at index 2. Next, the word B is inserted at index 8. Next, the word C is inserted at index 3. Next, the word D is inserted at index 4. The word E collides with word B already occupying index 8. To resolve the collision, the *link_index* is decremented until the first empty cell is found. This cell is cell 10 (the initial value of the *link_index*). Word E is inserted into index location 10. The value in index 8 of the link array is assigned 10. This allows a trace from 8 to 10 to be saved so that later when the word E is searched for in the hash table the trace from location to 8 to 10 will be saved. Next, the word F is inserted at index 5, which is unoccupied. Next, the word G, with hash index 3, collides with word C already occupying this location. The *link_index* is decremented to 9 and G is inserted into this location. The link array assigns the value 9 to index location 3. Finally, word H collides with index 8. The *link_index* is decremented to location 7, the first empty location. Word H is inserted into index 7. The link array is updated by putting the value 7 at index 10 (a collision chain from 8 to 10 to 7 is formed).

The completed hash table is shown in Figure 12.5.

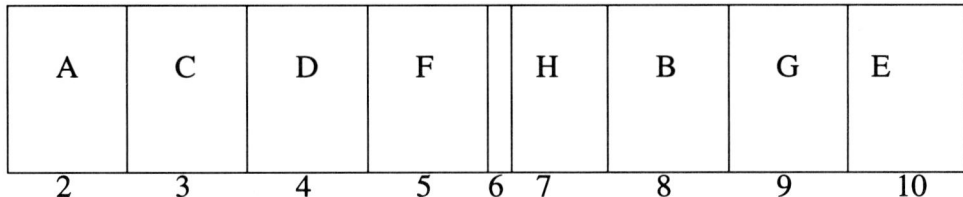

Figure 12.5 Collision resolution using coalesced chaining.

We compute the expected number of probes for the hash table depicted in Figure 12.5. Words A, B, C, D and F each require 1 probe. Word E requires 2 probes. Word G requires 2 probes. Word H requires 3 probes. Therefore, the average number of probes equals 12 / 8 or 1.5 probes.

If linear chaining had been used, the hash table shown in Figure 12.6 would exist.

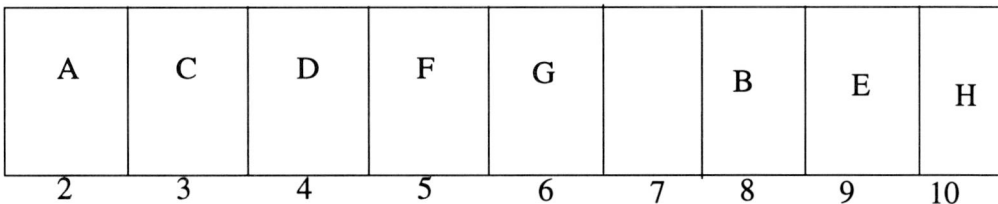

Figure 12.6 Collision resolution using linear chaining.

Hash Functions and Tables

The average number of probes for the hash table of Figure 12.6, using linear-chaining, is computed as follows: Words A, B, C, D, and F require 1 probe as before. Word E requires 2 probes. Word F requires 3 probes. Word G requires 4 probes. Word H requires 3 probes. Therefore the average number of probes equals 17 / 8, almost 50 percent more than the table constructed using coalesced chaining.

Because coalesced chaining resolves a collision using a cell that is generally not adjacent to the occupied cell, the long collision chains so typical of linear chaining are not produced. This causes the average number of probes to remain small even in the presence of load factors that approach 1. In the next section, we perform a simulation that compares the performance of linear chaining with coalesced chaining.

12.4.4 Simulation that compares linear with coalesced chaining

The focus of our effort in this section is to simulate the construction of hash tables using either linear chaining or coalesced chaining. To accomplish this, we idealize the hash function by using a random number generator with uniformly distributed index values across the range of the hash table.

Listing 12.9 presents the details of class COLLISION_RESOLUTION. This class encapsulates the simulation of linear and coalesced chaining.

Listing 12.9 Class COLLISION_RESOLUTION

class COLLISION_RESOLUTION

creation
  make

feature

  table: ARRAY [BOOLEAN]

  link: ARRAY [INTEGER]

  rnd: RANDOM_NUMBER

  size: INTEGER

  probes: INTEGER

  link_index: INTEGER

```
make (table_size: INTEGER) is
  do
    !! table.make (1, table_size)
    !! link.make (1, table_size)
    size := table_size
    !! rnd.initialize
  end

linear_chaining (load_factor: REAL) is
  require
    legal_load_factor: load_factor < 1.0
  local
    index: INTEGER
    upper: INTEGER
    hash_index: INTEGER
  do
    initialize_table
    upper := (size * load_factor).truncated_to_integer
    from
      index := 0
    until
      index = upper
    loop
      index := index + 1
      rnd.next
      hash_index := rnd.value_between (1, size)
      probes := probes + 1
      from
      until
        table.item (hash_index) = false
      loop
        hash_index := hash_index + 1
        probes := probes + 1
        if hash_index > size then
          hash_index := 1
        end
      end
      table.put (true, hash_index)
    end
  end
```

```
coalesced_chaining (load_factor: REAL) is
  require
    legal_load_factor: load_factor < 1.0
  local
    index: INTEGER
    upper: INTEGER
    hash_index: INTEGER
    previous: INTEGER
  do
    initialize_table
    upper := (size * load_factor).truncated_to_integer
    from
      index := 0
    until
      index = upper
    loop
      index := index + 1
      rnd.next
      hash_index := rnd.value_between (1, size)
      probes := probes + 1
      if table.item (hash_index) = true then
        from
        until
          hash_index = 0
        loop
          previous := hash_index
          hash_index := link.item (hash_index)
          probes := probes + 1
        end
        from
        until
          table.item (link_index) = false
        loop
          link_index := link_index - 1
        end
        hash_index := link_index
        link.put (hash_index, previous)
      end
      table.put (true, hash_index)
    end
  end
```

Unordered Collections

```
initialize_table is
  local
    index: INTEGER
  do
    from
      index := 0
    until
      index = size
    loop
      index := index + 1
      table.put (false, index)
      link.put (0, index)
    end
    probes := 0
    link_index := size
  end

end -- class COLLISION_RESOLUTION
```

In the simulation it is assumed that there are no duplicates among the inserted words.

Listing 12.10 shows an application root class that exercises each of the collision resolution procedures under a wide range of load factors.

Listing 12.10 Class APPLICATION to test collision resolution algorithms

```
class APPLICATION

creation
  start

feature

  collisions: COLLISION_RESOLUTION

  load_factor: REAL

  start is
    do
      !! collisions.make (1000)
      from
        load_factor := 0.0
      until
        load_factor > 0.85
```

HASH FUNCTIONS AND TABLES

```
    loop
       load_factor := load_factor + 0.05
       output_results_linear_chaining
       output_results_coalesced_chaining
    end
    load_factor := 0.9
    output_results_linear_chaining
    output_results_coalesced_chaining
    load_factor := 0.95
    output_results_linear_chaining
    output_results_coalesced_chaining
    load_factor := 0.96
    output_results_linear_chaining
    output_results_coalesced_chaining
    load_factor := 0.97
    output_results_linear_chaining
    output_results_coalesced_chaining
    load_factor := 0.98
    output_results_linear_chaining
    output_results_coalesced_chaining
    load_factor := 0.99
    output_results_linear_chaining
    output_results_coalesced_chaining
    load_factor := 0.993
    output_results_linear_chaining
    output_results_coalesced_chaining
    load_factor := 0.996
    output_results_linear_chaining
    output_results_coalesced_chaining
    load_factor := 0.999
    output_results_linear_chaining
    output_results_coalesced_chaining
    io.read_line
  end

output_results_linear_chaining is
   do
      collisions.linear_chaining (load_factor)
      io.putstring ("Load factor ")
      io.putreal (load_factor)
      io.putstring (" Using linear chaining --> ")
```

```
      io.putreal (collisions.probes / (1000.0 * load_factor))
      io.new_line
    end

  output_results_coalesced_chaining is
    do
      collisions.coalesced_chaining (load_factor)
      io.putstring ("Load factor ")
      io.putreal (load_factor)
      io.putstring (" Using coalesced chaining --> ")
      io.putreal (collisions.probes / (1000.0 * load_factor))
      io.new_line
    end

end -- class APPLICATION
```

The output of Listing 12.10 is quite interesting and provides the basis for comparing the efficiency of each of the collision resolution algorithms. This output is given below in Table 12.1.

Table 12.1 Output of Listing 12.10

Load factor 0.05 Using linear chaining --> 1
Load factor 0.05 Using coalesced chaining --> 1
Load factor 0.1 Using linear chaining --> 1.06
Load factor 0.1 Using coalesced chaining --> 1.08
Load factor 0.15 Using linear chaining --> 1.07333
Load factor 0.15 Using coalesced chaining --> 1.06
Load factor 0.2 Using linear chaining --> 1.185
Load factor 0.2 Using coalesced chaining --> 1.1
Load factor 0.25 Using linear chaining --> 1.148
Load factor 0.25 Using coalesced chaining --> 1.128
Load factor 0.3 Using linear chaining --> 1.19667
Load factor 0.3 Using coalesced chaining --> 1.16667
Load factor 0.35 Using linear chaining --> 1.25714
Load factor 0.35 Using coalesced chaining --> 1.21143
Load factor 0.4 Using linear chaining --> 1.3725

Table 12.1 Output of Listing 12.10 (continued)

Load factor 0.4 Using coalesced chaining --> 1.255
Load factor 0.45 Using linear chaining --> 1.34889
Load factor 0.45 Using coalesced chaining --> 1.30889
Load factor 0.5 Using linear chaining --> 1.454
Load factor 0.5 Using coalesced chaining --> 1.336
Load factor 0.55 Using linear chaining --> 1.60364
Load factor 0.55 Using coalesced chaining --> 1.31091
Load factor 0.6 Using linear chaining --> 1.65167
Load factor 0.6 Using coalesced chaining --> 1.37667
Load factor 0.65 Using linear chaining --> 2.07692
Load factor 0.65 Using coalesced chaining --> 1.41077
Load factor 0.7 Using linear chaining --> 2.00857
Load factor 0.7 Using coalesced chaining --> 1.46286
Load factor 0.75 Using linear chaining --> 2.97467
Load factor 0.75 Using coalesced chaining --> 1.48133
Load factor 0.8 Using linear chaining --> 3.40125
Load factor 0.8 Using coalesced chaining --> 1.51125
Load factor 0.85 Using linear chaining --> 3.85529
Load factor 0.85 Using coalesced chaining --> 1.59059
Load factor 0.9 Using linear chaining --> 4.93555
Load factor 0.9 Using coalesced chaining --> 1.70111
Load factor 0.9 Using linear chaining --> 3.76444
Load factor 0.9 Using coalesced chaining --> 1.65667
Load factor 0.95 Using linear chaining --> 13.5621
Load factor 0.95 Using coalesced chaining --> 1.72
Load factor 0.96 Using linear chaining --> 7.14271
Load factor 0.96 Using coalesced chaining --> 1.79792

Table 12.1 Output of Listing 12.10 (continued)

Load factor 0.97 Using linear chaining --> 12.3454
Load factor 0.97 Using coalesced chaining --> 1.72165
Load factor 0.98 Using linear chaining --> 12.0224
Load factor 0.98 Using coalesced chaining --> 1.77551
Load factor 0.99 Using linear chaining --> 14.396
Load factor 0.99 Using coalesced chaining --> 1.7404
Load factor 0.993 Using linear chaining --> 9.95166
Load factor 0.993 Using coalesced chaining --> 1.79758
Load factor 0.996 Using linear chaining --> 12.9849
Load factor 0.996 Using coalesced chaining --> 1.75703
Load factor 0.999 Using linear chaining --> 18.7447
Load factor 0.999 Using coalesced chaining --> 1.74374

It is evident from the output that the average number of probes for coalesced chaining remains relatively constant over the entire range of load factors. This is quite remarkable considering that there are not too many examples of algorithms that exhibit roughly constant performance as the load on the system increases. With balanced binary search trees, the search time increases logarithmically as a function of the size of the tree.

For linear chaining, there is a rapid increase in the average number of probes for load factors greater than 0.6. This may be explained by the clustering effect described earlier.

The reader may notice some irregularities in the average number of probes as the load factor approaches 1. This may be accounted for by the variations in the random number sequences used to simulate the hash function. As the load factor approaches 1, linear chaining in particular becomes unstable and quite sensitive to variations in the random number stream from one load factor to another.

It is interesting to substitute a real hash function for the simulated hash function used in class COLLISION_RESOLUTION of Listing 12.9. Fortunately this is relatively easy to do since a real hash function was designed in Section 12.4.2. We substitute index locations produced by this real hash function in place of those generated randomly and compare the results with those produced from Listing 12.10.

Listing 12.11 shows the details of a revised class COLLISION_RESOLUTION. In this class the hash index is supplied as a parameter (computed in the application class) to both *linear_chaining* and *coalesced_chaining*.

Listing 12.11 Revised class COLLISION_RESOLUTION

class COLLISION_RESOLUTION

creation
  make

feature

  table: ARRAY [BOOLEAN]

  link: ARRAY [INTEGER]

  size: INTEGER

  probes: INTEGER

  link_index: INTEGER

  make (table_size: INTEGER) **is**
    do
      !! table.make (1, table_size)
      !! link.make (1, table_size)
      size := table_size
    end

  linear_chaining (hash_index: INTEGER) **is**
    require
      legal_hash_index: hash_index > 0 **and** hash_index <= size
    local
      index: INTEGER
      i: INTEGER
    do
      probes := probes + 1
      i := hash_index
      from
      until
        table.item (i) = **false**
      loop
        i := i + 1

```
        probes := probes + 1
        if i > size then
          i := 1
        end
      end
      table.put (true, i)
    end
  coalesced_chaining (hash_index: INTEGER) is
    require
      legal_hash_index: hash_index > 0 and hash_index <= size
    local
      index: INTEGER
      previous: INTEGER
      i: INTEGER
    do
      probes := probes + 1
      i := hash_index
      if table.item (i) = true then
        from
        until
          i = 0
        loop
          previous := i
          i := link.item (i)
          probes := probes + 1
        end
        from
        until
          table.item (link_index) = false
        loop
          link_index := link_index - 1
        end
        i := link_index
        link.put (i, previous)
      end
      table.put (true, i)
    end
  initialize_table is
    local
      index: INTEGER
```

HASH FUNCTIONS AND TABLES

```
      do
        from
          index := 0
        until
          index = size
        loop
          index := index + 1
          table.put (false, index)
          link.put (0, index)
        end
        probes := 0
        link_index := size
      end
  end -- class COLLISION_RESOLUTION
```

Listing 12.12 shows the root application class that uses the hash function presented in Listing 12.7 and drives the simulation that once again compares linear-chaining to coalesced chaining.

Listing 12.12 Revised class APPLICATION for comparing linear and coalesced chaining

```
class APPLICATION
creation
  start
feature
  hash_table: HASHING

  collisions: COLLISION_RESOLUTION

  load_factor: REAL

  input_file: PLAIN_TEXT_FILE

  output_file: PLAIN_TEXT_FILE

  start is
    local
      index: INTEGER
      hash_index: INTEGER
    do
      !! hash_table.make (1000)
```

```
!! input_file.make_open_read ("words.txt")
!! output_file.make_open_write ("output")
!! collisions.make (1000)
from
   load_factor := 0.05
until
   load_factor > 0.95
loop
   load_factor := load_factor + 0.05
   collisions.initialize_table
   input_file.close
   !! input_file.make_open_read ("words.txt")
   from
      index := 0
   until
      index = (1000 * load_factor).truncated_to_integer
   loop
      input_file.readline
      if input_file.last_string.count > 3 then
         index := index + 1
         hash_index := hash_table.hash (input_file.last_string)
         collisions.linear_chaining (hash_index)
      end
   end
   output_file.putstring ("load_factor = ")
   output_file.putreal (load_factor)
   output_file.putstring (" linear chaining -> ")
   output_file.putreal (collisions.probes / (load_factor * 1000.0))
   output_file.new_line
   io.putstring ("load_factor = ")
   io.putreal (load_factor)
   io.putstring (" linear chaining -> ")
   io.putreal (collisions.probes / (load_factor * 1000.0))
   io.new_line
end
from
   load_factor := 0.05
until
   load_factor > 0.95
loop
   load_factor := load_factor + 0.05
```

Hash functions and tables

```
        collisions.initialize_table
        input_file.close
        !! input_file.make_open_read ("words.txt")
        from
          index := 0
        until
          index = (1000 * load_factor).truncated_to_integer
        loop
          input_file.readline
          if input_file.last_string.count > 3 then
            index := index + 1
            hash_index := hash_table.hash (input_file.last_string)
            collisions.coalesced_chaining (hash_index)
          end
        end
        output_file.putstring ("load_factor = ")
        output_file.putreal (load_factor)
        output_file.putstring (" coalesced chaining -> ")
        output_file.putreal (collisions.probes / (load_factor * 1000.0))
        output_file.new_line
        io.putstring ("load_factor = ")
        io.putreal (load_factor)
        io.putstring (" coalesced chaining -> ")
        io.putreal (collisions.probes / (load_factor * 1000.0))
        io.new_line
      end
    end

end -- class APPLICATION
```

The output to Listing 12.12 is shown below in Table 12.2. The previously obtained results with a random number generator substituting for a real hash function are shown in parenthesis in boldface for linear chaining only.

Table 12.2 Output for Listing 12.12

load_factor = 0.1 linear chaining -> 1.39 (**1.06**)
load_factor = 0.15 linear chaining -> 1.52667 (**1.07**)
load_factor = 0.2 linear chaining -> 1.54 (**1.18**)
load_factor = 0.25 linear chaining -> 1.584 (**1.14**)
load_factor = 0.3 linear chaining -> 1.66 (**1.19**)

Table 12.2 Output for Listing 12.12 (continued)

load_factor = 0.35 linear chaining -> 1.67429 (**1.25**)
load_factor = 0.4 linear chaining -> 1.7525 (**1.37**)
load_factor = 0.45 linear chaining -> 1.81333 (**1.34**)
load_factor = 0.5 linear chaining -> 2.04 (**1.45**)
load_factor = 0.55 linear chaining -> 2.22909 (**1.60**)
load_factor = 0.6 linear chaining -> 2.64167 (**1.37**)
load_factor = 0.65 linear chaining -> 2.84154 (**2.07**)
load_factor = 0.7 linear chaining -> 3.15286 (**2.00**)
load_factor = 0.75 linear chaining -> 3.568 (**2.97**)
load_factor = 0.8 linear chaining -> 3.9725 (**3.40**)
load_factor = 0.85 linear chaining -> 5.40588 (**3.85**)
load_factor = 0.9 linear chaining -> 7.42444 (**4.93**)
load_factor = 0.95 linear chaining -> 9.42842 (**13.5**)
load_factor = 0.1 coalesced chaining -> 1.34
load_factor = 0.15 coalesced chaining -> 1.44667
load_factor = 0.2 coalesced chaining -> 1.475
load_factor = 0.25 coalesced chaining -> 1.476
load_factor = 0.3 coalesced chaining -> 1.48
load_factor = 0.35 coalesced chaining -> 1.51429
load_factor = 0.4 coalesced chaining -> 1.575
load_factor = 0.45 coalesced chaining -> 1.58889
load_factor = 0.5 coalesced chaining -> 1.622
load_factor = 0.55 coalesced chaining -> 1.67818
load_factor = 0.6 coalesced chaining -> 1.73667
load_factor = 0.65 coalesced chaining -> 1.83538
load_factor = 0.7 coalesced chaining -> 1.89286
load_factor = 0.75 coalesced chaining -> 1.96667

Table 12.2 Output for Listing 12.12 (continued)

load_factor = 0.8 coalesced chaining -> 2.04125
load_factor = 0.85 coalesced chaining -> 2.14471
load_factor = 0.9 coalesced chaining -> 2.25111
load_factor = 0.95 coalesced chaining -> 2.35789

In comparing the results of using a real hash function with a simulated hash function it is clear that the real hash function turns in a poorer performance except at load factor 0.95. At this load factor the result obtained using the simulated hash function is an anomaly and should not be taken seriously. The results are expected. A real hash function tends to induce some clustering because it does not produce a totally random sequence of index values. Since the results are in most cases not significantly different we can conclude that the real hash function generally performs well.

12.5 Summary

- A BIT data type requires the numerical specification of the number of bits associated with each element of this type. A typical declaration, *bit_pattern*, is bit_pattern : BIT 8

- A set is a basic abstraction in mathematics and in computer science. It is an unordered collection of elements with no duplicate elements allowed.

- A hash function maps an entity such as a string or some other data structure to an integer. This integer may be used as an index into a table called a hash table.

- If a hash function is properly constructed, the hash indices associated with an arbitrary set of words will appear to be uniformly distributed (i.e., randomly distributed) across the range of values defined for the hash table. If the hash function is poorly designed then the distribution of hash indices will not be uniform and will exhibit clusters.

- A properly constructed hash function produces an unordered collection since an ordering of elements has been removed by hashing (dicing) the elements so that they are randomly distributed.

Unordered Collections

- In a good hash function there should be no obvious relationship among the equivalence class of words that produce the same hash index for a specific hash function.
- The two fundamental problems associated with constructing hash tables are:

  Designing a good hash function that randomly distributes indices across the hash table.

  Designing a collision-resolution algorithm that finds a new index location for a word in the event that the hash index is currently occupied by another word.
- The steps associated with this hash function are:

1. Break the string into groups of 5-bit vectors.
2. Form clusters of 15 bits from right to left.
3. Rotate the nth cluster by n - 1, beginning with n = 2.
4. Use the xor operator to combine successive clusters.
5. Convert the resultant 15-bit cluster to an integer.
6. Fold the integer to the size of the table using the remainder operator.

- The load factor of a hash table is defined as the ratio of the number of elements currently stored in the table, divided by the size of the table.
- The effect of large collision chains is to increase the average number of probes associated with insertions (and later lookup) in the table.
- The average number of probes for coalesced chaining remains relatively constant over the entire range of load factors. This is quite remarkable considering that there are not too many examples of algorithms that exhibit roughly constant performance as the load on the system increases. With balanced binary search trees, the search time increases logarithmically as a function of the size of the tree.
- For linear chaining there is a rapid increase in the average number of probes for load factors greater than 0.6.

12.6 Exercises

1. Explain the output of Listing 12.2.
2. Implement the INTEGER_SET (given in Listing 12.3) using BIT 64. Perform a benchmark test that compares the efficiency of this implementation with that of Listing 12.3.

EXERCISES

3. Repeat Exercise 2 using BIT 128.

4. Repeat Exercise 2 using BIT 256.

5. Compute the decimal equivalent of the binary numbers:
   (a) 10100010
   (b) 00111000
   (c) 10111001
   (d) 00101101

6. Write the binary equivalent of the decimal numbers (part of the Boeing fleet):
   (a) 727
   (b) 737
   (c) 747
   (d) 757
   (e) 767
   (f) 777

7. Discuss the following alternative implementation of the method *present* in INTEGER_SET. Explain every line of code. The variable *num_one* is initialized to be the binary number 1.

   present (element : INTEGER) : BOOLEAN **is**
   require
       non_negative_element : element >= 0
       within_range: element < capacity
   local
       index: INTEGER
       bits: BIT 32
       res: BIT 32
   do
       index := element // 32
       bits := elements.item (index) ^ (element \\ 32)
       res := bits and num_one
       Result := res @ 32
   end

8. Discuss the following alternative implementation of the command *insert*. Explain each line of code.

   insert (element : INTEGER) **is**
   require

```
        non_negative_element : element >= 0
        within_range: element < capacity
        not_present : not present (element)
local
        index: INTEGER
        bits: BIT 32
do
        index := element // 32
        bits := num_one ^ -(element \\ 32)
        elements.put (elements.item (index) or bits, index)
        number_elements := number_elements + 1
ensure
        number_elements = old number_elements + 1
end
```

9. Explain in detail the hash algorithm given in Listing 12.7.

10. Design a simulation that investigates the size and number of collision chains in a hash table constructed using linear chaining. Vary the load factor from 0.25 to 0.95 and compute statistics on the number of chains and the average size of each chain for each load factor.

11. A hash table of size 15 is to be constructed with the following hash values:

    h (A) = 5
    h (B) = 7
    h (C) = 12
    h (D) = 15
    h (E) = 7
    h (F) = 5
    h (G) = 12
    h (H) = 15
    h (I) = 7
    h (J) = 12

    Show the hash table if linear chaining is used. Compute the average number of probes required to find one of the symbols in the table.

12. Repeat problem 11 using coalesced chaining. Discuss and compare your results.

13. We wish to investigate a variation of coalesced chaining. Suppose we initially allow the hash index to assume values from 1 to size1 < size (the hash function folds its results onto a smaller range than the full size of the table). For values of size1 equal to 1/2 size, 3/4 size and 4/5 size perform a simulation that compares the performance measured by average number of probes to that of the original coalesced chaining algorithm. Explain what advantage there might be in using this variation of coalesced chaining.

14. Simulate a hash table of size 1000 using linear chaining. Assume that the first 400 insertions have a probability of access that is 10 times the next 500 insertions. Use a weighting function on the number of probes to compute the average number of probes for an insertion.

Chapter 13

Applications of Binary Trees

13.1 Heap sorting

Why, you might be asking, are we returning to the subject of sorting in this chapter? Sorting was discussed in Chapter 3. An exceptionally efficient and therefore important sorting algorithm, *heapsort*, is based on a special type of tree structure called a **heap**. The heap data structure, a binary tree, provides the basis for understanding the heapsort algorithm. The heapsort algorithm is therefore an important application of binary trees.

It is not unusual for an algorithm to be intimately associated with a data structure. As you will see shortly, heapsort provides a dramatic example of such an intimate association. The heap is the abstraction through which we view and rationalize the transactions that comprise the sorting algorithm. Without the heap abstraction as our "viewer" it is quite difficult to understand this sorting algorithm. To demonstrate this, we shall first view the transactions, which in the case of heapsort are interchanges of data within the array being sorted, as naïve observers. The array to be sorted is given in Figure 13.1.

| 4 | 1 | 8 | 9 | 3 | 2 | 5 | 7 | 10 | 6 |

Figure 13.1 Array to be sorted.

Heap Sorting

Observe the sequence of interchanges (sorting transactions) that occur as the *heapsort* algorithm performs its job. The results are shown after each transaction in Figures 13.2 to 13.31.

| 8 | 1 | 4 | 9 | 3 | 2 | 5 | 7 | 10 | 6 |

Figure 13.2 Array after interchanging 8 with 4.

| 8 | 9 | 4 | 1 | 3 | 2 | 5 | 7 | 10 | 6 |

Figure 13.3 Array after interchanging 9 with 1.

| 9 | 8 | 4 | 1 | 3 | 2 | 5 | 7 | 10 | 6 |

Figure 13.4 Array after interchanging 9 with 8.

| 9 | 8 | 5 | 1 | 3 | 2 | 4 | 7 | 10 | 6 |

Figure 13.5 Array after interchanging 5 with 4.

| 9 | 8 | 5 | 7 | 3 | 2 | 4 | 1 | 10 | 6 |

Figure 13.6 Array after interchanging 7 with 1.

APPLICATIONS OF BINARY TREES

| 9 | 8 | 5 | 10 | 3 | 2 | 4 | 1 | 7 | 6 |

Figure 13.7 Array after interchanging 10 with 7.

| 9 | 10 | 5 | 8 | 3 | 2 | 4 | 1 | 7 | 6 |

Figure 13.8 Array after interchanging 10 with 8.

| 10 | 9 | 5 | 8 | 3 | 2 | 4 | 1 | 7 | 6 |

Figure 13.9 Array after interchanging 10 with 9.

| 10 | 9 | 5 | 8 | 6 | 2 | 4 | 1 | 7 | 3 |

Figure 13.10 Array after interchanging 6 with 3.

| 3 | 9 | 5 | 8 | 6 | 2 | 4 | 1 | 7 | 10 |

Figure 13.11 Array after interchanging 10 with 3.

Heap sorting

| 9 | 3 | 5 | 8 | 6 | 2 | 4 | 1 | 7 | 10 |

Figure 13.12 Array after interchanging 3 with 9.

| 9 | 8 | 5 | 3 | 6 | 2 | 4 | 1 | 7 | 10 |

Figure 13.13 Array after interchanging 8 with 3.

| 9 | 8 | 5 | 7 | 6 | 2 | 4 | 1 | 3 | 10 |

Figure 13.14 Array after interchanging 3 with 7.

| 3 | 8 | 5 | 7 | 6 | 2 | 4 | 1 | 9 | 10 |

Figure 13.15 Array after interchanging 9 with 3.

| 8 | 3 | 5 | 7 | 6 | 2 | 4 | 1 | 9 | 10 |

Figure 13.16 Array after interchanging 8 with 3.

APPLICATIONS OF BINARY TREES

| 8 | 7 | 5 | 3 | 6 | 2 | 4 | 1 | 9 | 10 |

Figure 13.17 Array after interchanging 7 with 3.

| 1 | 7 | 5 | 3 | 6 | 2 | 4 | 8 | 9 | 10 |

Figure 13.18 Array after interchanging 1 with 8.

| 7 | 1 | 5 | 3 | 6 | 2 | 4 | 8 | 9 | 10 |

Figure 13.19 Array after interchanging 1 with 7.

| 7 | 6 | 5 | 3 | 1 | 2 | 4 | 8 | 9 | 10 |

Figure 13.20 Array after interchanging 1 with 6.

| 4 | 6 | 5 | 3 | 1 | 2 | 7 | 8 | 9 | 10 |

Figure 13.21 Array after interchanging 4 with 7.

HEAP SORTING

| 6 | 4 | 5 | 3 | 1 | 2 | 7 | 8 | 9 | 10 |

Figure 13.22 Array after interchanging 4 with 6.

| 2 | 4 | 5 | 3 | 1 | 6 | 7 | 8 | 9 | 10 |

Figure 13.23 Array after interchanging 2 with 6.

| 5 | 4 | 2 | 3 | 1 | 6 | 7 | 8 | 9 | 10 |

Figure 13.24 Array after interchanging 2 with 5.

| 1 | 4 | 2 | 3 | 5 | 6 | 7 | 8 | 9 | 10 |

Figure 13.25 Array after interchanging 1 with 5.

| 4 | 1 | 2 | 3 | 5 | 6 | 7 | 8 | 9 | 10 |

Figure 13.26 Array after interchanging 1 with 4.

| 4 | 3 | 2 | 1 | 5 | 6 | 7 | 8 | 9 | 10 |

Figure 13.27 Array after interchanging 1 with 3.

| 1 | 3 | 2 | 4 | 5 | 6 | 7 | 8 | 9 | 10 |

Figure 13.28 Array after interchanging 1 with 4.

| 3 | 1 | 2 | 4 | 5 | 6 | 7 | 8 | 9 | 10 |

Figure 13.29 Array after interchanging 1 with 3.

| 2 | 1 | 3 | 4 | 5 | 6 | 7 | 8 | 9 | 10 |

Figure 13.30 Array after interchanging 2 with 3.

| 1 | 2 | 3 | 4 | 5 | 6 | 7 | 8 | 9 | 10 |

Figure 13.31 Array after interchanging 1 with 2.

After tracing through the 30 interchange transactions that show heapsort in action for this small sorting problem, can you detect the underlying logic that drives this algorithm? If you are like most of us the answer will probably be "no."

Heap Sorting

Observing interchanges in the array is the wrong view of this sorting algorithm. As we have seen from the example presented above, there is nothing terribly obvious about the sequence of interchange transactions that occur with heapsort. Other simpler sorting algorithms can be explained right at the level of interchange transactions in the array. Bubble-sort is an example of such a simple sorting algorithm.

In order to understand the driving force behind heapsort, we need to examine a new specialized type of tree structure, the heap.

13.1.1 The heap data structure

A heap data structure is a binary tree derived from an array in which each node has a value that is equal or greater than its children.

How does one derive a binary tree from an array? We illustrate this process in Figures 13.32 and 13.33. Figure 13.32 contains an array with elements x_1 through x_{10}. Figure 13.33 shows the corresponding binary tree derived from this array.

The element in the first index location becomes the root node of the tree. The element in index two becomes the left child of the root. The element in index three becomes the right child of the root. The element in index four becomes the left most grandchild of the root. The elements in successive index locations of the array fill up each level of the binary tree from left to right.

Because of the manner in which a binary tree is derived from an array, the leaf nodes of such a tree can differ in level by at most one. The general shape of a binary tree that is a heap is shown below:

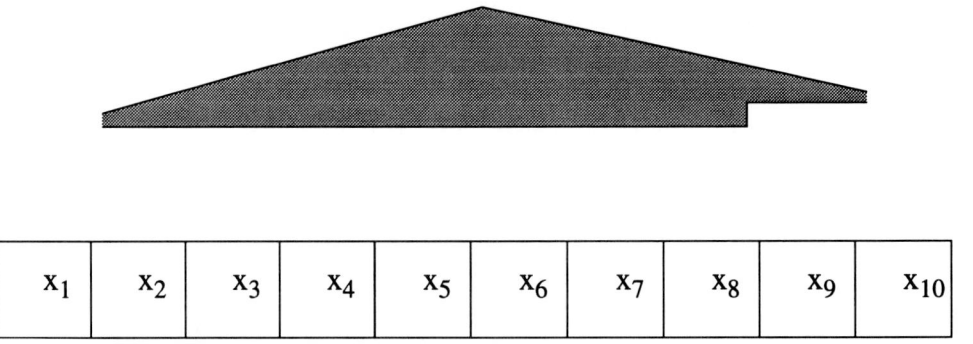

Figure 13.32 Array with elements x_1 through x_{10}.

Applications of Binary Trees

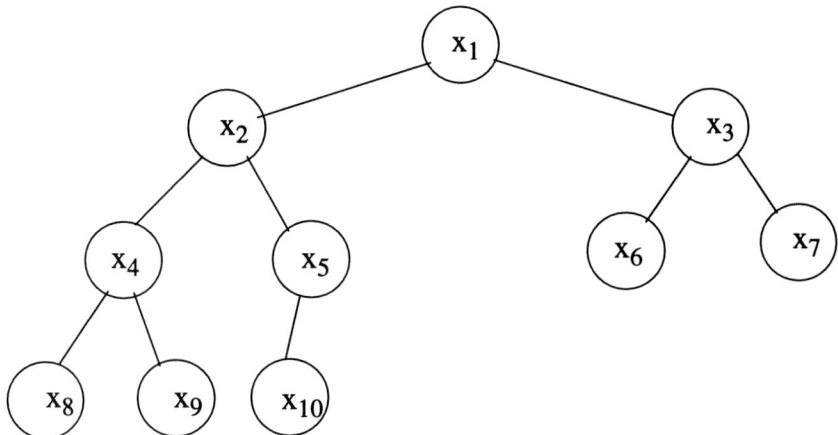

Figure 13.33 Tree derived from array of Figure 13.32.

If the tree shown in Figure 13.33 were a heap, then it would be necessary that $x_1 > x_2$, $x_1 > x_3$, $x_2 > x_4$, $x_2 > x_5$, $x_3 > x_6$, $x_3 > x_7$, ..., $x_5 > x_{10}$.

From the property that each node in a heap has a value that is greater than or equal to the value of its children we can make the inference that the root node must contain the largest element in the tree. If this were not so we would have at least one node that violates the heap property (See Exercise 1).

13.1.2 Overview of *heapsort* algorithm

formheap -- interchange the elements so that the array corresponds to a heap
from i := size
until i = 1
loop
    interchange the data in index 1 and index i -- The largest element is put in index i
    rebuildheap (i - 1) -- Rebuild heap but exclude the elements with index greater than i - 1
    i := i - 1
end

The first step partially orders the data in the array but, most importantly, assures that the root node contains the largest element. Since the

HEAP SORTING

root node corresponds to the element in index 1, the effect of *formheap* is to force the largest array element into index 1.

In the loop, the element in index 1 (the largest among the *i* elements) is interchanged with the element in index *i*. This transaction destroys the heap property of the tree because the root node does not necessarily contain the largest of the remaining *i - 1* elements. The command *rebuildheap* (*i - 1*) performs additional interchanges on the tree that yields a new heap among the first *i - 1* elements (we do not wish to touch the element *i* that has just been properly positioned).

In the next two subsections we examine the operations *formheap* and *rebuildheap*.

13.1.3 The procedure *formheap*

The first step in the *heapsort* algorithm is to perform a sequence of interchange operations on the array so that the array maps to a binary tree that satisfies the heap property (i.e., each node in the heap has a value equal or greater than that of its children).

The algorithm, written as an Eiffel procedure, is given in Listing 13.1.

Listing 13.1 Procedure *formheap*

```
formheap is
  local
    i, j, node: INTEGER
    values: ARRAY [REAL]
    temp: REAL
  do
    values := data  -- data is a public attribute stored elsewhere
    from
      node := 1
    until
      node = size
    loop
      node := node + 1
      i := node
      j := i // 2  -- j is the parent of i
      from
      until
        i = 1 or else values.item (j) > values.item (i)
      loop
```

```
            temp := values.item (j)
            values.put (values.item (i), j)
            values.put (temp, i)
            i := j
            j := i // 2  -- j is the parent of i
         end
      end
   end
```

We illustrate the formheap procedure using the data shown in Figure 13.1 and reproduced in Figure 13.34.

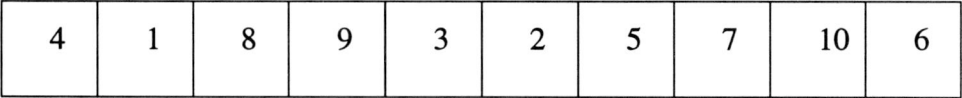

Figure 13.34 Array before invoking formheap.

The binary tree corresponding to the array of Figure 13.34 is shown in Figure 13.35.

In words, the algorithm presented in Listing 13.1 says the following: *For each node starting at node 2, compare the node with its parent. If the node is larger than its parent, then interchange the node with that of its parent. Then compare the parent node with its parent (if one exists) and again interchange the nodes if the child has a value that is larger than that of its parent. Continue this process until either the root node is reached (node 1) or a child node is not larger than that of its parent.*

If we apply this algorithm to the tree shown in Figure 13.35, the following transactions occur: (1) interchange node 8 and 4 (since child is larger than parent), (2) interchange 9 and 1 and then 9 and 8, (3) interchange 5 and 4, (4) interchange 7 and 1, (5) interchange 10 and 7, 10 and 8, and 10 and 9, (6) interchange 6 and 3.

These are the exact transactions shown in Figures 13.2 to 13.10. The heap is shown in Figure 13.36. As expected, the largest element in the tree, namely 10, has been forced to the root node.

Heap sorting

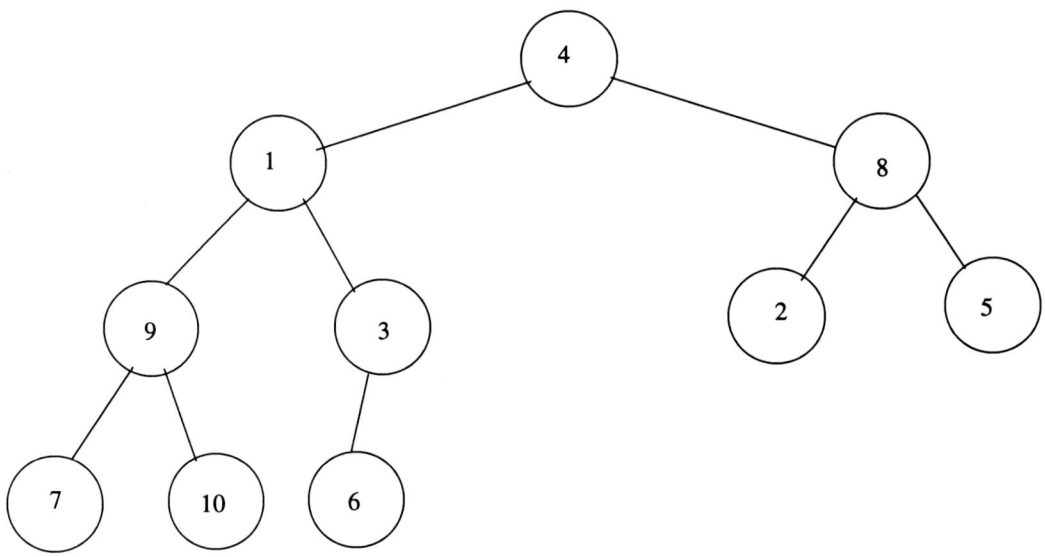

Figure 13.35 Tree corresponding to array of Figure 13.34.

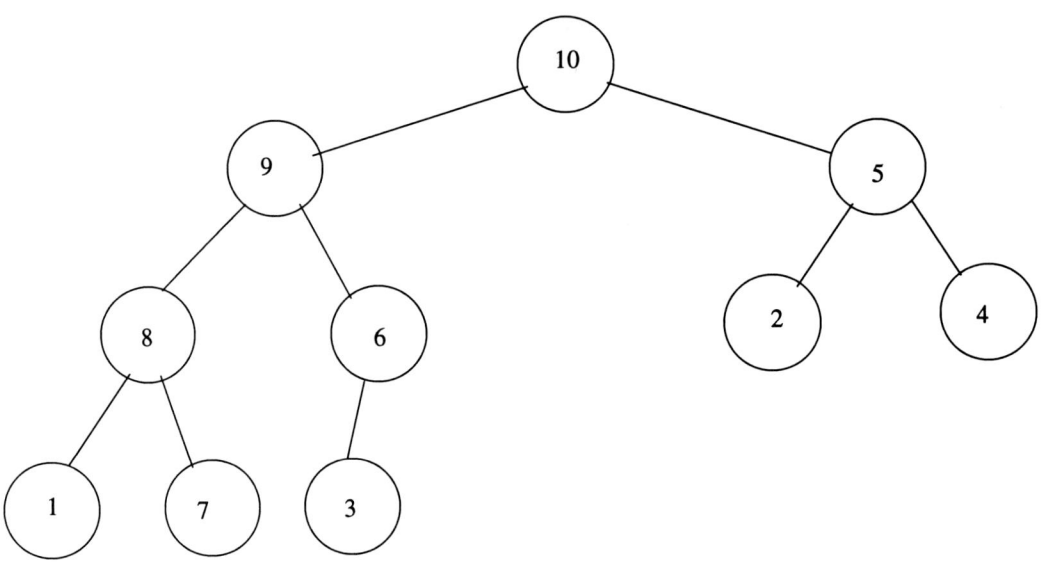

Figure 13.36 Tree resulting from procedure *formheap*.

The largest number of interchange operations for a given node is limited by its level in the tree. The worst case level would be approximately $log_2 n$, where n is the number of nodes in the tree. Since this upper bound applies to each of the n nodes in the tree, the upper bound on the number of interchange operations required to convert the original tree (array) to a heap (a new array that maps to this heap) is $O(n log_2 n)$.

13.1.4 The procedure rebuildheap

Once the element stored in the root node (10 in our example) is interchanged with the element in the highest index (index 10 in this example—interchange elements 10 and 3), the heap property of the tree is destroyed. The procedure *rebuildheap* must be invoked in order to restore the heap property to the tree.

The procedure *rebuildheap* which takes a parameter that represents the number of nodes remaining under consideration (we wish to exclude the node just moved from the root position) is presented in Listing 13.2.

Listing 13.2 Procedure *rebuildheap*

```
rebuildheap (k: INTEGER) is
  local
    i, j: INTEGER
    values: ARRAY [REAL]
    temp: REAL
  do
    values := data  -- data is a public attribute stored elsewhere
    i := 1
    j := 2
    if k >= 3 and values.item (3) > values.item (2) then
      j := 3
    end  -- node j is the larger child of node i
    from
    until
      j > k or else values.item (j) <= values.item (i)
    loop
      temp := values.item (j)
      values.put (values.item (i), j)
      values.put (temp, i)
      i := j
      j := 2 * i  -- node j is the child of node i
```

Heap Sorting

```
            if (j + 1) <= k then
               if values.item (j + 1) > values.item (j) then
                  j := j + 1
               end
            end  -- node j is the larger child of node i
         end
      end
```

In words, the algorithm of Listing 13.2 works as follows: *Starting at the root node, determine the larger of the root node's children. If the larger child has a value greater than its parent, then interchange the child and parent nodes. Next, compute the larger of the children of the previous larger child (if children exist). Again, interchange the child and parent nodes if the child node contains a value larger than that of its parent. Continue this process for all of the nodes under consideration (given by the input parameter).*

If one applies this process to the tree of Figure 13.36 after node 10 has been interchanged with node 3, the following transactions occur: (1) interchange nodes 3 and 9, (2) interchange nodes 8 and 3, (3) interchange nodes 3 and 7. This corresponds exactly to the transactions shown in Figures 13.12 to 13.14. The rebuilt heap structure is shown in Figure 13.37. The second largest element, 9 in our example, has been forced to the root position. This element will next be interchanged with element 3. Then the heap will again be rebuilt with only eight elements.

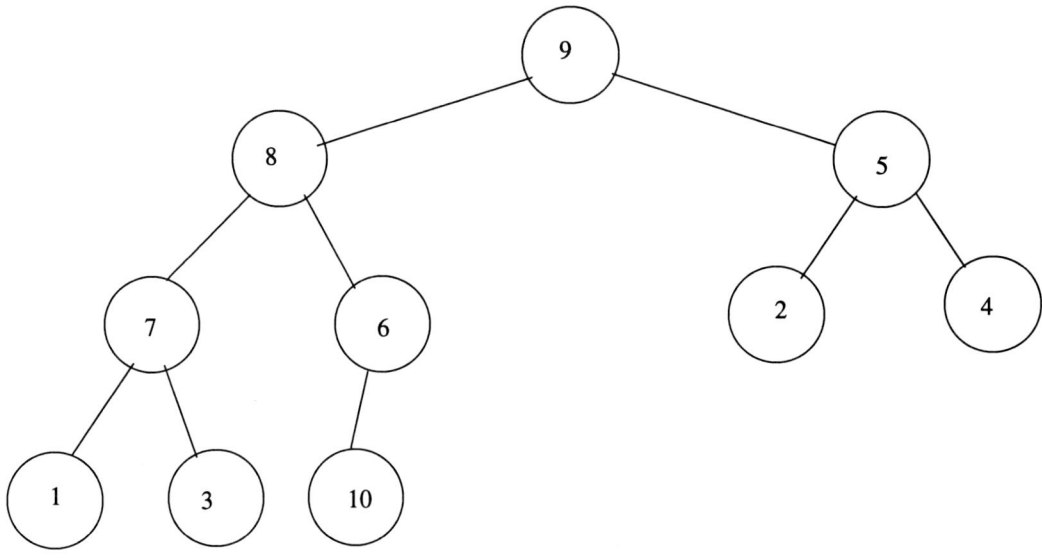

Figure 13.37 Tree resulting from procedure *rebuildheap*.

Applications of Binary Trees

The largest number of interchange operations that can occur in rebuilding the heap is $log_2 n$, where n is the number of nodes in the tree. This operation must be performed n times (see the heapsort algorithm given earlier). Therefore the algorithmic complexity associated with repeatedly rebuilding the heap is $O\ (nlog_2 n)$. Since it was shown earlier that the first step, *formheap*, is of complexity $O\ (nlog_2 n)$ and the remaining steps (rebuilding the heap after interchanging the root element with the current right-most element) is of the same complexity, the overall *heapsort* algorithm is therefore of complexity $O\ (nlog_2 n)$.

A fair question to ask is how does the speed of *heapsort* compare to that of *quicksort* (presented in Chapter 3)? We consider this question in the next section.

13.1.5 Speed of *heapsort* versus *quicksort*

As you may recall from Chapter 3, *quicksort* has an average-case complexity of $O(nlog_2 n)$. We have seen in the previous section that *heapsort* has the same complexity but for worst-case. The *heapsort* algorithm is more robust than quicksort since it guarantees $O(nlog_2 n)$ performance under all conditions. The *quicksort* algorithm slows down significantly when the data becomes more ordered.

Listing 13.3 presents the details of a class SORT that encapsulates the *quicksort* and *heapsort* algorithms. Listing 13.4 shows an APPLICATION class that loads an array with the same sequence of 1 million random numbers and measures the time to sort these numbers with both *quicksort* and *heapsort*. In addition to comparing the sorting times, class SORT also counts the number of swap operations required of each of the sorting algorithms. The results are interesting.

Listing 13.3 Class SORT

```
class SORT
 -- Encapsulates heapsort and quicksort
creation
   make,
   create

feature

   data: ARRAY [REAL]

   data_copy: ARRAY [REAL]
```

Heap sorting

```
size: INTEGER

rnd: RANDOM_NUMBER

swaps: INTEGER

make (sz: INTEGER) is
  do
    !! rnd.initialize
    size := sz
    !! data.make (1, size)
    !! data_copy.make (1, size)
    load_random_data
    data_copy.copy (data)
    swaps := 0
  end

create (values: ARRAY [REAL]  sz: INTEGER) is
  do
    size := sz
    !! data.make (1, size)
    !! data_copy.make (1, size)
    data.copy (values)
    data_copy.copy (data)
  end

reset is
  do
    data.copy (data_copy)
    swaps := 0
  end

load_random_data is
  local
    index: INTEGER
    value: REAL
  do
    from
      index := 0
    until
      index = size
    loop
      index := index + 1
      rnd.next
```

```
          value := 100.0 * rnd.next_value
          data.put (value, index)
        end
    end

  verify: BOOLEAN is
    local
      index: INTEGER
      dta: ARRAY [REAL]
    do
      Result := true
      dta := data
      from
        index := 0
      until
        Result = false or index = size - 1
      loop
        index := index + 1
        if dta.item (index) > dta.item (index + 1) then
          Result := false
        end
      end
    end

  quicksort (lower_index: INTEGER  upper_index: INTEGER) is
    local
      pivot_index: INTEGER
    do
      pivot_index := partition (lower_index, upper_index)
      if lower_index < pivot_index - 1 then
        quicksort (lower_index, pivot_index - 1)
      end
      if pivot_index + 1 < upper_index then
        quicksort (pivot_index + 1, upper_index)
      end
    end

  heapsort is
    local
      i: INTEGER
      temp: REAL
      values: ARRAY [REAL]
```

Heap sorting

```
        do
            values := data
            formheap
            from
                i := size
            until
                i = 1
            loop
                swaps := swaps + 1
                temp := values.item (i)
                values.put (values.item (1), i)
                values.put (temp, 1)
                rebuildheap (i - 1)
                i := i - 1
            end
        end

feature {NONE}

    partition (first_index: INTEGER; second_index: INTEGER): INTEGER is
        require
            first_less_than_second: first_index <= second_index
        local
            pivot_value: REAL
            move_right: INTEGER
            move_left: INTEGER
            temp: REAL
            values: ARRAY [REAL]
        do
            values := data
            pivot_value := values.item (first_index)
            from
                move_right := first_index
            until
                values.item (move_right) > pivot_value or move_right = second_index
            loop
                move_right := move_right + 1
            end
            from
                move_left := second_index
            until
```

```
            values.item (move_left) <= pivot_value
        loop
          move_left := move_left - 1
        end
      from
      until
        move_right >= move_left
      loop
        swaps := swaps + 1
        temp := values.item (move_left)
        values.put (values.item (move_right), move_left)
        values.put (temp, move_right)
        from
        until
          values.item (move_right) > pivot_value or move_right = second_index
        loop
          move_right := move_right + 1
        end
        from
        until
          values.item (move_left) <= pivot_value
        loop
          move_left := move_left - 1
        end
      end
      swaps := swaps + 1
      temp := values.item (move_left)
      values.put (values.item (first_index), move_left)
      values.put (temp, first_index)
      Result := move_left
    end

formheap is
  local
    i, j, node: INTEGER
    values: ARRAY [REAL]
    temp: REAL
  do
    values := data
    from
      node := 1
```

Heap sorting

```
      until
        node = size
      loop
        node := node + 1
        i := node
        j := i // 2
        from until
          i = 1 or else values.item (j) > values.item (i)
        loop
          swaps := swaps + 1
          temp := values.item (j)
          values.put (values.item (i), j)
          values.put (temp, i)
          i := j
          j := i // 2
        end
      end
    end

  rebuildheap (k: INTEGER) is
    local
      i, j: INTEGER
      values: ARRAY [REAL]
      temp: REAL
    do
      values := data
      i := 1
      j := 2
      if k >= 3 and values.item (3) > values.item (2) then
        j := 3
      end
      from
      until
        j > k or else values.item (j) <= values.item (i)
      loop
        swaps := swaps + 1
        temp := values.item (j)
        values.put (values.item (i), j)
        values.put (temp, i)
        i := j
        j := 2 * i
```

```
            if (j + 1) <= k then
              if values.item (j + 1) > values.item (j) then
                j := j + 1
              end
            end
          end
        end
end -- class SORT
```

Listing 13.4   Application that compares sort time of *heapsort* and *quicksort*

```
class APPLICATION

creation
  start

feature

  tm: TIMER

  sorting: SORT

  Size: INTEGER is 1000000

  start is
    do
      !! sorting.make (size)
      !! tm
      tm.start_timing
      sorting.quicksort (1, size)
      tm.end_timing
      io.putstring ("%NNumber of interchanges = ")
      io.putint (sorting.swaps)
      io.new_line
      if sorting.verify then
        io.putstring ("Quicksort of size ")
        io.putint (size)
        io.putstring (" has been verified.%N")
      else
        io.putstring ("Quicksort of size ")
        io.putint (size)
        io.putstring (" has not been verified.%N")
      end
```

HEAP SORTING

```
        tm.report
        sorting.reset
        tm.start_timing
        sorting.heapsort
        tm.end_timing
        io.putstring ("%NNumber of interchanges = ")
        io.putint (sorting.swaps)
        io.new_line
        if sorting.verify then
           io.putstring ("Heapsort of size ")
           io.putint (size)
           io.putstring (" has been verified.%N")
        else
           io.putstring ("Heapsort of size ")
           io.putint (size)
           io.putstring (" has not been verified.%N")
        end
        tm.report
     end

  end -- class APPLICATION
```

For *heapsort*, 19,587,985 interchanges were necessary during a typical run. Each run, of course, produces slightly different results because of the different set of random numbers used to fill the array. For *quicksort*, using the same random data, 4,445,841 interchange operations were necessary. The execution time for *heapsort* was 13.23 seconds, whereas for *quicksort* it was 6.21 seconds. It is certainly not obvious why *quicksort* outperforms *heapsort* by over a factor of 2 in execution time. Both algorithms are of complexity $O(nlog_2n)$. It must be remembered that the complexity of an algorithm reflects the growth of the computation time as a function of problem size as the size approaches infinity. It would be expected that for large problem sizes the performance ratio of 13.23 / 6.21 would be approximately maintained as long as the input data were not ordered. As an exercise you are asked to perform a benchmark comparing the performance of these two sorting algorithms when the data approaches being sorted.

13.1.6 Concluding remarks about *heapsort*

We have seen a dramatic example of the intimate relationship between a data structure (*heap*) and an algorithm (*heapsort*). Without viewing the transactions (array interchange operations) from the frame of ref-

Applications of Binary Trees

erence of the heap tree structure it would be quite difficult to interpret and understand the complex sequence of events that ultimately produce an ordered array. This example underscores the fact that the way in which one represents information (the choice of data structure) can greatly influence the efficiency of the underlying operations that can be performed on the data.

13.2 A "learning" tree

One of the first computer programs that captured my imagination many years ago was a game called "Guess the Animal." I was new to computer science, and the game is relatively simple. The computer asks the user a series of questions that have "yes" or "no" answers. Based on the user's responses, the computer guesses an animal that the user is thinking about. If the computer is unable to guess the user's animal, it prompts the user to enter this animal. It then prompts the user to write a "yes/no" question (i.e., a question that has an answer of "yes" or "no") that distinguishes the new animal from the animal closest in the database.

A sample dialog for a simple game might be:

Computer: Does the animal bark?
Person: y
Computer: Is the animal a dog?
Person: n
Computer: What is the animal that you were thinking about?
Person: bear
Computer: Input a yes/no question that distinguishes a bear from a dog:
Person: Is animal crazy about honey?

Computer: Do you wish to play again?
Person: y
Computer: Does the animal bark?
Person: y
Computer: Is the animal crazy about honey?
Person: y
Computer: Is the animal a bear?
Person: y
Computer: I have guessed your animal.

Computer: Do you wish to play again?
Person: y

A "LEARNING" TREE

Computer: Does the animal bark?
Person: n
Computer: Is the animal a cat?
Person: n
Computer: What is the animal that you were thinking about?
Person: elephant
Computer: Input a yes/no question that distinguishes a elephant from a dog
Person: Does the animal have a large trunk?

Computer: Do you wish to play again?
Person: n

  The initial database consisted of a 3-node tree containing a root node with the string "Is the animal a dog?" The left child of the root node (a leaf node) contained the string "dog." The right child of the root node (another leaf node) contained the string "cat." When the user responded "y" to the question "Is the animal a dog?" the leaf node with the string "dog" was replaced by a new node with the question "Does the animal have a large trunk?". This new interior node has two leaf nodes as children. The left of these nodes contains the string "bear" and the right the string "dog."

  Figures 13.38 and 13.39 show the game tree before and after the user's input.

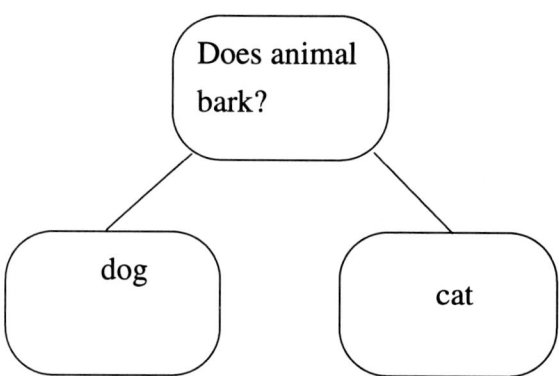

Figure 13.38 Initial game tree.

APPLICATIONS OF BINARY TREES

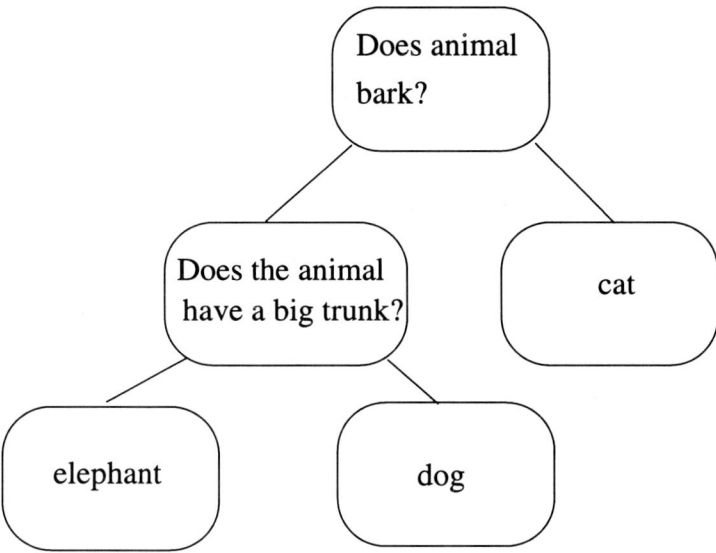

Figure 13.39 Game tree after user's input.

Suppose the user answered "y" to the first question (a "y" answer always results in moving to the left, whereas a "n" answer always results in moving to the right down the tree) and then "n" to the next question. When prompted, the user enters the new animal, coyote, and the question, "Does the animal hunt rabbits and deer?" This would lead to the game tree shown in Figure 13.40.

The process for constructing the game tree should be clear. Each time the computer fails to guess the user's animal, it replaces the guessed animal with a new question node. This new question node has two leaf nodes—the new animal and the guessed animal. The game tree, therefore, has the property that all nodes except leaf nodes have two offspring.

A "LEARNING" TREE

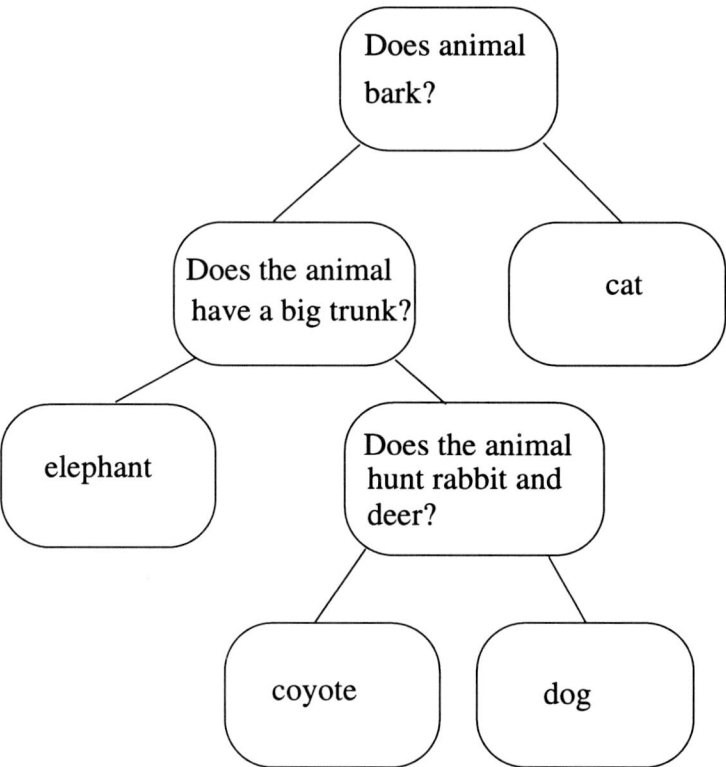

Figure 13.40 Game tree after second user's input.

In order for the program to "learn" from its mistakes (failures to guess correctly), it must continue to expand its game tree based on user input. In order not to lose all of its useful information from one game to the next it must be able to store its game tree on disk. Eiffel provides for "persistent storage" in class STORABLE. This capability is illustrated in the implementation details to be shown below.

There are three classes that define the design of this system: ANIMAL_NODE, ANIMALS, and the root class GUESS_ANIMAL. Listing 13.5 shows class ANIMAL_NODE.

The public attributes of each ANIMAL_NODE are *question*, *animal* (each of type STRING), *left*, and *right* (each of type ANIMAL_NODE). The commands include *make_question*, *make_animal*, *set_left* and *set_right*.

Listing 13.5   Class ANIMAL_NODE

```
class ANIMAL_NODE
creation
  make_question,
  make_animal
feature
  question: STRING

  animal: STRING

  left: ANIMAL_NODE

  right: ANIMAL_NODE

  make_question (q: STRING) is
    require
      non_void_question: q /= void
    do
      question := clone (q)
    end

  make_animal (a: STRING) is
    require
      non_void_animal: a /= void
    do
      animal := clone (a)
      question := clone ("Is the animal a")
      left := void
      right := void
    end

  set_left (node: ANIMAL_NODE) is
    do
      left := node
    ensure
      left = node
    end

  set_right (node: ANIMAL_NODE) is
    do
      right := node
    ensure
```

A "LEARNING" TREE

```
        right = node
      end

end -- class ANIMAL_NODE
```

Before discussing the details of class ANIMALS, the most complex of the three, let us examine the details of the root class, GUESS_ANIMAL. This is, in fact, how the program was designed. The root class identifies all of the necessary public queries and commands of class ANIMALS. Listing 13.6 presents class GUESS_ANIMAL.

Listing 13.6 Class GUESS_ANIMAL

```
class GUESS_ANIMAL

inherit
  STORABLE

creation
  start

feature

  ask: ANIMALS

  start is
    local
      play_more: CHARACTER
      ans: CHARACTER
      new_animal_name: STRING
      new_question: STRING
    do
      !! ask
      io.putstring ("Retrieve previous database (y/n)?")
      ans := user_response
      if ans = 'y' then
        ask ?= retrieve_by_name ("animals.dta")
      else
        ask.initialize
      end
      from
        play_more := 'y'
      until
        play_more = 'n'
```

```
loop
  ask.reset
from
until
  ask.done
loop
  io.putstring (ask.yes_no_question)
  ans := user_response
  ask.process_response (ans)
end
io.putstring (ask.yes_no_question)
ans := user_response
if ans = 'y' then
  io.putstring ("%NGames over! ")
  io.putstring ("The computer has deduced the answer.%N")
  io.putstring ("Clever to think of a ")
  io.putstring (ask.current_animal)
  io.putstring (".%N")
else
  io.putstring ("What animal were you thinking of? ")
  io.readline
  new_animal_name := clone (io.laststring)
  io.putstring ("%NInput a yes/no question that distinguishes ")
  io.putstring (new_animal_name)
  io.putstring (" from ")
  io.putstring (ask.current_animal)
  io.putstring (": ")
  io.readline
  new_question := clone (io.laststring)
  io.putstring ("%NIs the answer yes or no (y/n)? ")
  ans := user_response
  if ans = 'y' then
    ask.add_question (new_question, new_animal_name, 'y')
  else
    ask.add_question (new_question, new_animal_name, 'n')
  end
end
io.putstring ("%NContinue game (y/n)? ")
play_more := user_response
end
```

A "Learning" Tree

```
        ask.store_by_name ("animals.dta")
      end

   user_response: CHARACTER is
      do
         io.readchar
         Result := io.lastchar
      from
      until
         Result = 'y' or Result = 'n'
      loop
         io.readchar
         Result := io.lastchar
      end
      ensure
         Result = 'y' or Result = 'n'
      end

end -- class GUESS_ANIMAL
```

The game begins with the question, "Retrieve previous database (y/n)?" If the user responds "y" the command *retrieve_by_name ("animals.dta")* is invoked. Since class GUESS_ANIMAL is declared as a descendant of STORABLE, it can directly access all of the features of STORABLE. If a file "animals.dta" exists and the file access is successful the object *ask* will be non-*Void* otherwise it will get the value *Void*. Class ANIMALS, which object *ask* is an instance of, must also be a descendant of class STORABLE. The first time the user plays this game, or later if the user wishes to delete the existing database and start over, the answer to the question quoted above would be "n." In this case the command initialize is invoked. This establishes a new game tree with only dog and cat as leaf nodes (see Figure 13.38).

The inner loop prompts the user with a series of questions. The *process_response* command serves as an iterator that moves down to the left if the user responds with a "y" and down to the right if the user responds with a "n." When a leaf node is reached one final question is asked (the computer's guess of animal). If the user responds with a "y," the computer triumphantly announces that it has deduced the correct animal. If the user responds with a "n," the computer prompts the user for the new animal and a relevant question to differentiate the new animal from the computer's guessed animal.

The code reveals several important queries and commands that are directed at *ask*, the single instance of class ANIMALS (the game database). We identify these below.

The command *reset* is invoked through the object *ask*. This causes the tree iterator to start at the root of the game tree. The query *done* sent to *ask* and is used to terminate the inner loop. When *done* is True, the tree iterator has reached a leaf node.

The query *yes_no_question* is invoked on *ask* and output using *putstring*. The command *process_response* is invoked on *ask*. The query *current_animal* is sent to *ask* and output with *putstring*. Finally, the command *add_question* is invoked through *ask*.

When the user wishes to end the game, the command *store_by_name* is invoked on *ask* with "animals.dta" as the file name.

Based on these queries and commands, an interface to class ANIMALS is presented in Listing 13.7.

Listing 13.7   Interface to class ANIMALS (short form)

class interface ANIMALS

feature

-- Queries
animal_node: BOOLEAN -- Returns True if node is a leaf node

current_animal: STRING

done: BOOLEAN -- Returns true when current_node is a leaf node
yes_no_question: STRING -- Prompts user

-- Commands
add_question (q: STRING; new_animal_name: STRING; ans: CHARACTER)
   require
     is_animal_node: animal_node = **true**
     appropriate_ans: ans = 'y' **or** ans = 'n'
     non_void_question: q /= void
     non_void_animal_name: new_animal_name /= void

initialize -- Used to start a new data base

process_response (ans: CHARACTER)
     -- Move to left child if answer is 'y' otherwise to the right

A "LEARNING" TREE

    require
       appropriate_ans: ans = 'y' **or** *ans = 'n'*

  reset -- Sets nodes to root of tree

end *-- class ANIMALS*

    As with all Eiffel interfaces, the important protected details of the class are not shown. These include the attributes that allow the tree to be traversed. Determining the public interface to a class based on the needs of client classes (class GUESS_ANIMAL in this case) is a good practice. Of course, the interface details might be modified later when the system is fully implemented and tested.

    The full details of class ANIMALS are shown in Listing 13.8.

Listing 13.8   Class ANIMALS

class *ANIMALS*
 -- Encapsulates game tree
inherit
  STORABLE

feature *{NONE}*

  root: ANIMAL_NODE

  current_node: ANIMAL_NODE

  previous_node: ANIMAL_NODE

feature
  -- Queries
  done: BOOLEAN **is**
    -- Returns true when current_node is a leaf node
  do
    Result := (current_node.left = void) **and** *(current_node.right = void)*
  ensure
    Result = **true implies** *current_node.left = void* **and** *current_node.right = void*
  end

  animal_node: BOOLEAN **is**
  do
    Result := current_node.animal /= void
  ensure

```
      Result = true implies current_node.animal /= void
   end

yes_no_question: STRING is
      -- Prompts user
   do
      if current_node.animal = void then
         Result := clone (current_node.question)
      else
         Result := clone (current_node.question)
         Result.append (" ")
         Result.append (clone (current_node.animal))
         Result.append ("? ")
      end
   end

current_animal: STRING is
   do
      Result := current_node.animal
   end

 -- Commands
initialize is
      -- Used to start a new data base
   local
      left_child, right_child: ANIMAL_NODE
   do
      !! root.make_question ("Does animal bark? ")
      !! left_child.make_animal ("dog")
      !! right_child.make_animal ("cat")
      root.set_left (left_child)
      root.set_right (right_child)
      current_node := root
   end

reset is
      -- Sets nodes to root of tree
   do
      current_node := root
      previous_node := void
   end
```

A "LEARNING" TREE

```
process_response (ans: CHARACTER) is
    -- Move to left child if answer is 'y' otherwise to the right
  require
    appropriate_ans: ans = 'y' or ans = 'n'
  do
    if not done then
      previous_node := current_node
      if ans = 'y' then
        current_node := current_node.left
      else
        current_node := current_node.right
      end
    end
  end

add_question (q: STRING; new_animal_name: STRING; ans: CHARACTER) is
  require
    is_animal_node: animal_node = true
    appropriate_ans: ans = 'y' or ans = 'n'
    non_void_question: q /= void
    non_void_animal_name: new_animal_name /= void
  local
    new_question: ANIMAL_NODE
    new_animal: ANIMAL_NODE
  do
    !! new_question.make_question (q)
    !! new_animal.make_animal (new_animal_name)
    if ans = 'y' then
      new_question.set_left (new_animal)
      new_question.set_right (current_node)
    else
      new_question.set_right (new_animal)
      new_question.set_left (current_node)
    end
    if previous_node.left = current_node then
      previous_node.set_left (new_question)
    else
      previous_node.set_right (new_question)
    end
  ensure
```

```
        previous_node.left /= void and previous_node.right /= void
    end
```

end -- class ANIMALS

Class ANIMALS contains three protected attributes: *root*, *current_node*, and *previous_node*, each of type ANIMAL_NODE. The attributes *current_node* and *previous_node* are used by *add_question* and *process_response* to iterate through the tree.

The query *yes_no_question* uses the fields *question* and *animal* of ANIMAL_NODE when a leaf node is queried.

The command *initialize* establishes a 3-node tree, containing a root with the question, "Does animal bark?" and two leaf nodes, "dog" and "cat."

The *process_response* command advances the protected attribute *current_node* down to the left or right (depending on the value of the parameter *ans*) and moves *previous_node* to the old value of *current_node* only when *current_node* is not a leaf node.

The command add_question creates two new nodes given by the local variables new_question and new_animal. Depending the value of the parameter *ans*, the *new_question* node has *new_animal* as its left child and *current_node* (the old animal leaf node) as its right child or the reverse. The *new_question* node is made to replace the previous leaf node by linking *previous_node* to the *new_question* node.

13.3 Summary

- It is not unusual for an algorithm to be intimately associated with a data structure. Heapsort provides a dramatic example of such an intimate association.

- A heap data structure is a binary tree derived from an array, in which each node has a value that is equal or greater than its children.

- How does one derive a binary tree from an array? The element in the first index location becomes the root node of the tree. The element in index two becomes the left child of the root. The element in index three becomes the right child of the root. The element in index four becomes the left-most grandchild of the root. The elements in successive index locations of the array fill up each level of the binary tree from left to right.

- The general shape of a binary tree that is a heap is shown below:

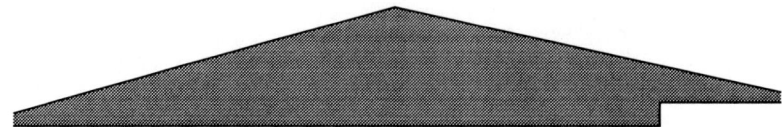

- The heapsort algorithm is more robust than quicksort since it guarantees $O(nlog_2n)$ performance under all conditions. The quicksort algorithm slows down significantly when the data becomes more ordered.
- The way in which one represents information (the choice of data structure) can greatly influence the efficiency of the underlying operations that can be performed on the data.

13.4 Exercises

1. Prove that in a heap data structure the root node contains the largest value in the tree.

2. Use class SORT given in Listing 13.3 to solve this problem. Compare the execution time of *heapsort* with *quicksort* as the input data becomes more and more ordered. Clearly show how you measure the degree of ordering of the input data, and perform several simulation experiments for different degrees of ordering in the input data. Output the sort times for *heapsort* and *quicksort*.

3. "Walk" through the code of Listings 13.5, 13.6, and 13.8 and create a database consisting of 10 animals. Sketch the game tree that corresponds to your input data.

Appendix A

Interface to String Class

class interface STRING

  creation
    make

  feature -- Access

    has (c: CHARACTER): BOOLEAN
      -- Does string include 'c'?

    hash_code: INTEGER
      -- Hash code value.

    index_of (c: CHARACTER; start: INTEGER): INTEGER
      -- Position of first occurrence of 'c' at or after 'start';
      -- 0 if none.

    item (i: INTEGER): CHARACTER
      -- Character at position 'i'

    item_code (i: INTEGER): INTEGER
      -- Numeric code of character at position 'i'
    require
      index_small_enough: i <= count
      index_large_enough: i > 0

shared_with *(other: like Current): BOOLEAN*
    -- Does string share the text of 'other'?

substring_index *(other: STRING; start: INTEGER): INTEGER*
    -- Position of first occurrence of 'other' at or after 'start';
    -- 0 if none.

True_constant: *STRING* is "true"
    -- Constant string "true"

infix "@" *(i: INTEGER): CHARACTER*
    -- Character at position 'i'

feature -- Comparison

  is_equal *(other: like Current): BOOLEAN*
    -- Is string made of same character sequence as 'other'
    -- (possibly with a different capacity)?

  infix "<" *(other: STRING): BOOLEAN*
    -- Is string lexicographically lower than 'other'?
    -- (False if 'other' is void)

feature -- Conversion

  linear_representation: *LINEAR [CHARACTER]*
    -- Representation as a linear structure

  mirror
    -- Reverse the order of characters.
    -- "Hello world" -> "dlrow olleH".
  ensure
    same_count: count = old count

  mirrored: *like Current*
    -- Mirror image of string;
    -- result for "Hello world" is "dlrow olleH".
  ensure
    same_count: Result.count = count

  to_boolean: *BOOLEAN*
    -- Boolean value;
    -- "true" yields 'true', "false" yields 'false'
    -- (case-insensitive)

  to_c: *ANY*
    -- An integer which a C function may cast into a pointer

-- to a 'C' form of current string.
   -- Useful only for interfacing with C software.

to_double: DOUBLE
   -- "Double" value;
   -- for example, when applied to "123.0", will yield 123.0 (double)

to_integer: INTEGER
   -- Integer value;
   -- for example, when applied to "123", will yield 123

to_lower
   -- Convert to lower case.

to_real: REAL
   -- Real value;
   -- for example, when applied to "123.0", will yield 123.0

to_upper
   -- Convert to upper case.

feature -- Duplication

   substring (n1, n2: INTEGER): like Current
      -- Copy of substring containing all characters at indices
      -- between 'n1' and 'n2'
   require
      meaningful_origin: 1 <= n1
      meaningful_interval: n1 <= n2
      meaningful_end: n2 <= count
   ensure
      new_result_count: Result.count = n2 - n1 + 1

feature -- Element change

   append (s: STRING)
      -- Append a copy of 's' at end.
   ensure
      new_count: count = old count + s.count

   append_boolean (b: BOOLEAN)
      -- Append the string representation of 'b' at end.

   append_double (d: DOUBLE)
      -- Append the string representation of 'd' at end.

append_integer (i: INTEGER)
  -- Append the string representation of 'i' at end.

append_real (r: REAL)
  -- Append the string representation of 'r' at end.

copy (other: like Current)
  -- Reinitialize by copying the characters of 'other'.
  -- (This is also used by 'clone'.)
ensure
  new_result_count: count = other.count

extend (c: CHARACTER)
  -- Append 'c' at end.
ensure
  item_inserted: item (count) = c

fill_blank
  -- Fill with blanks.

head (n: INTEGER)
  -- Remove all characters except for the first 'n';
  -- do nothing if 'n' >= 'count'.
require
  non_negative_argument: n >= 0

insert (s: like Current; i: INTEGER)
  -- Add 's' to the left of position 'i' in current string.
require
  string_exists: s /= void
  index_small_enough: i <= count
  index_large_enough: i > 0
ensure
  new_count: count = old count + s.count

left_adjust
  -- Remove leading blanks.
ensure
  new_count: (count /= 0) implies (item (1) /= ' ')

precede (c: CHARACTER)
  -- Add 'c' at front.
ensure
  new_count: count = old count + 1

prepend (s: STRING)
  -- Prepend a copy of 's' at front.
require
  argument_not_void: s /= void
ensure
  new_count: count = old count + s.count

put (c: CHARACTER; i: INTEGER)
  -- Replace character at position 'i' by 'c'.
require
  index_small_enough: i <= count
  index_large_enough: i > 0

replace_substring (s: like Current; start_pos, end_pos: INTEGER)
  -- Copy the characters of 's' to positions
  -- 'start_pos' .. 'end_pos'.
require
  string_exists: s /= void
  index_small_enough: end_pos <= count
  order_respected: start_pos <= end_pos
  index_large_enough: start_pos > 0
ensure
  new_count: count = old count + s.count - end_pos + start_pos - 1

replace_substring_all (original, new: like Current)
  -- Replace every occurence of 'original' with 'new'.
require
  original_exists: original /= void
  new_exists: new /= void
  original_not_empty: not original.empty

right_adjust
  -- Remove trailing blanks.
ensure
  new_count: (count /= 0) implies (item (count) /= ' ')

set (t: like Current; n1, n2: INTEGER)
  -- Set current string to substring of 't' from indices 'n1'
  -- to 'n2', or to empty string if no such substring.
require
  argument_not_void: t /= void
ensure
  is_substring: is_equal (t.substring (n1,n2))

share (other: like Current)
    -- Make current string share the text of 'other'.
    -- Subsequent changes to the characters of current string
    -- will also affect 'other', and conversely.
require
    argument_not_void: other /= void
ensure
    shared_count: other.count = count

tail (n: INTEGER)
    -- Remove all characters except for the last 'n';
    -- do nothing if 'n' >= 'count'.
require
    non_negative_argument: n >= 0

feature -- Initialization

adapt (s: STRING): like Current
    -- Object of a type conforming to the type of 's',
    -- initialized with attributes from 's'

from_c (c_string: ANY)
    -- Reset contents of string from contents of 'c_string',
    -- a string created by some external C function.
require
    c_string /= void

frozen make (n: INTEGER)
    -- Allocate space for at least 'n' characters.
require
    non_negative_size: n >= 0
ensure
    empty_string: count = 0
    area_allocated: capacity >= n

setup (other: like Current)
    -- Perform actions on a freshly created object so that
    -- the contents of 'other' can be safely copied onto it.

feature -- Measurement

capacity: INTEGER
    -- Allocated space

count: INTEGER
  -- Actual number of characters making up the string

occurrences (c: CHARACTER): INTEGER
  -- Number of times 'c' appears in the string

feature -- Output

out: like Current
  -- Printable representation

feature -- Removal

prune (c: CHARACTER)
  -- Remove first occurrence of 'c', if any.
require
  true

prune_all (c: CHARACTER)
  -- Remove all occurrences of 'c'.
require
  true
ensure
  changed_count: count = (old count) - (old occurrences (c))

remove (i: INTEGER)
  -- Remove 'i'-th character.
require
  index_small_enough: i <= count
  index_large_enough: i > 0
ensure
  new_count: count = old count - 1

wipe_out
  -- Remove all characters.
ensure
  empty_string: count = 0
  empty_area: capacity = 0

feature -- Resizing

adapt_size
  -- Adapt the size to accommodate 'count' characters.

grow (newsize: INTEGER)
  -- Ensure that the capacity is at least 'newsize'.

    require
       new_size_non_negative: newsize >= 0

  resize (newsize: INTEGER)
      -- Reallocate space to accommodate
      -- 'newsize' characters.
      -- May discard some characters if 'newsize' is
      -- lower than the current number of characters.
    require
       new_size_non_negative: newsize >= 0

feature *-- Status report*

  Changeable_comparison_criterion: BOOLEAN is false

  consistent (other: like Current): BOOLEAN
      -- Is object in a consistent state so that 'other'
      -- may be copied onto it? (Default answer: yes).

  Extendible: BOOLEAN is true
      -- May new items be added? (Answer: yes.)

  prunable: BOOLEAN
      -- May items be removed? (Answer: yes.)

  valid_index (i: INTEGER): BOOLEAN
      -- Is 'i' correctly bounded?

invariant
  extendible: extendible
  compare_character: object_comparison = false

end *-- class STRING*

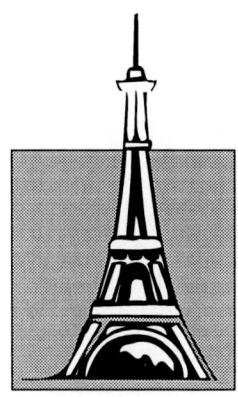

Index

; (semicolon), in Eiffel language 10–11
:= (assignment operator) 40–41
* (asterisk), multiplication operator 41–42
 (braces), export section 52
^ (caret)
    binary operator for raised to power 41–42
    BIT_REF class command 392
\\ (double backslash), remainder operator 41
// (double forward slash), integer division operator 41–42
= (equality operator) 41
!! (exclamation points), creation operator 38
> (greater than) 42
>= (greater than or equal) 42
/= (inequality operator) 41
< (less than) 42
<= (less than or equal) 41–42
- (minus sign), subtraction operator 41–42
+ (plus sign), addition operator 41–42
# (pound) command, BIT_REF class 392
+ query, POLYNOMIAL class 295
/ (single forward slash), binary division operator 42

A
abstract classes
    AIRPLANE class example 78–79
    and assertions 76–79
    SAVINGS class example 63–68
abstract data types (ADT)
    overview 2–6
    RECTANGLE example
        data model notation 3–4
        Eiffel implementation 7–10
        Pascal implementation 4–6
    See also Classes
accessing strings 118
ACCOUNT class example
    assertions 73–76
    CHECKING subclass 54–56
    deferred classes 63–68

INDEX

export scope 52–53
  inheritance 56–58
Ace files 10
activation record, defined 194
addition of long integers 283–284
Adelson-Velskii, G.M. 345
AIRPLANE class example
  abstract class with assertions 78–79
  JET subclass 53–54
algorithms
  average-case asymptotic
    complexity 97
  AVL trees
    deleting nodes 368–372
    inserting nodes 356, 366–367
  big O notation 97
  binary search, recursive 201–204
  binary tree traversal 302–304
  collision resolution, hash tables
    415–418
  computational complexity 92, 97
  defined 92
  efficiency 97–98
  partition 109–111
  relationship to data structures
    458–459
  simple search algorithm 126–128
  sorting
    bubble sort 98–101
    comb sort 101–105
    divide and conquer 108
    heapsort 437–459
    insertion sort 105–108
    magic number sort 104–105
    quicksort 108–116
    selection-sort 93–97
  weight-balanced trees, inserting
    nodes 373–376
  worst-case asymptotic complexity
    97
  See also Recursion

See also specific topics in this index
aliasing problems, STACK class 136
allocating storage for objects 38
ancestor classes 12
and
  BIT_REF class command 392
  Boolean operator 42
and then, Boolean operator operator
  42
animal guessing game
  See Learning tree
ANY class 52
APL (average internal path length)
  See Average internal path length
  See Binary trees
applications
  binary trees
    heap sorting 437–459
    learning tree 459–471
  lists
    long integers 281–289
    polynomials 289–296
  mathematical
    long integers 281–289
    polynomials 289–296
  queues
    random number generator
      258–263
    waiting line simulation 263–278
  stacks
    calculator 226–234
    infix expression, converting to
      postfix 221–234
    recursive routine, converting to
      iterative routine 207–221
    solitaire poker game 234–255
  See also Examples
ARRAY class
  commands 88
  interface 88–89
  queries 88

routines, example 89–91
arrays
   algorithms
      bubble sort 98–101
      comb sort 101–105
      efficiency 97
      insertion sort 105–108
      quicksort 108–116
      selection-sort 93–97
   ARRAY class 88–91
   deriving binary trees from 444–445
   dynamic 87
   examples
      recursive binary search 200–204
      tennis players 48–50
   sorting problems 92
   static 87
   See also Heap sorting
   See also String class
assertions
   examples
      abstract class, AIRPLANE class 78–79
      ACCOUNT class 73–76
   inheriting 76–79
   overview 70
assigning objects, CAR class example 40–41
assignment operator (:=) 40–41
as_string command, LONG_INTEGER class 289
asterisk (*), multiplication operator 41–42
attributes
   adding to descendants 56
   assigning to objects 38
   changing values with routines 45–46
   defined 7
   initializing with creation routines 38–39

and read-only semantics 8
redefining with inheritance 56
vs. routines 68–69
See also Queries
See also Routines
automatic garbage collection 39
average internal path length
   AVL trees 345
   comparing to balanced tree 331–334
   computing 304–306
   randomly generated search trees 334–341
   testing for AVL balance 353–354
   traversal algorithms 302–304
   weight-balanced trees 372
   worst case 334, 372
average-case asymptotic complexity 97
average_internal_path_length query BINARY_T class 307, 311–312
AVL trees
   average internal path length, worst case 372
   balanced, defined 351–352
   deleting nodes
      algorithm, discussion of 368
      rotational corrections 368–372
      vs. inserting nodes 368
   height-balanced, defined 345
   history of 345
   inserting nodes
      algorithm, discussion of 356, 366–367
      paired rotational corrections 358–361
      postconditions 366
      preconditions 366
      sample code 361–366
      single rotational correction 356–357
      vs. deleting nodes 368

INDEX

leftrotate command 349–351
rightrotate command 349–350
testing 353–354
vs. weight-balanced trees 372,
 381–384

B
back_node query, LIST_TYPE class
 163
balance, determining for binary trees
 comparing to balanced tree 331–334
 computing average internal path
  length 304–306
 randomly generated search trees
  334–341
 testing for AVL balance 353–354
 See also Average internal path length
 See also AVL trees
 See also Weight-balanced trees
balanced search trees
 See AVL trees
 See Weight-balanced trees
basic object types, default values 40
behavioral model 3
big O notation 97
binary operators 41–42
binary trees
 arrays, deriving from 444–445
 average internal path length
  AVL trees 345
  comparing to balanced tree
   331–334
  computing 304–306
  randomly generated search trees
   334–341
  weight-balanced trees 372
  worst case 334, 372
 balance, determining
  comparing to balanced tree
   331–334
  computing average internal path

length 304–306
randomly generated search trees
 334–341
testing for AVL balance 353–354
commands, list of 307
defined 299–302
heap sorting 437–459
implementing 307–312
learning tree 459–471
levels, defined 301
nodes
 deleting 321–326
 determining if present 307–310
 displaying 302
 inserting 316–320
 traversal order 302–304
 types of 299–301
perfectly balanced 305
queries 307
resemblance to natural trees 301–
 302
rotating 346–351
search-time performance 306
subtrees 299–300
traversal algorithms 302–304
See also AVL trees
See also Search trees
See also Weight-balanced trees
BINARY_T class
 assertions 307–308
 commands 307, 311–312
 constrained generic parameter 310
 implementing 308–310
 interface 307–308
 queries 307, 311–312
binding mode 24
binding storage
 See Storage
BIT data type
 declaration 389–390
 integer set example 394–400

BIT_REF class
  commands 391–392
  example code 392–394
  interface 390–391
  queries 391–392
bits
  See BIT data type
  See BIT_REF class
blocking
  commands 16
  queries 16
BOOLEAN object type
  default values 40
  operators 42
braces (), export section 52
branching 42–44
bubble sort algorithm 98–101

C

calculator application 226–234
caller, defined 46
can_move query, LIST_TYPE class 162
capacity query, stacks 134
CAR class examples
  assigning objects 40–41
  creation routines 38–39
  reclaiming storage 39
card game application 234–255
caret (^)
  binary operator for raised to power 41–42
  BIT_REF class command 392
case-sensitivity 9
CHARACTER object type, default values 40
characters, arrays of
  See String class
CHECKING subclass examples
  export subclause 58
  redefine subclause 57–58
  rename subclause 59–60
child classes 12

children, binary trees 299
class libraries 81
classes
  abstract 63–68
  ancestor 12
  child 12
  collections 389
  components, list of 50–51
  containers 20, 131–132
  creation routines 38–39, 51–56
  deferred 63–68
  defined 2
  descendant 12
  descendants, creating 54
  elseif clause 43
  ensure clause 70
  ensure then clause 77
  export subclause 58
  external views 11–12
  generic 20–21
  inheritance 56–63
  inspecting, with *short* tool 11–12
  instances, creating 9–10, 20–21
  as logical unit 37
  as modules 37
  names, as object types 38
  notational conventions 9
  parent 12
  as physical unit 37
  and programs 38
  redefine subclause 57–58, 68
  rename subclause 58–60
  require clause 70
  require else clause 77
  select subclause 60–63
  short tool 11–12
  subclasses 12
  See also Examples
  See also specific class names
client, defined 8
cloning objects 41

coalesced chaining 416–418
code blocks, control structures 42–45
code reuse
    See Reusability
collections
    See Hash functions
    See Set operations
collision, defined 401
collision chains, defined 416
collision resolution algorithms
    coalesced chaining 416–418
    comparing 418–432
    linear chaining 415–418
comb sort algorithm 101–105
combining bits 392
commands
    ARRAY class 88
    BINARY_T class 307, 311–312
    BIT_REF class 391–392
    blocking 16
    defined 4
    DEQUE class 183
    doubly-linked, converting to 176–179
    inheritance 12–13
    LIST_TYPE class 162–163
    naming conventions 46
    ORDERED_LIST class 174–175
    queues 143
    RANDOM_NUMBER class 260
    STACK class 133–134
    STRING class 118–120, 473–480
    UNORDERED_LIST class 151, 155, 167
    UNORDERED_LIST_D class 168, 174
    See also Queries
    See also Routines
    See also specific command names
comparing strings 118
computation
    performing 45–46
    vs. storage 68–69
computational complexity 92, 97
concrete parameters 20–21
configuration files 10–11
constraining generic parameters 176
container classes
    defined 20, 87
    list of 132
control structures 42–45
converting strings 118
copying
    objects 41
    strings 118
creation operators 38
creation routines
    CAR class examples 38–39
    creating classes 38–39
    creating subclasses 53–56
    export section 52
    overview 10
cursor, defined 151
cursor query, LIST_TYPE class 163

D

data models
    defined 3
    notation 4
data structures
    defined 3
    relationship to algorithms 458–459
    See also Arrays
    See also Binary trees
    See also Lists
    See also Queues
    See also Search trees
    See also Stacks
declaring
    BIT data types 389–390
    objects 38
default export section 52
deferred classes

INDEX

ACCOUNT class example 63–68
and assertions 77–79
delete command, BINARY_T class
assertions 308
iterative version 320–326
See also Insert command;
BINARY_T class
deleting items
AVL trees
rotational corrections 368–372
vs. inserting nodes 368
balance considerations 345
binary trees
assertions 308
tree with no children 321–323
tree with one child 324–325
tree with two children 325–326
search trees 320–326
stacks 133
See also specific Remove commands
DEQUE class 182–184
deques, as lists 182–184
deriving binary trees from arrays
444–445
descendant classes 12
destroying objects 38–39
detaching storage 39
dice game, late binding example
24–33
dicing
See Hash functions
dictionary, hash table example
401–415
DICTIONARY abstract data type 389
differentiate query, POLYNOMIAL
class 295–296
discrete-event simulation 263.278
divide and conquer algorithm 108
do statement 46
dog obedience, polymorphism example 22–24
do_it_recursively, recursion example

189–192
double backslash (\), remainder operator 41
double forward slash (//), integer division operator 41–42
doubly-linked lists 176–179
dynamic arrays 87
dynamic binding 22–24
dynamic container classes 132

E
early binding 22–24
efficiency of algorithms 97
Eiffel, overview
; (semicolons), use of 10–11
abstract data types (ADT) 2–6
Ace files 10
assertion handling 70
attributes 7–9
basic object types, default values 40
case sensitivity 9
classes 2–6
list of components 50–51
commands 3–4
compared to C++ 37
configuration files 10–11
container classes 20
creation routines 10
encapsulation 6–11
external routines 46–48
external views 11–12
generic classes 20–21
history of 37
inheritance 12–13
instances
creating 9–10, 20–21
defined 3
Interactive Software Engineering
(ISE) 10
internal views 11–12
late binding 22–24

Index

logical unit 37
Meyer, Bertrand 12
notational conventions 4, 9
objects 3
physical unit 37
polymorphism 22–24
queries 3–4
recursion 189
reusability 13
short tool 11–12
uniform access 12
Eiffel is a wonderful language, recursion example 189–192
elseif clause 43
empty query
   LIST_TYPE class 162
   queues 143
   stacks 134
enabling bits 391
encapsulation 6–11
end statement 46
ensure clause 70
ensure then clause 77
entry nodes, binary trees 301
equality operator (=) 41
error handling 69–70
examples
   abstract class with assertions, AIRPLANE class 78–79
   ACCOUNT class
      assertions 73–76
      CHECKING subclass 54–56
      deferred classes 63–68
      export scope 52–53
      inheritance 56–58
   AIRPLANE class
      abstract class with assertions 78–79
      JET subclass 53–54
   arrays
      recursive binary search 200–204
      tennis players 48–50

assertions
   abstract class, AIRPLANE class 78–79
   ACCOUNT class 73–76
assigning objects, CAR class 40–41
CAR class
   assigning objects 40–41
   creation routines 38–39
   reclaiming storage 39
CHECKING subclass
   export subclause 58
   redefine subclause 57–58
   rename subclause 59–60
creation routines, CAR class 38–39
deferred classes, ACCOUNT class, 63–68
dice game, late binding 24–33
dictionary, hash tables 401–415
dog obedience, polymorphism 22–24
do_it_recursively, recursion 189–192
Eiffel is a wonderful language, recursion 189–192
exception handling, MATH class 70–73
export scope
   ACCOUNT class 52–53
   CHECKING subclass 58
FLOWER class, rename subclause 59
hash tables, spelling checker dictionary 401–415
income tax computation, routines 46
inheritance
   ACCOUNT class 56–58
   queue example 14–20
INTEGER example, abstract data types (ADT) 3
iteration, sum of integers 45

late binding
   dice game 24–33
   dog obedience 22–24
learning tree example, STORABLE class 459–471
MATH class
   exception handling 70–73
   preconditions 70–72
PARENT and CHILD classes, select subclause 60–63
permutation group example, recursion 196–200
polymorphism, dog obedience 22–24
preconditions, MATH class 70–72
print_recursively, recursion 193–196
reclaiming storage, CAR class 39
RECTANGLE example
   data model notation 3–4
   Eiffel implementation 7–10
   Pascal implementation 4–6
recursion
   binary search of sorted arrays 200–204
   Eiffel is a wonderful language 189–192
   permutation group example 196–200
   print_recursively 193–196
   run-time stack 192–194
redefine subclause, CHECKING subclass 57–58
rename subclause
   CHECKING subclass 59–60
   FLOWER class 59
routines, income tax computation 46
run-time stack, recursion 192–194
search trees
   determining balance 332–334
   randomly generating 334–341
searching, recursion example 200–204
select subclause, PARENT and CHILD classes 60–63
spelling checker, hash tables 401–415
STORABLE class, learning tree example 459–471
subclasses
   ACCOUNT class 54–56
   AIRPLANE class 53–54
sum of integers, iteration 45
tennis players, array 48–50
See also Applications
exception handling 69–70
   MATH class example 70–73
exclamation points (!!), creation operator 38
exit nodes, binary trees 301
exponential interarrival time 263–264
export subclause
   ACCOUNT class example 52–53
   default values 52
   unordered lists with duplicates 174
external views
   defined 2
   inspecting with *short* tool 11–12

F

fields 3
find_occurence query, UNORDERED_LIST_D class 174
first-in-first-out protocol 142
FIXED_STACK class, in game application 248–255
FLOWER class, rename subclause example 59
forward slashes (//), integer division operator 41–42
from-until-loop construct 44–45
front query, queues 143

front_node query, LIST_TYPE class 163
function routines 45–46

G

garbage collection 39
generic classes 20–21
generic parameters
   BINARY_T class 310
   defined 20–21
   ORDERED_LIST class 176
Gonnet, Gaston 346, 372
greater than (>) 42
greater than or equal (>=) 42
Guess the Animal game
   See Learning tree

H

hash functions
   collision resolution algorithms
      coalesced chaining 416–418
      comparing 418–432
      linear chaining 415–418
   designing 403–404
   implementing 404–411
   indices 401–404
   real vs. simulated 425–432
   testing 411–415
hash tables
   defined 401
   spelling checker dictionary example 401–415
   See also Hash functions
heap, defined 437
heap sorting
   formheap procedure 446–449
   heap data structure 444–445
      largest value 445
   learning tree application 459–471
   overview 445–446
   rebuildheap procedure 449–451
   speed 458
   transactions, tracing 437–444
   vs. quicksort algorithm 451–458
   See also Binary trees
height-balanced, defined 345
Hoare, Tony 108
hybrid language, defined 37

I

if-then structure 42
if-then-else structure 42–44
implementation vs. interface 45
implies, Boolean operator 42
income tax computation example 46
index
   defined 48, 87
   See also Hash functions
inequality operator (/=) 41
infix expression, converting to postfix 221–234
inheritance
   assertions 76–79
   attributes, redefining 56
   classes 56–63
   commands 12–13
   examples
      ACCOUNT class 56–58
      queue example 14–20
   export subclause 58
   extension 56–57
   ORDERED_LIST class 175–176
   postconditions 76–79
   preconditions 76–79
   RANDOM_NUMBER class 261–262
   redefine subclause 57–58
   rename subclause 58–60
   restriction 56
   and reusability 13, 56
   routines 12–13, 56–63
   select subclause 60–63
   selective export 58
   specialization 56–63

subclasses 12–13
in unordered lists with duplicates 168–174
UNORDERED_LIST_D class 174
initialization
  objects 40
  strings 118
  See also Creation routines
inorder command, BINARY_T class 307, 311
inorder traversal 302–304
input/output routines 46–48
insert command
  AVL trees 361–367
  BINARY_T class
    iterative version 319–320
    postconditions 308
    preconditions 308
    recursive version 316–318
    See also Delete command, BINARY_T class
  INTEGER_SET class 399
  ORDERED_LIST class 174
  queues 143, 145
insert_after command
  doubly-linked version 178
  UNORDERED_LIST_D class 168
insert_before command
  doubly-linked version 178–179
  UNORDERED_LIST class 167
  UNORDERED_LIST_D class 168
insert_before_occurence command
  UNORDERED_LIST_D class 168
insert_front command
  UNORDERED_LIST class 167
inserting items
  AVL trees 356–368
  balance considerations 345
  binary trees 316–320
  BINARY_T class 308, 319–320
  doubly-linked lists 178–179

insertion sort algorithm 105–108
INTEGER_SET class 399
ORDERED_LIST class 174
queues 143, 145
stacks 133
UNORDERED_LIST class 167
UNORDERED_LIST_D class 168
weight-balanced trees 373–381
insertion sort algorithm 105–108
inspect construct 44
instances
  creating 9–10, 20–21, 38
  defined 3
  generic parameters, replacing with concrete 20–21
  of problems 92
  See also Abstract data types (ADT) 3
  See also Objects
INTEGER object type
  default value 40
  operators 41
INTEGER_SET class
  feature sections 398–399
  implementing with BIT 32 394–398
  inserting items 399
  vs. UNORDERED_LIST class 399–401
integrate query, POLYNOMIAL class 296
Interactive Software Engineering (ISE) 10, 37
interarrival time 257, 263–264
interface
  ARRAY class 88–89
  BINARY_T class 307–308
  BIT_REF class 390–391
  LONG_INTEGER class 282
  STRING class 121–122, 473–480
  UNORDERED_LIST class 151–156
  vs. implementation 45
  See also specific class names

internal use only
   See Protected section
internal view, defined 2
internal-path balanced (IPB) 372
intersection operation, sets 394
IO object 46–48
IPB (internal-path balanced) 372
is a kind of, relationships 56
is_avl query 353–356
ISE (Interactive Software Engineering) 10, 37
is_present query, SEARCH_TREE class 314–316
item query
   ARRAY class 88
   BIT_REF class 392
item_after query
   UNORDERED_LIST class 155, 167
   UNORDERED_LIST_D class 168, 174
item_after_occurence query
   UNORDERED_LIST_D class 174
item_at_cursor query
   LIST_TYPE class 162
item_before query
   UNORDERED_LIST class 167
   UNORDERED_LIST_D class 168, 174
item_before_occurences query
   UNORDERED_LIST_D class 174
items
   determining presence in set 394, 399–401
   See also Nodes
iteration 44–45
iterative routine, converting from recursive routine 207–221

K
keyboard input, routines 46–48
keywords, notational conventions 9

L
Landis, E.M. 345
Las Vegas poker game application 234–255
last-in-first-out (LIFO) protocol 133
late binding
   dice game example 24–33
   dog obedience example 22–24
leaf nodes, binary trees
   defined 300
   order of traversal 302–304
learning tree
   classes 462–466
   sample dialogs 459–462
   STORABLE class 462–471
left child, binary trees 300
left subtree, binary trees 299
leftrotate command
   AVL trees 349–351
   weight-balanced trees 378
less than (<) 42
less than or equal (<=) 41–42
levels, binary trees 301
   See also Average internal path length
LIFO (last-in-first-out) protocol 133
linear chaining 415–418
linear data abstractions 87
linked lists 157
linking code 11
lists
   applications
      long integers 281–289
      polynomials 289–296
   defined 149
   as deques 182–184
   doubly-linked, converting to 176–179
   linked 157
   ordered 174–176
      implemented as a priority queue 184–186
   as priority queues 184–186

as queues 181–182
specification for 149–150
as stacks 179–181
unordered
    data abstraction 150–151
    with duplicates 168–174, 179–184
    implementing 156–167
    interface 151–156
LIST_TYPE class
    commands 162–163
    implementation 157–162
    queries 162–163
load factor 266, 416, 432
logical operators 41–42
logical unit, basic 37
long integers application 281–289
LONG_INTEGER class
    addition of long integers 283–284
    creation routine 288–289
    implementing 284–288
    interface 282
    internal representation 282–283
looping 44–45

M

magic number sort 104–105
mapping
    See Hash functions
MATH class examples
    exception handling 70–73
    preconditions 70–72
mathematical applications
    long integers 281–289
    polynomials 289–296
measuring strings 119
memory
    See Storage
methods
    See Routines
Meyer, Bertrand 12, 37
minus sign (-), subtraction operator
    41–42

modifying strings 118
modules 37
mutator routines 52

N

naming conventions 46
nested if-then-else structures 43
next query 157
nodes
    defined 299–301
    deleting
        AVL trees 368–372
        search trees 320–326
        tree with no children 321–323
        tree with one child 324–325
        tree with two children 325–326
    determining if present 307–310,
        314–316
    displaying 302
    inserting
        AVL trees 356–367
        search trees 316–320
        weight-balanced trees 376–381
    order of traversal 302–304
    rotating 346–351
    values, comparing 312
    weight, defined 373
    See also AVL trees
    See also Binary trees
    See also Search trees
    See also Weight-balanced trees
not
    BIT_REF class command 392
    Boolean operator 42
notational conventions
    classes 9
    data models 4
    Eiffel keywords 9
number_occurences query,
    UNORDERED_LIST_D class 174
numbers, sorting 92

See also Sorting algorithms
num_elements query
    queues 143
    stacks 134

O

object-oriented language, defined 37
objects
    assigning 40–41
    attributes, initializing with creation routines 38–39
    changing internal state 45–46
    cloning 41
    copying 41
    creating 38, 51–56
    declaring 38
    default values 40
    defined 3
    destroying 38–39
    equality, defined 41
    operators 41–42
    reference semantics 40
    routines
        assigning based on class 38
        invoking 45
    state information, accessing 45–46
    storage, attaching to 38–39
    types
        declaring 38
        list of 40
    value semantics 40
    See also Routines
operations
    See Commands
    See Queries
operators
    := (assignment) 40–41
    !! (exclamation points), creation 38
    BOOLEAN object type 42
    equality (=) 41
    inequality (/=) 41
    INTEGER object type 41
    logical operators 42
    REAL object type 42
or
    BIT_REF class command 392
    Boolean operator 42
or else, Boolean operator 42
ordered lists
    See ORDERED_LIST class
ORDERED_LIST class
    commands 174–175
    implementation 175–176
    as a priority queue 184–186

P

parameters
    generic, replacing with concrete 20–21
parent classes 12
    select subclause example 60–63
parsers 389
partition algorithm 109–111
Pascal, limitations of 6
path length
    See Average internal path length
permutations, generating 196–200, 207–221
    See also Recursion
persistent storage 459–471
physical unit, basic 37
+ query, POLYNOMIAL class 295
plus sign (+), addition operator 41–42
pointers, in lists 151
poker game application 234–255
polymorphism 22–24
POLYNOMIAL class
    creation routine 294
    implementation 291–294
    queries 295–296
polynomials application 289–296
pop command, stacks 133
postconditions

defined 70
inheriting 76–79
postfix expression, converting from infix 221–234
postorder command, BINARY_T class 307, 311
postorder traversal 302–304
command, BIT_REF class 392
preconditions
   defined 70
   inheriting 76–79
   MATH class example 70–72
preorder command, BINARY_T class 307, 311
preorder traversal 302–303
present query
   LIST_TYPE class 162
   set operations 394, 399–401
print_recursively, recursion example 193–196
priority queues
   as lists 184–186
   waiting line application 263–278
   See also Queues
PRIORITY_QUEUE class 184–186
problems, instances of 92
procedure routines 45–46
programming
   constructs 42–45
   by contract 70
programs, defined 38
protected section 8
protocols, defined 132
push command, stacks 133
put command
   ARRAY class 88
   BIT_REF class 391

Q

queries
   + query, POLYNOMIAL class 295
   ARRAY class 88

average_internal_path_length query, BINARY_T class 307, 311–312
back_node query, LIST_TYPE class 163
binary trees 307
BINARY_T class
   implementing 311–312
   list of 307
BIT_REF class 391–392
blocking 16
can_move query, LIST_TYPE class 162
capacity query, stacks 134
cursor query, LIST_TYPE class 163
defined 4
DEQUE class 182–183
differentiate query, POLYNOMIAL class 295–296
empty query
   LIST_TYPE class 162
   queues 143
   stacks 134
find_occurence query, UNORDERED_LIST_D class 174
front query, queues 143
front_node query, LIST_TYPE class 163
integrate query, POLYNOMIAL class 296
is_avl query 353–356
is_present query, SEARCH_TREE class 314–316
item query
   ARRAY class 88
   BIT_REF class 392
item_after query 155
   UNORDERED_LIST class 167
   UNORDERED_LIST_D class 168, 174
item_after_occurence query, UNORDERED_LIST_D class 174

item_at_cursor query, LIST_TYPE
    class 162
item_before query
    UNORDERED_LIST class 167
    UNORDERED_LIST_D class
        168, 174
item_before_occurences query,
    UNORDERED_LIST_D class 174
LIST_TYPE class 162–163
naming conventions 46
next query 157
number_occurences query,
    UNORDERED_LIST_D class 174
num_elements query
    queues 143
    stacks 134
+ query, POLYNOMIAL class 295
POLYNOMIAL class 295–296
present query
    LIST_TYPE class 162
    set operations 394, 399–401
queues 143
RANDOM_NUMBER class 260
reverse_list query, POLYNOMIAL
    class 295
STACK class 133–134
STRING class 118–120, 473–480
top query, stacks 133
UNORDERED_LIST class 150–151,
    155, 167
UNORDERED_LIST_D class 168,
    174
See also Attributes
See also Commands
See also Routines
See also specific class names
queues
    applications
        random number generator
            258–263
        waiting line simulation 263–278

commands 143
counting 143
dynamic implementation 143–145
empty, checking for 143
first-in-first-out protocol 142
implemented as
    UNORDERED_LIST_D 181–182
inserting items 143
next item, accessing 143
queries 143
removing items 143
See also PRIORITY_QUEUE class
queuing theory 257–258
quicksort algorithm 108–116
    speed 458
    vs. heapsort algorithm 451–458

R
random number generator application
    258–263
RANDOM_NUMBER class
    Ace file 261
    C functions 260–261
    commands 260
    data model 258–260
    inheritance 261–262
    queries 260
    test program 262–263
read-only semantics 8
REAL object type
    default value 40
    operators 42
reclaiming storage, CAR class
    example 39
RECTANGLE example
    data model notation 3–4
    Eiffel implementation 7–10
    Pascal implementation 4–6
recursion
    activation record, defined 194
    arrays, searching 200–204

defined 189
examples
  binary search of sorted arrays 200–204
  converting to iterative routine 207–221
  do_it_recursively 189–192
  Eiffel is a wonderful language 189–192
  permutation group example 196–200
  print_recursively 193–196
  run-time stack 192–194
mechanics, statement of 194
See also Binary trees
recursive stack
  See Recursion
recycling storage 39
redefine subclause
  CHECKING subclass examples 57–58
  UNORDERED_LIST_D class 174
  when to use 68
reference semantics 40
remove command
  INTEGER_SET class 399
  LIST_TYPE class 162
  queues 143
  UNORDERED_LIST_D class 174
  vs. pop command 145
remove_after command
  LIST_TYPE class 163
  UNORDERED_LIST_D class 168, 174
remove_back command, UNORDERED_LIST_D class 174
remove_before command 155
  LIST_TYPE class 163
  UNORDERED_LIST_D class 168, 174
remove_front command, LIST_TYPE class 163
rename subclause, examples
  CHECKING subclass 59–60
  FLOWER class 59
require else clause 77
reusability
  defined 132
  and inheritance 13
  list code
    as deques 182–184
    as priority queues 184–186
    as queues 181–182
    as stacks 179–181
reverse_list query, POLYNOMIAL class 295
reversing bit patterns 392
right child, binary trees 300
right subtree, binary trees 299
rightrotate command
  AVL trees 349–350
  weight-balanced trees 378–379
root nodes
  binary trees
    defined 299
    order of traversal 302–304
  heap data structure 445
rotating
  binary trees 346–351
  bits 392
routines
  adding to descendants 56–58
  assertions 70
    inheriting 76–79
  assigning based on class 38
  blocking in descendants 56, 58
  defined 45
  delimiters 46
  documenting 69–79
  income tax computation example 46
  invoking 45
  mutators 52

naming conventions 46
parameter lists 46
postconditions 70
preconditions 70
protecting 69–79
redefining with inheritance 56–63
renaming 58–63
return type 46
self-documenting 70
vs. attributes 68–69
See also Creation routines
See also Examples
See also Inheritance
See also Recursion
See also specific query names
run-time stack, recursion example 192–194

S

search trees
  AVL trees, defined 351–352
  balance, defined 345–346
  balance, determining
    comparing to balanced tree 331–334
    computing average internal path length 304–306
    randomly generated search trees 334–341
    testing for AVL balance 353–354
  defined 312–314
  deleting nodes 320–326
    balance considerations 345
  implementing 326–331
  inserting nodes 316–320
    balance considerations 345
  internal-path balanced (IPB) 372
  nodes, determining if present 314–316
  speed 306
  weight-balanced trees 372–376

See also AVL trees
See also Binary trees
See also Weight-balanced trees
searching, recursion example 200–204
SEARCH_TREE class
  deleting items 320–326
  implementing 326–331
  inserting items 316–320
  items, determining if present 314–316
  See also BINARY_T class
  See also Search trees
select subclause, PARENT and CHILD classes example 60–63
selection sort algorithm 93–97
semicolon (;), in Eiffel language 10–11
service time probability density function 257
set operations 394–401
set_balance command 354
shifting bits 392
short tool 11–12
simple objects
  See Objects; types
simple search algorithm 126–128
single forward slash (/), binary division operator 42
solitaire poker application 234–255
SORT class 451–458
sorting algorithms
  bubble sort 98–101
  comb sort 101–105
  divide and conquer 108
  heapsort 437–459
  insertion sort 105–108
  magic number sort 104–105
  partition 109–111
  quicksort 108–116
  selection sort 93–97
  shrink_factor 102–105
  SORT class 451–458
sorting problem, the 92

spelling checker, hash tables example 401–415
STACK class
  aliasing problems 136
  commands 133–134
  dynamic implementation 139–142
  queries 133–134
  short form 137–138
  static implementation 134–136
  storage, creating 136
  test program 138–139
stacks
  applications
    calculator 226–234
    converting infix expression to postfix 221–234
    converting recursive routine to iterative routine 207–221
    solitaire poker game 234–255
  capacity 134
  counting 134
  deleting items 133
  empty, checking for 134
  implemented as UNORDERED_LIST_D 179–181
  inserting items 133
  last-in-first-out (LIFO) protocol 133
  as lists 179–181
  recursive 192–194
  top element, accessing 133
state information, accessing 45–46
static arrays 87
static binding 22
static container classes 87, 132
STD_FILES class 46–48
STORABLE class, learning tree example 459–471
storage
  allocating 38
  detaching 39
  persistent 459–471

vs. computation 68–69
STRING class
  commands 118–120, 473–480
  feature sections 117–120
  interface 121–122, 473–480
  queries 118–120, 473–480
  routines 117
  simple search algorithm 126–128
  test program 122–126
strings
  See Hash functions
  See LONG_INTEGER class
  See STRING class
subclasses
  creating 53–56
  defined 12
  examples
    ACCOUNT class 54–56
    AIRPLANE class 53–54
subtree, binary trees 300
sum of integers, iteration example 45

T

target objects, creating 41
tennis players, array example 48–50
terminal output routines 46–48
testing
  AVL trees 353–354
  strings 122–126
top query, stacks 133
torque, defined 346
traversal algorithms 302–304
trees
  See AVL trees
  See Binary trees
  See Search trees
  See Weight-balanced trees
types
  basic, default values 40
  declaring for objects 38

U

uniform access 12
union operations, sets 394
universal export 52
unordered collections
   See Hash functions
   See INTEGER_SET class
unordered lists
   data abstraction 150–151
   with duplicates 168–174, 179–184
   implementing 156–167
   interface 151–156
UNORDERED_LIST class
   commands 151, 155, 167
   implementation 156–167
   interface 151–156
   queries 150–151, 155, 167
   vs. INTEGER_SET class 399–401
UNORDERED_LIST_D class
   commands 168, 174
   implementation 168–174
      as a deque 183–184
      doubly-linked 176–179
      as a queue 181–182
      as a stack 179–181
   inheritance 174
   queries 168, 174

V

value semantics 40
visiting
   See Traversal algorithms
Void, initial value 40

W

waiting line simulation 263–278
weight-balanced trees
   average internal path length 372
   inserting nodes 376–381
      algorithm, discussion of 373–376
   leftrotate command 378
   rightrotate command 378–379
   vs. AVL trees 372, 381–384
worst case
   asymptotic complexity 97
   average internal path length 334, 372